Students
Teaching,
Teachers
Learning

Students Teaching, Teachers Learning

Edited by

N. Amanda Branscombe, West Georgia College

Dixie Goswami, Clemson University

Jeffrey Schwartz, Greenwich Academy

Foreword by

James Britton and Nancy Martin

BOYNTON/COOK • HEINEMANN
Portsmouth, NH

Boynton/Cook Publishers, Inc.
A Subsidiary of Reed Publishing (USA) Inc.
361 Hanover Street
Portsmouth, NH 03801-3912
Offices and agents throughout the world

The editors and publisher wish to thank the following for permission to reprint material:

Chapter 6, "The Drudgery and the Discovery: Students as Research Partners," by
Jeffrey Schwartz, was previously published in the February 1988 issue of *English
Journal*. Copyright 1988 by the National Council of Teachers of English. Reprinted with
permission.

A variation of Chapter 7, "On the Move in Pittsburgh: When Students and Teacher
Share Research," by Jeffrey Schwartz, was previously published in *The Writing Teacher
as Researcher*, ed. Donald A. Daiker and Max Morenberg. Copyright 1990 by Boynton/
Cook Publishers, Inc. Reprinted with permission.

Chapter 9, Part 2, "Cross-Age Tutoring in South Carolina: Coming of Age," by J.
Elspeth Stuckey, was previously published in the Spring 1988 issue of *The Bread Loaf
News*. Reprinted with permission.

Chapter 15, "Meeting Strangers in Familiar Places: Teacher Collaboration by Cross-
Visitation," by Susan Lytle and Robert Fecho, was previously published in the February
1991 issue of *English Education*. Copyright 1991 by the National Council of Teachers of
English. Reprinted with permission.

Library of Congress Cataloging-in-Publication Data

Students teaching, teachers learning/N. Amanda Branscombe, Dixie Goswami,
   Jeffrey Schwartz, editors.
         p.   cm
   ISBN 0−86709−299−8
   1. Teacher-student relationships−United States. I. Branscombe, N. Amanda.
II. Goswami, Dixie. III. Schwartz, Jeffrey
LB1033.S873   1992
371.1′023−dc20

Cover designed by Tom Allen
Printed in the United States of America
93 94 95 96   10 9 8 7 6 5 4 3 2

Contents

Foreword

To us here in London, it comes as a transatlantic call—a call we can not resist. After all, what we are being invited to do is to join a conversation, a conversation with some people we know and some whom we meet for the first time in their writing. We think of Prospero, whose isle, as Caliban found it, is full of voices. In Ken Macrorie's words, "I find myself enjoying most what those teachers and students had to say. Their words were clear and moving." And he sees his role as a respondent, of "showing the consequences of the writing in a reader's mind." And that, if we may join him, is what we should like to indicate—briefly and selectively as necessary, no more than a word here and a word there.

The sense of participating in a conversation is above all the effect of the editorial plan—the matching of a text with the responses of readers. What we have therefore is an interpretive exchange representing equally the views of students, of teachers, and of observers looking in on the exchange. Chapters in many lives, it seems to us, here meet and interweave as they create a picture of life in a classroom. And it is a picture above all of collaborative activity, focusing on the sharing of power and the release of new energies.

As Amanda Branscombe and Charlene Thomas have put it, "Collaboration, laboring together, is an essential construct in teacher/student inquiry. . . . It is the taproot of a shared community that often anchors that community as it experiences growth, dissension, success, and change. Its interactive nature is one of the community's means of building shared knowledge."

Again as Cindy Myers comments upon the collaboration of students with their teacher, Jeff Schwartz: "Jeff had a choice. He could have carried out the same inquiry on his own. . . . Imagine what his inquiry would have been like then. I think that Becky's and Lindsay's work took Jeff deeper into the research—engaged *him* more with the work, kept him going at it, made him think more, made him see more. . . . Is it not true that if we don't have the students' viewpoint of the data, we might be off base in judging what the data mean?"

What we find quite unforgettable about the stories is the courage they represent when cultural conflicts arise. There is no shirking the issues, even when differences have to remain unresolved. As we read the stories of classroom dynamics, of interaction and collaborative endeavor, we meet much that is unexpected; alternative cultural patterns highlight contrasts and leave problems that will not go away. There is for example the full and sensitive discussion of cross-cultural anxieties about schoolchildren on a journey "eating in the streets" — how black teachers set a higher standard for black students and how those students react and respond.

There is, in Chapter 10, the story of a black teacher's struggle to come to terms with the demands of the university community at Harvard, the agonies of compromising his sense of language, of culture, of race. The chapter culminates in Nanzetta Merriman's "Vision of a Field Negro." This is a piece he wrote with the help of Judith Diamondstone, a fellow doctoral student at Harvard and joint author with him of Chapter 10. In his introduction he speaks of his origins: "I did not begin this journey. My father began this journey in Grenada in the early 1900s. Then he knew he wanted indoor plumbing, a floor not made of dirt, and a better life for a family. The contributions and achievements that my children, my caramel angels, will make to society will be focused on the vision that is bound by tradition. I got here from the blood, sweat, tears, and love of my ancestors, parents, sisters, my wife and children."

And his vision is grounded in a sense of "the field Negro," the descendant of the workers in the field who make up "the core black tradition." The twofold tasks of Nanzetta and Judith, engaged in creating a "portrait" of him, combine to raise issues that explore the unforeseen and sometimes disturbing aspects of collaboration — how a partnership is able to persist in the face of hostility and criticism.

It seems to us that publishers' lists abound in records of successful practices in the classroom, philosophically grounded sometimes, and sometimes little more than gimmicks. What we have in this set of records and responses is not in that "successful practice" category; rather, it records problems that persist and attempts to deal with them that sometimes fail. Ike Coleman, for example, records how successful collaboration in one year may fail to transplant into another group, another year. And, on the other hand, the story of Charlene Thomas reports the lifelong effects of a brief and unfinished schooling at the age of sixteen with Amanda Branscombe as teacher and Shirley Brice Heath as advisor. In their intermittent encounters over the period from 1981, when Charlene had one child, to 1988, when she had four more children, Amanda discovered that Charlene was still keeping records of her children's education and using the ethnographic recording methods she had learned in school as a means of doing so. What is evident is the lasting effect of her confidence in what education could achieve for her children, and her success in planning and putting it into operation. It is a triumphant story that reaches its point when Charlene's two older sons win school awards for academic excellence and when she "is beginning to believe that she must be more political so that she can be heard. ... She believes that our leaders must listen to people who live in and survive the struggle of the underclass."

We believe this a good note on which to conclude a brief preface to a book on student/teacher collaboration—collaboration in the classroom—and who knows how far a little experience of such collaboration can go? It is evidence of this sort that makes the book a very unusual and arresting account.

JAMES BRITTON
NANCY MARTIN

Section One:
Students Teaching

In classrooms where teachers are conducting classroom research, students too can become inquirers and sometimes collaborators in inquiry. When this happens the classroom changes. Students and teachers form new relationships based on negotiation and trust. Expertise is shared. The focus of a class shifts to include student voices. Students become more responsible for *how* as well as *what* they learn.

The students in these chapters come from a variety of backgrounds: from the South, the North, and overseas; from urban and rural, private and public schools; from elementary, middle, and high school grades, including children with learning difficulties or in accelerated programs. At every age they are engaged with language purposefully, not only for communication, but also as a way to understand and take control of their lives. These students are welcomed as colleagues in classroom research, as cross-age tutors of English and science, as teachers of Greek and French. They collaborate with their teachers on inquiries about how good readers read, how literary discussion works, how stereotypes are created and overcome, how oral histories are edited for publication, or how ethnographic methods serve a young mother studying her children's literacy and trying to change public policy.

More important than the actual processes studied are the reflections — through talking and writing — on what it means to raise dynamic questions, to risk change, to negotiate with one or more other people. This is teacher research extended beyond the lonely office of the solitary instructor. The kind of "attentive looking" Anne Martin describes in Ellen Schwartz's classroom is enhanced in conversation with students or other teachers who look and learn together.

While these chapters report how learning is enhanced through collaboration and systematic reflection, they do not propose easy answers or suggest foolproof methods. Rather they raise messy questions about what happens when students and teacher share authority in and out of schools and when they become excited together about the kind of authentic learning that can't be measured on standardized tests.

Following each chapter are responses that tell stories, raise questions, push the argument further, and carry on a conversation with the author that we hope will extend as well to the readers of this book.

3

1

Student and Teacher Co-Researchers
Ten Years Later

N. Amanda Branscombe
Charlene Thomas

Collaboration, laboring together, is an essential construct in teacher/ student inquiry. Metaphorically speaking, it is the taproot of a shared community that often anchors that community as it experiences growth, dissension, success, and change. Its interactive nature is one of the community's means of building shared knowledge. Its multiple perspectives and the coordination of those are other essential aspects necessary for the creation of a community identity that values and practices cooperation, negotiation, shared space, and shared power in order to solve problems and make decisions. Because of these dynamics and others involved in true collaboration, teachers who advocate classroom practices that incorporate collaboration often find themselves in precarious situations with their students and with administrators, other teachers, and parents. After all, collaborative work changes one's perception of what's important, what works, and what's acceptable in schooling.

The teacher researcher movement in education has encouraged collaborative learning and shared inquiry by proposing that teachers and students work together on topics that relate to their community, their language, their writing, and so on. Many teachers who have used classroom research and have engaged in collaborative inquiry with students and other teachers are now questioning whether such inquiry offers students anything more than a novel experience. True, we are aware that students score higher on their standardized tests during and after they have collaborated with their teachers in classroom research (Heath & Branscombe 1985). We have also found that students develop positive attitudes about school when they collaborate in classroom research (Goswami & Stillman 1987). In fact, we have documented situations in which children's lives have been temporarily changed so much that they become leaders in their school and valued members of their community (see Chapter 9). However, our testimonials aren't enough. We want to know more about what happens when students and teachers collaborate. We want to know how effective those methods are for students' daily lives. Finally, unlike most university researchers who maintain contact with their collaborators through professional organizations, conferences, and academic networks, classroom research collaborators (teachers/students) often lose contact because of high school graduation, students moving, and students attending other schools within the same district. Just as with the university researchers' need to maintain contact, we, teacher researchers, have a need to know how and what our classroom research collaborators are doing. We also want to know the long-term effects of our research just as the university professors. This was one of the reasons that I contacted Charlene Thomas, one of the student collaborators in the 1981–82 classroom research project that Shirley Brice Heath, my ninth-grade basic English students, and I had done.

During my first visit with Charlene, I found that she was eagerly making plans to write her own story. She explained that she had been preparing to write it for some time and had been reading autobiographical pieces in *Reader's Digest*, *People*, and *Jet* as models. She said:

> One of my dreams is to write my story and my family's story. It was because of my work back in ninth grade with Shirley Heath and Amanda Branscombe that I got to thinking that I would write my own story. I started thinking about writing my story because I think that it might help others like me deal with their problems. That year, they helped us learn about school and work and how to do them. Then they had each of us doing projects about our neighborhoods. They worked with me in a project about Dede, my first child, and the ways I read to him. To do that they showed me how to use a tape recorder to tape mine and Dede's words. Then they got me to write field notes to help me remember what happened. I've been doing that ever since.
>
> Last summer I didn't have nothing to do, so I started writing down stuff when I had a mind to. I was planning on moving to a city that is about fifty miles away because I had heard that I could get better education opportunities for my children and better after-school programs for them. I decided that while I was making plans to move, packing up, and getting moved I could write. I didn't write every day

'cause it was too much. I did try to write whenever I put my mind to it. What you read here is my story!

This chapter is the result of our renewed contact and collaboration. It will chronicle how Charlene has used and continues to use the ethnographic methods she learned as a student researcher in the collaborative project with Heath and me. Furthermore, it will describe what it means to her to be an ethnographer of her children's lives and of her neighborhood. Finally, it will suggest that the role of participant observer has a distancing and objective aspect that allows an individual to see the reality of his/her world, neighborhood, and family, while not being crushed by those systems.

Background

Throughout the 1981–82 school year, I engaged in a collaborative classroom research project about language and literacy with my ninth-grade basic English students and Shirley Brice Heath (Heath & Branscombe 1985; Branscombe 1987). Because Charlene and I met during that study, a brief summary of it and our first collaborative inquiry with her seems necessary.

The original classroom research project had several phases. The first phase, a letter-writing exchange between my eleventh- and twelfth-grade expository writing students and my basic ninth-grade English students, occurred during the first semester of that school year. The second phase was developed when Heath and I realized that the older students' course was only one semester. That phase involved Heath corresponding with the ninth graders to ensure that they continued to have a real audience and purpose for their writings.

The third phase, use of ethnographic methods, evolved because of that correspondence. Heath decided to invite the students to become co-researchers who studied their community's oral and written language. She pointed out that if they chose to join her, they would have to have some systematic way of sending her the information they were gathering. Because of her interest in ethnography and their interest in her work, we all agreed that they would learn various ethnographic-data-gathering methods. Heath explained that those methods should include field notes, observations, interviews, tape recordings, administering and tallying surveys, collecting various kinds of writing samples, as well as analyzing their data. Because the students had a desire to learn those methods (to become co-researchers and provide Heath with information about their communities' language use) and knew that someone really needed and wanted their data, they not only learned how to use the methods but were also willing to work for accuracy and clarity in the use of those methods. Furthermore, they were willing to learn how to use those methods as they did their work; this sequence was preferable to mastering a method and thereafter applying it to a situation. Their use of ethnographic methods led to the fourth phase of the classroom research project.

Heath and I designed various team projects for the students so that they could practice their ethnographic approaches and gather the data she had requested. After we designed them, the students discussed all of them, modified some, omitted others, and added their own. The final list included some of the following: (1) a study of baseball language and its rule structure, (2) a study of the ways people read to young children, (3) a comparative study of rap music and Elizabethan poetry and prose, (4) a comparative study of rules and strategies for video games and English grammar, (5) an autobiography of each student and a videotaped presentation of those for Heath, (6) a class newspaper, (7) a study of poetry written by two of the students, (8) a study of games and contests and their uses in the English classroom, (9) a study of the ways publishers write textbooks, workbooks, and standardized tests, (10) a survey administered by students on writing and reading behaviors in their communities, (11) a study of the folktales and folklore in their communities, (12) audiotaped interviews and written observations of people at work within their communities and people talking about literacy and learning, and (13) a study of questioning strategies used by teachers, students, and others.

Charlene was one of the students in the class. She took part in the letter-writing exchange and did her project on her young son, De, and his language learning. Although she dropped out of school during November of the 1981 school year because of a school absentee policy, she continued to collaborate with Heath and me about his language development and daily activities (Heath with Thomas 1984). At that time she was sixteen and a ninth grader in my basic English class. She had missed the previous year because of her mother's prolonged illness and death and Dede's birth (her first child). When she found that she was pregnant with her second son, Tutti, she decided to drop out of school permanently.

Charlene's original project with Heath and me consisted of reading to De, tape-recording those sessions, and taking field notes of their interactions and his activities. I occasionally visited Charlene to monitor the project, give her more tapes and materials, and gather the data she had collected. Heath would write to the two of us, provide books and materials, and comment on the project's progress. By school standards Charlene was not literate, from a literate environment, or even a marginal student. A detailed account of her literacy development (Heath 1984) indicated that before this project she had never written a letter, read a book, or succeeded in a formal learning situation. Neither

Heath nor I had any reason to believe that she would follow through with the project; however, she did. In late February 1982, she provided us with her first field notes. According to Heath (1984) the field notes contained specific details of De's speech, her attempts to get De to label objects and people in the room, conversations others had with De, and his daily activities.

Because of Charlene's initial efforts, Heath and I encouraged her to read to De on a regular basis, talk with him about those reading events, and record her impressions of his interest during those events. In June 1982, we discovered that when Charlene had reading sessions with De she made him sit or stand in front of her and "say" the object pictured in the book. Then she read the story to him as he stood or sat quietly looking at the cover of the book. If he moved during the reading event she disciplined him. I quickly intervened by modeling a reading session with Dede. I had him sit by my side or in my lap, so that we could both see the pictures and print. Because Tutti was a "lap baby," I explained that he should be present during the reading events and involved with the interactions.

Charlene adjusted her reading style so that both children were sitting with her and noted that reading to De became much easier as a result of that intervention. After that, she began constructing her own strategies for the reading sessions and recorded those strategies through her use of the audio tape or her field notes. Next, she began to experiment with times to read to them, ways to hold the book so that all could see, ways to talk to and question them about the stories, and ways (such as pointing to the text) to focus their attention on the print and pictures.

Because of the early reading events and Charlene's interaction with De and Tutti during those events, they began to develop a predisposition for reading and rudimentary notions about literacy and schooling. All three looked forward to their story time. De retold stories that had been read to him, and attempted to write stories, his name, the alphabet, and his numbers. Because of his age, Tutti watched De and listened. Charlene maintained her role as participant observer during the sessions and provided us with the notes she had made about those reading events. But during that time, neither the children nor Charlene developed their literacy notions to the point that they could be described as proficient practitioners of mainstream literacy events.

In October 1982, I moved. As a result of that move, I maintained minimal contact with Charlene; however, from 1982 to 1984 she continued to take field notes, mail Heath and me letters and tapes, and visit with me when I stopped by. We lost regular contact with Charlene and the children during the next few years because of my sporadic visits, the children's school schedule, and Charlene's home and work situations. During those years Heath and I did not encourage Charlene to continue with her field notes. In fact, we had no idea whether she even remembered the ninth-grade research project, much less utilized any of the ethnographic tools she had used earlier with the children. In 1988 I contacted Charlene to find out what had happened to her.

When I found Charlene I discovered that she had had three more children (twin boys and a girl). I also learned that she had moved several times within the community and was currently living in a six-room frame house with her two brothers, some friends, and a boarder. According to her, she had been living in that situation for about a year. Before that, she and her family had lived in a trailer that had burned. It seemed that each time she faced a crisis (a fire destroying their trailer, a report of parental neglect, relatives telling the family to get out, etc.) she chose or was forced to move. In her view, these moves had not caused the family any problems because De and Tutti still attended the same school.

When I asked Charlene about the children's schooling, she explained that the school's staff had added to her problems by retaining De in first grade because he was two points below the system's cutoff score on the Stanford Achievement Test, was very active and somewhat immature, and had a parent who seemingly wasn't interested in his schooling (because she was a cook who worked for hourly wages and couldn't get off work to meet the school's scheduled conferences). She also recounted that Tutti was viewed as a troublemaker and fighter who couldn't get along with others in his kindergarten class.

Her earlier expectations of school success for her children had been destroyed. According to her, she just wanted to keep De and Tutti from being tested and placed in a special education program like the one she had experienced. She noted that she couldn't understand the school system's assessment of De and Tutti since they did well on their schoolwork, report cards, and test scores. Furthermore, she noted that De loved to read. She recounted numerous times when he would sit at the kitchen table and read to Tutti and his twin brothers as she cooked dinner. She said that she took him to the library to get books because she couldn't afford to buy as many as he read.

When I asked if she had any records of De and Tutti's schoolwork, she opened a drawer that contained a two-year collection of data consisting of their papers, report cards, standardized testing reports, as well as letters to her about their progress. After examining those and talking with De and Tutti, I, too, questioned the incongruities between the children's standardized scores, their grades, and their teachers' subjective complaints regarding neatness, correctness, and behavior.

It was through the questions and concerns I had about De and Tutti's schooling that I inadvertently discovered that Charlene had continued to use her ethnographic skills to gather data on her children and their schooling. Her use of data collection caused me to ask her why she had saved all of the children's schoolwork. With a surprised look, she noted that she had learned to do that during *our* research project about De and Tutti. I then began to question her about other ways she had used these research methods. She noted that she employed them all the time. She elaborated her point by describing her methods for doing her own self-initiated study about alimony payments and the laws regarding them so that she could get her ex-husband to pay her appropriately. She pointed out that that study had helped her know how to get information from the local library about alimony, interview some legal services employees, gather data from court proceedings regarding her divorce, and so on. As she talked, she explained that her work with Shirley and me had given her methods to use so that as an adult she could gather the data necessary to go to the court, the housing authority, the mental health workers, the welfare office, and the school and tell them her side of the story. Furthermore, she noted that when she went to those people with her data, they listened.

The Story: "There ain't no once upon a time here!"

My name is Charlene Thomas. I am a single mother at the present time and am trying to do my best to raise my children. I am not working, because work would cause me to lose my children's benefits. I tried working outside the home but found that I could not attend school meetings or care for my children when they were sick. I also found that my hourly wage was less than what I could get from government benefits. Even though I do not work outside the home, I am a full-time mother who is interested in my children doing the best that they can in school and in life. I have had my two oldest children attend school experiences at a local university and day camp. I did this so that they would stay off the streets and continue to learn during the summer.

Dede, he was smart and would catch on fast. He liked to have me talk to him and read books Shirley and Ms. Branscombe gave me. I like children, so it weren't a problem to do it. I could see how excited he got about books and school. Now, Tutti, Dede's little brother, would be around when I was talking and reading to Dede. I didn't pay much attention to what Tutti was doing but he must have been listening 'cause he loves books and reading more than Dede.

Now that they are in school, Tutti is so smart that he is going to be a smart child. He's going to make it. I'm working with Dede and trying to make him realize how things is. I got to be hard on him because he want it all without working. He want to be grown before his time. It seems like if I talk to him, it helps a little. See, I make him do book work every day even though he's not in school. Tutti, he just reads or does on his own. He just sits back and observes, listens at you or Dede doing his work, and then catches on all at once. That's hard for De. He sees Tutti going up to their room and doing work 'cause he wants to. Then I makes him go up and do work that I pick out for him. If I let him do like Tutti he won't do nothing except draw. He draws all the time. Like I say, he just wants to be grown before time.

The twins, they do the best they can. It just takes them longer, and they don't take to books like the others. They had to stay back in Head Start an extra year. They are just now learning to say their ABC's, to count, and to tie their shoes. It takes them so long to put learning together. I think I can teach them right from wrong and how to get a job. They won't ever be like the others. Asalia, the baby, she as smart as De and Tutti were. She already looks at books and points to pictures when I say the word or says the word when I point to pictures. She's only three and doing pretend reading. She knows her name when she sees it and is learning to spell it. She's putting on her shoes, buckling them, and even trying to tie the twins' for them. She talks all the time.

There's not no life out there for the kids if they don't make it for themselves in school. Now, I'm trying to encourage them about what's right and giving them a place to learn. When they reach the teenager stage I hope they'll honor me as to what I am and always respect me and my teachings. If I can teach them, help them get their lessons, and work with them steady until they get out of high school, who knows maybe three of them will be able to go to college. Who knows!

Like I wrote earlier, I am moving to another town 'cause I hear that I can get more for the children. This new place has after-school programs, better school services for the twins, more government help, and the YMCA. Some folks are shame to use that kind of help. I don't see a problem with taking it, if it means I can raise my children better. I've been thinking about doing this for a long time. Before I decided to move, I went over to see the schools, the town, the people in the agencies, and the housing. I like them a lot. The only thing I didn't like was that the school people told me my children would go to different schools. All three of the youngest go to school together. Dede, he will go to another school 'cause he's in third grade. I don't like that. I'm going to try and see will they switch him over to the same school as the others. All the kids have to walk since it's not five miles from the house. I'm going to carry them because I never have let them go that far over to school.

I have made helping my children be all that they can my goal in life. My other two goals are to help other people with their children and to help older people with trips to the grocery or doctor. Because I help Ms. Branscombe and have helped Shirley, I am able to write and tell ways I learned to get my children to love school and reading. I also try to counsel teenagers about the problems of being a single, teenage mother.

I work hard, sets my mind to a goal, and achieves it. I also try to problem-solve to accomplish my goals. You see, I have saved five hundred dollars for the down payment on a house and am saving the necessary money for insurance and property taxes. Owning a home is one of my lifetime dreams. My daddy owned his house until it burned. My mama and daddy thought that owning a house was one way of being who you are. I know I can get this dream for me and my children. I am trying to get my house through Habitat. I read about it in Reader's Digest. *It's where you can help people help you get a house. They takes a house that needs work and helps you with it. Then you pay them so much a month. If you leave, you can sell it, give them their loan money, and keep any that's left. I have told them that my children and I can help them. The children can carry paint cans, do clean-up work, carry wood and nails, and other stuff. I can cook for them. If I don't get the house through them (Habitat), I will save more money and get one another way.*

Amanda's Comments

After Charlene finished writing this section, she couldn't decide what to write next. I suggested that she write about her own memories of her children's early years or her own childhood. None of my suggestions seemed to fit her design for the chapter. Finally, after several false starts and several months had passed, she decided that we should write about the ways she had used "them field notes and stuff" over the last two years. She noted that she wanted to write about getting into the housing project, moving to the new town, and finally trying to move into her own home. She noted that the opportunity to reflect on those events by using her field notes and her writings would allow her to have more awareness about those events and would act as a record for her as she wrote her family history.

A Talk with Charlene

When I decides I want something, I think a long time about how to get it. I guess I think about what I have done to get things and then decide if doing like that will work this time. I wanted to move out of that house with my family and into the projects so my kids could have a bedroom. I tried going over and filling out the forms. I didn't hear anything from them, so I went back. They said that they had me on "The List!" I got a letter saying that I made too much money.

I was working at a family steak place cutting up stuff for the salad bar and frying chicken. They weren't paying me nothing except hourly wages so I couldn't figure it out. I had five children and made about $130 a week. I decided that I better find out how folks got into them projects. I started asking people who lived over in there, in the ones I wanted to live in, how they got there. Some told me to send a letter saying why I wanted to move and why I needed to live there. Some told me to get some peoples who know me to write for me. Then I asked around to see who'd be moving from the apartments I wanted. When I found that out I got me some references and wrote a letter about why I wanted to live in the projects. I told them in that letter that I have five children and didn't make enough money to pay for my rent, lights, and heat through the winter. I told them where I wanted to live, so my kids would be messing with no drugs. Finally, I told them that I know some of the apartments over in that section of the projects would be vacant soon. It took a few weeks, but I got my letter saying that I could move into the ones I wanted.

I stayed in there for a little over a year. We took good care of it, and I even had me some flowers in front of the porch. But the kids from up the street started hanging out at the playground behind my place. Dede and Tutti, they wanted to go over there and play with them kids. I knowed they were messing with drugs 'cause I could see out my kitchen window. When that started, I decided I needed to move.

When I started thinking about moving, I thought I'd leave and go to another town. I had always lived around my grandmama, daddy, and brothers and had them there to help. I thought it would be nice to try raising my family on my own. I had a sister up in Ohio. I thought about moving up there with her, but when we went to visit I knew that wasn't for me. I had another sister who lived about forty miles away. She was doing okay over there. When I went to visit her, I rode around. It seemed like the best place for me. I took several trips over there to see how I liked it. Then I started trying to meet people to see what they had to say about it. I went to the food stamp place and the welfare place and talked to them. I drove around to the schools to see what they were like. I got the newspaper and read it whenever I went. After a few visits, I decided I wanted to live there. Once I made up my mind I went back and started filling out forms, writing letters, and making application. When I got them through, I moved.

It been different. We had two tornadoes last year go down our street. At first I lived in the projects. A fast food place was across the street. There was noise all of the time, day and night. Now, I moved into a house which is better. I am still trying to get my own house, but I'm making friends and taking older peoples to the grocery and doctor. I really likes working with them and helping them. I also brought my family here with me. My sister up in Ohio was having a terrible time, so she's here now. My brothers are within fifty miles of us. If we need them, we can get them. See, I think we can help each other cause we are a family. We can raise our children together. We ain't got Mama, but we got each other. If we all pull together, we can have the courage to face life.

Charlene's Comments about Learning

When I asked Charlene about getting an education she explained that she might go back after the children had theirs. In the following statements she comments about schooling, education, and learning.

Maybe when I get my kids out I can go back to school, but not right now. It ain't the time for me to go to school. I tried it. I tried it again just recently. Now, I know that I got to go all the way back and learn everything. School ain't the place for me either. Never was. It just didn't work for me. It put a lot out of my life. See, if I go to school it'll be like before. I'll have to have somebody to look after my children and help them get ready for the rest of their education. I would be going to school and getting my lessons when my children needed me to help them with their lessons. I couldn't go to their assemblies or conferences. I think I need to stay with the children and their education now.

I got enough education to get by. See, I had a choice. I could either go to school and do what was right by the teachers and my lessons, or I could stay at home and be the mother who's tending to my children. I made my choice to be a mother. Schooling, I can always go back and get it. I can't go back and be a mother and change those kids after they're grown up.

It's not like I don't do any learning. I read books. I read the newspaper and magazines. I also observe the children while they learn. I write about what I see them doing. I write other stuff too. For example, sometimes I just sits back and watch them as they are getting their lessons. I watch to see who's gonna ask the other one a question. I'll watch to see who's gonna finish first. While I'm observing, I'm learning the stuff they are learning and learning from what they're doing. I also learn when they asked me to help them. Dede, he is almost ahead of me. The work he's bringing home now, I might not be able to understand it. It just different. Maybe when they get older, then I can go back to night school and get a degree. I have to steadily work along with them. If I do that steady working, I'll be ready for night school.

Somebody might wonder where I got interested in knowing about children. I learned about them from my grandmother. She was keeping children at her home. When she had to run an errand or go somewhere I'd keep them. Back then there wasn't nothing wrong with kids watching kids. Kids became a question to me. I would just take up a child and start playing with it, changing it, washing it, and learning about it. I would watch everything that child did, everything it said, and try to make sense out of the way it acted. Sometimes, all I could say was that that's children. That's why they be doing that. Other times like when they started to walking and talking, they made more sense to me. I knew I had done the same things that they be doing so that helped me make sense of them. Then I would try to guess what step they might be taking next. I did the baby sitting for my grandmama all of my life, until I moved here. Doing it helped me learn what was natural for a child to be doing and what wasn't.

My mama wasn't around but for six months after I had Dede. She died then. She had the cancer. Even before that she was so sick, she couldn't help me. She tried to help me, but there just wasn't no time for Mama and me. I guess Mama thought, "Charlene, she done made her bed hard, and she's gotta learn the hard way how to raise her children. I ain't gonna be here to help her."

When Shirley and Ms. Branscombe asked me about working with them, I was eager to do it 'cause I do love to watch children. It's fun to me to see who's gonna do what when. It's fun to me to watch them learn. From my studying and working as an ethnographer, I've learned about the way children learn in books and from what's happening around them. I know that if things aren't right in the home, the children can't think straight. They'll be worried about what's happening there instead of their schoolwork. See, the children know what's going on. See, they've got it all up in their heads. They watch, observe, and then put it all together just like Tutti done. All we can do for them is give them a place to learn that don't have all of that fussing and fighting and drugs. We can also give them the materials they need. I got paper and books and stuff for my children to use at school and at home. They don't ever have to worry about not having paper, pencils, and books.

Then we also gotta talk to them about what they are learning. I'll have Dede working on a math problem. He'll be having trouble and ask me a question. I try to help him by asking him that same question without him knowing it. Then he'll think some more and finally turn around and just work that problem. That's why I say that children got it up in their heads and we just gotta help them get to it.

Charlene's Comments on Being an Ethnographer

After we had discussed the methods Charlene used to talk with agencies, officials, and others, I asked her several questions about whether she thought ethnographic methods helped her. Some of those questions related to her ability to state what steps she used. Others related to what it meant to her to consider herself an ethnographer. Still others related to her notions of power and her need to have her story heard outside of her family and community. Finally, I asked why she did not use those steps to get more education. I have summarized her responses.

According to Charlene, seeing herself as an ethnographer allows her to have several roles (mother, observer, worker, recorder, and writer), which make up an identity of success rather than a member of the underclass. By being an observer, she is able to confront bureaucratic agencies, fail to get what she wants, step back, and start over. She recalled doing field notes for Shirley. According to her, she would write the best she could, think nothing had been omitted, and then find that Shirley would write asking for more detail or more information. She also explained that when she thought she had gotten to the end of a project, Shirley would ask for more. Charlene noted that having to deal with the agencies is no harder than having to gather data. According to her, "You just have to be willing to be patient and go back and back and back. The ones who don't try, don't go back, but give up are the ones who don't get what they want. They don't have the courage to face life."

Concluding Comments

Since 1981—82, this is the fourth chapter that has been written about the literacy development of Charlene and her family. When I first walked into her home in 1981, I did not see books, magazines, notebook paper, pencils or crayons, newspapers, family pictures, but I did hear the television and radio playing at all times. When I walked into her new home this past week, I saw novels that Charlene had been reading, children's books that the children read to each other, notebook paper, pencils, crayons, a photo album that documented the children's lives, magazines, a Bible, and paintings on the wall. I also saw a small television in the other room that the children are allowed to watch after they have done their homework, played outside, and talked with Charlene about their school day and their work. In her first home, the furniture simply served its utilitarian function. In her latest home, the furniture is both functional and attractive. Her schooling experience had been a failure when I first met her. Her children's schooling experience is becoming more and more successful. This past year, her two oldest sons won school awards for academic excellence. Dede won two essay writing awards for his essays on Christmas and fighting drugs. Tutti received awards for having the top standardized scores in math and reading for his grade level. Furthermore, he was awarded a certificate as an outstanding academic student in the second grade.

These aren't the only changes in Charlene's life. She is beginning to believe that she must be more political so that she can be heard. At this point, she is attempting to get local and state officials to allow her to help them in their fight against drugs, gangs, dropping out of school, and their efforts to help single mothers. Although she has contacted the mayor in her hometown and has written several local television talk show hosts to get them to work with the problems she sees facing children, she has found that they will not listen to her. Charlene believes that our leaders must listen to people who live in and survive the struggle of the underclass. Furthermore, she has said that the problems she sees are deeper and more complex than telling children to "just say no to drugs."

Works Cited

Branscombe, N. A. 1987. I gave my classroom away. In *Reclaiming the classroom*. See Goswami and Stillman 1987.

Goswami, D., and P. Stillman, eds. 1987. *Reclaiming the classroom*. Portsmouth, NH: Boynton/Cook.

Heath, S. B. 1984. The achievement of preschool literacy for mother and child. In *Awakening to literacy*, ed. H. Goelman, A. Oberg, and F. Smith. Portsmouth, NH: Heinemann.

Heath, S. B., and N. A. Branscombe. 1985. "Intelligent writing" in an audience community: Teacher, student and researcher. In *The acquisition of written language: Response and revision*, ed. S. W. Freedman. Norwood, NJ: Ablex.

Sinclair, H. 1978. Conceptualization and awareness in Piaget's theory and its relevance to the child's conception of language. In *The child's conception of language*, ed. A. Sinclair, R. J. Jarvella, and W. J. M. Levelt. New York: Springer-Verlag.

Response

Ethel White

My comments with regard to "Student and Teacher Co-Researchers: Ten Years Later" are based on my observations and experiences as a teacher, educational director, and director of a Head Start program where we served 240 children from less advantaged homes. My response also reflects my current work as director of a day-care center serving infants and school-age children whose parents are working or going to school. On a more personal note, my responses are influenced by my own experiences as the single parent of an adopted daughter whose academic performance was quite short of what the teacher expected; this teacher's approach, however, focused narrowly on academics without regard to the whole child.

My idea of collaboration and shared experiences in the raising of today's children began in the Head Start programs, where agencies kept close relations with the children's parents. There, collaboration between teachers and parents was aimed at promoting optimal performance of children and optimal development of parental skills as the principal influence in the children's growth and development.

In those instances where true partnerships evolved between the parent and teacher, we found that changes and improvement took place not only between the children and the agency but between the agency and the entire family. Parents became more assertive, and were more likely to risk group involvement and participation. They began to be more likely to seek other means of self-improvement and to search actively for employment if they did not have a job. Many were hired as permanent aides in our program and moved up to positions of increased responsibility when they were exceptionally competent or gained new academic skills.

Parents were encouraged from the outset to become team players and to reinforce the activities of the center in their homes — which they did on an informal basis through:

1. observation of techniques used in the center
2. self-study, training, workshops
3. planning, preparation, and use of available resources as teaching tools

4. action (implementation)
5. evaluation (informal).

Parents were also involved in group discussions, decision-making activities for the center and the overall program, curriculum planning, meal planning, and budgets.

The processes involved appeared to give parents (1) a sense of what was needed and (2) a road map of where they were going. They developed a sense of belonging, acceptance, and "connectedness." They became more "open," took an increased level of interest in their child, and showed enthusiasm about bringing their child to the center. We frequently referred to them and they referred to us as members of a "family." We could see them lose the tendency to avoid trying new tasks because they feared failure. We saw self-confidence and pride in their children emerge.

This approach could be and was employed in other aspects of their lives to solve problems in the family and in their community. Parents frequently came in to discuss other activities, problems, and concerns. In other problem-solving situations, advice or confirmation was sought from our teachers and other members of the staff.

These processes helped our agency turn into a place for experimenting with new ideas and approaches in a nonthreatening manner. Professionals were involved in center activities, but so were the parents' peers. When parents realized success or reached a milestone or completed a special project with their child, we were there to encourage them and applaud their efforts.

If their project or approaches were unsuccessful we were there to say, "It's OK," "Here's another way you may want to try," "Let's try again," or "I tried something like this and tried several times before it really worked."

We were there to help construct alternate ways or methods to achieve their goals.

What seems so often lacking in the lives of many young adults is

1. a set of achievable goals
2. a plan of action to reach stated goals (the ability to think things through)
3. the courage and confidence to try
4. a support system (cheerleaders or co-collaborators).

The heroine in this chapter, Charlene, realized that when she used the ethnographic method she got results and reached her goals. Since success triggers confidence and the boldness to try again, Charlene began to use this tool in other aspects of her life. Success "feels good" and is a rare commodity in the lives of the less privileged.

All of us as parents and teachers must realize that the experiences and life-styles of those we serve today represent such a broad and unique mix that we can never expect to be successful in our work with children unless we take into account the experiences and dynamics of each child's situation. Then, we need to employ approaches that foster a sense of direction, belonging, and acceptance of whatever level the children operate from. This, coupled with encouragement and support, enthusiasm and joint efforts, produces far greater results and commitment. All of us, children especially, are emboldened by success, and thrive when nurtured with praise.

I would also note that parents desire very much to be productive, self-supporting citizens but are frequently overwhelmed with the staggering cost of survival in the workplace — so much so that they become dependent on the system. This does not mean that they lack ambition or that their children are doomed to failure. We give up far too easily on parents and children and don't really listen when their attitudes don't conform to our professional expectations.

My daughter's preoccupation with the circumstances of her existence, from home to foster home, from foster home to foster home, and from foster home to adoptive home, of course, was her primary interest. Her interest in academics would be delayed until she could feel secure and know that she would not have to move again, know that she had a "forever home" and adults in her life who would be with her forevermore. Her academic success was tempered by a need for belonging, acceptance, and connectedness. She could not focus her energies and efforts on academics when her life was in turmoil and continuous change. Her academic progress might have advanced earlier with the aid of an understanding teacher who knew that you cannot separate a child's academic growth from his/her emotional needs entirely. The opportunity to foster that sense of belonging, that need for acceptance, could have found root in the classroom in partnership with the home.

As we look at our family structures, there are so many deviations in structure and in situations that we must take into account in our planning and implementation of our classroom offerings, methods, and delivery of quality education.

Our search for quality education, for excellence in the classroom, and for maximum development of all children will be greatly influenced by the extent of involvement of parents, students, and teachers as partners in the learning process.

2

The Round Table
Emergent Curriculum in a Primary Class

Ellen Schwartz

In one of my early years of teaching, and my first year at my present school, I had a student who was going to miss the first days of school because of a family trip to Louisiana. In a home visit, I suggested to Marie and her mother that they look for things native to Louisiana that we don't have here in Vermont, and bring some back to share with us.

Marie found soybeans and rice growing in Louisiana and brought them back, still on the stem. The rice especially became a source of interest and investigation for the first graders. They had all eaten rice, and were curious about the difference between rice as they knew it and rice in the wild. I set up a corner for Marie's finds and supplied the children with hand lenses and a mortar and pestle which they used to hull the rice. I got some library books about soybeans and rice, and together we looked at pictures, discussed growing conditions and things we eat that use soybeans or soy products, and wondered at how the rice got from its raw state to its more familiar processed form.

As the children worked and we developed more activities, some began to draw and write (or dictate) about their discoveries. This work went up on the wall near the raw materials. One afternoon, a colleague came into my room after school and commented to me about the rice and soybean material, "What an interesting idea for a center." I felt at once complimented and insecure. The fact that this colleague, herself a teacher of long standing, found what I was doing to be interesting was reassuring to me as a neophyte. At the same time, I was nervous about not knowing what a "center" was, and beyond that, by the implication that I had come up with the idea for one, which was not at all how the corner had developed. I thought that perhaps I *should* be coming up with ideas for "centers," but at the same time I liked the idea of presenting possibilities (as with the assignment I had set for Marie) and responding to what the children brought in.

At the time, I wasn't able to articulate what I was doing, except very generally. My sense was that the sources of my curriculum were different from what they appeared to be or were assumed to be, not just by this colleague, but also by those teachers who presented and participated in various workshops on curriculum development that I attended over the course of that year.

The summer after that school year I attended my first Summer Institute at The Prospect Center in North Bennington, Vermont. Through Prospect, I was introduced to the idea of the "emergent curriculum." Simply put, this is an approach to developing curriculum in which the teacher draws on the interests of the students.

The idea of tapping students' interests is nothing new. Writing in 1916, John Dewey said, "The problem of instruction is thus that of finding material which will engage a person in specific activities having an aim or purpose of moment or interest to him, and dealing with things not as gymnastic appliances but as conditions for the attainment of ends" (155).

The process approach to writing, gaining in popularity in some school districts, is an example of a current educational practice that allows student interest to shape a piece of curriculum. Individualization of instruction, when not reduced to marching each child through the same text or workbook at a different rate, can be another means of wedding children's interests to their school lives.

What was added by the ideas I encountered at Prospect was the notion that through attentiveness to children's interests and activities — individually and across the class — I could not only meet individual needs but also provision my class with materials and ideas that would respond to interests alive in the group. In this way I might enable us to collectively pursue lines of inquiry in which the children as well as I would play a formative role.

One of the assumptions about learning that underlie this view of children, learning, and curriculum is that people are by nature active seekers after meaning. In any classroom of young people (or adults), I assume that each person is trying to make sense of the various experiences that the group offers. In so doing, individuals relate experiences in class to their wider worlds of experience, which is another way of saying that children's lives provide a context for their school experiences. I state this as an assumption because to me it seems an inevitable quality of human nature. As humans, we can't help but try to connect things up, though how each of us does so is unique, which makes for a richly varied texture in any classroom where attention is paid to people's ways of viewing the world.

The Role of Observation and Record Keeping

Through the Prospect Summer Institute, I was taught systematic approaches to observing children and their work that have been invaluable to me in developing the instinctive inclinations expressed in the rice and soybean "center." When I observe, I am looking for those places where individuals and groups of children are active, invested, and engaged; where their interest and imagination are fired; where they sustain themselves energetically. I am looking at what they do in these areas, with whom they work, and how they enact their ideas. The places I look may be, literally, areas of the room such as the block area, sand and water table, or class library. They may also be thematic areas such as castles, dinosaurs, or planets.

My own stance becomes one of observer and questioner as well as instructor. While the children are engaged in making and doing, I may well be offering instruction or engaging in conversation with them about their work, but at the same time I am reflecting on what I see them doing and on the understandings that are taking form, rather than coming in with a preconceived notion of how they *should* understand *my* (or some mandated) curriculum.

I won't be able here to detail all I have learned about observing and documenting children's school experiences. (The two monographs by Patricia Carini included in the bibliography discuss observation and documentation in greater depth.) I would, however, like to say a few words about the kinds of records I keep. I have found these records to be a core component of the emergent approach to developing curriculum, because they enable me to remember daily incidents and give me access to a body of such incidents, providing me with data about my class in which I can discern themes, patterns, and points of interest, which then suggest curriculum areas or topics worth pursuing.

Like many teachers, I keep records of books read by my students, of written work in progress or completed, and of academic skills in which they exhibit strength or the need for further instruction. But the heart of my record keeping is the set of narrative records I keep on each child and the journal I write about the class as a whole. In the individual records I note, in addition to the aforementioned academic items, choices made by the child at the daily activity time. In addition I write brief weekly or biweekly narratives on each child, in which I note such things as what the child actually did at the chosen activities, what aspects particularly engaged him or her (or didn't), friendships (with whom? around what?), expressions of feeling (prompted by what? with what degree of intensity?), perhaps a remark made by the child that caught my ear, or a playground incident, or something I've noticed about the child's physical bearing. I don't try to be exhaustive; if I did, writing these records would be a daunting task. Rather, I count on the fact that I will have all year to get to know the child, and that although each week's entry is itself only a tiny slice, over time the records will build up, and a portrait of the child will emerge.

I also bear in mind that the records will provide only one dimension, and that I will be looking at the child also through his or her own work products, the observations of others (teachers, paraprofessionals, the principal), and the parents' insight. Each of these will provide a context for the others, and in the end, what I feel I gain is a bit more understanding of the child's particular way of coming at the world, not a total picture. I am leery of phrases like "total picture" (or "whole child") because ultimately I feel that every child I teach remains a mystery to me, however knowable he or she may be in certain aspects.

To give the flavor of these records, I reproduce here several weeks' entries about one child, Ana:

> *Week ending 9/5:* Shy first morning, mostly alone. By afternoon, very engaged with others, especially at building long Unifix train across the room. Bouncy with excitement as it neared completion. — Let me put my arm around her; contact with Ana is more physical than verbal. — Loves the guinea pig. — At group time often on her stomach, sometimes seems somewhere else. — Giggly with Bonnie.

> *Week ending 9/12:* Brought in her guinea pigs. Wants to be with the pigs all the time. Chose them at activity time, with Rose and Marilyn. At math time also wanted to be with the pigs. — Over to me with many little problems, "I can't write because someone stacked my chair." Acts a bit helpless. — Wants to be with Mae a lot, to sit next to her at group time.

> *Week ending 9/18:* Modeling clay alone, very involved. Made a house and garage for Snoopy, then Snoopy sleeping. Wrote about Snoopy in her journal. — Seems more tuned in at group. Volunteers a bit now in discussions. — Modeling clay Wednesday with Mae and Marilyn, all working on "Snakeland." — Sometimes seems helpless about things like opening the door, and other kids can tend to patronize her a bit.

My journal provides a counterpoint to the individual records, for in it I turn my attention more to group themes and dynamics than to individual children. (Of course, one can never totally distinguish between the two, nor is that my intention.) Here I might recount group discussion, note themes and activities that are a locus of energy for a number of children, or identify places where children's interests intersect. Writing the journal helps me to stand back from the focus on individual children and to look at them also as group members. Here is a typical entry:

10/19/86

A spontaneous discussion after story about snakes. This was the Spider tale in which an innocent snake gets killed. Shane declaiming that "Many people think snakes are bad but they're really very good." Someone said, "Except poisonous snakes." Spencer and Shane trying to explain that a snake can be poisonous and good at the same time. I'm not sure what the others made of this, as we had to end the discussion to go to gym.

Kids making boat models. Lots of discussion about whether they would float. (Chuck: "It'd float 'cause it's lighter than water.") But no one wanted to try floating their models because they said they'd get soggy and ruined. We talked about it at meeting, and the kids decided to try and float an abandoned model tomorrow.

One thing I'm most excited about is what's happening with the Spider stories — the stories themselves, the oral tradition, the tie-in to slavery, which became a connection to the Columbus story & what happened to the indigenous peoples. It's the first year that I've felt the Columbus Day thing had some meaning to the kids. Kids are mesmerized by the idea of slaves bringing their stories with them. Several kids retold whole Spider stories to Mr. Y [a parent who had visited the room]. I'm thinking I should do more with singing and dramatization.

In sketching out an overview of the idea of emergent curriculum and of my own history with it, I have intentionally compressed lived experience. However, it is the particular experiences of students and teachers that breathe life into ideas about teaching and learning. After describing the setting in which the children and I work, I shall recount the growth of a particular study with a particular class of children, in an effort to illuminate both the vitality I have found in this approach to teaching and the classroom dynamic it makes possible.

The Milieu: School and Classroom

The study I'll describe here took place with a pre-first class at Putney Central School. Putney Central is the only public school in the town of Putney, Vermont. The school has approximately 250 students in grades K through 8, and like the town, the student body is nearly all white. In terms of socioeconomic class, however, the school is less representative of the town. While the schoolchildren come from primarily working-class, poor, and middle-class families, the town also includes upper-middle-class and wealthy families, most of whom send their children to private schools.

Fifteen children, ten boys and five girls, were placed in the pre-first for the 1986–87 school year. These children had finished kindergarten, and based on the kindergarten teacher's observations and Gesell screening, were considered to be "developmentally young"—not ready for first grade. (At the end of the pre-first year, these students usually go into first grade.)

Children in this class had a daily activity time for work on projects of their own choosing. Regularly available were drawing, painting, modeling clay, junk material constructions, block building, marble chutes, dramatic play, sand and water table, needlework, papercraft, puppetry, board games, puzzles, story records, reading, and math materials and games. In addition, there was frequently a special choice such as cookery, collage, mural work, clay, weaving, papier-mâché, mask making, candle making, experiments, or particular projects related to class or individual undertakings. In addition to the activity time, there were periods of the day when children were expected to write and draw, read or engage with books, work on math, or work on particular science or social studies activities assigned by me.

The Conversation Begins

The activity time provides a fertile ground both for the children to explore activities and media of their own choosing and for me to take note of what activities and materials most excite which children and what themes appear in their work. In this class, castles and royalty were recurrent motifs, particularly in the block area, at the sand and water table, and in dramatic play. Tad, a prolific and dramatic storyteller, enlivened this play with ongoing sagas about his royal family of cats. King Petey was the first character he introduced. Early in the year, Tad was frequently to be found at the sand and water table, building castles, dungeons, mouse holding tanks, swimming pools, and other accoutrements for Petey. There were invariably other children with him, and I noted with interest that they easily and genuinely got swept in the Petey building and the stories. I kept waiting for the complaints ("I want to make something else, but Tad is hogging the sand"), but they never came. Petey had become a presence at the sand table.

The flavor of Tad's Petey stories can be felt in this dictated example:

> There was King Petey. The wagons were coming with cough cure and cigars for the head jailer cat and food for King Petey. One day there was a war coming. The war came closer and closer to the castle. The dungeon gates opened. But they walked right into the dungeon. King Petey's jailers quickly closed and locked the dungeon door.
>
> One day there was a terrible storm. The moat went round and

round, and almost knocked down the stone castle. But it didn't. The
storm lasted for days and days and nights and nights.

After five hundred days the storm stopped but then the wagons
were getting ready to come again. When they came, the castle was
almost out of food. Finally the wagons came. The end. Happy King
Petey.

Meanwhile, children in the block area began to build castles and
other structures for Petey as well. The children in my class talk freely
with each other about their undertakings. Much of this takes place
informally as they work. Children circulate to see what others are
doing. (It's always interesting to me to note which children do this
most frequently, and what they do when they are watching: look
silently, ask questions, talk about technique, offer suggestions, express
appreciation.) There is more formal conversation at group meetings,
when children show and tell about their projects or the group discusses
various topics.

All this conversation allows for a theme, technique, character, or
idea suggested by one individual or group of children to get developed,
reworked, or embellished by others. I note which ones *do* spread
among the children, what is done with them, and which aspects seem
to hold the greatest appeal. When I saw King Petey taking over the
block area and children making junk constructions for him, I thought,
"Here is something worth paying attention to."

My own role goes beyond observing, of course. Sometimes I link
up children whose work or ideas seem to have the potential to spark
one another's thought and activity by making them aware of one
another's pursuits. At other times I centerstage a piece of work or an
idea by devoting group discussion time to it. For instance, when King
Petey seemed to be catching hold among groups of children, I set aside
some group time for the telling of Petey stories, the showing of completed
projects, and the planning of new ones.

As I watched the children's block play more carefully, I began to
hear some children talking about Arthurian characters, whom they had
met through the movie version of "The Sword in the Stone." I also
noticed — in the block area, in dramatic play, and on the yard — a high
degree of interest in war play, not surprisingly among the boys. The
war play revolved not so much about Arthurian characters as about GI
Joe, Masters of the Universe, and Rambo.

I also looked at what was going on in the children's dramatic play,
in addition to the war themes. Magic came up frequently, and in a
class where the girls were so outnumbered, I took particular note of
the fact that a girl was a catalyst in this area. She was often the creator
of original fairy tales with all manner of magical happenings, which the
children developed into short plays. Another child explored a different

facet of magic through creating and presenting magic shows for the class.

From the outset, this group had impressed me as particularly imaginative in its response to stories. I had begun the year by telling the African stories of Ananse (Spider), and teaching the children related chants and singing games from both African and Afro-American traditions. I have often chosen these stories — or Native American stories of Coyote — to start the year, when I don't really know the group yet. This is in part because they seem to "take" with almost any group of children, in part because they can lead in many different directions, and in part because I like them myself. This class took to them in a way others had not, both in their spellbound attention at story time and in individual recastings of the stories. As with King Petey, Spider became a fixture in the class, available to children for their own storytelling.

Rose, in the following two stories, has taken the character of Spider and woven it into her own tales:

> This is my spider and this is his cousin that's sick and he's been in bed for a while but they've been out of their bed tricking their mother, playing when they're not supposed to 'cause their mother sent them to bed at 1:00.
> This is my rainbow that's shining up on them. The sun's right after the rainbow.
> Sometimes they get out of bed when they're not supposed to. They get into the barn and get onto the horses and then they jump off the horses and get into the hay. Then they go back into the house and go to sleep when their mother's coming.

> Spider's little butterfly — and he caught it, and his little cousin caught the butterfly. His little cousin caught a snake and he had to let it go. It's inside the little jar 'cause he had to wait till his mother comes. Then when he goes to his Aunt Spider he plays with the snake and he gets grounded when he comes home. His brother goes to his aunt, too. See, Spider's the aunt's little brother. And when he goes to bed and when his mother leaves again he goes outside and play.

Though her stories are far removed from the folktale mode, both involve trickery, one of the central motifs of the Ananse tales. At the same time, these stories incorporate themes of family and family relationships, which turned out to be central to many of Rose's stories over the course of the year.

The Ananse stories meant something quite different to Spencer. One day, when I finished a tale, someone asked which story I was going to tell next. I said that it was called "Why Spiders Live in Ceilings." Spencer said, "Oh, I know why spiders live in ceilings," and he dictated and illustrated the following story:

Why Spiders Live in Ceilings

Spider lived in a corner on the floor, in a dark corner. And then one day when Spider was sleeping — he was like a spoon, he could tip and spring up — while he was sleeping an animal saw him. Now while he was sleeping this animal liked to eat bugs like spiders. He thought that he should pounce on the legs. Then he pounced on the legs.

But at this time people were working and only a part of the ceiling was finished and they dropped a box and it fell on the animal and the animal made the spider spring up and crash into a dark corner in the made-part ceiling. And that's why Spider never goes down, because he knows that the same thing will happen and he made a new spider web and then he was never troubled.

What stands out to me in Spencer's story is his feel for the folktale genre, his use of turns of phrase that give his story a folktale ring. In his final "that's why" line, in which the story becomes an explanation for all time, he has captured a folktale convention. Phrases like "And then one day" and "But at this time" carry a resonance of the Spider stories he had been hearing.

Perhaps not surprising in a group so drawn to stories was an interest in history. I complemented the Ananse stories with cognates from the New World, inviting the children to find similarities and differences. This led quite naturally to my telling them of how these stories came to this country: the story of the slave trade. Some children responded by making models of slave ships, others by dramatizing aspects of the story, and still others by raising questions at group times that led to yet more thought-provoking discussion. A particularly compelling question was "Why hadn't the slaves just run away?" I told them about the Underground Railroad (and taught "Follow the Drinking Gourd," which remained a favorite song throughout the year). We talked about the dangers of getting caught, and children debated about whether it was worth the risk.

How did I get from King Petey, war play, magic, and the slave story to King Arthur? I cannot spell out the progression step by step; it was in part an intuitive leap. But it was based on what I think of as the conversation of teaching.

This conversation includes much real talk: among the children, between the children and me, and between us all and the wider world. But our conversation is more than talk. The children also "converse" via their drawing, building, dramatic play, and other expressive activity, even when such activity is not actually accompanied by talk.

My role is in part to respond in an ordinary, daily way to what the children bring up. But it is also to reflect on what they are saying (verbally and otherwise) in the context of the wider world, asking myself what areas of human knowledge or endeavor are suggested by the interests arising among the children. And then it is to find ways of making those areas of human inquiry accessible to the children.

With this class I thought about some strands that had been coming up — castles, royalty, magic, story, war, and history. These, along with the specific references to "The Sword in the Stone" on the part of a few children, suggested to me that the stories of King Arthur and a study of "castle times" might be of interest to this group. And so my response to what I had been witnessing among the children was to introduce this material, to see where it would lead us.

The Conversation Continues — Focus: King Arthur

I began our study by reading to the children from a book called *Living in Castle Times*. This story, told from a child's vantage point, is full of small pictures detailing aspects of daily life. It took us several weeks to read, because there was so much on each page, and each page led to discussion of these details. The children were particularly interested in comparing the particulars of life then and now.

A subgroup got interested in technical aspects of castles. I brought in library books that showed cutaway pictures of castles, and Macauley's *Castle*. This group did some intensive work with blocks, trying to reproduce elements of a castle, such as turrets and arrow loops. Others, who were more drawn to moats and drawbridges than to the finer points of castle architecture, worked with sand and water.

I started to tell the Arthurian legends. I wasn't able to find many versions I could just read to the class, because the language was geared to older people. So I retold the stories in my own words, trying to keep some of the particular vocabulary of the time and teaching the children those words and phrases, so that the stories would have something of an authentic ring. (It was interesting to note points at which this vocabulary found its way into the children's writing, as in the use of the word "squire" in Henry's Questing Beast story; see p. 33.) I told these stories on and off from November through most of the school year. On and off because while some children were passionate about the stories, and would have liked nothing better than to hear them all year long, the interest of others would wane, and I needed to honor that. Furthermore, I have a commitment to introducing children to a variety of genres, writers, and cultures through the story time. A local library had several LP records of Arthurian legends, and I was able to borrow those to indulge the appetites of those children who wanted "more Arthur."

I also made a couple of assignments. Coats of arms figured in the Arthurian legends, at times quite crucially, as a means of identifying an armored knight as friend or foe. Each child designed and made a personal coat of arms. This began with a homework assignment: each student was to interview family members about the meaning of his or her first and/or last name, about how he or she was named (e.g., children who were named for someone could choose to find out about their namesakes), or about his or her family history. What came back was a range of stories, from elaborate name tales to the fact that a grandfather had come from Canada and had had a dairy farm. Each child's next task was to find a way to visually represent some element or elements of his or her own story. They sketched these on blank coats of arms that I had cut out of heavy-duty cardboard (the kind used for large appliance boxes). Once they had their designs worked out, they painted them onto the card.

Another assignment was a collaborative project. I cleared off a large section of bulletin board for a mural about the Arthurian tales. Working singly or in pairs (their choice), children selected a story and created a cut-paper representation of it, or of a high point in it. When their artwork was completed they dictated their version of the story, and the dictation went up with the visual work. Two particularly nice touches were a castle with a three-dimensional drawbridge and a knight on a horse crossing it, and a moveable sword in the stone. Children added to the mural as new stories were read.

They also used the bulletin board as a place to hang related material. One child added a picture of the real coat of arms for his family name, which his parents had found and given him. Children who were doing weighing experiments discovered that the flour they were using was King Arthur brand. Up went the illustration from the flour bag.

I was able to borrow some slides of European castles, including one with a fresco featuring Merlin. In addition, I arranged for two seventh and eighth graders who had made a finely wrought castle model to bring it to my class. They shared with my children their expert knowledge of knights and castles, as well as answering technical questions about their model making. This in turn set off a new rash of castle models among my students, this time with more attentiveness to detail than was visible in their earlier attempts, and many activity periods spent on "getting it right." Lego, as well as our junk material supply, turned out to be material well suited to this endeavor.

The children have a daily writing and drawing period. Although I occasionally give assignments during this time, most days the students are free to choose topics for writing and drawing. Children's interest in retelling Arthurian legends in their own words, as in the following examples, indicated to me that they were making this material their own. Additionally, each story was a window for me on a particular child's take on a story he or she had heard. (Some of these stories were written by the children; others were dictated.)

The Questing Beast

A knight was chasing a beast. The beast had heads that looked like dog heads. The beast sounded like all of the dogs were screaming.

The knight tried to catch the beast. He met the king—King Arthur. He got a horse from Arthur.

Arthur's horse died. Arthur was sitting under a tree. A knight came riding by looking for the beast. He asked Arthur if a big beast came by. Arthur said yes. The knight really wanted a new horse. A squire came by with a fresh horse for King Arthur. The knight rode away on it. Then another guy came by with another horse just for King Arthur.

—Henry

Merlin

Merlin was a magician. He made the hand go up in the lake and give Arthur the sword. He could change into a boy or a fox or anything in the world.

—Ana

The Sword in the Stone

King Arthur was the only one who could pull the sword out of the stone. He became the king of all England. That is true—he did.

—Paul

The Lady in the Lake

The lady in the lake is saying to Arthur and Merlin that they may go and take the sword and the sheath only if they return something and she will tell them when she is ready.

—Mae

Beaumains

Sir Lancelot was fighting with Beaumains. Lancelot is the guy who saved Guinevere. They're playing in the woods, charging each other. Beaumains is the person who came to a castle when King Arthur was celebrating a holiday. He asked King Arthur if he would make him a knight.

Later on a lady came and she asked King Arthur if he'd send one of his knights to help her sister locked in a castle by the baddest knight in the world and that knight is the Red Knight. Beaumains asked Arthur if he could go and Arthur said yes.

—Noah

As with the Spider stories, the Arthurian tales provided fertile ground for new, child-created stories, such as:

Merlin put some magic into a big log and the thing with the log on top of it moved and crashed into the castle and suddenly the North Tower crumbled. And a rock came suddenly and it made a humongous hole in the walls. People were shooting arrows from the battlements. People fell dead from the battlements. In the morning there was lots of blood splashed on the ground. In the afternoon there was blood globbed on the ground. The blood flamed at sunset. And suddenly there were trumpets ringing in the air that Arthur had conquered his sister's town. And a flashing of swords filled the town. The end.

—Spencer

This is the horse and King Arthur. Today is cold and windy so King Arthur got up and started his stove. King Arthur's horse is tied up with a rope and there's a little hitch and that's the rope that King Arthur holds onto to stay on his horse.

—Henry

Tad, who had introduced King Petey back in September, developed that character (whose name he changed to Peter, having decided that Petey wasn't a suitably royal name for a king), and introduced other members of his royal family of cats in a series of stories he wrote:

The Party

King Peter went to the party. They stayed for ten days and ten nights. They caught lots and lots of fish. They dined on mints and slices of quince and they stayed all night. King Peter went back to his castle. His kittens painted him. Luckily, his kittens painted him yellow, the color he is. King Peter noticed that his kittens had painted him.

The Battle

Chief Guard Twit went to a battle. He stayed for all night long. He stabbed the dragon. The horse was standing in a river of blood. Chief Guard Twit and the other knights had a lunch break. They had dragon sandwiches. Happy knights. The job was done.

The War

Royal Prince Friendly was at the castle. He was having a big feast. They were having dragon soup. But suddenly they heard a trumpet. King Peter ran to see what was going on. He told Friendly to tell the knights that they had a battle. The knights fought for twenty days and twenty nights. Finally the battle was done. Peter and Friendly were almost killed. They lived. They were so happy that they decided to have a big feast.

I could describe more class activity, for instance the way impromptu dramatization developed into short plays. However, I think the examples already cited suffice to give the flavor of the work we were doing, and it is not my intention here to catalogue the full curriculum. My focus is on how the activities and ideas originated, and in particular on the active involvement of children in the process.

King Arthur and "Big Ideas"

Any topic of study or any discipline can be entered from a multitude of perspectives and can lead in endless directions. In the Arthur study described up to this point, emphasis was placed on legend, daily life, castle architecture, and family history as topics, and on drawing, painting, drama, building, storytelling, and writing as media of expression.

Just as the study led us into legend, family history, building, and storytelling, it also led into what I think of as wider ideas. I'm referring to themes that were not so explicitly linked to Arthurian legends and times, but that in our class discussions grew out of consideration of the Arthur material. One such theme was good and evil; another was truth and fiction; a third touched on male/female stereotypes.

I first noticed the issue of good and evil come up in a discussion about Sir Kay: whether he was a "good guy" or a "bad guy" and what his character was like. When I later read the story of Beaumains, the hero was clearly Beaumains, and Kay a villain. This brought the question back to the foreground.

One child commented, "In every bad person there's still a little bit of good, and in every good person there's a little bit of bad." The children were intrigued with this notion; it was one of those ideas that took hold in the group (it always interests me to see which ideas fascinate each group). They began to talk about it in terms of themselves, being good people who sometimes do naughty things (many examples here!). Then they returned to Beaumains:

Student 1: In the King Arthur story Kay wasn't treating Beaumains right and when Kay came after him — Kay charged with his spear — then Beaumains drew his sword from his holder and they charged each other and Beaumains knocked Kay off and took his shield and his spear.

Student 2: And that was bad. Beaumains used his little bit of bad in hurting Kay and in taking his sword.

Ellen: Can you say why you think that was bad?

Student 2: Because it was somebody else's thing. He shouldn't have tooken it from him.

Student 3: He should have asked Arthur for it.

Student 4: Well, he needed it.

Ellen: What do people think about that? Was it OK for Beaumains to take something that was not his because he needed it?

This question in turn led to further discussion about whether it is ever justified to take something that is not one's own, whether necessity (to fight for one's life) is a valid reason.

I guide these discussions in much the same way that I guide the curriculum: by putting out questions for the children to address or highlighting a question raised by a child. Since my aim is to foster thoughtfulness, the ability to probe beneath the surface, and serious consideration of the ideas of others, I try to listen for those points in the discussion where I can interject a question to deepen the dialogue or to draw the larger group to consider a point raised by one child ("Was it OK to take the sword if it was needed to survive?"). I also requested clarification at times ("Can you say why you think that was bad?"). Another role I take on is "memory holder" for the group (some children also take on this role). For instance, the discussion from which this excerpt is drawn came several days after the initial comment about every bad person having a little bit of good. I began this discussion by reminding the group of that idea, and asking children to comment on it.

The sorts of questions raised in this discussion recurred at other points, sometimes raised by children, sometimes by me. The strong interest in war play provided a backdrop that made these particularly compelling and personal discussions. The children had something at stake; they cared. And for me, it was a more comfortable way of dealing with the war play than simply condemning it (or condoning it, or ignoring it).

A schoolwide celebration of Martin Luther King's birthday provided another arena for the consideration of these ideas. In the context of the stories of King and of Rosa Parks, we were talking about violence and nonviolence. Why didn't King and Parks and the bus boycotters of Birmingham just fight? A child brought up GI Joe and Rambo as characters who fight for what is "right." There was a heated discussion about whether they are "good guys" or "bad guys" because they fight and kill. All the children identified them as "good guys," and the characters they vanquish as "bad guys," but they grappled with the killing part. There were no clear conclusions, more the feeling of people working through a dilemma, trying to figure out what they felt about it all. And I discovered, for the first time, how these powerful characters from the children's television world can become part of the curriculum. Previously I had shied away from the whole subject of those television heroes, allowing my own discomfort to blind me to possibilities to probe more deeply.

Another large theme that came up was that of fiction and nonfiction. Tad, who could spin a yarn so convincingly that his classmates would believe it was true, was, at the same time, *very* interested in the line between fiction and nonfiction. It is for me a hard line to define. So when he asked whether the Arthurian legends were truth or fiction, I was hard pressed to give him a simple (and satisfying) answer. I said that to the best of my knowledge not everything in the stories was literally true, but that people who were digging back have found artifacts and sites that they associate with Arthurian times, and that some historians think there might really have been a King Arthur, though it was impossible to be certain. I brought in library books that showed some of the historical finds.

The children's response was to try to figure out with each succeeding tale which parts of the stories were true. Once this question had been opened up, the discussion after each story would inevitably include an effort to figure out which parts had really happened and which were made up. A new child joined the class on a day when I was in the middle of a Gawain story. One of the first things that the others brought up in introducing him to the Arthurian legends was the issue of truth and fiction; it seemed important to them to set him straight on that.

The children's book *Sir Gawain and the Loathly Lady* created an opportunity for discussion that was of particular value in this class where the girls were so outnumbered. In this story, Arthur's life depends on his ability to find out "what it is that women most desire." I stopped before reading the part that tells how Arthur found the answer and had each girl in the class answer the question for herself. We then had a full-group discussion about the question. When across-the-board claims or stereotyped answers were suggested we could check them out; the girls became a sounding board for their validity. I also asked the children to think about other girls and women they knew. Would the claims they were suggesting hold for their mothers, sisters, grandmothers, female friends? In the end, the children could not arrive at a common answer. We returned to the story. Arthur asks many women, and from each gets a different answer. ("Just like us," commented a child.)

The Loathly Lady saves Arthur's life by telling him the answer: "What all women most desire is to have their own way." I prompted more discussion here, concerned that the expression "have their own way" fueled a stereotype. As we talked about real-life instances, what came out is that *all* the children — boys and girls — wanted to have their own way.

These class discussions allowed me to see a different sort of interest developing among the children. They were at a place where (sometimes) children related something quite particular (Sir Kay, GI Joe, the Martin Luther King story) to a larger question. As with the development of themes, I assume that the larger questions will vary from group to group, and thus it is my job to be attentive to those that come up in each particular class, and to respond. I am, of course, also a moderator, ensuring that a variety of voices are heard and that major questions and thoughts don't get lost.

The Emergent Curriculum and Issues of Authority

In my first year at Putney Central I had a child in my class who was the son of farmhands, and at home did calf chores alongside his father's cow chores. He had seen calves born, had helped his dad treat sick cows, and knew of the disaster to the herd when an epidemic spread through it. On all these subjects this child (who, incidentally, came to first grade identified for special education in speech and language) could speak, draw, and write eloquently, if sparsely. When questions about cows arose to which he didn't know the answer, he knew how he could find out, and would do so, instead of fudging an answer. I considered him an authority on the subject, as did his classmates.

I often think of this child when I reflect on authority in the classroom, both my own and the children's. "Authority" is a loaded word, particularly in the school context. At its root is "author," which suggests a person productively engaged in creating a work. It also has overtones of ownership. An author is active, which brings back to mind the assumption I set out earlier: that people are active in the pursuit of meaning. It was this child's experience with cows, the meaning with which he imbued this experience, and his ability to call upon his knowledge that made him an authority. Equally, his authority remained dynamic because of his willingness to consider questions that pushed at the frontiers of his knowledge and to go back to the farm or to the library in pursuit of further information.

What I have described in the emergence of curriculum around Arthurian legends is not a shift towards classroom democracy in the literal sense; nor do I think it reasonable (or honest) of me to pretend that my classroom will become a democracy in which I will be the children's equal in all ways. The shift that is embedded in the emergent approach to curriculum is one of stance. It requires of me as a teacher to stand back as I observe and reflect on the life of the class, and to tailor my work as introducer, assigner, and instructor to what I absorb via observation and reflection.

One aspect of my work is to respond to the children on a day-to-day basis about their work and ideas, to note patterns and themes and to highlight them in group discussions, to point out to a child the work of another that might hold interest for him or her, and to look for opportunities to teach skills in the context of the children's work. At the same time, I am storing up images, ideas, motifs, and preferred modes of expression and mulling them over in terms of the larger world. This larger world encompasses the community in which we live, but also the world of ideas, handed down to us in literature, art, science, history, geography, mathematics, and other disciplines. My work here is to discover arenas in that larger world in which the children's questions are explored, and then to choose suitable ways to introduce that material, activities that will draw the children in and provide them with opportunities to express their understanding of the material. At the same time, I need to remain attentive to what children do with what I introduce—my cues for how the study will unfold.

In this way, the curriculum becomes a collaborative venture. That is, it becomes as much my job to listen, look, and respond as to initiate, and the children have a hand in initiating via their own work (for instance, the sand and water play, block building, dramatics, and storytelling). Of course, there are differences between us. By dint of my age and education, I have come into contact with areas of the world with which the children are less familiar. Also, as the teacher I have a slew of responsibilities that they don't share—responsibililities to my own standards for what should be going on, as well as responsibilities to common goals and programs of the school, responsibilities to parents, and responsibilities mandated at the district and state levels. At the same time, I don't want to take over total responsibility for the children's learning.

There are always times when I introduce or assign work because I deem it necessary or because of external requirements. What I am suggesting is not that the emergent approach take over as a panacea for all that ails schools. I am by nature cautious of such sweeping claims for *any* method or material, and feel that our societal inclination toward educational cure-alls has gotten us into grave difficulties, by turning our gaze toward models or programmatic solutions rather than toward the particular individuals who people our schools. While not at all proposing another model, I am suggesting that this approach to curriculum is one way of enacting what Dewey suggests as an alternative to "the doctrine of formal discipline" when he urges us to discover "typical modes of activity, whether play or useful occupations, in which individuals are concerned, in whose outcome they recognize they have something at stake, and which cannot be carried through without reflection and use of judgement" (156). In retelling the story of how one area of curriculum grew with one class, I intended to illustrate how, in a day-to-day and week-to-week way, a teacher can both see points of activity and interest (through observation and record keeping) and create spaces in classrooms for them to be explored further (through linking what is learned from such records to curriculum planning).

Changing the teacher's stance necessarily alters the roles of student and teacher. The point is not that everything should emerge from the children, but rather that the curriculum, like other areas of classroom practice, can become a dialogue between students and teacher. If this is to be a true dialogue, one that takes its shape from the children's emerging voices and not just that of the teacher, then the teacher cannot have fully mapped out the terrain beforehand. This is not to say that one does not plan. Rather, it implies that one plans in a way that leaves room for surprises, that lets the work of the class — like a conversation — travel down unexpected byways.

Because I start with the assumption that I set forth early on — that as humans we share an inclination to create meaning out of experience — I don't worry about the byways leading us in different directions than I might have anticipated. My job is not to judge the ultimate worth of a child's interest, but to pay close attention, to keep probing (much as I would have the children probe) for what lies below the surface or beyond the present horizon, and then to translate that into potential new directions for the group. I must learn to become as active in listening and responding as in setting out material or "giving lessons."

My own effort to incorporate this way of working into my classes has, over the years, deepened my appreciation of the potential present in the small moments that comprise a school day and of the depth of thought visible in the young children I teach. In spite of the difference in our ages, the children have been able to revitalize my own thinking about such issues as war play and "good guys/bad guys" by offering fresh perspectives when my own risked stagnation. In this way, I am reminded that it is not only curriculum that emerges or grows out of the collaborative work of people engaged in an educational endeavor. At the core, it is our understanding that is ever emerging. As I reflect back on the Arthur study, I see that my own understanding of the possibilities inherent in the Arthurian legends has altered and deepened thanks to the many perspectives offered by a group of six- and seven-year-olds who were my colleagues as well as my students.

Note

This essay was first presented in a somewhat different form at a seminar called Early Identification of Children's Strengths held at The Prospect Center, North Bennington, Vermont, in April 1987. The thought-provoking questions raised by Prospect staff members David Carroll and Susan Donnelly helped me to translate what was at that point the day-to-day life of my class into a description of curriculum. I am also indebted to Patricia Carini and to The Prospect Center for introducing me to ideas about the emergent curriculum and for the reflective environment they have made available. Judy Ashkenaz and Anne Martin generously provided me with invaluable editorial assistance. All names of the children have been changed to protect their privacy.

Works Cited

Carini, P. F. 1979. *The art of seeing and the visibility of the person.* North Dakota Study Group on Evaluation Monograph Series. Grand Forks: University of North Dakota.

———. 1982. *The school lives of seven children: A five-year study.* North Dakota Study Group on Evaluation Monograph Series. Grand Forks: University of North Dakota.

Dewey, J. 1916. *Democracy and education.* New York: Macmillan.

Gee, R. 1982. *Living in castle times.* London: Usborne.

Hastings, S. 1985. *Sir Gawain and the loathly lady.* New York: Lothrop, Lee & Shepard.

Macauley, D. 1977. *Castle.* Boston: Houghton Mifflin.

Response

Anne Martin

Curriculum as "the conversation of teaching" and "a dialogue between students and teachers" — what an apt metaphor for the complex learning (on the part of the teacher as well as children) that takes place in this pre-first-grade classroom! Ellen's class feasts on words — stories, discussion, folktales, history, song, literature — and the children engage in "expressive activity" that mirrors some of the themes and elegant language ("The blood flamed at sunset") that they have imbibed. By her intense participation in the conversation, which requires standing back to listen, observe, and reflect, Ellen keeps the dialogue alive, always growing and often taking unexpected turns and twists. The children and Ellen develop a language, both spoken and symbolic, in which they learn to communicate with each other and make connections.

While primary teaching in all schools is focused on what is generally referred to as "language arts," the term unfortunately tends to be narrowly interpreted to mean daily drill in reading, handwriting, and spelling, accompanied by many work sheets and "seatwork." Somewhere along the line, the true "arts" are dropped in favor of tightly bounded lessons presented by the teacher to the students with varying amounts of success. Where the lessons fail, schools often blame the backgrounds or temperaments of the children who are unable to fulfill the school's expectations. Even where curricula are planned for greater student participation, such as the introduction of the "learning centers" that so puzzled Ellen at the start of her teaching career, materials and work sheets at each station are usually prepared with a specific outcome in mind. "Centers" imply bounded figures that can be measured, located, and defined ahead of time.

In Ellen's classroom, there is always "room for surprises," and her approach "lets the work of the class — like a conversation — travel down unexpected byways." It is a delicious irony that the children in this class, designated "'developmentally young' — not ready for first grade," grapple with questions of morality, truth, social organization, war/peace, and other basic human problems, as they produce thoughtful work on topics like the King Arthur legend or delight in their discoveries in natural science. But the inherent capabilities of young children should not come as a surprise, nor are they only evident in the classrooms

42

of obviously gifted teachers like Ellen. In every kindergarten class I have taught over the years, children come to school with strong interests, knowledge, curiosity about the world, and an endless eagerness to learn. They also come with an unquenchable thirst for playing out their ideas and fantasies, which they express in many forms: blocks, house corner, arts and crafts, writing, speaking, sand, water, movement, outdoor play. How we respond to our youngest children as they first enter school and adjust to working within a group is probably a crucial factor in the rest of their school lives. If we fail to make use of children's strengths, experience, and inclinations in mapping out curriculum, we are bound to lose our main entry point to their paths of learning.

The collaborative learning Ellen describes is certainly dependent on some basic assumptions she states clearly: that all children seek to make sense of their world and relate their experiences in school to their own lives; that teachers can learn about children through observation and documentation of daily classroom events; that teachers can use what they learn about children to provide a setting and materials that support children's strengths and interests; that teachers need time for reflection. What Ellen implies but does not elaborate is that teachers also need colleagues to talk with, not only in a friendly capacity but as serious collaborators in the challenging task of working out new relationships within the classroom (a different "stance") and deepening our understanding of children's learning. Traditionally teachers were isolated in their classrooms, out of touch with each other, often lonely. Even now when we give so much lip service to "sharing," and "networking," it takes special effort and strong motivation to make the time and opportunities for teachers to come together to exchange knowledge and discoveries, just as children need to do.

One place where this happens is the Summer Institute at The Prospect Center in North Bennington, Vermont, where Ellen developed so much of her philosophy and practice. For two weeks each summer, about twenty-five teachers from all over the country come together for intensive study of children, children's work, classrooms, schools, and school issues. Much of the work takes place within structured group processes that are constantly adapted and revised to fit particular needs, topics, and times. Books and articles are read jointly, and participants bring along concerns and research projects that they would like to explore with colleagues. Other more informal work takes place over mealtimes; during rambles through the Vermont countryside; and in the evenings in the dorm, where people may gather in each other's rooms, and the sound of typewriters and word processors competes with crickets. The group varies from year to year, but there is a core of dedicated, involved teachers who have gradually taken on the responsibility for planning and organizing the sessions. In everything that has happened during Summer Institute over the years, there is the strong presence of Patricia Carini, former director of The Prospect Center, whose extraordinary work and depth of thought inspire other participants, moving them into new areas of understanding and endeavor.

While summer workshop contacts are intense and may sometimes be continued during the year, it is obviously important to have this kind of collegial support available at each school site. In many places, teachers (sometimes as a result of their experience at the Prospect Summer Institutes) have organized their own school or local teachers' child study groups. These groups may meet once a week or once a month, with members rotating responsibilities for organizing, planning, and carrying out a program that reflects the interests and needs of the particular school or school system. When a group of teachers is available as supportive friends and helpful colleagues, it is easier for a teacher to take risks, try out new ideas, follow through on classroom research. But even where this is not possible, teachers can change and grow and seek out whatever resources there may be in their own communities.

While the complexities of Ellen's classroom and thinking may appear a bit daunting, on one level she has fairly simple suggestions that are within reach of any thoughtful, committed teacher. One implication of Ellen's piece is that if we want children to be interested in school, it is important to supply them with intrinsically interesting things to do. Her casual listing of the children's daily choices does present us with a staggering array of materials and activities, and it is true that Ellen's classroom sounds exceptionally rich in materials, but many of them are basic and not necessarily expensive, such as paper, paints, crayons, sand, water, junk materials, library books, nature finds. Parents and other community members are often untapped resources for raw materials that lend themselves to many purposes. And most school systems, even restrictive ones, probably leave some room within curriculum guidelines for teachers to adapt the use of materials supplied.

A large range of materials and activities is obviously an asset, but even more important is the *time* for children to make use of materials in their own ways, to work informally with each other, to be permitted to engage in pursuits of their own with the understanding that these activities are considered worthwhile, and to have occasion to show and explain their work to the whole class. When children are given time to explore materials and talk to each other, the teacher has a chance to do what we all do almost automatically every day: to notice things children do and say. All teachers tend to bubble over with funny, sad, interesting, or just curious classroom stories that take hold of them and often won't let go. Out of this, with practice and time, can come the *attentive* looking, listening, and recording that Ellen describes so well, which allows teachers to notice and follow up on incipient studies and themes. We don't need to search far for fruitful subjects and themes: they pop up wherever there are children talking and playing within the context of a lively, reflective classroom. As Ellen indicated, even those ubiquitous Ninja turtles and other TV characters can be useful indicators of young children's search for what constitutes good and evil, the sources and play of power in society, the roles of children and adults within the family.

As every teacher knows, no matter how well a classroom may be going, there are many discouraging days at school, and we are usually our own severest critics. Moreover, the outside world is an increasingly dangerous, threatening, and uncaring place, especially for children. As teachers, we are caught between the small daily pressures and the larger crushing ones, as we take responsibility for helping children deal with a world that is often beyond our own understanding. Perhaps the only way we can keep going within our schools is to remain open to different ways of responding to children so that our interest in teaching gets constantly renewed. If we encourage children to be teachers of each other, just as we become learners in our own classroom, we will be able to welcome the contributions every child's "authority" can make to the group. But at the heart of all teaching and learning is *relationship*, more than specific lessons, topics, materials, methods. In order to survive in schools we need to keep building our own communication skills so that over time we can sustain an ever-expanding dialogue with children and other teachers.

3

Savoir ou Connaître?
Alternative Ways of Knowing in the Foreign Language Class

Wendy Strachan
Evi Zoukis

March 16: Michael has finished his presentation. We all
learned how to make a chocolate grasshopper. The ingredients
were all American but the process was all taught in Greek. A
success? Was the learning of Greek enhanced? Yes, a certain
amount of new vocabulary and phrasing was used, but couldn't
that be done in a regular classroom anyway? Yes, it could.
Something new did happen today, though. I wasn't the
instructor. I guess one shouldn't take that for granted. I
actually managed to stay out of it. . . .

This excerpt from Evi's teaching log encapsulates the uncertainties
faced by any teacher experimenting with alternative approaches to
learning in the classroom. In particular, however, it points to the
experience of foreign language teachers who routinely, albeit without
malice and for merely forty minutes a day, risk making their normally
vocal students feel like verbal incompetents. With limited vocabulary
and grammar, students in the foreign language class obviously cannot
express much of what is on their minds. They depend on the teacher
and on the text for what they learn to say. Typically, they practice

While this essay is written collaboratively, the point of view shifts. To clarify these shifts,
our initials — WS or EZ — follow each section heading. The first section is written
from Wendy's point of view.

46

grammatical structures and use vocabulary through a variety of activities, which range from memorizing foolproof patterns to creating individual sentences or essays. The contexts for such practice are secondary, facilitative only. They provide a framework, but are rarely a situation out of which an authentic need for linguistic communication arises. The onus for making the material meaningful and the activities purposeful thus falls on the teacher as the person who knows and understands the language. The role of the student seems necessarily confined to that of recipient-learner.

In twelve years of teaching French and Greek to middle school students in an American International School in Greece, Evi Zoukis had experimented with various methods. She had taught from what she refers to as "a somewhat random assemblage of ideas about what works." Sometimes she got new ideas from journals, sometimes from other teachers, sometimes from sessions at conferences. More often, suggestions for how she might improve her teaching were visited upon her from "without" — that is, by new textbooks or itinerant experts. She reacted to such upgrading efforts with some resistance. She felt an implicit assumption that she was somehow inadequate to the task of improving her own teaching although she believed that she, like other teachers, knew best what should and should not be done in her own classroom.

As one of those "itinerant experts," I met Evi five years ago. My work is in the teaching of writing, which for me has implications for all aspects of teaching and learning in schools. Evi participated in the first series of writing workshops I offered at her school. She became intrigued by the relationships between language and learning and between learning and patterns of social interaction and the implications for the foreign language class. She introduced learning logs to her classes. Students wrote to her about their classwork and their problems with the language. She taught writing as a process, taking time to do prewriting and revision of content before focusing on errors. At first, she used these processes mechanically and felt uncertain of their value. Over the course of subsequent workshops, however, the strategies became more meaningful. Going through the experience of being a student helped her become self-conscious about her own learning process. In her foreign language classes, keeping a log became a matter of course, revising a stage that simply could not be left out, and peer conferencing no longer a nightmare to be avoided at all costs. Evi was nevertheless conscious of a persisting dichotomy between her emerging theory of learning and her teaching practice.

Over the first three years of her involvement with what became the school's ongoing Writing Project, I had seen Evi come to value responsive instead of directive teaching and to believe in collaborative patterns of work in the classroom. The barriers that seemed to prevent her from really transforming the interaction in her classroom, however, were ones every foreign language teacher will recognize: the students' limited knowledge of the language, which places obvious limits on their capacity for self-expression, and their beliefs, based on experience, about how foreign language is taught and learned. We spent hours in intensive discussion of how and whether these limitations necessarily made foreign language learning an enterprise quite different from learning other kinds of subject matter. Evi talked; I listened and asked questions. When it became possible for me to offer a course at the school in classroom research for teachers, Evi saw this as an opportunity to investigate those barriers and limitations. An invitation to think through and articulate what she was learning from teaching was, more-over, an invitation to the reflective practitioner she knew herself to be.

In what follows, we offer an account of that investigation. In writing it, we have attempted to present different angles of observation without sacrificing the sense of their often simultaneous occurrence. From one angle, this account documents a sequence of activities that could be adapted for use in other classes. From another, it articulates the process of collaboration between teacher and students in the planning and presentation of course material. From a third angle, it comments on the process of researching one's own practice; from a fourth, it reflects on what it means to learn and know a foreign language. When the project was over, it was the fourth angle that most intrigued us. We discovered that the nature of the project, as it emerged both for the students and for us, came to be symbolized in distinctions we attached to the meanings of "know" that in French are expressed by two different verbs: *savoir* and *connaître*. *Savoir* means to know in the sense of knowing how to do something. It refers to knowing facts and possessing information. *Connaître*, on the other hand, means to know in the sense of being acquainted with and understanding. It is used to refer to knowing people and places. One would say, for instance: Je sais parler français (I know how to speak French) but Je connais la langue française (I know the French language). Implied in the use of *connaître* with *la langue* is a sense of the quality of knowing we associate with people and places. In the case of knowing the language, we mean knowledge at a spontaneous, felt level, not simply how to use it. Our account is thus, in addition, an account of a journey from *savoir* to *connaître* for both teacher and students.

The Teacher as Researcher: Finding a Focus (WS)

Language development is often narrowly conceived in foreign language teaching. Habits of correct use are encouraged with praise for right answers. Wrong responses are extinguished by meticulous correcting of errors and through practice in repeating correct forms. Acts of speaking and writing the foreign language are almost always invited as conscious acts. Language is not expected simply to flow out appropriately in context. Research in writing suggests that an overemphasis on error and correction inhibits the flow of language and the development of fluency in writing. The learner is either unwilling to express him or herself or keeps to the safety of what he is sure about. The traditional methods of teaching foreign language typically produce just such reactions. They probably also communicate similar messages about the nature and purpose of language.

One message is surely that one does not really need to say anything with a foreign language in order to learn it. (And, for some people certainly, that does seem to be true — they learn it anyway!) Another message is that it is best not to say something unless you know you are saying it correctly. We suspect that if one could become an invisible visitor in many foreign language classes, one would very often hear the teacher silencing student protests with the classic, "Never mind what you want to say. Just say what you can." Optimally, this could be viewed as encouragement to "use" the language from the start. Unfortunately, that is very rarely what is conveyed. Instead, the message is construed to mean "*Only* say what you can say *correctly.*" If the messages about the language are to change, however, the focus of attention needs to change or to be much broadened. Attention to the language might usefully shift to, or at least include, attention to learning, with language as the means of communication — in this case, the foreign language.

From research on composing and from our experience of learning in the workshop settings of the Writing Project we have learned that confidence and willingness to take risks can be fostered when the learner does not fear error, when learning draws on prior knowledge or experience — thus when passive knowledge is brought into active use — and when the language to be learned is contextualized by a meaningful situation that encourages purposeful activity. Of course, the "readings" in the foreign language textbook do provide topics and occasions that set contexts for the learning of vocabulary and syntax. Sometimes this context includes cultural information that is learned as students compose dialogues or paragraphs based on what is given. Opportunities for expression, however, all conform to the basic assumption: Language development proceeds from correct usage. The teacher, as the expert in the language, is the arbiter of that usage. The text typically makes the choice of material and structures to be learned. Knowledge flows principally in one direction: from teacher and text to student.

Evi, in her classes, had experimented with strategies she experienced in the writing workshops. She introduced learning logs and peer conferencing to vary the pattern of interaction and to encourage students to rely on themselves and each other as they learned. She knew she wanted to encourage more independence and to have students even more fully engaged and aware of their own skills, but it was not at all clear what kinds of changes she could initiate in a foreign language class and still fulfill her responsibilities as the teacher. She was also concerned about the meaning of what she might do. What would make it into "research"?

After searching through journal articles to see what others had done and finding no obvious model or match to her own situation, she realized she would simply have to trust her own judgment. As she commented in one of her teaching logs: "If I were to read that no similar projects have been done in the foreign language field, thereby confirming the innovative aspect of it, I would feel I'm on the right track. On the other hand, that could also be misleading. Being innovative doesn't necessarily mean being on the right track." She recognized also that she would have to give up wanting scientific precision and generalizability from her investigation. All the teachers in the Teachers as Researchers class wrestled with this issue, Evi more than others. We began the class by thinking about the concept of classroom research and examining samples of research by other teachers. As Evi saw it, "Attempting to define what classroom research is would be like describing each and every unique situation that each and every unique teacher is attempting to draw conclusions from by observing it closely." In the end, the pressure of time forced everyone to action.

Evi decided that students in two of her middle school classes, one a second-year Intermediate Greek class, the other an Advanced French class, could take on a project in which they did the teaching. In the Greek class, she planned to allow the students to select both the material and the approach to teaching it; in the other, she would select the material, but let the students decide how to go about teaching it and evaluating learning. Through documenting and analyzing the process of preparing and implementing their teaching plans, she hoped to see what effects such a process had on their language development and on the patterns of interaction in the classroom. More specifically, she asked: In classroom situations where students are able to teach, (1) is their learning of the foreign language enhanced and (2) is more meaningful teacher/student and student/student dialogue fostered? Evi's next step was to present the project to the students and to enlist not only their cooperation but also their collaboration.

Collaborating with the Students (EZ)

Expecting the student in a foreign language class to take on the role of the teacher could seem rather suspect. I legitimized it fairly easily to my two middle school classes, however, who seemed quite unable to resist — as we all would be — being invited to play an instrumental role in an investigation. I explained what it means to do classroom research and what I wanted to learn. I made it clear that this was to be a joint venture through which they would both teach and learn. The teaching would involve a new set of responsibilities given to them, and a new set of responsibilities given to me. I stated my research question very clearly, underlining that I would be observing them and collecting data all along. I solicited their cooperation in supplying as much of that data as possible, and as I anticipated, they seemed quite eager. We all knew from the start that we, as a team, would be looking for evidence of how and whether this activity would provide a better means of learning the foreign language than the methods we had used so far. We would all evaluate the teaching presentations and we would all keep logs of what we were doing.

Students in the Greek class were to make their own choice of a topic or skill to teach the others. I encouraged them to choose something they thought would be really fun and interesting for the class to learn. They seemed to like the idea of choosing their own subject matter, but had some reservations about being able to teach it in Greek. It seemed like a gigantic step beyond the traditional safety of even the most creative activity in any foreign language textbook. It was one thing to write a dialogue simulating a real situation, quite another to teach something and handle genuine, unpredictable dialogue with others. It also seemed to most of them, complete beginners the year before, too ambitious a venture for their basic vocabulary of approximately two thousand words. It seemed to require a level of fluency they did not yet possess. However, the mere fact of our beginning to discuss topics and plans made the project concrete and achievable. The first day evolved into a brainstorming session, an excerpt from which follows:

Evi: Let's talk about how we're going to plan the activity.

Tara: Can we write these steps down?

Evi: Sure. Well, what's first?

Lisa: Think of an idea.

Amy: Yeah, list your ideas.

Michael: Narrow it down to your two favorites.

Amy: See which one would be easier.

Evi: Is that how you're going to choose your activity? Any other considerations?

Mary Ann: Which is more interesting, fun, easy to find information on.

Evi: OK. (*writing on the board*) Then what?

Michael: Well, you have to get the information.

Evi: What would you call that?

Ben: Research!

Evi: How do you do research?

Tara: Talking to people.

Terry: Books.

Lisa: Using what you know.

Michael: Experiences.

Evi: It seems we have a particular problem, though. Can you guess what it's going to be?

Amy: The Greek—

Evi: Think of how you're going to use the language.

Ben: Dictionary.

Mary Ann: What you already know.

Tara: Talking to other people.

We continued in this fashion until we had devised a plan of how each student was to go about choosing a subject to present to the group, get the information, and finally, prepare this whole project in Greek. We made a list of expressions that all students would need in order to talk about and explain their subject, such as: Today I'm going to talk to you about. ... Look on the sheet that I passed out. ... Are there any questions? ... Do you understand? etc. I let the students suggest the expressions that they would need as well as try to give a Greek equivalent, or at least an approximation using the vocabulary they knew so far.

For the Advanced French class, I had selected the language content to be taught. I divided the chapters from the text and assigned a section to each student. The students felt no anxiety about working in French since they were competent speakers, but they were concerned about the new responsibility of teaching. In our first discussion of the project, they described some of the problems they anticipated:

Mark: Les autres n'auront pas d'intérêt. (The others will not be interested.)

Alice: La classe ne sera pas sérieuse. (The class won't be serious.)

Chris: C'est difficile de faire un test. (It's hard to make up a test.)

Manos: Je n'ai pas d'expérience. C'est difficile d'expliquer seulement en français. Je ne sais pas comment expliquer. Je n'ai jamais expliqué quelque chose à quelqu'un. On n'a jamais ça à mon ancienne école. (I have no experience. It is difficult to explain only in French. I don't know how to explain. I've never explained anything to anyone. We never did this in my old school.)

In both classes, the planning period that followed seemed time-consuming and stressful. Inevitably, a teacher embarking on a relatively new venture such as this is apprehensive and feels the need to justify every minute of every class period, making sure it can be categorized as "productive." I know such was the case with me. During the two weeks it took us to prepare the presentations, there were days when "very little," as I saw it then, was accomplished. On those days, students would stare at their folders wondering what to do next, or would converse (to my great discomfort) among themselves on issues totally unrelated to the project, or in the worst of cases, would totally reject the whole research idea with middle school language: "I hate doing this stuff. This is stupid. Why are we doing this anyway? Do we have to?"

In our logs, we recorded our reactions to the process and our accounts of plans and progress. I spent some time with Manos in the French group, suggesting ways in which he could learn how to explain things. Some days students became unwilling to take responsibility, wanting me to make decisions for them. I resisted. I conferenced with each of them, and then they met with each other to share ideas and report on their progress.

At the end of the two weeks, each student had put together a package that included a teaching plan, notes for the presentation, questions for the class, log entries, and sample teaching materials. They had analyzed their material and created a working vocabulary list, not only of new words needed to talk about their subject but also useful explanatory expressions that would serve as teaching tools. They had reviewed the oral explanatory part of their presentation with me in order to iron out difficulties and to acquire familiarity with it. They had made a list of possible problems that might arise, linguistic or otherwise, in an attempt to be as well prepared as possible. Once they were ready, we began the unit. Each student taught for two to three class periods. They presented the material, engaged the class in an activity with it, and evaluated their learning. I sat at the back of the room with my notebook and got ready to record what went on ... at least, that is what I tried to do, but it is easier said than done.

The Greek Class (EZ)

March 16: The presentations started today. Finally. I thought we would never get out of the planning stage. On the other hand, I knew that that would be one of my concerns. How important is teaching someone to make their favorite dessert in a foreign language? It seems like something unreal, contrived. What are we trying to prove? What am I trying to prove? ... Perhaps I should remove myself from trying to prove something constantly and just let the presentations go on — just observe!

As my journal entry at the beginning of this chapter notes, Michael chose to cook, and we made chocolate grasshoppers in the Domestic Science room. Tara taught calligraphy, Amy taught music appreciation, and Ben taught the rudiments of sailing using diagrams and pictures. Each student took two to three days to present a topic and teach the necessary language, involve the class in an activity, and evaluate what had been learned.

March 19: Tara is going to teach the class how to do calligraphy, specifically how to use the Gothic alphabet. She seems very nervous. First, she hands out a list of new words and expressions while introducing her subject in Greek:
Καλημέρα σας, σήμερα θα σας μάθω πως να γράφετε με καλλιγραφία ... αλλά πρώτα θα διαβάσουμε τις λέξεις. (Good morning, today I'm going to teach you how to write using calligraphy ... but first we'll read the words).

She seems to be "talking" rather than reading it — good. She proceeds to go through the list of words, asking the class to repeat them after her. She has chosen to give the forms that she will use rather than the words as they would appear in the dictionary. For example, the imperative forms of the verbs rather than the infinitives, which in the case of Greek, unlike English, differ. She is talking about the history of calligraphy at a level beyond what she or the students could normally comprehend. ... She pauses several times to ask: "καταλαβαίνετε? (Do you understand?)" ... Some aren't sure. She explains again. ... They seem more comfortable now — they are familiar with the list so they are more reassuring as an audience.

She demonstrates on the board and with a second sheet that shows a sample Gothic alphabet, explains with gestures and words what the students are to do: "κάντε ότι κάνω εγώ (follow my example)." Tom is puzzled, but then looks on his list and recognizes the expression. His moment of discovery is almost comical. I imagine a kindergarten class would very much resemble this one. The students begin to follow Tara's example ... she circulates and suggests techniques ... she gives directions for practice at home.

In evaluating Tara's presentation, students commented on their response to the high level of her language: "I didn't expect I would understand as much as I did. I guess it doesn't matter if you don't know every single word. You can guess some," said Michael. Such awarenesses are important in a foreign language class. Students gain confidence when they are encouraged to make sense of and use what they hear without being required to produce exact translations. When they guess, they also focus on language for learning, language as means, rather than on language only as rule-governed code.

What I noticed was that Tara presented the vocabulary in the forms she was going to use. That meant she was able to transform the word as it appears in the dictionary, following appropriate grammatical rules, to fit the context of her intended use. I was especially pleased with this because it showed she understood the limitations of the dictionary (parallel to its undoubted usefulness) and the purpose of language to communicate meaning. Typically in using a foreign language, students find a word in the dictionary, then insert it into a text unchanged. Changing it requires both knowledge of what to do grammatically and an attitude of concern for the meaning.

I also saw Tara use the language in ways she had never needed to before. She pushed herself to explain and the class responded. Both she as the teacher and her students were using Greek in a nonmechanical way. The motivation had shifted. Instead of merely completing a linguistic task in hopes of being able to reproduce it later in a "real" situation, the students were learning it in real situations and engaging in genuine dialogue. Tara had created the real need for understanding right in the classroom. As they talked among themselves, in Greek, they were not thinking of how to ask or answer a question correctly, nor even "trying" to "make up" questions. Instead, they asked questions because they had questions; they communicated to learn about something they wanted to do.

By the time we got to Amy's presentation a few days later, I was feeling more comfortable, but still very conscious of my own uncertainties. In my log, I noted:

> I think we're all getting used to the idea and the purposes of the project. Well, if not the exact purposes, the atmosphere of the project. I wonder if it's as open-ended in the students' minds as in mine. Or do they expect what's happening—is it all predictable? The way the project's going so far, it seems a pretty awkward attempt. It doesn't feel excellent although there is evidence of what I set out to look for: the kids picked what they wanted to teach, they are acting as teachers, and they are using the language and learning new words. Why isn't it enough? Did I expect some big breakthrough? I think I'm not quite sure what to expect. I feel like we're all blindfolded, but we still know we haven't left the classroom, so we grope through familiar surroundings even if we can't see. Sounds good—what does it mean? Who's the most unsure, me or the kids?

I also found it difficult to evaluate an individual student's work. I couldn't help thinking of Ben's self-image when I watched him. Everyone was impressed because he was surprisingly articulate. He has a good accent, but often he gave up and assumed the role that his peers had given him or, rather, that he had created for himself — the clown who can't do anything right. He and I talked a great deal while he was preparing his presentation. He came up with an excellent plan. He gave everyone a word list and a diagram of a sailboat and some sailing patterns. His speech was written out and mostly read, but it sounded articulate because he had spent time reading it over and over, and he obviously knew what he was saying (even though he wasn't secure enough to do it without the paper in front of him).

Did we evaluate Ben highly because we all expected him to do poorly? Amy, for example, wrote, "Ben's presentation was one of the easiest to understand. He spoke slowly and made sentences at our level. Not too complicated." It was true and I hadn't thought of that. It occurred to me that I should look at the student logs more carefully and analyze my own conclusions more carefully; that is, resist the tendency to bend the logs to what I think myself.

The Advanced French Class (EZ)

In the Advanced French class, we were doing something less radical. Although the students were doing the teaching, they did not choose what to teach. I had assigned Alice to teach the two verbs *connaître* and *savoir*.

She started out by commenting, in French, that we translate both verbs as "to know" in English because the English language does not make the distinctions that appear in the French. She then led the class through the conjugations of positive and negative forms of both verbs in the present and past tenses before going on to explain when to use each of them.

My journal entry for March 22 included a transcription of her explanation:

Alice: Connaître, c'est pour les personnes and les endroits. Michel, donne un exemple. (*Connaître* is for people and places. Michael, give an example.)

Michael: Je ne connais pas cette fille. (I do not know that girl.)

Alice: Bien. Charles, un autre. (Good. Charles, another.)

Charles: Je connais la ville de Paris. (I know the city of Paris.)

Alice: Bien. Le verbe savoir c'est comme "to know how" en anglais — par exemple, je sais jouer au tennis. Vous avez compris? (Good.

The verb *savoir* is "to know how" in English — for example, I know how to play tennis. Do you understand?)

Simple explanations (simpler than mine usually are) — without confusion. She asks the class to break up into pairs and write a small paragraph using both verbs. While the students work, she circulates among them and they ask her questions, seeming anxious to please her. Alice is articulate and the students understand her. Carl, a student who normally wastes time, was busy writing. At one point he asks:

Carl: Est-ce qu'on va les lire en classe? (Are we going to read these to the class?)

Alice: Oui, demain. (Yes, tomorrow.)

For the following day, Alice had devised a short test on the verbs themselves, after which the students shared their paragraphs with the class, as Carl had requested. The rest of the students read their paragraphs. I was impressed with what they had written and with their enthusiasm. I was convinced that they understood the lesson well. Perhaps Carl summed up the general feeling: "Now I understand. I used the verbs wrong before. Why isn't the book so simple?"

As I watched and wrote from the back of the class, I noticed how the students both imitated and deviated from what I do in the classroom. What they did made me question my own practice. Manos, for instance, did several activities with the initial text of the chapter that I don't normally do. I wondered whether I in fact go too fast and skip over the personalizing aspects of certain parts of the book because it seems boring to me. I also made judgments about my own reactions. I noted, for example, that Melanie had trouble at one point in her lesson and turned to Alice, who is a better student, and said, "You explain it, I can't." My immediate, guilty thought was: Should I count that against her? Early on in the project, I found myself looking for faults, perhaps out of concern not to see only what I wanted to see. My journal entry read:

> So the nature of my disapproval feels like it was purely personal. In other words I, still putting myself out of habit at the head of the pyramid, created a scheme, assigned everyone a role, and then expected it to be executed perfectly. Isn't that unfair, though, when one of the basic goals of the project is to allow the students to be the teachers? How far back should I remove myself?

Eventually I realized I was observing a new purpose for dialogue. The kind of dialogue taking place was created by students' desire to communicate among themselves and to share what they had written. I also became aware that for the first time, students were using French

to talk about using French. In other words, they were using the foreign
language to explain the foreign language in a nonmechanical way (that
is, without being forced by our customary oral drill format) and with
much more confidence than I had ever seen before.

The text belonged to those who taught it. Many students devised
creative ways to use the text and I thought the class seemed to be
having more fun than when I do it. Lisa, for example, came up with
two good ideas. First, she asked the students to write their own
questions rather than use the ones given in the book. To make up such
questions, they had to reread carefully and compose for themselves. I
wondered that I had never thought of doing that. She also had them
write a funny dialogue about skiing and they enjoyed reading and
listening for the humorous content, rather than for correct usage.
Certainly they were corrected less and the teacher interjected less. The
learners were able to talk more.

Looking Back (WS)

It is important to note that the students who participated in this project
were of very mixed cultural backgrounds. In the Advanced French
class, some were bilingual, their native tongue being Greek or Arabic,
so their automatic transferring and language skills were more developed.
Those students needed little explanation as to why, for instance, "table"
is feminine in French, or why adjectives can be made plural, since the
same features appear in their own language. An English speaker must,
at some point, be taught rules that seem wholly unnatural, illogical
even. Likewise, the difference between *connaître* and *savoir* is not
embodied in a single word in English and therefore needs to be
explained periphrastically. Interestingly enough, the native English
speakers were able to do just as well in their presentations as the
students of bilingual and trilingual backgrounds. Did this activity allow
students to become more fluent and to gain understanding of how a
foreign language is learned regardless of how much they already knew
about how languages work? Certainly here is an issue to pursue in
another project.

Assuming and maintaining the position of observer-recorder in the
classroom enabled Evi to keep her misgivings and anxieties to herself.
In general, she felt the students had very little sense of her being in the
room. In some lessons she did not say a word and felt no need to
intervene. Other days she wondered what she was seeing. She fluctuated
between thinking this was a really good activity and thinking it was just
a waste of time and that she was trying to give it significance it didn't
have. Was language learning really being enhanced? Or was it simply a
sense of "better" class, more motivated, more self-run? That in itself,

of course, was an outcome not to be simply dismissed. But in the midst of the activity, she wasn't able to gain the perspective that was possible later, when the classes had completed the cycle of student presentations.

During the general evaluation that immediately followed the presentations in both classes, students talked about each other, about themselves as teachers, and about what they had learned from the project. They agreed, in both groups, that this particular foreign language experience, being a new one, encouraged the class to work as a team and to receive and offer peer support and criticism. Everyone had used the foreign language not only to increase vocabulary and knowledge of grammatical structures but also to learn and understand something interesting and fun, to share ideas, and to refine their evaluating skills. In the Greek class, students had focused on learning how to explain new information and skills, using the foreign language as the means of communication. In the French class, students had focused on learning how to explain new grammatical structures and uses, also using the foreign language as the means.

It's significant that the students did not think their fluency in the language had increased. They acknowledged their own progress only in those particular words and expressions they had learned and used during the presentations. That they remembered those expressions was apparent weeks later. They would come across a phrase and comment, "I remember that, I used it in my presentation!" Not only did they notice this use of the new vocabulary, but they were able to put it in appropriate contexts in meaningful ways. For the first time, they were able to use the foreign language to discuss the processes of learning in class as well as the content. While clearly their fluency was increasing, they themselves did not believe it was.

The purposes for the foreign language use had thus more closely approximated natural, communicative mother tongue uses. Such uses enhanced ownership of the language. They also enhanced ownership of the learning process. Because teacher and students made plans together, wrote and shared logs documenting processes and progress, discussed how to present material, and developed ways of explaining, the students found out *how to learn* the foreign language. The strategies they used for their teaching were ones they could now consciously use for their learning. The teacher no longer needed to be the main speaker, nor the main source of information.

What does this mean in the foreign language class? Is the teacher abdicating responsibility through such a project? Venturing from known into imagined territory involves some risks. Teachers do have a responsibility to do what they think is best for their students. When they aren't sure, how do they decide what is best? For Evi, the question turned on her being able to demonstrate confidently that what she was attempting could be justified. She asked herself, "Was I determined to interpret certain observations in a way that would prove that the project was successful?" and "Was I at any point more concerned with proving the success of the project than with finding out what my students were really learning?" She questioned further "whether my data collection was scientific enough — i.e., detached enough — therefore valid enough to be of any use."

This is not the place to examine the issue of scientific reliability and its relevance to the nature and purposes of teacher research. What did become apparent, as we examined the collection of data about this particular research, were the ways this project added to students' language learning in that specific class. It was quite evident that Evi had not avoided responsibility. On the contrary, she had allowed the students to gain inside knowledge of their material in a way they had not done before. Every student had succeeded, even if only briefly, to move from *savoir parler* — knowing how to speak — to *connaître la langue* — knowing the language, as each became a teacher of a tiny part.

In this project that new sense of *connaître* vs. *savoir* was very much influenced by the planning stages, the identifying of objectives and goals by each student, and especially the personal interaction that is instrumental in making every teacher/student relationship unique, and that unforgettably colors the learning linked to it. As teachers, the writers of this chapter also gained a new kind of knowledge as to how "deeply" Evi's students were learning. What she often suspected them of understanding now became evident in their use of the language. The obstacles to foreign language learning were not so much removed as transformed by the teaching experience. The projects contextualized *what had been* and *what was being* learned and made it meaningful.

Such projects do not need to form the whole curriculum to be effective. As in learning to use their native language, learners of a foreign language need variation in the length and complexity of their assignments and variation in the intensity of their involvement. Whether or not Evi's students themselves recognized their growth in fluency, they did know that they valued the experience that involved them in developing the curriculum. Shortly after the project ended, Evi suggested to the French class that they go back to the text to finish certain parts. The students' reaction led her to observe in her log:

> Why do the students hate that book so much? It's impersonal, all grammar, no English, no pictures. It's exhausting to the eye of the middle school kid. Still they've learned many structures from it. The way we've used it matters — I can see that having it as an everyday text would be a disaster. They need variety. They need to feel like they're somehow involved in the material they're learning. It's

interesting how often in the Greek class—where the curriculum is a bit of this and a bit of that and we have no textbook—students do in fact help make the curriculum. They say things like "Why don't we ...?" or "Let's learn ...." This does not occur in a rigid textbook-driven class. I know, for example, that in the beginning French classes, students haven't ventured to suggest something different yet. On the contrary, they seem to be avoiding it ....

As she saw it: "My new responsibility was to give this opportunity to all my students, rather than take the easy way out and just do the teaching myself."

Summary Evaluation of the Project (EZ)

When students were involved in teaching their peers a foreign language, their fluency and their sense of ownership of the language increased in the following ways:

1. In both classes, ownership of the language appeared as a key factor that enhanced the learning of the foreign language because both projects contextualized the material into a unique experience that the students would not forget. As mentioned earlier, weeks after the project students commented several times when hearing a familiar expression, "I remember that, I used it in my presentation."

2. The fact that the students chose to use the new words in their presentations showed that they were able to find the words in one form in the dictionary and transform them into spoken forms, demonstrating they understood various grammatical rules and were able to manipulate the language to fit their own purposes. Their decision to do this on their own proves that they understood the limits of a dictionary (parallel to its usefulness); they were making an intelligent—nonmechanical—use of the foreign language.

3. Students learned new vocabulary both as presenters and as students. As presenters they created a nonconventional vocabulary list of words and expressions with which to teach their material. This made it necessary to spend more time than usual in order to become familiar enough with the words to use them for communicating, rather than just to pass a vocabulary text. As students they were introduced to vocabulary not found in their textbook but relevant to the presentations.

4. As their confidence and enthusiasm increased, so did their fluency. Students worked both individually and as a team, offering peer criticism and support and refining their evaluative skills. They synthesized their material into a whole that was communicable and

teachable. Their success in doing so gave each one of them a new sense of accomplishment in learning the foreign language.

Looking back, I feel that if I were to repeat the project, there are certain areas that could be improved. It is clear to me now that those chaotic moments in the planning stages where nothing seemed to be accomplished were really beneficial. When students didn't know what to do next, perhaps there were insufficient guidelines given by the teacher or we had spent insufficient time talking about planning. A list of guidelines and a checklist with which to monitor progress could be very beneficial and would supplement the journals.

Students were wrestling with several new tasks at the same time, namely how to provide questions rather than answers and, more important, whether or not to accept the authority and responsibility handed over by the teacher. By allowing them to talk about their frustrations and avoiding the trap of "taking over" and telling them what to do, I would have encouraged creative student/teacher and student/student dialogue. Involving them in discussions of the teaching process would have increased their understanding of the learning process as well.

Response

Mary K. Healy

My first responses after I read this study were immediate, quite personal, and more than a bit petulant: Mainly, the issues raised in Zoukis and Strachan's thoughtful piece made me again aware of my own frustration with the lack of plain common sense in so much of what we do in schools. *Why*, for example, when I was studying French, German, or Spanish at various times in my schooling, did I never have the opportunity to learn those languages in the ways that Evi so sensibly introduced in her classes? *Why*, when the benefits are so immediately obvious, is it almost impossible for teachers in most school districts to observe their colleagues teaching? *Why* is the notion that learning must be active for students so difficult to incorporate in lessons, when the positive results of active participation are immediately apparent? These questions, clearly more rhetorical than not, will serve as a general introduction to the points I wish to raise.

First of all, as the description of Evi's evolution as a teacher indicates, there are no easy transformations in teaching. The classroom pressures are too inexorable and immediate to allow the regular reflection that can help bring about change in practice. Teachers need the kind of distance permitted by engaging in classroom studies to begin to reconcile, as Zoukis and Strachan put it, the "persisting dichotomy between [Evi's] emerging theory of learning and her teaching practice."

During Evi's research she had the opportunity, over an extended period of time, to watch what happened in the classroom when someone else was teaching. Because her students were teaching the class, she had the time to observe a range of approaches in operation, note the reactions of the class, reflect on what she saw, and raise questions about her own methods and practice. Among the things she noticed were the lack of interruptions when the students were teaching, the slower pacing, the simplicity of explanations. All these she found instructive for improving her own teaching. In summing up her observations, Evi pointed out "the text belonged to those who taught it." She saw from a very different angle what she had known from her own experiences in the classroom — that most times when you teach something, you learn it.

As well as distance and time to reflect, teachers need to be freed from the isolation of the classroom. During Evi's research project, she had the advantage of a dual collaboration. One was her ongoing extended conversation with Wendy Strachan, which began with the first of Wendy's in-service courses that Evi attended and continued over five years to their latest collaboration on this article. And the second was the more immediate one with the students in her two language classes who became her partners in this joint investigation. Evi learned that by including the pupils in making decisions about the teaching/learning process, she helped them improve their learning of Greek and French and also improved her own understanding of what it means to teach a language effectively. Teaching/learning became a joint venture with her students, who were encouraged to be conscious of their own learning processes in new ways. The students in Evi's two classes saw learning from a new angle. They were allowed, in a sense, to do market research: to sample various approaches to teaching and thus find out which methods worked best for their own learning. In addition, Evi gave them the rationale for what they were doing and made them more conscious of what helped them learn more efficiently. Thus they clearly saw how their learning improved — in both content and organization — once they went beyond reliance on the textbook.

I will end with some concerns. In the excerpts from Evi's learning log that were included in the article, she reveals her continuing doubts about whether her research was "scientific" enough. From what we are given in the article, it seems that, for her, "scientific" means "detached." And this concern for detachment, for objectivity, has come up whenever I have worked with teachers on classroom-based research projects. I think it stems from the quantitative, experimental studies, usually in the social sciences, which teachers often read during their initial training. This research appears to have a "rigor" that teacher researchers often feel is lacking in their "soft" narratives of what occurred in their own classrooms. I've found no easy way to deal with this anxiety, except for immersing us all in reading and discussing a range of teacher researcher reports and studies. The most useful work I've found for this purpose is M. M. Mohr and M. S. MacLean's *Working Together: A Guide for Teacher-Researchers* (Urbana, IL: NCTE, 1987), which describes a group of teacher researchers' evolution in understanding the particular nature of their investigations.

So, improving the conceptual understanding of how teacher research differs from that of the positivist tradition is an ongoing process, best tackled through wide reading and discussion. But while that is going on, I also think teacher researchers might attempt to be more specific in detailing the parameters for their studies in their written reports. For example, when I finished reading the Zoukis/Strachan article, I was certainly in agreement with the conclusions. However, I had some specific unanswered questions about the investigation itself: What was the extent of Evi's observations in both her classes? How long were these class periods? How many students were in each class? What grading/evaluation system did she use? Did all the students in both classes participate in the study? What types of written evaluations of the process did the students make during the study? Did she read her own learning log comments to her students? In other words, as a teacher myself, I wanted to know the specifics of the situation in which the study had taken place so I could better judge the relevance of the findings for my own work with teachers. While the reflections of an experienced teacher who has raised questions about her own practice over an extended period of time are invaluable, these reflections have more impact when they arise from systematic documentation that can later be made available during the presentation of findings.

4

Coming Full Circle
As Teachers Become Researchers So Goes the Curriculum

Patricia Johnston

I'd like you to imagine a process of professional transformation as the teacher researcher learns from the subjects of her study. As participant-observer to an eighth-grade book discussion group, I kept at my side my field-note journal, a place where I jotted bits of conversation before the recorder was turned on, noted a hallway interaction, and penned my latest question. My writings reveal not only a pointed concern with the content of my study—the social construction of meaning—but beyond substance, show a poignant concern with the form of doing research. It was through these moments of writing and reading and silent reflection that one notion became quite clear: the teacher researcher had managed a quiet reformation. Curriculum was not to be the same.

> We're sitting in a circle at our desks. The desks are in the half-a-classroom we've come to think of as the "clubhouse." I sit with the six eighth-grade students who agreed to become part of my research, one thirteen-year-old boy and five girls. It is now May. We have met since January, and our work together is coming to a close. We have read and discussed books, have worked through interviews, and have sat together in family meetings. The date is set for a celebration dinner. But before the pizza is ordered, we meet for three class sessions to look at the processes of learning in which we engaged over the semester.

Students have been asked to keep journals over the semester we worked together. These journals were designed to be places where students would respond to their readings. They became, instead, the field notes of collaborators in classroom research. In our last three formal meetings our purpose for getting together was to think, write, and talk about a semester's work. The discussions are about the process of doing research, what it felt like, what students learned, what worked, and what they would do differently, if given opportunity. The discussions are their group analysis of the study, their impressions of the group, and their definitions of reading and the interpretive community.

Here, I heard Amber report, "I don't feel cornered or embarrassed when I say something. In a group I tend to be more objective. I'm not afraid to say what I believe, or disagree with anyone else. I know in my mind there is no right or wrong. . . . You're not judged on who you are, but on what you think." I also heard Asheley explain that the reading group was effective because it represented a significant mix of personality: Robert Smith is humorous and looks at things Asheley never would, whereas others are realistic, or full of ideas, or creative and observant.

What transpired was a paradigm shift. Students were asked to be the investigators of their own learning over a semester. How many times does that happen in classrooms? How often do we ask students to behave as Donald Schon (1983) suggests of the reflective practitioner, as artful learners? This "look at our own processes" is a radical departure from usual classroom histories. What it revealed altered forever my view of students, and my understanding of the kinds of work that could fit in a meaning-centered curriculum. When my students became student researchers I saw them as the intellectuals they are, struggling for their academic voices in an institutional setting that too often asked that they not speak. Instead, given the opportunity, these student researchers took responsibility for their own learning and for sharing their own ideas with others. Further, I saw the role of teacher anew: our function in schools can be to encourage the development and growth of the intellectual lives of our students. This has nothing to do with work sheets and workbooks and filling in the blanks or multiples choices. This has to do with the thoughtful consideration of a problem, making a decision about its essential questions (Sizer 1985), and taking a defensible position.

This experience suggested to me possibilities for classroom practice, much like the learning I had read about in Shirley Brice Heath's *Ways With Words*. Like the Main Town teachers in her ethnography, I had to adjust the curriculum not merely to permit student voice, but for student ideas, questions, needs, and intellectual lives to infuse the learning, and therefore, the curriculum. Believing that change could occur through even slight alteration, I did what I thought was a minor tailoring of standard practices. What I discovered is that even the smallest nip and tuck, when thoughtfully planned, can lead to an actual inversion of curriculum.

School Background

How do you get to know the students with whom you work? I think you start by looking beyond the classroom, even beyond the school. There are a few markers that help us better understand students; such markers make up the "surround" of students' reading and writing and literacy practice. Simply put, people are joined, or not joined, by neighborhood involvement, work, religious affiliation, school, and unspoken boundaries. Students bring messages of literacy and learning to the reading classroom from the communities where their lives are organized — where they first learn the rules of language and social interaction.

The Helping Hand signs posted along the tree-lined streets of this suburban neighborhood hint at the kind of community many consider theirs to be: friendly and caring. Monthly, groups of concerned neighbors meet in each other's living rooms to discuss ways of preventing vandalism, the wisdom of instituting curfews for children and adolescents, and a means of keeping Halloween pranks to a minimum. This is a Town-watch Neighborhood. That's one marker.

The school district is filled with similar small developments and neighborhoods that make up the community. One small village within this area even has its own mayor. Beautifully restored Victorian homes line quiet roads. The pace is slower here, somehow. In fact, local humor says there are only eight roads in this borough, but ten stop signs. The scuttlebutt is that borough police hand out tickets to those who don't make complete stops at corners; it's a way to control taxes. That's a second marker.

A third marker is a part of the community considered less mainstream and quite unlike other subdivisions. This "village" includes the apartment complexes and the housing projects that were built during World War II. A former landlord did not responsibly care for the properties, it is generally felt, though in more recent years a new landlord brought with him some fresh capital and some fresh ideas about the maintenance of property. Most of the district's Hispanic population lives in this area.

There is a main thoroughfare that runs through the school district, east to west. Not too far from one of its most busy intersections is the diner, the hub of much social activity. It's a place where people meet after events: after a dance or game on a Friday or Saturday night; after a chaperone duty or back-to-school night during the week; or after church services on Sunday morning. The diner is as telling about the community as are the playing fields of an active community sports program, the public library at either end of the district, and the new consumer area that lets you get your groceries, a new outfit, a haircut, and some fast-food dinner in one-stop shopping. The students involved in this work come from these neighborhoods, play for these soccer and baseball teams, and get parts in the youth group productions of these churches and synagogues.

If you were to visit the junior high school where my students spend seventh, eighth, and ninth grades, I think you would be favorably impressed. The school was constructed in 1967, a time when the design of public space often omitted openable windows, when occupants learned to depend upon central heating and air conditioning. Floor and wall tiles are pale gray-beige. Ceiling tiles, large rectangles of white acoustic tile, have been painted by art students. Years ago the art department decided to add color to the building; students worked in pairs or small groups to claim a tile for themselves, and to design and then paint the tile. Rock groups and cartoon characters are popular themes. Throughout the year posters predominate the extra wall space. Student council and class officer elections, yearbook sales, advertisements for dances, National Book Week banners, all compete for a place on the wall. The sense of the building is that it is orderly, attractive. Until the buses start to arrive at 7:50 a.m., it is quiet.

Standard Reading Curriculum

Traditionally, reading instruction in the junior high school has centered around the Planned Course Outline for seventh, eighth, and ninth grades. This is a kind of curriculum scope and sequence that outlines the goals, objectives, activities, and materials for each grade level. The official nature of the document suggests that it represents a guideline for instruction that has as much to do with uniformity as it does with accountability. Reading comprehension is clearly delineated, vocabulary study is outlined, study skills are classified, and oral language skills are explained.

My initial reaction to the Planned Course Outline was confirmed and reaffirmed through sixteen years of practice, reflection, and even experimentation: the document clearly states what to teach, but not how to teach it. I think all will agree this is professionally liberating. But is it? I wonder how many would care to think about what my practice, my head, and my instinct suggest — that the *what* of instruction changes when we look at the *how*. Process influences product as much as the parts make up the whole. How I suggest kids look at literature, and when and where and why we talk about a book, have as much to do with their learning as does a work sheet on main idea and supporting details. In other words, method determines content. Teachers create classroom contexts where meaning is made, context is affected by method, and method walks hand in hand with curriculum.

At the time of the work I'm reporting on here, the reading classroom in seventh grade was distinct from other subject areas, and it was discrete from content. Changes were then being made to transform reading curriculum in a districtwide effort to change to a middle school concept and philosophy. At the time of this study, however, reading occurred in isolation. More concerned with skills and subskills, the focus of the reading curriculum was part-to-whole. Students read for purposes of answering specific and predetermined questions, whether they were my questions or those of a publishing company. Instruction in reading comprehension, for instance, might include a unit on making inferences. Students would get some background information on the "skill" from me, a discussion might follow, and we'd practice making inferences. Eventually, I'd conduct a directed reading activity of a story especially prepared for its use of inference. Years later, when I conducted my own formal study of students' reading practices (Johnston 1987), I realized that when given permission and opportunity to respond to literature without teacher constraints, students were expert at putting two and two together; I merely had to listen to the terms and standards of their talk about books to finally hear and understand.

Examples of Change

Part of the seventh-grade curriculum was a unit on study skills. A workbook was the basis of the study skills unit. Chapter one had about four work sheets that more or less asked students to check off someone else's preconceived notions of what a good student is. It didn't take too much thought for students to recognize what was the correct answer, what it was they should believe a good student is. Students could easily get 100 percent on the workbook pages without having given any consideration or real thought to the topic. It didn't take too much thought for me to begin asking, "What am I teaching? What are students learning?" It was, decidedly, time for change.

After reviewing the workbook chapter I realized that the purpose of these blanks and checklists and outlines was for students to understand what a good student is and does and thinks and how one behaves. Why not, instead, look to the resources that surround us? Why not look to our families, our classmates, our teachers, and our coaches to find one example of a good student? The curriculum changes in this manner: students were to decide on one student they already considered exemplary, come up with a list of qualities they felt this person had, share the lists with classmates, then come up with questions they would need to ask the good student to find out what "good" really means. My twelve-year-olds were on their way to their first ethnographic interviews.

We began with modeled interviews. As students began to create possible questions for their interviews they decided their next step was to play out their questions, to see if the questions actually asked what they needed to know to complete the assignment. I was the first interview guinea pig as student after student practiced asking me questions, note taking, having a conversation with another about being a student. Part of what astonished the seventh graders was the news they got from the interview: Their teacher had once been a seventh grader. More astonishing was that I attended "school" as an adult, when I really didn't have to. Most astonishing was that I continued to refer to myself as a student and could talk about present study habits of reading and organizing and listening to others. Students eventually practiced interviewing each other, shared ideas for questions, and began to understand that interviewing was a significant way to learn.

Further, these practices provided the basis of discussions to follow. We talked about proper interviewing techniques, the same ones I had learned at the University of Pennsylvania with adult learners. I warned them of the vagaries of tape recorders, told them to check batteries before entering the field. Each knew of the protocol of arranging interview appointments and scheduling follow-up times for possible backup questions. Students came back to class with suggestions of questions that "worked," and thoughts about "What do I ask next when all he says is 'yes' or 'no'? What's wrong with what I ask?" Students began to question their own questions, and to analyze the definitions of common words they claimed they already understood: What does discipline mean, for instance? Is time something that can be managed? Are there strategies for learning? How do I know that something is really learned?

It didn't take long to see that another kind of learning was taking place in my classroom. As interviews were completed and answers to questions were brought in, we developed study groups to help analyze the material. Students had to write up their findings to answer the research question "What is a good student?" and not merely provide answers to questions with no synthesis or integration of thought. This was, after all, a full-scale investigation. Several excerpts from my field notes from that period reveal what I had observed and what I had felt was happening in the classroom:

> It seems to me that students are taking pride in their work. I don't
> have to remind the kids to put their names on their papers before I

collect their folders; instead, students are using their full names, their middle names, their given names. What does that mean?

I think what I enjoyed most about today's activity was that David became the illustrator for the class. My one artistic soul had simply made an illustration for his project, something he always does for most of his work. Everyone is now commissioning him to make covers or designs for their work. What is going on here? Is it because kids are able to walk around the room and make this space their own that lends to their sharing ideas and talents? Is it because they are enjoying this that they are naturally curious about what others in the class are learning?

Today Kristen explained why drafting is an important part of the process of getting the work done: "I made my rough copy, and as I went through it I found out how to do it right." That strikes me as a legitimate, and authentic, way to write.

At the same time that I was learning about creating a classroom context that was different from the traditional arrangement of desks and chairs and distribution of books and papers, I was also learning about instruction in reading and writing. Students' findings became the texts read in class, and their analysis became the stuff from which we developed categories and classifications of appropriate student behavior. Some students took it upon themselves to find the negative case — to interview someone they knew not to be a good student — or to try their hand at triangulation — interviewing a series of randomly selected students and looking for patterns in their data.

Jeff writes, "I asked my mom what's one adjective [sic] for a good student. She answered with 'eager.' My mom said to become a good student you always have to be competing with yourself and working to your ability. ... Everyone can be a good student within themselves." Jeff's teacher is compelled to think that Jeff knows a good deal about language: he knows how to ask a question that forces someone to summarize in a word, and he knows that one word suggests many pictures, many behaviors, many ideas for his mom and for himself. Jeff and his mom also know about learning and the possibility to achieve through desire and decision making. Much was learned about Jeff and his language processes, particularly when understood in contrast to previous curriculums of checklists and work sheets.

Tim writes, "A good student is a combination of two or three things. Number one is paying attention in class so that he/she can understand and hear the material that is being presented. Number two is to ask questions in class when there is information that he/she isn't clear about and doesn't completely understand. Number three is practicing and studying every day in preparation for tests in the future sometime." Tim's teacher reads many things in this paragraph. There is a coherence to his writing: a synthesis of ideas gathered throughout the interview. Tim is able to highlight several points that impress him the most. There is the possibility for application: Tim now knows that paying attention is important, asking questions matters, and test preparation is an ongoing affair. His teacher also sees a sensitivity and awareness of representation of gender conventions for public writing. Much was learned about Tim and his reasoning processes, particularly when understood in contrast to previous curriculums of checklists and work sheets.

Kathy writes, "Kim gave me two examples of how she studies for tests. For a final, Kim gets together with her friends and they quiz each other and then skim the book over. The second example is for a math test. Kim saves all her homework and does a couple of problems on each page. She checks to see if the answers match with the homework. When I asked Kim about her homework habits, she said she didn't have a particular place or time to do it." Kathy's teacher understands Kathy better after having read this essay passage. Kathy, it appears, understands the notion of main idea and supporting details. Further, what is impressive is Kathy's sense of audience—of clarifying information for the reader's benefit—and her sense of self—her writer's voice is fronted. Much was learned about Kathy and her descriptive processes, particularly when understood in contrast to previous curriculums of checklists and work sheets.

Student-as-researcher had begun. I came to feel that classroom was more like laboratory. There were other study skills chapters to rearrange and invert. A chapter that asked students more fill-in-the-blanks about the parts of a textbook easily converted into an investigation of what makes a good textbook. After researching the field of textbooks students decided how the parts provided readers with information. In turn and in time, they created their own books: *How to Make It in the Seventh Grade, Choosing Your Junior High Wardrobe, Everything You Need to Know About Nintendo, The Road to Popularity*, and so on, and so on. Much like Ken Macrorie's (1980) work with the I-Search paper, students used alternatives to traditional research texts: Parents provided information on boating, a family hobby and the focus of one student's textbook; the computer lab teacher helped a student explain how the parts of a computer could be identified in an appendix. The important thing is that topics and the processes undertaken to gather information belonged to the students. They made decisions; students found they could understand the function and format of an index without benefit of a dummy index on a workbook page.

Later, a study skills chapter on maps, graphs, and charts led the students to create classroom, schoolwide, and communitywide surveys. This information was graphed and charted. The room became a repository for archival information on favorite rock groups, the most popular brand of sneakers, hours spent on homework each night ... you get the idea. Directions were written using real road maps for reaching real destinations; students then reported if the directions were clear, how they could have been worded differently, and what was successful.

Because my students had become researchers over the year, I felt confident that they could handle a major culminating activity for the fourth marking period. Since I taught reading and since theirs was a reading class, it seemed appropriate to ask what they know about a good reader. And so, that became the focus of our final project together. This four-part ethnographic study had students conduct a case study interview of at least one person they knew to be a good reader, collect data for one week in their communities and schools and homes of all observable literacy practices, write a personal story of their own histories as readers and writers, and conduct a final thoughtful analysis of the research topic.

The classroom was filled with activity, with talk, with work, with reading and writing, with students going to others for help, with some coming to see me for clarification and, at times, direction. I was the facilitator and coach. They were the teachers. We were all learners. Final projects were read and reread, compared, analyzed, discussed. Again, these reports became the texts of our reading lessons, and students shared their experiences of researching as well as their research itself. "Did you know that the textbook is the focus of our science class? We hardly ever do anything without using that textbook." "Does reading the cereal box every morning count as reading?" "My Mom says that she never gets enough time to write letters, but that she has to write every day to keep track of all her errands." "A good reader is one who likes to read." "A good reader doesn't always stay with the same book, but changes a lot, or reads a couple different books at once." "Good readers talk about the books they read." "I always get a book for Christmas from my grandmom. They're in a special place in my bedroom. It's fun to see them now, and to see how different they are."

This is what the discussions in my classroom came to sound like; these represent the ideas of observers, contributors, intellectuals. I was struck and am repeatedly re-impressed by the sound and the look and the feel of instruction in such an environment. As a personal aside, I feel like I have come full circle, too: Teacher became researcher for the sake of students' becoming the same. Student-as-researcher suggests a restructuring of present curriculum. Part of that new design speaks to five notions that have emerged from my classroom practice:

1. The present talk and literature on cooperative learning are interesting, compelling, and useful to teachers as they create different

classroom configurations. I argue that cooperative learning is a structure that is imposed on students (see, for instance, Kagan 1990). It strikes me, therefore, as a somewhat unnatural practice in light of what I saw happening in my classroom. Students didn't need to be put into triads or to be told that one person would be the recorder and another the reporter. Instead, in an unstructured setting I saw people helping themselves when they needed it, learning on their own terms and in their own way.

2. Part of my present work involves the *Pennsylvania Comprehensive Reading Plan II* (1988). Students' learning about their own learning is a fundamental part of this framework for language and literacy. I found that as a teacher researcher I encouraged my student researchers to be reflective learners. As I shared with my students my processes for learning I modeled practices that enabled them to see themselves as strategic learners. Learning became synonymous with the doing, discovering, trying out in false leads, risking, and finally, enabling that student research generated. In time, an understanding of personal assessment and growth became contingent upon insights into the processes of learning.

3. As we have seen, all students become contributors. Moreover, they create an audience for each other's work that is interested and participatory. Conferencing is not something that is done on schedule and for purposes of reaching a reading or writing summit, but collaboration arises from a need to collaborate. In other words, students do in school what we all do in the real world: we seek the audience we need to get the hearing that will help us move our work along. As adults in the world we take responsibility for our figuring out our next steps; so can kids in classrooms.

4. Students bring experiences and information to school from the contexts in which they live their lives. When students become researchers they begin to see that their knowledge counts in classrooms. The received message is that what they say is valuable. As I worked with Asheley and Amber, Robert Smith and the other eighth graders of my formal research study, for instance, I found they had much to teach each other and me. Listening to their response in group discussion taught me about my students beyond their school roles; I learned from readers, real people who live real lives. They knew much about books and about the content of response; under their tutelage I became a learner of text construction and the construction of a human truth through literature (Johnston, in press). I learned, I think, because I heard. That happened, I suspect, because of trust.

5. Curriculum design must speak to the how of instruction. My concern is that teachers' voices be included in the development of curricular

change. I speak of a view of curriculum that is vital and, therefore, conversational. A discourse model of curriculum design speaks of reflection upon the how of classroom practice. The model builds upon the kind of risking, instruction, learning, and reflection that are already a part of the thinking and the work of the teacher researcher. The commonly shared chat about what worked and what didn't work is what we professionals have come to rely upon to inspire colleagues and build morale Monday to Friday, September to June. This talk of the faculty room, our proverbial trials and errors, needs to go beyond the level of passing anecdote to a status of recorded information.

A Re-vision of Student-as-Researcher

I am reminded again of the work of Heath in *Ways with Words*. In a first-grade social studies lesson on community helpers, the teachers asked students to tell a story about the job of the police officer. I remember that the Roadville children thought the teacher was asking that they "tell on," or find some instance of the officer's failure to comply with rules. The Trackton children were accustomed to "tellin' a story," a fabrication of truth, an exaggeration of facts for humorous intent. The concept of storytelling is problematic, for what was praised at home could be seen as a digression, disturbance, or disobedience in the classroom.

When students bring their experiences to the classrooms, when they are asked to become researchers of their lives, the problematic becomes an opportunity for all to learn. It becomes interesting, compelling, informative, enriching; it helps us to examine our own existences and find the shadings of similarity and difference. Students as researchers look for nuances in meaning when they must extend beyond the familiar and the comfortable.

When students become researchers, my fundamental understanding of what it means to be a teacher gets recast in my own mind and in my own practice. I found that my own formal research project was among the most powerful learning experiences I've encountered. The work made me reconceptualize. I had to break through fixed categories and well-learned ideas. I'm talking here not only about my notions of learning and reading and writing, but even more about societal standards and political understandings I finally "got." I saw the complexity of human relationships, the networkings of families and schools, the place of communities and school boards, and myself with my own decision-making processes that didn't quite fit any longer. And, that's what I decided that my students could experience also. If I have a hidden agenda for my classroom it is that I want them to know the power of their thoughts and the power of their language. I want them to see themselves as the intellectuals they can be: to look at problems critically, to know that they can trust their own knowledge, to understand that they can be independent because they know what original thought is because they have experienced it firsthand. Then I will know that I have done my job. Then I will be satisfied as a teacher and as a researcher. They'll be the investigators, they will construct the questions out of their need to know, they will, in effect, invert the curriculum they study, and my students will consider before they answer, and wait before they close.

Works Cited

Heath, S. B. 1983. *Ways with words: Language, life, and work in communities and classrooms*. New York: Cambridge University.

Johnston, P. 1987. *Social scenes of reading: A study of eighth-graders' talk about books*. Ann Arbor, MI: University Microfilms.

———— In press. Student readers and the "elevated, glorified discussion." In *Creating a classroom of learners: An integrated literature-based approach to instruction*, ed. D. Ogle and T. Estes. New York: Longman.

Kagan, S. 1989/1990. The structural approach to cooperative learning. *Educational Leadership*. 47(4): 12–15.

Lytle, S., and M. Botel. 1988. *Pennsylvania comprehensive reading plan II*. Harrisburg: Pennsylvania Department of Education.

Macrorie, K. 1980. *Searching writing*. Rochell Park, NJ: Hayden.

Schon, D. 1983. *The reflective practitioner: How professionals think in practice*. New York: Basic Books.

Sizer, T. 1985. *Horace's compromise: The dilemma of the American high school*. Boston: Houghton Mifflin.

Response

Nancie Atwell

Although I left my own classroom at Boothbay Elementary School three years ago, I'm just writing up the final piece of research that my students and I conducted together. Many of the kids in my last group had been writing since the third grade, and a collaborative inquiry afforded them a moment in time to stand back, contemplate, and celebrate their histories as writers. I asked each student, "What's the best thing that's ever happened to you as a writer?" As Patricia Johnston noted of her eighth graders, the stories that my eighth graders told by way of response represented "the ideas of observers, contributors, intellectuals" — and writers.

After the class had shared their stories with each other, four students and I sorted, re-sorted, and then characterized the responses. In the process we identified the kinds of experiences that had made writing in school worthwhile for these young writers and had helped them understand what writing is good for.

Many of my students said that others' responses to their writing were benchmarks giving my students a sense of themselves as writers. A special education student who was mainstreamed into my classroom remembered a time when I had showed a piece of her writing to the class on an overhead transparency, to demonstrate how writers can reveal character through dialogue. She explained, "No one had ever read one of my pieces to the class as an example of good writing." Another girl told about how her mother and grandfather wept in response to a poem she had written about the death of her grandmother. "It's not like I wanted to make them sad," she said, "but we could all be sad together. It helped." And one writer remembered her letter to *Kind* magazine, protesting laboratory experiments on animals, and the conversations it inspired. She commented, "Some people changed their minds because of what I wrote." These young people could answer one of the most important questions about any piece of writing — "Who is it for?" — because their teachers had worked hard at bringing real audiences for their writing into the classroom and had made the unnatural seem natural.

Other students described collaborative projects with classmates as favorite memories. Two girls had written and performed a play in fifth grade, and two boys collaborated on a parody as eighth graders. They revealed something that I had forgotten as a teacher of writing: the power of two minds at play together. For the remainder of that school year I invited all the writers in my classes to develop and share ways that they could join forces on projects.

Still other eighth graders described personal milestones in their writing careers, including the completion of major pieces of writing — a three-act play and a novel — as well as attempts to master new genres — essays and free verse poetry. One boy wrote, "In fifth grade I remember I tried two new things in one week. I used dialogue in a story, and I wrote a poem. Ever since that week, I felt confident about myself as a writer." Another writer referred to a journal entry that she had written in my classroom about an ordeal that had devastated her family: "When I wrote about the tragedy, it was like I got it out of my mind and onto the paper. After that, I didn't have to think about it any more."

These responses helped me more fully understand how idiosyncratic writing can be and how important it is for individual students to be able to make big decisions about their writing. Permitting kids to spend months of class time on such extensive projects as a novel and a play, trusting them to cope with difficulty, was a major step for me as a teacher; in the end, these difficult writing experiences were the ones that had meant the most to the writers. But at the same time that I allowed students to make decisions about their writing, I also provided direction by nudging individual kids, hard, to branch out and try unfamiliar genres, and by encouraging students with painful personal situations to write as a way to get some control over their responses. Instead of envisioning a scope and sequence of eighth-grade writing skills, I began to recognize what Patricia Johnston saw in her changed program: a *discourse model* of curriculum design that begins to account for the complexity of human relationships.

Only two of my students mentioned positive evaluations as high points of their experiences as writers. One boy remembered the day the state department of education reported the eighth-grade assessment results, when he learned that he had scored within the 91st percentile in writing. He explained, "It was the highest of all of my test scores, by a lot. It's like the governor said to me, '*You* are a writer kid.'" The only student who singled out a high grade in English as his best memory was a boy who had transferred into my room from another school system.

Our findings gave me new respect for my eighth graders. They spoke and wrote as writers, not as kids in an English class. Their confidence and authority, and their *interest in* considering and sharing their histories as writers, were by-products of an approach to teaching that said to students, your ideas and experiences matter. When teachers conduct research in our classrooms, we learn that kids' knowledge counts. But as Johnston observes, when kids become researchers, then they, too, learn that their knowledge counts.

5

Student-Sustained Discussion
When Students Talk and the Teacher Listens

Sara Allen

"Second-semester seniors are impossible to teach!" I moaned one dreary February Monday in our faculty room. "I prepare, but they don't. Half of them aren't even doing the reading! I ask a question. They just sit there and watch. I feel like such a fool as I answer my own questions!" Muttered responses assured me I was not alone. Second-semester seniors are impossible to teach, at least in conventional ways. Even the supposedly ideal conditions of my private school life — small classes, selected students, four classes instead of five or six — are no protection against student disengagement. My attempts to change the traditional fare by offering "Dramatic Poetry" instead of "Poetry" or "The Nineteenth Century Novel" hadn't wooed this group. They had had enough of the predictable English class discussion: teacher question, student response, and teacher evaluation. In *Classroom Discourse: The Language of Teaching and Learning*, Courtney Cazden claims that "The three-part sequence of teacher initiation, student response, teacher evaluation (IRE) is the most common pattern of classroom discourse at all grade levels" (29). No wonder my students were turned off, refusing to play the usual teacher/student game. They'd been doing this for twelve or more years!

"Why not let them do the discussion themselves?" my ever-ready-to-try-new-ideas department chair challenged. "You can be an observer. Take notes. Tell them what you see. They've been in English classes for years and years. They know how to talk about reading."

"You mean teacher research?"

"Yes. Describe what you've noticed about how they talk and listen in class now. Show them you know something about what is going on. Tell them they can figure out the poem. See what they'll do."

I'm used to trying out new ideas, plunging in, and seeing what will happen. Dixie Goswami's course at Bread Loaf had taught me something about looking at a class; Deborah, my department chair, had always encouraged experimentation. Though I knew that I might be in for some chaos, I was willing to risk that. I was desperate.

Such was the beginning of "student-sustained discussion" in which I turned the talk about literature over to the students, and watched to see what would happen. For the next six weeks, through units on Frost's dramatic dialogues and Robert Pack's and Pamela Hadas's dramatic monologues, students talked together about reading. They were unsure, giggly, embarrassed. Some refused to talk. But once a brave girl initiated discussion, others responded. They argued, agreed, disagreed, and paused, creating heavy silences. They floundered, but, convinced by my physical removal from the circle of desks that I would not interfere, they gingerly explored their new freedom. I played observer, taking notes on who talked, who responded, and who remained silent. At the end of each class, I told them what I'd observed about the way they were talking together; sometimes I offered suggestions ("Silence gives people a chance to think," "You could say you agree with Ann instead of just thinking it," or "Susan's question helped focus the discussion"). I resisted the temptation to instruct them about the literature. Though we were tentative, erratic, frightened, we felt released from the bounds of the teacher-directed, question-and-answer, you-must-know-certain-things approach. The class came to life as it hadn't in all that long month.

The students' greatest frustration was their inability to push the discussions to a general level. Used to the certainty of a teacher's directing questions, confirmation of their responses, and the underlying assurance that they could achieve right answers, they keenly felt the absence of the old authority. I never offered to appoint a leader; this *was* a radical shift for all of us. None of us, teacher included, knew what new order might result, if any. We knew only that we didn't want to quit.

One day I asked permission to ask a question to help with Frost's "Home Burial." It didn't help. Some started to whisper together in ways they hadn't since I'd let go of the teacher's role. I backed off. A few days later, they got bogged down in the confusions Frost craftily creates around "truth" and "lies" in "The Witch of Coos." I asked a question about that issue and, this time, they willingly pursued the elusive "truth." Apparently the question I asked was *their* question; I had begun to "read" their discussion better. We spent five days on "The Witch of Coos," five days in which we discussed the poem and the class discussion together, weaving a new kind of conversation none of us had experienced before.

Much of the talk was about discussion: What is frustrating? What enables you to move to a more general level of discussion? What prevents you? Can some of you assume the roles the teacher used to assume? Can you believe in what your peers say? Under what conditions? I assured them that the poem was hard, tricky. One day I summarized the previous day's discussion. They joined right in, pushing the discussion even further. As we talked together, they no longer treated me as the teacher; I, too, was a student. They argued with me, ignored what I'd said, or countered with questions of their own. They laughed when a classmate raised her hand, which acknowledged how different this kind of discussion was for all of us. Old habits like raising hands no longer applied.

That first year was an experiment; we felt our way, but we weren't very sure what we'd discovered. We liked the excitement of doing something new; we liked the openness and the freedom. We didn't like the confusion, the dead ends, and the lack of systematic ways of proceeding. I wasn't even sure I'd try this kind of discussion again. An NCTE Teacher-Researcher Grant kept me going.

Teacher Researcher

Just writing the proposal for an NCTE Teacher-Researcher Grant changed my approach to my teaching. I had to figure out what I was trying to do and why. I had to propose ways I would gather information and make all this explicit to an unfamiliar audience at NCTE. This forced me to formalize my study of student-sustained discussion, and to map this new territory—collaborative teaching and learning.

As I taught the course in the second semesters of the next two years, I developed and refined my collection of data. I devised questionnaires and assigned journal entries to provide information about students' changing responses to the class format. I kept my own teacher journal. Studying talk is hard; unlike writing, it's ephemeral, said and gone. Previously, I'd scrambled to jot down who talked (but not what each said) and to mark the patterns of each day's discussion. For the semester of the grant, my third time through the course, I audiotaped each class and hired a graduate student in education at the University of Pennsylvania to transcribe a few of them. One of the best research and teaching tools turned out to be the video camera. Worrying about the effect of the camera on class discussion, I'd initially resisted a colleague's suggestion that I videotape some classes. But the camera proved nearly as unobtrusive as the tape recorder, and the students talked apace, no holds barred.

The young woman who transcribed the tapes became an active

participant in the project. Early in the semester she visited the class to meet the students and observe a conventional, teacher-led discussion. She observed and took notes on each student-sustained discussion I wanted her to transcribe. She joined the study group I formed to describe the transcriptions, thus offering another perspective on the class.

Gathering information, loosely called data, was easy. Figuring out how to read it was not. Luckily, I'd met someone with an approach that made sense. Cecelia Traugh, Head of Middle School at Friends Select School in Philadelphia, suggested an approach formulated by her colleague Patricia Carini, who established The Prospect Center and School in Bennington, Vermont. She has developed an oral inquiry process to look closely at students' and children's learning. For the research project, Cecelia and I formed a small study group with two other teachers and the transcriber to look at transcripts of the tapes of class discussion. We met periodically during the semester.

The Prospect inquiry process builds on the multiple perspectives of several people talking and observing together. The process keeps the participants focused on description and checks the urge to judge or evaluate. Each description of a student-sustained discussion began with a reading aloud of the entire transcript of that class. We then gave impressions of the whole discussion. Each person spoke in turn and I as chair took notes, summarizing the talk of the group after each round. To look more closely, we always chose a small chunk to describe in detail. Again, we went around, each person speaking in turn and the chair summarizing. The resulting accumulation of observations provided insights that went far beyond what I as a single observer could gain from studying the class or the transcripts. This kind of collaboration supported and deepened my research.

I brought the videotape into the study group fairly late in the year. We were astounded by how much more we could see. From the audiotapes, we could study talk (frequency of speaking, tone of voice, strength of voice). From the videotapes we could see everything else that was going on in the room: who was listening, who chatting quietly with a neighbor, who looking out the window, who writing. The body language of each speaker showed us attitudes we couldn't pick up from the writing of the transcript or the speech of the audiotape. We could see gestures, movements of head and eye, and body posture that affected each person's speech and revealed his or her engagement in the class. We could see those who listened intently though they did not speak. With both the videotape and the transcript at our fingertips, we could look again and again at one class. I've continued to use the videotapes for further study and to demonstrate both student-sustained discussion and descriptive teacher researcher techniques.

The Research and the Class

The research project intensified our experience as teacher and class. The students were stimulated by the sense of something special going on. Occasional visitors, including the transcriber, an art teacher, and the academic dean added to the sense of adventure. One boy wrote, "I found this dramatic poetry class to be somewhat revolutionary. A mostly student-run class. ... I appreciated the fact that the teacher respected us enough to let us go." Another said the "idea of a student-led discussion fascinated me and sparked a different kind of interest in this course."

Suddenly how a class went, usually a subject for separate student or teacher chat in the halls or faculty room, became part of our daily conversation. We talked together about teaching styles, the purposes of talking (and listening), and connections between talking and writing, writing and learning. I talked with students after class, in the halls, during lunch, in a conference room. The class was no longer confined to my room or to a whole group talking as a body.

I reported the study group's observations to the class: that they stayed close to the text; that different students assumed different roles (Alice asked her own questions, John asked leading questions like a teacher, Sam liked to make statements); that they were anxious to reach some kind of consensus. I told them early on that they were like the first readers of a new text, and that they had to use their own experience with reading to create their own interpretations—and that going around and around was not an uncommon way for people to talk together about something new. We talked about how we make meaning and whether that meaning is objective and "out there" or subjective and the creation of each, individual mind. That became the central issue of the course: Was there an interpretation to be discovered, a "final truth" right-thinking people all agreed upon? My letting go of the talk of course implies that there is not, that each reader creates meaning and that although these meanings overlap and can be shared, they are not "out there," final, correct, or incorrect. For some, this was liberating, for others, a challenge to the way they'd been taught all their lives. A challenge to the way they'd learned to be successful.

Perhaps that is why this class was especially difficult. Though divided equally between boys and girls, the group was unevenly divided in every other way. Some of the boys were sure of themselves as students; some had been in "advanced" English courses. Three boys, confident, articulate, and intelligent, loved to argue. Two were friends who had shortcuts in their talk with each other that left others out. The girls, on the other hand, had been in "regular" courses; they were unsure of themselves, inarticulate in class (though not in the halls), and tentative. After the first day's experiment, Lauri told me in the cafeteria that she hated that day's class: "There was too much arguing. I can't participate in that kind of discussion. Sam just went on and on. Are we going to have more of these discussions? I hope not."

One boy and two girls chose to remain silent. The girls listened attentively. The boy grinned at those who spoke as if to mock their foolishness. (That all three wrote copiously in their journals suggests that they were not disengaged.) One girl, angry at the boys but powerless to counter them on their ground, shouted challenges across the room. These oppositions were too close to the stereotypical images of dominant males and compliant females. We were all concerned. Classes became shouting matches among three boys, and no one seemed strong enough to overwhelm them into silence or, better yet, to change the talk from argument into discussion. Classes were lively, students were engaged, but too many people felt excluded. The girls, unable to battle in the boys' terms, nonetheless refused to agree with their interpretations. "Write it in your journal!" became their counter. "That's where you put your own interpretation." But that option felt like a retreat into subjectivity. We were stuck. Until I turned them into researchers.

I decided to show them part of the tape of an especially difficult class on Frost's dramatic poem "Witch of Coos." Once they got over the shock of seeing themselves on the screen, I forced them to look closely at about three minutes of the class. I insisted that they use the close descriptive technique I'd been learning in my study group. The trick was to stop them from judging: "Sam is hogging the class again." "Susan should be quiet." "John shouldn't interrupt like that." I insisted that each judgmental comment be transformed into a statement. This was quite a challenge. "OK, Sam is talking during most of this tape." "Laura is trying to talk and yells when Sam interrupts." "Tom interrupts." Each wrote down as much as he or she could see as I played the same segment over and over. The observations were fascinating for all of us. They noticed that the boys sat together on one side of the room, leaned back in their chairs, and argued with one another; the girls sat on the other side of the room and leaned forward over their desks to listen to and watch the arguing boys. They thought this odd, and we talked about the dominance of the few boys, the passivity of many of the girls and the rest of the boys. Several people objected to the kind of talk going on in this course but felt helpless to do anything about it. But the talk about the dynamics of the class helped to change the situation. Suddenly we were all thinking and talking about discussion: Should the boys argue? Who got left out? Should everyone in the class get a chance to speak? Were we ever going to agree on an interpretation of a poem? Should we? Is there a correct interpretation of a poem? What is the point of discussion? Surprisingly and unexpectedly, the course had become a collaboration in which we discussed not only literature but fundamental issues of how we form meaning in the context of a classroom.

And it worked. Their discussion changed. I met with the three arguing boys outside of class to ask if they could find other, more inclusive ways of talking and listening. One day, I asked them not to talk for twenty minutes. I asked another to be aware of the "That's a stupid idea" expression he often wore whenever anyone disagreed with him. I suggested that everyone scramble their order, not sitting in the same places every day. I urged silent girls to talk and the challenging girl to try to find a way to work with rather than against the arguers. I did cautiously move into the circle of the discussion, offering a nod of support to a tentative student, a gesture of "Cool it!" to another, a genuine question or opinion. And I continued to offer observations after each class.

One day, almost out of the blue, they had a class in which the boys did not argue, more girls talked, and discussion was more like a conversation than an argument. They began with a new poem, read it silently and then aloud, and then began talking together. I participated later in the discussion, asking a question, offering an opinion. At one quiet point, I said, "You're moving. This is a nice conversation." But I was not at the heart of the discussion. They were. They groped, but they returned again and again to the central images of the poem itself (a dramatic monologue called "Secrets" by Robert Pack) as their way to understanding. The poem is elusive, and they did not "finish," but there was a sense of common enterprise in their attempt.

The tone of class had changed significantly — and everyone knew that. One of the arguing boys described the class in his journal:

> The atmosphere was relaxed, yet everyone was focused, either on the poem or on the person speaking. ... People were more satisfied because they felt more a part. People were more sensitive while not being too emotionally attached to their ideas. People were working together, sharing ideas, giving and taking, trying to reach some level of common idea and feeling.

They had, in essence, changed the nature and the purpose of talk from a defense of "right ideas" to a mutual exploration of possible meanings. They had transformed that class — with support but not direction from me.

We talked about the class for half an hour together as we tried to figure out why it was so much more comfortable than usual. They noted the absence of argument and anger, the inclusiveness of the talk, the listening. Laura said, "You boys never listen to us!" and Sam retorted with a groan, "Why does that issue always come up down here [at Springside, an all-girls' school, which coordinates with his all-boys' school in eleventh and twelfth grades]?" We wondered if "arguing" and insisting on right answers were something the boys were more comfortable with—if "conversation" felt more comfortable for the girls. One boy wondered if the purpose of all this was to get everyone to talk or to find the answer. He was convinced the "truth" was most important, and skeptical that everyone talking together could achieve that.

The answer to that boy's query is that, in a sense, the meaning that we make together is a kind of truth. And that meaning may change according to who the reader is and who is in the group. I assume that students construct meaning themselves in a complex process determined by who they are and what they bring to their reading. Talking is one way they find out what they think; listening to others' perspectives can alter their understanding. As one student expressed it:

> My classmates are there to present their ideas of each poem. Each of their ideas added pieces to each poem which I might not have seen or understood. It is important to talk to others to get a full picture or idea of the poem, so I talk to others to understand more or to debate a point I do not agree with.

The "full picture" is, ultimately, constructed by the student, the individual learner.

Writing is another way they find out (and show) what they think. These students wrote journal entries, papers, and a final exam. The final exam exemplifies how students can use both writing and talking to think their ways through a poem. Wanting the exam to reflect the course, I arranged for a class discussion to precede their actual exam. Before the exam day, I handed out the poem (Ezra Pound's "River Merchant's Wife: A Letter") and told them to write a journal entry in which they showed their thinking as they read. They brought the poem and their writing to the exam. During the "exam," they first talked together about the poem and then wrote an interpretation. The grades were based on my evaluation of the whole process: journal entries, talk during the discussion, and the final interpretation. Everyone was so thoroughly prepared for the exam that this was the most heated discussion of the term. Everyone contributed something, even the stubbornly silent boy. The two argumentative boys dominated the discussion again, this time espousing an interpretation most of their classmates opposed. People were forced to examine their thinking more deeply while maintaining faith in their own readings. Though they could not reach consensus, they were full of energy, ready and eager to write their own understanding of key points of the poem. The talk made them firm in their own assertions, clear and well focused.

The energy from the discussion carried through their writing; they presented their ideas with passion and conviction.

Student Response

As I've already indicated, student-sustained discussion changed the ways we talked and what we talked about. Handing the talk over to the students also made significant changes in the way students thought about themselves as learners. After that final exam, the two arguing boys stayed behind, partially to "check out" their interpretations, but mostly to chat. "I can just see me in a big lecture next year," said the one who was going to a large university. "I'll stand up in the middle and yell, 'Wait a minute! I don't agree with you at all!'" He would no longer accept the voice of any authority without question. In his final course response, this student wrote:

> This class has been very important in helping me learn how to read deeper and with more insight. I was learning to do this ... at the end of 11th grade, but even then the teacher usually helped us reach our own conclusion. Now I feel it's easier to come to my own conclusions and I feel more confident about them. I think I've probably gotten better at discussing my ideas too. I'm more open to other people's ideas and better at defending my own.

When students do the real talking, they feel a responsibility that goes beyond simply being allowed to express their thoughts. One student discovered a new sense of authority, which led him far beyond "right" and "wrong" answers:

> The students responded because they were the ones in control, they were teaching and learning, speaking and listening. There was no one person who had the last word, the right word that others would be judged by. Everyone was equal, and this gave people a chance to look into themselves, their thought processes, their independence, their communication skills, and their ability to function in a group.

Another found herself trusting her classmates' perceptions as a way to trusting her own. She realized the power she has to decide what she will think:

> I noticed that these class discussions in which the teacher was not involved helped me to become more confident about my classmates' opinions as well as my own. At first I felt shaky about accepting my classmates' ideas and I always needed the "OK" from the teacher. Now I accept ideas more willingly at my own discretion which has also helped me become more confident about my own thoughts. I think these discussions were so beneficial. I have never had a class

like that, but they are so much more helpful than discussions where the teacher lectures.

One boy, finding especially intense connections between the work we did and his own thoughts and feelings, shows that such learning can engage students in meaningful personal ways:

> This was a time in my life where I had begun to open up more in school, be more of myself and so I began to express myself more. . . . This class has helped me to express myself through my learning . . . and through my writing of the journals and papers.

As another put it:

> This course is not about English, it's about improving one's ability to speak his or her mind.

These responses showed me that turning the talk over to the students could be a way to turn the learning over to the students — and that the risks had been worthwhile. If students could come to believe in their power to create meaning, as individuals and in a group, they could believe in their power to create their own lives. The leap is not large, as these responses illustrate. If they feel they are responsible for what they think and know, they also feel responsible for how they live. When learning and knowing go beyond acquiring knowledge for a test, we have begun to "educate."

Further Changes

What emerged from this course and the research is a clearer understanding of Nancy Martin's words in *Reclaiming the Classroom* (1987):

> Once a teacher moves out of the traditional position of being the giver of questions and the receiver of right or wrong answers, there is no more certainty. (24)

So the revolution one student noticed has occurred. There are no final readings of a text, no certain ways a class will go, no certain ways of proceeding that work for all students. But the uncertainty has opened up new understandings about how students learn. The REsearch, as Ann Berthoff (1987) calls the looking at what goes on in our classrooms, forced me to ask questions not only about student talk and listening but about writing and reading. I am forced, again and again, to examine the fundamental assumptions that underlie what I do and say in the classroom. I am forced to study my own practice, and to change.

The uncertainty has also forced me to articulate more explicitly what I am doing and why. I continue to do classroom research, focusing on the ways I turn talk over to the students on all levels. Courtney

Cazden's *Classroom Discourse* helped me see that students need a kind of scaffolding (see Cazden 1988, Chapter 6) or structure to allow them to move from where they are as individuals or a class to new learning. I can provide that support if I know what they are thinking. I find out by asking for a question, observation, or response from each student. Or I ask them to bring in a favorite passage and explain the choices. One or two can launch a half-hour discussion even among seventh graders. Or I can form small literature groups that allow students to talk together about a book. (I eavesdrop on those conversations, taking notes about who talks, who listens, who is engaged.) I have had seventh graders sustain a whole-class discussion together after several days of small group discussions.

With seniors, I try to make my ways of proceeding explicit so they can agree or disagree with my basic assumptions. At least, they'll know what mine are. I often begin a unit with a "reflection." I choose a word that emerges from the reading (such as "memory" or "marriage" or "control"); I ask them to write words, phrases, sentences that come to mind, and take notes in a summary as each reads his or her list aloud. I give them copies of the summary and refer back to it during the unit. Or I ask them to do the summary and present it to the class the next day. This process not only expands each individual's thinking but shows connections among responses. This practice shows how group talk can create new, fuller, more detailed thinking.

Now, I know better how and when to have student-sustained discussions. The scaffolding comes from a variety of experiences in the classroom. We will have talked together about the purposes of talk in the classroom and the relationship to learning. They will have had practice talking together in pairs or small groups. That talk may be focused around a question I ask, a passage I give to them, or a question derived from full-class discussions. Before a student-sustained discussion, I may have them write or read for a few moments or look over their notes in their reading journals. Then they feel they have some sense of familiarity with or control of what they have read. (Another teacher I know appoints a leader who is to call on students; he tells the class to come prepared with genuine questions for a "class-run class.") Afterwards, someone (a student or the teacher) will do a summary of the discussion, presenting it to the class that day or the next. Though our responses to the literature may be tentative, though we may have a sense that our views could change even by the end of the semester, and though we may still have differences of opinion within the group, we will have a sense that everyone has been engaged in creating meaning. Distinctions between teacher and learner become less certain: everyone is teaching, everyone learning. We think together.

Works Cited

Berthoff, A. E. 1987. The teacher as REsearcher. In *Reclaiming the classroom*. See Goswami and Stillman 1987.

Cazden, C. B. 1988. *Classroom discourse: The language of teaching and learning*. Portsmouth, NH: Heinemann.

Goswami, D., and P. Stillman, eds. 1987. *Reclaiming the classroom*. Portsmouth, NH: Boynton/Cook.

Martin, H. 1987. On the move: Teacher researchers. In *Reclaiming the classroom*. See Goswami and Stillman 1987.

Response

Courtney Cazden

In his sympathetic and critical introduction to *The New Literacy*, Willinsky (1990) defines it as

> those strategies in the teaching of reading and writing which attempt to shift the control of literacy from the teacher to the student; literacy is promoted in such programs as a social process with language that can from the very beginning extend the student's range of meaning and connection. (8)

In placing this work "within a theater of educational and intellectual developments" (3), Willinsky reminds us that this book, and we (like all innovators), have roots, especially in the Dewey "progressive education" movement of an earlier era. We need to understand that heritage not just to pay our respects, but to avoid its failures — failures that Dewey himself discussed in *Experience and Education* (1938), a short retrospective commentary written near the end of his life.

One problem we share with our earlier colleagues is figuring out how best to incorporate into our understanding of the active learner our own roles as the active teacher. Three examples from the teaching of writing may help to explain my concern.

First, language educators in both England and New Zealand have expressed ambivalence over the effect on classroom practice of descriptive United States research on children's invented spelling. Yes, they say, it is good to have this picture of children's intuitive knowledge. But unaccompanied by descriptions of how teachers can help children build on that knowledge, such research seems to paralyze teachers and lead them to give up even reasonable and helpful aids.

Second, in two important articles, black language arts educator (and now MacArthur fellow) Lisa Delpit (1986, 1988) argues for the importance of deliberate teaching of the "culture of power" to black children.

Finally, teachers who do in fact supplement rich immersion in a writer's workshop with minilessons may wrongly feel that the latter are old-fashioned and shouldn't even be necessary in a perfect "whole language" classroom. For example, a first-grade teacher in Alaska invited me to visit his classroom to see the writing program he was justifiably proud of. For more than an hour, the children wrote and then listened while many took turns reading aloud from "the author's chair." Only as I was leaving the room, and the teacher was shifting the class from writing to math, did I notice on the overhead projector in the corner a transparency with a child's story prepared for a class discussion of some editing conventions. Here, in fact, was a classroom with a rich "social process with language" plus instructional detours to call children's attention momentarily to important matters of form. But that detour wasn't considered worthy of being shown off, much as I would have valued it.

Sara Allen's report (Chapter 5) seems to me important less for one more illustration of what students can do than for the details with which she describes her own roles. In this account, the New Literacy objective is interpretation as "the creation of each individual mind," and the means is "student-sustained discussion." But Sara did not just withdraw and assume she had thereby done the right thing. She listened, more intently than before; she acknowledged the students' frustration with "their inability to push the discussion to a general level"; and she found ways to insert an occasional question that was "their" question, because she had "begun to 'read' their discussion better." As she rightly acknowledges, "A teacher's voice *can* be helpful, can encourage students to make new connections or see something in a different light" (personal communication, 11/21/89).

Then she designed an exam that elegantly reflected the course by evaluating a miniversion of the students' process of learning to read a poem: "journal entries, talk during the discussion, and the final interpretation." In short, she figured out ways to support her active learners with the best kind of active teacher.

That alone would merit praise and publication. But thanks to the NCTE grant, Sara went further: collaborating with her students in researching their own patterns of talk. The danger in any kind of classroom deregulation is that inequalities may increase. That happened here: In a heterogeneous group of "advanced" boys and "regular" girls, some of the boys dominated discussions. "Classes were lively, students were engaged, but too many people felt excluded." In other classrooms, patterns of exclusion might follow lines of ethnicity or social class.

As with her dilemma about questions, Sara found effective ways to intervene. It is not easy, even for graduate students being trained as researchers, to watch a videotape and make observations instead of judgments. Sara and her students learned something:

> The talk about the dynamics of the class helped to change the situation. ... Surprisingly and unexpectedly, the course had become a

collaboration in which we discussed not only literature but fundamental issues of how we form meaning in the context of the classroom.

When even such collective self-reflection was not enough to achieve more affirmative interaction, Sara intervened more directly. She spoke to some of the students privately; she suggested that students not sit in the same seats every day; and at least once, she asked "three arguing boys" not to speak at all for twenty minutes. And here too, with respect to discussion process as with respect to content, she sometimes moved right into the discussion — to hold back one student or support the participation of another.

When I finished writing *Classroom Discourse* (Cazden 1988) in 1986, I was sure I had said all I knew about that important aspect of teaching. Now, four years (and five Bread Loaf summers) later, I understand better where new ideas for practice will come from. Forms of classroom talk suitable to new visions of active learners will be created, not by researchers like me, but by classroom teachers like Sara Allen. Then, again like Sara, they must write about what they have done. And tell the whole story.

Works Cited

Cazden, C. B. 1988. *Classroom discourse: The language of teaching and learning*. Portsmouth, NH: Heinemann.

Delpit, L. 1986. Skills and other dilemmas of a progressive black educator. *Harvard Educational Review* 56: 379–85.

———. 1988. The silenced dialogue: Power and pedagogy in educating other people's children. *Harvard Educational Review* 58: 280–98.

Dewey, J. 1938. *Experience and education*. New York: Collier-Macmillan.

Willinsky, J. 1990. *The new literacy: Redefining reading and writing in the schools*. New York: Routledge.

6

The Drudgery and the Discovery
Students as Research Partners

Jeffrey Schwartz

In 1986–87 I conducted classroom research on what happens when high school writers use an electronic network. I used student research assistants to help me with the mechanics of the project as well as with the collection and analysis of data. In the preface to *Reclaiming the Classroom*, Dixie Goswami (1987) writes that "working with teachers to answer real questions provides students with intrinsic motivation for talking, reading, and writing, and has the potential for helping them achieve mature language skills" (ii). In addition to conducting research with a whole class, I worked intensely with a pair of students as research partners. Quickly I found that collaborating with two student research assistants was as interesting to me and as educational as the information we were digging up.

Students become active learners when they are engaged in a discovery process. They also observe and save data a teacher may miss. In two writing classes I explained to all of my students that we were involved in an inquiry and that I would be conducting research as they were. The focus of the research, for them, was a comparison of three communities who shared writing on an electronic network: Sewickley Academy, their private school outside of Pittsburgh, Pennsylvania; Wilsall High School, a school of only forty-nine students in a ranching town in Montana; and Little Wound High School on the Pine Ridge Reservation in Kyle, South Dakota. I tape-recorded key discussions, interviewed case subjects, collected surveys before, during, and after the course, kept a research journal, and saved all of the student exchanges among the three schools as well as the additional formal and informal student writing. In addition to a letter exchange, students at the three schools shared interviews, stories, essay drafts, revisions, and oral histories during the semester-long course. My students reflected on their stereotypes and how they changed, saved *all* their writing, and raised their own questions about comparative life-styles, family, religion, career ambitions, community history and problems, school, and the like. They wrote frequently during the course about what they were discovering. When I spoke at state and national conferences, I asked students for permission to share their writing, and I reported the response of other teachers to what we were doing. Students felt they were part of a unique project.

With an NCTE Teacher-Researcher Grant, I hired Lindsay de Haven and Becky Downs, two bright, motivated, enthusiastic students, who were accomplished writers. I knew they would be trustworthy and responsible and that I would enjoy working with them over a period of months. Collaborating with individual students is more like teaming up with two colleagues. The three of us worked together for a year, sharing the drudgery as well as the discovery of research.

Time is a teacher's most precious commodity, even more valuable when the teacher is conducting research. My two student research assistants gave me time. They helped photocopy massive amounts of student writing and spent hours typing twenty-seven students' answers to open-ended questions. We spent one afternoon counting the number and speed of hundreds of electronic messages in an effort to document that the computer was essential in student exchanges.

But the students weren't hired to be clerks. From our very first meeting, I tried to involve Becky and Lindsay as co-researchers. At the beginning of the project, I wrote to them:

> I see us as partners in this research. That means that I want to share with you the drudgery as well as the discovery ahead. All three of us will be involved in the mechanical work of photocopying and filing lots of writing. You'll also have as much responsibility as you want in activities such as interviewing, observing classes, writing your own field notes, and bringing to our weekly discussions any insights, questions, or hunches you might have about what we're looking for. I have a focus and set of questions in mind, but I'm sure that these will change as we move along. You can be very helpful by asking questions and making suggestions when they arise.

In our first meeting I went over the background of the project and the nature of classroom research. We discussed the key issues of our project, the central questions, methods of collecting and analyzing data, a timetable, and their role as student researchers.

As my research partners, Becky and Lindsay proved most valuable when they contributed a point of view I couldn't have seen without them. This happened in the group interviews, on the revision of the midsemester survey, and in our analysis of the data. Case studies were one way to observe individual students in more depth. I began by interviewing three case subjects alone. Twice during the semester Becky and Lindsay conducted a group interview of the subjects, once in the first month of our research and again on the last day of the course. A group interview encourages discussion rather than interrogation. Conducting it without me allowed student interviewers to control one aspect of the project, and it allowed the subjects to express themselves differently, if not more honestly, than if they were speaking to a teacher.

Before the interview we talked about planning good open-ended questions but staying flexible to interesting sidetracks or surprises. I also suggested topics I was interested in (attention to audience, stereotypes, attitude toward the project), but I encouraged them to think of their own. The students planned, arranged, conducted, and transcribed the interview (forty pages' worth) before we met to analyze it. Since they would be conducting a follow-up interview, we discussed *how* the interview was conducted as well as *what* they found out. We examined what happened: the results of good questions, as well as the contradictions, repetitions, interruptions, misinterpretations, colloquial expressions, and incomplete answers. We talked about the way the two of them worked together, about productive and nonproductive sidetracks ("the importance of knowing when to intervene when the conversation begins to go off on a tangent and when it's best to stay silent" — Becky), the meaning of pauses, the slow emergence of thoughts ("Spit it out!" Lindsay said she wanted to tell them when she was transcribing), and those delightful moments when the group discussion took off on its own "wavelength." Discussing the transcripts was a real lesson for all of us.

The two student researchers asked many of the questions I would have asked. But they also found information I may not have discovered — information, for example, that contradicted my hypothesis about writing to a real audience. In the following excerpts, taken from the first group interview, the student subjects' names have been changed.

Dave: Well, I think with teachers in general, I think I usually tend to write what I think they want to hear.

Becky: Uh-huh.

Dave: And I don't care, I mean, if people say they don't do that. But, fine, but I think you get better grades if you do.

Lindsay: Uh-huh.

Becky: Uh-huh.

Dave: So, I, if I was writing to Mr. Schwartz, I'd try to write more like what he'd want to hear, and if I was writing to them in South Dakota, I'd write what Mr. Schwartz would want to hear because he'd see it anyway.

Becky: (*Laughs*) Yeah, I think. . . .

Dave: I mean, it's just, I mean it's just the way I write, I write to teachers. I think you get better grades that way.

Lindsay: Um, hmm.

Becky: Right. So like, if Mr. Schwartz, like wasn't reading these at all, like, if he was just, like, if you were just sending them over the modem to these people, like, they'd be totally different.

Dave: Oh, totally different, probably.

In that discussion about anticipating an audience, one student very honestly asserts that his true audience is the teacher. This led me to question my own hypothesis that writing to a real reader would change the rhetorical context. For at least one student, at the beginning of the project, that was not true.

Student researchers elicited responses I never could have at other moments in the interview. For example, at one point the students have read about some of the serious problems on the reservation, and they want to know why the Indians stay there. Since the interviewers did *not* have the answer, the question was real.

Dave: But I don't understand why they just don't leave and like. . . .

Lindsay: I don't know. Can they? Or is it sort of like they can't?

Becky: Yeah, can. . . .

Sam: They — I don't think they can.

Dave: No, yeah, no, no, they're uh, allowed to leave but it's just that, I don't know, their tribal or whatever. . . .

Nancy: But they . . . their lives.

Lindsay: Or maybe it's just family closeness or something.

Nancy: Where would they go? 'Cause they already have their schools established and I mean if they just leave. . . .

Sam: Yeah, right, Alan? [Alan is a sixth student who has wandered into the room.]

Becky: Do they, like, go to school, like, free — like the government pays for all that stuff for them if they stay on the reservation or —

Nancy: I think it's just like a regular public system.

Becky: Oh.

Sam: Yeah, 'cause they—some of them—no.

Lindsay: Well, um. ...

Nancy: But it was an Indian name.

Sam: What was it called? Little Wound High School?

On another occasion the students' answers would have sounded premeditated or forced had I been the interviewer:

Lindsay: Is there any point in all this, do you think? In this sort of project? Do you think it's gonna help you?

Sam: I, I think it's great.

Nancy: I think it's kinda ... it's interesting.

Sam: You learn about somebody else's, somebody else's society, and it's in America. ...

Becky: Uh-huh.

Sam: ... and, I mean, think about all the different, all the different places in America. It makes everything seem more, um, intense, and it makes me, it makes it seem like this community is, is more than we make it out to be sometimes.

Becky: Uh-huh.

Sam: Because I'm looking at these people talk about their community and, um, it's kinda neat.

Lindsay: Um, hmm.

Sam: Do you know what I mean?

Becky and Lindsay: Yeah!

Becky: It makes you think about your own culture. ...

Sam: Yeah.

Becky: Uh-huh.

Sam: ... it's like a whole other world to us—the way we live, the way we, like, we think and act. (*Mumbles*) Yeah, so that's good.

In revising the midsemester questionnaire, the student researchers contributed a valuable and necessary outside point of view. We teach our students that it's productive to test a draft on a reader, but how many times do teachers "test" an exam or questionnaire on students before they hand it out? Before this research project, I never would have thought to test questions on students before the final version. After compiling a three-page survey intended to elicit responses to my classes' writing progress and their understanding of other cultures, I shared a draft with my research partners. Lindsay's comments helped me to see more clearly how a student would approach the survey. On one question about students' attitudes toward the project, she wrote, "This isn't going to be easy. This is an evaluation of sorts. Won't everyone put '5 Extremely Interested'?" When I asked, in my own words, "What have you learned about generalizing from data?" Lindsay wrote in the margin, "stereotypes?" Yes, of course. When she wrote "difficult" or "this will be tough," I listened carefully, and in some cases I eliminated or revised a question according to her advice. As co-workers in this research project, our traditional student/teacher roles were sometimes reversed. The student had the authority to suggest changes in a teacher's draft, and the teacher learned to be more sensitive to a real audience.

In our analysis of data — in the meetings where we phrased hypotheses and drew conclusions — the student research assistants and I worked most effectively as colleagues. In our discussions of survey and interview results, we raised real questions and figured out answers together. In March, when we started to analyze features in students' writing to see how it had changed over the previous semester, I asked myself and Becky and Lindsay, "What changes do you expect to find?" We isolated one example of the three-way electronic exchanges: the fourteen letters written over three months between one student at Sewickley and another at Wilsall. We looked closely at what distinguished the letters from other writing, what features indicated context and attention to a reader, what reasonable explanations might account for what we saw, what constituted change from the first letter to the last. Together we constructed, tested, and altered hypotheses that sometimes matched, and sometimes did not match, what we found. Without my research partners, I would not have faced the data as early as I did, nor examined it from as wide a perspective. Meeting with them kept me thinking actively about the research.

In addition to helping me, Lindsay and Becky learned more about research than others normally do in high school or undergraduate English. "Research in education is a postgraduate luxury," Garth Boomer (1987, 5) argues in "Addressing the Problem of Elsewhereness: A Case for Action Research in Schools." By participating actively in a real inquiry, my student research assistants learned to think and behave as researchers. Halfway through the first semester; Becky wrote,

> As our work has progressed, I have discovered that in order for the results to be as unbiased and truthful as possible, we must be willing to revise and rework the original hypothesis as new data comes to light. With this task in mind, I am quickly becoming aware of how many variables are significant to this project and how they are inter-related. ... As for the actual analyzing, I am just beginning to learn the techniques of picking out thought patterns and significant comments relevant to our topic of study from questionnaires and interviews.

Equally important is the ability to recognize new aspects of data. An example of this from our own project was the discovery that as the students wrote to their peers in other cultures and backgrounds, they became increasingly aware of their own surroundings.

At the end of the school year in June, Lindsay wrote,

> I truly feel we both have gotten so much more out of this project than we ever imagined. ... The project gave me a chance to become comfortable with a new writing context, too, and helped me to discover a new angle to teaching. I felt the joy of discovery, the pains of "hacker's cramp," the frustration of the occasional (*not* frequent) difficult case study, and the headache from too much of it all. But I want to say that the excitement I felt from being a part of such a unique project outweighed all the not so interesting parts. As you so well put it, I really feel we shared with you the drudgery as well as the discovery. ..."

The excitement and discovery all of us experienced from this project suggest that both teachers and students can benefit from sharing in a process of inquiry. Studies about how students learn to do research in science reveal the same thing. In *Notebooks of the Mind*, her book about thinking in different disciplines, Vera John-Steiner (1987) describes how apprenticeships form the scientific thinker:

> Learning by being with a knowledgeable partner is a more effective method of developing a particular language of thought than learning from books, classes, or science shows. The crucial aspect of these informal or formal apprenticeships is that they provide the beginner with insights into both the overt activities of human productivity and the more hidden inner processes of thought. (200)

In classroom studies in English, too, students can learn about what it means to raise real questions and to conduct research. Teachers can learn to examine more closely what happens in the classroom. Both can learn together about the role of language in the creation of meaning.

To collaborate with students, teachers need, above all, to trust them. Teachers lead and model but also have to relinquish some of the authority they may be accustomed to. They have to trust the students to think on their own and to contribute intelligently and responsibly to the research project. When students know that their insights and opinions do matter, they will contribute their best work. Involving individual students as partners in research does not necessarily mean paying them (as it did in my funded project), though some sort of compensation in credit is necessary and fair. It may not even be limited to two research assistants. Possibly a whole class can participate as actively in projects of inquiry. According to George Hillocks (1986), inquiry is the most effective focus of instruction (249). Boomer (1987) goes further than that to propose that "all students at all levels must be researchers and all teaching should be based on the methods of research, if we are serious about learning" (8).

Involving students as partners in research means working with them more as colleagues than in traditional student/teacher roles. As partners, they should be expected to write about and to discuss the research, as well as contribute to the mechanics of collecting the data. When teachers share their research with their students, they will find that they will learn in new ways together.

Works Cited

Boomer, G. 1987. Addressing the problem of elsewhereness: A case for action research in schools. In *Reclaiming the classroom*, ed. D. Goswami and P. Stillman. Portsmouth, NH: Boynton/Cook.

Goswami, D. 1987. Preface to *Reclaiming the classroom*, ed. D. Goswami and P. Stillman. Portsmouth, NH: Boynton/Cook.

Hillocks, G. 1986. *Research in written composition*. ERIC report. Urbana, IL: NCTE.

John-Steiner, V. 1987. *Notebooks of the mind*. New York: HarperCollins.

Response

Cindy Myers

Jeff points out well how "students become active learners when engaged in a discovery process." We all know it's true. But even with knowing the power that classroom research has for us, we don't naturally involve the students in our inquiries, or we aren't sure how to do it, and that needs to change.

Involving students isn't easy. I've experimented with having students who are in a revolving advisory group give me suggestions about our classroom. I've also had students, as research assistants, work with younger students on their writing and meet with me to reflect on that as well as on their own writing. But with the revolving group, there were problems with continuity, and meeting with the research assistants became a scheduling problem. All of these students helped me see what writers needed, but I never felt as if I were involving them enough.

I see from Jeff's experience that part of the problem was lack of organization. Jeff had carefully worked out ways for gathering and analyzing data, and he already knew when and how he could use two research assistants. I tried setting up a structure *with* my students because I wasn't sure what they could manage, and I thought we should figure it out together. But I think the structure of Jeff's project allowed the students to quickly get into valuable in-depth work and become engaged in the research themselves. Lindsay's comments show the enthusiasm and involvement they felt from being part of the project, and as Jeff pointed out, the amount of work accomplished and the findings of the research were directly affected by Becky's and Lindsay's work.

What strikes me is that Jeff had a choice. He could have carried out the same inquiry on his own, gathering and analyzing the data himself, not having students participate in the actual research. Imagine what his inquiry would have been like then. I think that Becky's and Lindsay's work took Jeff deeper into the research — engaged *him* more with the work, kept him going at it, made him think more, made him see more. Can we risk the loss of that as we carry out our research? Do we not all need the motivating power that working as partners with our students can give us? Also, is it not true that if we don't have the students' viewpoint of the data, we might be off base in judging what the data mean?

So how do we manage involving our students in classroom research which already takes extra time? Consider this: *All* of your students become, in a sense, your research partners when you make clear your intention to learn from them and you show them how to become "engaged in a discovery process" about themselves.

I stumbled upon that realization three years ago while experimenting with learning logs. Almost daily I asked my students to write about what they were learning, what they noticed about themselves and their work, goals for their learning, or their progress toward their goals. At the end of each quarter, they read over their logs, thought about their work, and told me in writing what had happened to them in English that quarter, quoting anything from their logs that seemed especially important.

By the end of the third quarter, my students became strikingly fluent in telling what they saw in themselves, not only in their logs but during conferences in class. They grew more analytical as they pointed out what they noticed in their reading and writing. For example, one student showed me quickly and accurately an overall picture of the writing she'd done for the year when she wrote:

> Some papers I worked well on one thing but it was needing another thing. For example my paper *Room Two Hundred Twelve* all I did was describe this room, nothing else just description. On my paper *U2* I didn't describe enough. So that kind of tells you something. I wish I had more writing time to write one paper with everything in it. If I could do this all the time I would become a very good writer. In the future I'll do this so I can be a better writer.

I saw the students go after goals they set for themselves, goals that were usually on target and realistic. They explained reasons for their progress or lack of progress and noted any sudden change that took place as one student did in this entry from December: "During this week in my reading log I have written my opinions and feelings rather than explaining the whole story. It came out really good. It was easier and it took a lot less time."

Because of what they wrote and told me about in class, I learned how to approach these students better. I felt as if I were working alongside them, moving them along, discovering *with* them instead of watching, listening, and putting together the data on my own. I realized that their ideas, along with my observations, made a more complete picture of how students learn to read and write and that all of them had become, in a sense, my research partners. I need the students' views in order to have an accurate picture of what's happening to them, and using the logs the way we did opened up a manageable way to give them a voice and involve them in a discovery process about themselves.

I'm certain that the work these students did with their logs made them learn more than any other students I'd had. As one student put it, "At the beginning of the year I thought all the goals and writing what you learned was dumb but now I see that it has a great impact on what you remember at the end of the year."

I also think they viewed their work and themselves more seriously, as one student did when she wrote, "It's important to be able to write and read because without it, you wouldn't be able to be a person. You have to be able to express yourself."

I didn't have any students work with me on analyzing their logs, although I wish I had. Jeff's experience reminds me of the need for that. I think anyone who's carrying out an inquiry needs to explore the possibilities for having the students work as Becky and Lindsay did in Jeff's classroom. I also think we have to reach for Garth Boomer's proposal which Jeff quoted, that "all students at all levels must be researchers and all teaching should be based on the methods of research, if we are serious about learning."

We can and must create a "research environment" in our classrooms involving all of the students as much as possible. Maybe that means involving a whole class in gathering and analyzing data for an inquiry, or maybe it can mean involving the students in looking at themselves and their work throughout the year. Students are asked so infrequently in our schools to analyze their own work and to think about their own learning that at first they often have little to say. But when we show our students how to look at themselves, when we invite them to help us learn from them, they become more interested in the learning, they take more control over their own learning, they progress more, and they show us what we could not see on our own.

7

On the Move in Pittsburgh
When Students and Teacher Share Research

Jeffrey Schwartz

Shared inquiry, as it is described in this book, depends on trusting students to contribute to their own learning. From Ellen Schwartz's emergent curriculum in pre-first grade to Marilyn Cochran-Smith's collaboration with two student teachers, you'll see teachers listening to their students and being changed by them. But collaboration between students and teacher — or between teacher colleagues, as Susan Lytle and Robert Fecho write in Chapter 15 — is never easy. Sharing inquiry means negotiating a new balance of power in the classroom. It means sharing genuine questions that rarely have simple answers and that sometimes shake us from the comfort of long-held, fundamental beliefs. It means risking failure, and in the case of Rich Murphy and Jan Kazmierczak, examining what went wrong. Sharing inquiry means changing to a focus on learning, where language is the instrument to talk, think, create, question, argue, share, and reflect. The result of shared inquiry is more engagement in both content and the processes of learning. Students and teacher learn together, sometimes by surprise, inside and outside the classroom.

In writing process classrooms, there is already the core of an interactive model of learning when students make decisions about their own writing, when they write for real purposes and real readers, and when they learn from their peers. In classrooms where the teacher proposes to learn with his or her students, roles of authority begin to break down even more. In a shared inquiry, students see the teacher learn, and they learn by teaching. Both students and teacher see themselves as makers of meaning and as providers and takers of skills and information. When this happens the writing classroom changes again. As Paulo Freire (1972) writes:

> Through dialogue, the teacher-of-the-students and the students-of-the-teacher cease to exist and a new term emerges: teacher-student with students-teachers. The teacher is no longer merely the one-who-teaches, but one who is himself taught in dialogue with the students, who in turn, while being taught, also teach. They become jointly responsible for a process in which all grow. (67)

When students are welcomed into the dialogue of learning, they have more invested in the class and therefore take more responsibility for their own learning. In a situation governed by real questions, students can't help but become inquirers.

In the 1987–1988 school year I extended the work with two student researchers (described in Chapter 6) to include an entire class. The course at Sewickley Academy, called The History of Pittsburgh, was coordinated with a history class at Clairton High School, about an hour and a half away in Clairton, Pennsylvania. Six teachers in English, history, and computer science planned a course with common assignments to offer high school students a chance to do original research into their communities and to share that research, along with questions, notes, letters, and essays using the computer for electronic mail.

Clairton is a working-class town centered around what was once the biggest coke works in the world. In 1987 over half of the heads of households were unemployed. Since the town has been bankrupt, there is no regular police or fire department. Last year Clairton students attended a condemned elementary school in shifts while they waited for the state to finish rebuilding their former high school. The day my students and I visited Clairton, we drove through the Mon Valley, where Pittsburgh's industry had been centered for one hundred years. The enormous steel mills we passed in Homestead, Duquesne, Braddock, McKees Rocks, and, finally, Clairton were closed or nearly silent—"like ghost towns out west," one of my students said.

Sewickley, by contrast, is one of the towns where steel barons used to own summer homes. It's one of the most affluent towns in the Pittsburgh area. Students who live there are likely to go home to three-story, one-family houses, not segregated housing projects. Most students drive to Sewickley from dozens of outlying areas, some on scholarship, but all eager for an education that will prepare them for college. The school they attend is beautiful and looked to the Clairton kids "like a college campus." The day the Clairton students visited Sewickley, they got off their bus and stood frozen, for what seemed like five minutes, till one student called another's name and all met for the first time. By the end of the day, their teachers couldn't coerce them to leave.

It would be easy to stereotype the kids at Sewickley as "stuck up, rich wimps," as one of my students put it, or, as he continued, to stereotype Clairton kids as "poor, poorly dressed, [and living in] slum-like houses." Our course was an investigation into those images, where they come from, and how they change. In coming to terms with each other, students had to confront their stereotypes about public and private education, as well as the economic, racial, religious, and ethnic differences between and also within the two schools. They had to leave their classroom to do that, they had to learn from each other, and they had to write about what they saw.

What made this course unusual was not just the collaboration between Sewickley and Clairton — two economically different communities that shared a common history in Pittsburgh — but also the focus of the course on inquiry. Writing would be used for real purposes — to investigate, reflect on, and communicate what we found. The computer would be the tool for writing, and, with its local bulletin board service, the tool for communicating as well. Ten students participated in Sewickley; twenty from Clairton. Six teachers worked on the project, with further support from other faculty and administration at the two schools, and grants from the Pennsylvania Museum Commission and the Bread Loaf School of English.

From the beginning of the course, I told the class we would focus on writing and inquiry, as much as we would on local history. In the course description, I wrote that

> most of the activities you participate in will be as much about *how* to discover information as they are about *what* you discover. We are all learners when we conduct research by asking genuine questions, creating and testing hypotheses, observing, finding answers, and writing about what we find. Since writing is one of the best ways to learn, we will write often to explore ideas, to make connections, and to share results. This will lead us at times to examine language — how we use words to think and communicate, and how to be better writers.

In the History of Pittsburgh class, students and teacher shared the process of finding out. We welcomed questions as a basis for developing the course. Students began with questions about their own pasts and continued with questions about Clairton and about the nature of making judgments. Students electronically mailed each other questions about town government, ethnic origins, career ambitions, jobs, school, percentage of minorities, religion, and what they did for fun in their spare time. Some questions could be answered from experience; others had to be discovered through outside research.

A Lot More Than the Facts

As students pursued their own questions, they had to choose the best method for finding out. Would answers best be found in a book? a formal interview? an informal conversation? a class discussion? a survey? a lecture outside class? a phone call to town hall? a trip to the public library? a close observation? Students used all of these methods. They interviewed and wrote about parents, grandparents, administrators, teachers, older residents of their towns, the first woman architect in Pittsburgh, a former managing director of the Civic Light Opera, among others. They brought to class an author, a filmmaker, an officer from the local historical society, and a longtime resident of Sewickley who lived in the first post office west of the Allegheny Mountains. They conducted schoolwide surveys, assembled statistics from the public library, the town hall, and the school's development office, read books, talked on the phone, dug up old photos, and attended outside lectures. They learned that different questions require different sources of information. In the process they learned the difference between traditional research and what we called inquiry. In her self-assessment of her work at the end of the course, Heather wrote:

> I discovered more than any book or newspaper could tell me. I found out what it was like to actually live through those years. ... Inquiry teaches a lot more than the facts. It teaches the feelings, the emotions, and most of all the truth about the people instead of the events. And isn't that really what history is about anyway?

Students also learned that new information leads to new questions. To become an independent learner, Andy wrote, "all it takes is a little know-how on how to find information. Once you find a book ... you can then follow up the leads it drops, and become almost like a detective, searching for clues on whatever your particular interest is." When we read Thomas Bell's *Out of This Furnace* to find out about immigrant labor in the Pittsburgh steel mills, students supplemented the book with pamphlets about unions, books about the Orthodox Church and the Serbian alphabet, and a map of a local mill. We asked, Where can we find out more about Braddock, the center of *Out of This Furnace*? Where can we find out more about Eastern European customs and food? What are hruskas, and how do they taste? One student, Lacey, invited the class to her home for her family's traditional Orthodox Christmas meal. Her father translated the names of the homemade breads, described the significance of the meal, and finished by telling of his own days working in the mills. Another student, Darren, interviewed his grandfather about working in Aliquippa, a mill town closer to Sewickley. His interview was published in a national magazine. Still another, Laura, invited Dave Demarest, the writer who reprinted *Out of This Furnace* and who wrote its Afterword, to come to our school; he showed slides and talked about Braddock and the history behind the book. Demarest was followed by Tony Buba, an internationally acclaimed documentary filmmaker, who specializes in films about Braddock, where he still lives. Buba came the same day the students from Clairton visited. He talked with pride and anger about changes in the Mon valley, how community history had to be preserved, and how we can generalize about life in the Pittsburgh area by examining its particulars. Laura had arranged his visit too.

The Process of Knowing

The questions that persisted between Sewickley and Clairton showed the students struggling to know themselves and to communicate as truthfully as possible to someone else. Meaning is slippery, they discovered. Students grew to understand the power that they had to influence how others saw them. One day in class, before they met in person, Lacey reported a three-hour phone conversation she had with her Clairton correspondent the night before. She said they described who everyone was, what they looked like, and other information that hadn't been forthcoming in the letters. They were also more blunt than they had been in the letters. "Are you all rich? We're all poor," the Clairton student said. That was our first confirmation of how we feared Clairton would see us.

"I hope they don't think we're geeks," Kathy said. There was a lot of concern throughout the correspondence that Clairton wouldn't be able to see beyond the economic differences between the two schools. Both sides, though, tried hard to correct any false conceptions. In a letter from Clairton to Andy before they met, Fred wrote:

> What I meant when I said that everyone thinks that Clairton is a bad city is that because we're considered an economically distressed city people think that a lot of bad things go on here. Like a lot of robbery and stuff like that. It's real surprising the stereotypes the surrounding areas have about us; like Pleasant Hills, T. J., and some other areas. I just wish I could show everyone like that, that it's not true. Our city isn't one big slum like some of them think either. I mean there are a few bad areas, but if you take for example the neighborhood I live in it would fit in almost any community, as a normal friendly place where the neighbors all get along and know that they can rely on one another if they need to. . . .

Before the Clairton students visited Sewickley, a common expectation was:

> I think (but I don't hope) that the Clairton students are going to resent us big-time when they meet us. In letters we can hide the facts that we live in beautiful houses, wear expensive clothes, and attend an incredible, gorgeous, expensive school. I also think they might not want us to see their school now. But I'm not sure.

After the Clairton students visited, though, my students were delighted by how well it went:

> First of all, I had a great time! I think I expected a lot of differences, so many that they would get in the way of "the project." But they didn't, which was fabulous!
>   In general, they (the kids) were really open (and open-minded) & it happily surprised me.

In building a more informed picture of her community, she found:

> It was hard to explain that not everyone who goes to SA is affluent and that not all people who go to SA are from Sewickley. My guests were on the lighter side of shock when they found out that I chose SA over other schools. It was like ... "How can your school be *that* good?"
>   Another "topic" that surprised them was the number of kids here on scholarships. Why get a scholarship to a high school?

Because we were involved in an inquiry, we continued to examine our expectations, to raise questions, and — always — to write about what we found. Writing and talking heightened our sensitivity about stereotyping, but meeting in person made us confront even more how images are formed, how we make judgments and are judged, and how really difficult it is to change someone's mind. James Britton (1987) writes:

> As human beings, we meet every new situation armed with expectations derived from past experience or, more accurately, derived from our interpretations of past experience. We face the new, therefore, not only with knowledge drawn from the past but also with developed tendencies to interpret in certain ways. It is in submitting these to the test of fresh experience — that is, in having our expectations and mode of interpreting either confirmed or modified — that the learning, the discovery, takes place. (16)

Knowing, as Britton says, is a form of doing. "There is no simple sense in which we *apply* a poultice to a swelling. In any confrontation, what we know must be reformulated in the light of what we perceive and our knowledge is thus forever on the move" (19). To learn, we found, we couldn't stay still. Sometimes we had to leave the classroom; other times we had to bring the outside in.

Certain questions became a framework from which we could test what we were learning against what we already knew:

- What do I already know about this subject/idea/person/place/experience?
- What do I expect to see? What questions do I have?
- What did I observe?
- What did my observations confirm? What surprises were there?
- What questions were answered? What conclusions can I draw?
- What new questions are raised?

In talk and in writing, students reflected continually on how their expectations were matched or not. They were always revising their preconceptions based on their observations, experiences, and reading. For the students and for me, the course was about coming to know: the process of raising questions, gathering information, and testing assumptions.

The Limits of Communication

As students tested their expectations, they struggled to stay open-minded, to observe and listen carefully, and not to generalize too quickly based on one observation or one interview. We found that no matter how much information we had from primary or secondary sources, it was never enough. After she met her Clairton correspondent, one of my students said in class, "You think you knew them from letters, but now I feel like I don't know them at all." Every new point added to our understanding but also complicated the perspective. When we visited Clairton, we observed their school, their neighborhood, and even saw the outside of some of their homes. We were continuing to understand something about how they lived. As Laura said later, though, if we could have lived with the Clairton students in their houses, we would have come to understand even more. At the same time our knowledge grew, we recognized its limits. To be sensitive to that was to increase our understanding of how communication and language work. We are always trying to say what we mean (and to infer beyond what we see).

Katie became very aware of the relative completeness of any picture, when she was the first to describe the town of Sewickley for her outside readers:

> Looking back, when I decided to write about the intersection [of Beaver and Broad Streets], I thought that it would be a fairly easy job. I thought, "I live here, don't I?" Soon afterwards, I began my "easy" job. Immediately, I had to eat crow. I began to realize that I had never before ripped apart Sewickley to see what makes it tick. I quickly saw that the essay was going to be much more than description.
> As I sat at the corner in the park, I had the chance to observe

people. I was already aware of the dichotomy between rich and poor. However, that corner came to symbolize the split. By that I mean that the poor rarely crossed Beaver Street to get to the specialty shops. They stayed for the most part in the front of Mellon Bank and on the benches of the park.

As for being a teacher in this situation, it was such a strange feeling to know that I was going to be representing Sewickley to Clairton. It was both exciting and nerve-wracking. I felt great knowing that I would be the one to say that Sewickley is more than rich people, specialty shops, and big houses. However, I was very concerned with presenting the full picture. It was very tempting to emphasize the poorer people, because everyone thinks that everyone in Sewickley is rich. However, I had to present a balanced picture. I constantly worried that the picture would not have some type of equilibrium. In this case, I truly felt the responsibility of being a teacher.

Katie understood where stereotypes come from, and she struggled for that impossible balance she associated with teaching, or with a type of authority she recognized she, too, could share.

Shifting Authority in the Classroom

As students participated in our collective inquiry, they learned that they, as well as the teacher, could contribute new information and affect the direction of the class. This new authority for them led us all to question the traditional role of student and teacher. We became "jointly responsible for a process in which all grow" (Freire 1972, 67).

In sharing inquiry our roles had to change. There were times when students saw me as learner — not someone with all the answers — and times when they saw themselves as teachers. The atmosphere of the classroom had to change, too. "There was a special rapport among everyone in the class," one student wrote in her final evaluation of the course. Another wrote, "With all of the informality in the class structure itself, we had a chance to be both teachers and students." Even the notion of "teaching" had to be redefined not only as providing information and transmitting the answers, but also as raising questions, reflecting, creating and sharing ideas. Teaching — or learning — could happen with a whole class, between two partners, or even by oneself. One student wrote about what she taught herself after suffering through a painful misunderstanding with her Clairton partner: "In this experience, I was both a learner and a teacher. I taught myself that comments that I had felt were genuine and personal had been seen by another as impersonal and boring. This showed me how easy it is to misconstrue others' intentions."

Research suggests that building responsibility and sharing authority are crucial for secondary school students. In 1984 Theodore Sizer reported that "no more important finding has emerged from the inquiries of our study than that the American high school student, *as student*, is all too often docile, compliant, and without initiative" (54). "Put the burden of learning on them," he says. "Such responsibility will liberate energy now lost because of the impersonality and the patronizing inherent in the lockstep routines of many schools" (67). In their studies of writing and learning, Judith Langer and Arthur Applebee (1987) conclude that "despite the process- and context-oriented research of the past two decades, [the traditional teacher-centered classroom] continues to undergird contemporary approaches to schooling, including the approaches of the teachers we studied." They continue:

> Though persistent and widespread, this model of teaching militates against many of our goals for writing and learning. It emphasizes the teacher as transmitter of knowledge, rather than the students as active agents who must interpret and reinterpret what they are learning; it emphasizes testing and evaluation, rather than work in progress; and it emphasizes declarative rather than procedural knowledge (knowing *that* rather than knowing *how*). To summarize bluntly, given traditional notions of instruction, it may be impossible to implement successfully the approaches we have championed. (138–39)

We know from researchers like Perl and Wilson (1986) that when writing is taught effectively, students take on new roles of authority, and the structure of the classroom changes:

> Traditional assumptions about how writing happened, of who could learn from whom, or of who owned or had access to knowledge, had, for the most part, vanished. No longer were teachers the sole sources of knowledge in their classrooms. Instead, they created settings in which students wrote for and learned from one another. And when they were no longer constrained by the need to write merely to please their teachers, some students, some of the time, discovered a freedom and depth of expression they had rarely known before. (251)

Furthermore, they found that "teachers who inquired into the nature of their teaching taught writing in the same spirit of inquiry" (253). Nancie Atwell (1987), too, argues "for a redistribution of the power of ideas and a new kind of classroom seating plan. When each student initiates the writing process by taking responsiblity for finding out what he or she has to say, everyone sits at a big desk" (181). For effective writing and learning to happen, the classroom has to change. Students need to be trusted to be learners and to share authority with their teachers.

After the History of Pittsburgh course was over, I met several times with two students to look at what was different about our course. What conditions made it possible for us to shift authority so that students and teacher learned together? One of those students, Laura Gratton, spoke with me about the results of our project at the Miami University "Writing Teacher as Researcher" conference in 1988. To sum up, these are the conditions we found that created the shift in authority in our class:

1. *Posing real questions*. In order to learn with students and to show them that their answers matter, the teacher has to ask genuine questions. I had to accept the fact that I did not know every answer in order to encourage my students to teach me.

2. *Students and teachers sharing expertise*. In class students shared their expertise about different religions, different ethnic backgrounds, working-class vs. upper-class neighborhoods, history of the U.S. Steel union, and their own personal history. When they wrote to Clairton, or when the Clairton students visited, Sewickley students had another audience with which they could share their expertise on school and community. Students also shared varying expertise with each other on the use of computers for telecommunication and word processing. At both schools there were students who knew more about electronic bulletin boards than their teachers. Students shared information they had to research. They conducted a survey at SA on public/private schools and student jobs; they attended lectures on local history and how to conduct oral histories; they interviewed outside experts; they compiled statistics on minorities, class size, etc; they shared outside reading.

3. *Sharing decisions*. In her final evaluation of the course, one student wrote, "Most effective was all the freedom — how we had a say in what we did." I had to plan, but also stay flexible enough for students to influence the direction of the course. Visiting Clairton, inviting speakers, and sharing a Serbian Christmas dinner were activities based on student suggestions. Students were able to choose their own topics, influence the pace of our reading, and — through mid-course surveys — comment on the successes or failures of the course and make suggestions for change. In their final course assessments, they participated further in the evaluation process. Students also took responsibility for managing aspects of the class. Each student had a different job that contributed to the group. These included managing the electronic bulletin board, keeping a class notebook, hosting guest speakers, and conducting outside research.

4. *Creating a sense of community*. It was important to create an atmosphere, based on trust, that would allow students to experiment, to share their feelings and insights, and to try new things. "At first

all of the informal writing and lack of grades frustrated me, and I'm sure I didn't make a secret of it. But, now, looking back, I realize how helpful it all was. My writing improved in that I'm a lot more honest than I used to be. I'm not afraid to add my opinions and feelings anymore. ... By writing informally, without the pressure of being graded, we could be honest, experiment, without being afraid."

5. *Hands-on experience*. The course got students to go outside of the classroom and to learn by doing. One student wrote at the end of the course that "the process of inquiry is much more beneficial than regular research you do in history. The thing that makes it different is the hands-on experience. When you do research that's in a book or article the only thing you find out is what another person has learned. It isn't your own views. This is what separates inquiry from traditional research." She added, "Taking action on a subject to find information with your own hands and eyes makes a person remember that forever."

6. *Respect for the little guy*. Another student wrote, "I think the most important thing I learned, through all of my experiences with the History of Pittsburgh class, is that everyone, no matter how small, or seemingly insignificant they are, has something important to offer his community. ... I have discovered a new way to find information, to dig into the things the little guy has to say, because sometimes his story is more factual than any encyclopedia." From conducting original community research, examining their own histories, and reading about the little guy in the steel industry, they learned that they, too, can make history.

7. *Providing models of inquiry*. As the students wrote about and conducted research, they saw me model a process of raising questions, examining expectations, and writing before and after our class trips. Speakers who visited the class also spoke on their own research and, through films, slides, speaking and writing, demonstrated their own values about lifelong learning, respect for community, and methods of interpreting the universal in the particular.

8. *Focus on process of learning as well as the content*. At the end of the course, Laura had written, "What you learn is only as interesting as how you learn it. If you copy information from an encyclopedia, your paper will probably be as boring to read as it was to write. And furthermore, what idiot couldn't look something up in the encyclopedia? You have to have fun when you research — you have to think of a way that will make it interesting to you personally. Then you can be enthused about it and your paper will show your enthusiasm." Our ideas of learning had to be based on a model of

shared inquiry and participation, not the old transmission model where expert information passes unidirectionally from teacher to student. Even the definition of the classroom changed to mean *where* we learn—outside as well as inside a school.

My students and I were involved in this inquiry together. Each of us taught; each of us learned. To allow that to happen, I had to give up the traditional authority I was used to bringing to the classroom. Since I was an English teacher in a collaborative, interdisciplinary course whose content material was history, it was easy for me to assume the role of learner. There was so much I didn't know about Pittsburgh. I wanted to be able to learn with my students, and to build in the flexibility for them to follow their own leads. At the same time, I had to offer a structure and guidelines from which students could freely roam. That freedom is a funny thing in a school system. It angered colleagues who saw it as too lenient or breaking the rules. It made the teacher and students uncomfortable who are used to predictable routines and centralized authority. But when it works, it makes students responsible for their own learning. It redistributes the power of the class, not equally, but so that it's not exclusively in the hands of the teacher.

Four months after our original visit to Clairton, I drove back with Laura for the open house of the new Clairton High School. Despite the resignation of two superintendents, the three-month delay of the opening, and a lawsuit between the school and the city, the school opened to the excitement of the whole town. There were hundreds of visitors on tours of the new building when we were there. People seemed to share the sense that this beautiful school would be a fresh start for Clairton's children. Even the owner of the Blue Bird, a busy all-night restaurant, planned to go over to see the new school before he went home to bed. We had found him resting in the window of the Blue Bird, where he signaled us to come in. Listening to him tell about the history of the restaurant his father began in 1923, we were both reminded—teacher and student—how much fun it is to find out something unexpectedly and how the classroom doesn't have to stand still.

Works Cited

Applebee, A. N. 1981. *Writing in the secondary school*. Urbana, IL: NCTE.

Atwell, N. 1987. Everyone sits at a big desk: Discovering topics for writing. In *Reclaiming the classroom*, ed. D. Goswami and P. Stillman. Portsmouth, NH: Boynton/Cook.

Bell, T. 1976. *Out of this furnace*. Pittsburgh: University of Pittsburgh Press.

Britton, J. 1987. A quiet form of research. In *Reclaiming the classroom*, ed. D. Goswami and P. Stillman. Portsmouth, NH: Boynton/Cook.

Freire, P. 1972. *Pedagogy of the oppressed*. New York: Herder and Herder.

Langer, J., and A. N. Applebee. 1987. *How writing shapes thinking*. Urbana, IL: NCTE.

Perl, S., and N. Wilson. 1986. *Through teachers' eyes*. Portsmouth, NH: Heinemann.

Sizer, T. 1984. *Horace's compromise: The dilemma of the American school*. First report from a study of high schools, cosponsored by the National Association of Secondary School Principals and the Commission on Educational Issues of the National Association of Independent Schools. Boston: Houghton Mifflin.

Response

Deborah E. Keyes

A model of shared inquiry between students and teachers, Jeff Schwartz's project raises some provocative questions about the ways we teachers have traditionally approached research in our classrooms. For the past two years I have been involved in collaborative research that has some similarities with Jeff's Sewickley-Clairton inquiry. Participating in one project, entitled "Grants for Students," and closely following the other have led me to ask, Why should we include research in our curriculums? And, if we do, How can we best teach the research process?

For years I dutifully suffered reading through the required term papers, wading through treatises about the effect of mud levels on the duckbilled platypus, long-winded histories of the Civil War, and endless tabulations of Major League batting averages. Occasionally, the choice of subject might have been interesting, but invariably, the student had located or borrowed just enough information from a few sources to satisfy the length requirement and had thrown it together in a random collage of facts and quotations. Having read volumes of wooden, voiceless prose, I could agree with Carol Booth Olson (1987) that the research paper is too often "a passive enterprise in which the student merely analyzes and restates the results of someone else's intellectual inquiry, an inquiry that he or she may have no personal involvement in" (133).

"Grants for Students" began as a search for ways to more actively engage students in their research process and to enable them to feel a greater sense of ownership and authority as learners. Instead of a research paper, I asked my students to write a grant. They could either design a research or creative project or propose a solution for a need they saw in their school or community life. While grant writing in my classroom began simply as an attempt to replace a worn-out assignment, it soon mushroomed into a project with far-reaching and unanticipated effects.

I was not prepared for the dramatic changes in my classroom that grant writing brought about. Suddenly my students were in charge of their ideas and I was no longer the authority. Their topic choices alone were more personal, diverse, and speculative than I had seen from a class of high school students. They ranged from developing a new form of therapy using laughter to combat cancer, to investigating the perils and pitfalls of left-handedness, to positing a new program for preserving marine archeological sites.

I soon noticed a significant shift in the way students chose topics. Whereas before they looked for a subject about which they could regurgitate information, now they began by formulating questions that would help them extend their own knowledge of the topic. The topics themselves often represented new approaches or theories that had evolved from the students' own attempts to express and refine their ideas. Nancie Atwell (1987) observes that true authorship begins with a "struggle to discover and clarify what one thinks" and that when we deny that step, we usurp our students' authority (180). Although that step had been missing from my previous teaching, it had become an essential part of writing these grants.

As my students found their voices, my classroom was transformed. Lucy Calkins (1986) notes that in contrast to the way fiction and narrative writing is taught, school-assigned research is often a "voiceless" process (282). We expect our students to take notes and find a thesis in silence, when, in reality, students need opportunities to talk about their research. Erik, a student who proposed his own design for building the Challenger in America's Cup Race, made sure he found enough conference time. As he wrote his grant, I watched him metamorphose from a cynical, uninvolved student to an impassioned writer and talker.

Concerned that the average layperson would not understand his grant, which contained a great deal of specialized vocabulary, Erik wrote four drafts of his proposal. After completing each draft, he held a conference with me and asked if I understood what I had read. Though he said the most difficult part of writing his grant was "sounding as though he knew what he was talking about," from my position as a sailing novice, Erik sounded very knowledgeable. As Erik became the teacher and I the student, we both had to redefine our senses of authority.

The deeper my class and I got into this project, the more apparent it became that Erik and my other students were better qualified to talk about this project than I. In March I invited them to speak to a group of teachers at a state convention about their process of writing their grants and how that differed from other research they had done in school. A seasoned author of term papers himself, Erik summed up the difference for his attentive audience: "Writing a grant focuses on why you want to do something, not on what you're going to do. The project is to make a project."

For Erik the major value of this project was being able to use his own research process and design his own format, although this had been more demanding. "The grant makes you work harder than most projects. Because you are doing research which you've created, you cannot just plagiarize facts out of a few sources. You must instead gather these facts together and make them into relevant arguments for your own proposal. This requires much more thinking and comprehension than does simple fact gathering and reporting."

Jessica, on the other hand, described a different kind of process in researching her grant on the use of music in Japanese festivals. Whereas Erik began by reading every available issue of *Sail* magazine and writing multiple drafts, Jessica started by looking for "gaps" in what had already been published about Japanese festivals. She found that while these books briefly mentioned the role of music, they did not go into any depth. A musician herself, she decided to try and fill that particular gap. Rather than study how music was used in each festival, she looked for common elements she could compare to learn how music functioned within the various events. Once she had located these elements, she came up with seven questions to help her organize and write her proposal.

Jessica and Erik were two students out of a class of twenty-five. As I watched them work, I grew to understand that researching, contrary to what my fixed classroom procedures had assumed in the past, was a richly varied and idiosyncratic process. As a teacher-facilitator, I had to allow for and appreciate these differences in my planning.

For Jessica, the value of this grant was finding an original topic and "developing theories." And she too became my teacher. From the start Jessica had a philosophical problem with the assignment. She wrestled with finding a balance between the actual facts she was researching and the fictional proposal she was forming from them—fictional because she wasn't going to receive money to carry it out. Because the proposal wasn't real, she had a hard time knowing how far to go. For example, did it matter if she talked to an expert or mentor, or could she just pretend?

As I listened to Jessica's concerns, I was struck by the truth of her dilemma. I had designed what I thought was a real-world research project and yet I had only gone halfway. I realized that if designing and writing a proposal were to be authentic, I had to create a vehicle whereby students could, indeed, apply for actual grant monies. Furthermore, the projects they were fashioning deserved to be funded.

In the spring of 1989, my colleague Anita Kurth and I received an innovative grant in education from the Maine Department of Education and Cultural Services to create such a vehicle, and "Grants for Students" expanded into a statewide project. A board composed of students, teachers, and community members awarded six grants in June 1990 to eleven student/teacher teams. The funded projects included cultivating tomato seeds that have traveled in space, raising awareness of adolescent eating disorders, and videotaping an interview with a well-known American author.

The "Grants for Students" project invites students to mine a vein of interest, a pursuit that our concern for covering the curriculum seldom addresses. Ethan, one of this year's grant recipients, spent his summer tracking thunderstorms across Central Maine. He applied for the grant because none of his science courses in high school went into depth about his own particular interest, meteorology, and because local libraries lacked sufficient information about thunderstorms. This grant will not only enable him to track down more data from other areas of the country, but will give him valuable "hands-on experience finding out how thunderstorms happen."

All too often we ignore the power that comes from what our students already know and are interested in. "The History of Pittsburgh" and "Grants for Students" took surprising and rewarding directions because students assumed leadership roles based on a growing confidence in their own authority as learners. Both projects provide ways for teachers to tap into that power and use it to transform their classrooms. Once that change begins to take place, teachers can leave behind old, ineffective ways of teaching and learn with their students in a true partnership.

Works Cited

Atwell, N. 1987. Everyone sits at a big desk: Discovering topics for writing. In *Reclaiming the classroom*, ed. D. Goswami and P. Stillman. Portsmouth, NH: Boynton/Cook.

Calkins, L. 1986. *The art of teaching writing*. Portsmouth, NH: Heinemann.

Olson, C. B. 1987. A sample prompt, scoring guide, and model paper for the I-search. In *Practical ideas for teaching writing as a process*. Sacramento, CA: California State Department of Education.

8

Giving Their Words Back to Them
Cultural Journalism in Eastern Kentucky

Carol Stumbo

> To grasp the meaning of a thing, an event, or a situation is to
> see it in its relations to other things: to see how it operates or
> functions, what consequences follow from it, what causes it,
> what uses it can be put to.
>
> John Dewey

Not too long ago, as I was visiting one of the elementary teachers in
the writing program that I coordinate in our district, I was reminded of
why the so-called experts in education worry me. I was spending the
afternoon in an older elementary school built sometime in the late
1930s by the Works Progress Administration. Many of the schools in
our district are in older buildings, but in spite of the worn condition of
this one, the students were bright and receptive. The teacher obviously
cared about the students in her classroom. She had just finished video-
taping some of them reading pieces of their writing and she wanted to
share some of that with me. She had been touched by the story of one
child in particular. The teacher had asked the children to imagine what
it would be like to be an animal of their own choice for one day. It was
the type of assignment that I avoid because it seems too removed from
the students' own experiences, but I am sure that the teacher thought

124

it would encourage creativity and help her teach personification in her reading class.

The student whose writing the teacher had been impressed by had a fatal muscular disease and was confined to a wheelchair. In the exercise, the child wrote about what it was like to be a bird. In a simple voice, she talked about how difficult it was to come to school in her new form. She couldn't reach her food in the cafeteria. She had to avoid some friends because they would "squeeze" her too hard. In spite of the fact that her form was awkward, the student wrote that she still felt "human" inside. Near the end of the piece, the child wrote, "It's all right though because I can fly away when I get tired, and go home." The teacher mentioned the story to me because she was impressed with the girl's courage and how well she was handling her disease. "She doesn't seem bothered at all by it," she told me. "She is always so cheerful."

As I drove home that afternoon, I thought about the piece of writing and the power that writing has. Although I would never have given the assignment, it seemed to me that because of it, the child was able to discuss the helplessness and fatigue that she felt about her own situation. I also thought about how at times we are symbol makers without knowing it. I didn't understand how the child created, almost unconsciously, a set of symbols that spoke eloquently of her own pain or how any of us really lays down the "line of words" that Annie Dillard (1990) has written about in *The Writing Life* (3).

That incident has become important to me because, in a way, it symbolizes much of what happened to me as I conducted a research project with my students last year. What occurred that afternoon in that classroom is the type of experience that can't be put on a chart or in a kit. It makes those of us who think we understand writing or the teaching of writing a little less certain. It is the type of education that teachers can only know about if they are willing to watch children thoughtfully. The incident also reminded me of the power that writing has to change things in a classroom. When we bring our experiences, our lives, into the classroom, the whole learning transaction is changed, as Lucy Calkins (1983) has said. The classroom becomes a different place: "When we regard students as unique and fascinating, when they become case-study subjects even while they are students, then the children become our teachers, showing us how they learn" (7–8).

This is a study of myself as a teacher of writing and those students that I worked with during the course of a year. It is a journey of sorts — one that led in directions that I did not anticipate and to conclusions that I was sometimes not prepared for, but it is one that I am not likely to forget. More than anything it is an attempt to understand the students in my own classroom. Ken Macrorie (1987) has written that research often gets lost in numbers, charts, and graphs that don't matter to anyone. "The fear of contaminating an inquiry," he argues, "by touching or interacting with the 'subjects' is out of place in studying an activity as human as the making of meaning" (46). After watching the students in my classroom for a year, I think he is right. My research had everything to do with the young people I teach.

When I returned home in the summer of 1988 from the Bread Loaf School of English in Vermont, I was anxious to begin a research project that I had talked to Dixie Goswami about. My original plan was to ask students in the magazine class that I teach in eastern Kentucky to do case studies of other students. Although my intent didn't change over the course of the school year, the manner in which we carried out that intention at times did.

I began with what I thought was a reasonable assumption. Since so much of what another teacher and I were doing in our magazine production class involved students in decision making and research, I thought it would be appropriate to expand upon those activities. In a sense, what I was asking students to do was to examine *what* they were learning in the classroom and *how* they were learning it. One of the first things that I did was discuss the project with my students. It was important to have their approval. If they were not receptive, the idea for the project wouldn't work. As usual, my students surprised me. They were willing to participate. Their willingness helped me deal with some of my own fears and reservations. After our initial discussion, I was less concerned by the question a teacher had raised when I mentioned the project to her: "What is the point of turning students into researchers?" She thought that asking students to conduct research was a violation of their rights and a relinquishment of my responsibilities as a teacher. My students didn't seem to think so.

Launching an Oral History Magazine in Wheelwright, Kentucky

My school is located at the far end of our district, almost at the end of the road, in fact. In 1985, after I had attended a summer workshop conducted by Eliot Wigginton of *Foxfire*, I returned to Wheelwright ready to try a different approach with my students. Another teacher at the high school and I decided to begin *Mantrip*, a magazine in which we would publish oral histories that we had collected. The focus of *Mantrip* was to be the town that we taught in. Since its creation in the early part of this century, Wheelwright has been a "company town," not unlike the numerous other coal camps that can be found in the hills of eastern Kentucky. Miners lived in rows of "shotgun" houses, small homes constructed almost overnight, until Inland Steel Corporation of

Chicago, Illinois, bought the town in the early 1930s and began to improve living conditions. The company believed that good living conditions made for better workers. Homes were renovated, a golf course built, and a swimming pool constructed for miners and their families. In time, *Inland Steel News*, a company publication, hailed Wheelwright as a "model coal town" and promoted it as an example of what could happen under the generous ownership of a large corporation.

In the 1960s, however, that world collapsed for the people of Wheelwright. No one knew for certain why the company decided to leave town. People attributed the departure to everything from increasing union unrest to the fact that Inland had secured coal resources closer to its plant in Illinois. Whatever the reason, in the midsixties, Inland left Wheelwright without much warning. One morning the public learned that the company had sold the town, and the people of Wheelwright were devastated. Videotaped interviews that my students and I have watched show residents who were stunned, almost in tears. "I don't know why they did this," one older woman said. After more than sixty years of ownership, the residents were free but there was little rejoicing. Without the company, the economic future of the town was threatened and residents knew very little about how to make decisions for themselves.

When I came to the school in the late 1970s, the student population was declining. Many of the miners had left the community when Inland did. Some had gone to work in Illinois and others to jobs at different mines. Approximately three hundred students were attending the high school and it had a reputation within our district as a difficult place to work. The situation was so bad that many teachers refused to work at the high school even as substitutes. There were horror stories of teachers being driven from the school. In the past, students at the high school had been the sons and daughters of well-educated people or miners who were ambitious for a better way of life. The current students were not known to be either highly academic or motivated. Many of the people living in the town were older residents; others were simply unemployed. Most of the older residents were caught up in the past. Citizens still talked of the days when the company owned the town, and although the town was making efforts to recover, it was not an easy time.

I had never felt more needed or more frustrated as a teacher than in those first years at Wheelwright. Although I worked hard at teaching, I knew I was not reaching most of the students. Some of my students went on to college and did well, but I knew that they would have done so in any case. There was a great deal of violence and vandalism at the school. Fights broke out unexpectedly in the hallways or on the school grounds. Students were sometimes sullen, often disinterested in what was going on in the classroom. I wanted to find some way to reach them if I could.

The students who worked on the first issue of *Mantrip* were an odd mixture — some were bright and motivated, others could barely read, but they did some good work and helped one another. The magazine began as a six-week project within a traditional classroom, but eventually, because of the demands of putting together two issues of the magazine, we created a special class. In time, students were doing some important work and being recognized for that. "Mantrip" is the name that miners give to the car that transports miners underground. The creation of the magazine gave us a chance to examine in a thoughtful way what happens to people who have been so dependent on a company for so long when technology begins to change an older way of life. We also thought the interviews would provide the students with a reason for writing.

Students conducted interviews in the community with older residents, transcribed and edited those for publication, and handled all the responsibilities for sales and presentations dealing with the magazine. Eventually, we were selling our magazine in twenty-some states, we had a substantial subscription list, and the students' work was being recognized by organizations across Kentucky. We applied for and received a grant from the Kentucky Oral History Commission to do a study of the black community in our area. Students who were considered at the bottom of the educational system in our district were making frequent presentations to educators, and kids from Wheelwright were entering and winning districtwide writing competitions. Something good was happening at our school and with our students, and I wanted to understand more about it. In the car on our way back from interviews, my students and I always discussed what we had learned as a result of our work, we analyzed what material we were finding or how they thought we should proceed, but when I sat in an audience and listened to them describe why the class was important to them and what they had learned from it, I knew that I didn't really understand how some of that had come about. I listened to students talking about acquiring the courage to express their own opinions or feeling more confidence in themselves and I wasn't sure I knew why that had happened. I could see the results of the class — more energy, more involvement on the part of all of us — but I wasn't really sure what was happening or why.

Raising Questions for Research

If you had asked me or the teacher who worked with me about what we had observed over the four years that we had been working with the students in our magazine class, we could have given you an answer that would have consisted of something like, "The students are more involved. They make more decisions. They are learning more grammar and writing skills. They have a greater appreciation of their heritage." While I felt that all of that was true and that many of those assertions could be supported, I felt uneasy about some aspects of the class. Were students really learning as much as they would have in a traditional writing class or were all of us demonstrating more energy simply because we had escaped the deadly routine of a traditional classroom? And even if I accepted the fact that the type of evaluation that we were doing was adequate, intellectually where did it lead? What action could we take based on that information to improve the class? Without some additional understanding of what was happening, we could only continue to re-create the existing class year after year. What did we really know about students' writing or their ability to think that would help us improve the class?

Intuitively, I felt that more was occurring in my classroom than I was aware of. Over the four years we have worked on the magazine, many people have visited our classroom—everyone from education students to ministers. Some of the people have thought that it was wonderful that students should be interviewing older people. Others have been skeptical about the value of the work. I think most of them understand that the work is far from being simple or easy, but I wanted to be able to answer their questions thoughtfully. In order to do that, I wanted to look at our classroom in a different way. We had to "look and look again." "If I set out to find an answer to some classroom matter, I am a learner," Nancy Martin (1987) has written, "but in engaging in the inquiry, I am initiating a small piece of research — two sides of the same coin" (23). That was the coin I wanted to look at. In *Experience and Education*, John Dewey (1938) has written, "Activity that is not checked by observation of what follows from it may be temporarily enjoyed. But intellectually, it leads nowhere. It does not provide knowledge about the situations in which action occurs nor does it lead to clarification and expansion of ideas" (87).

Although our efforts were based on the model created by Eliot Wigginton, I thought that we were headed in a slightly different direction. The creation of oral history projects does not guarantee an instant connection between the young people doing the interviews and older members of the community. After sitting in the kitchens and living rooms of people with students over the five years, I know that does not happen automatically. As was true when we began our magazine, there are students in the class today who know about the older way of life. Most, however, do not. It is foreign to them and they have to make an effort to understand the lives and times of the people that we interview. The element that binds these students to the older people is the language, and that was what I hoped we could look at together.

Setting Up the Study

Since all knowing, including all scientific inquiry, aims at under-standing, it proceeds by taking the thing inquired out of its isolation. Search is continued, until the thing is discovered to be a related part of some larger whole. (Dewey 1938, 34)

The main purpose of our collaborative study was to look at what happened as students edited the interviews they had conducted with members of their community for publication in our magazine. But we did not want to look at that one element in isolation. It seemed impossible to separate editing from factors such as the student's sense of himself or herself as a writer or the relationships that students established with each other and members of the community. Whenever possible, we wanted to make connections.

Three student researchers joined me in this study. Brian, Amy, and Pam were seniors, enrolled in the magazine production class for a second year. Together we decided to limit the number of students we researched to three. All three student subjects were girls, and all were also taking the magazine class. Tonja was the only one enrolled in the class for a second year. Missie and Tona were both new to the class. From the beginning, we discussed the project with the three students who had agreed to let us "study" them. For this essay, I will focus on two of the case subjects since their work provides such an interesting contrast.

Our research data were collected from four primary sources: my teaching journal, reflections and analyses written by the students whose editing methods we were studying, interviews by student researchers of the student subjects, and analyses of texts (including drafts of the interviews and other writing from class).

In the first meeting that I had with my co-researchers in September, we made the decision to focus our inquiry on the process of editing because it was at the heart of what we were doing. We wanted to learn (1) what kind of decisions students make as they work through this editing process, (2) what role the teacher plays in those decisions, and (3) what impact this work has on students as writers and learners.

Early into the study, though, we found that the students we were researching didn't really know how to talk about their editing process. Tonja's early statements in the interviews showed that she had not thought deeply about her decisions in editing:

Lisa [her partner] and I started at the first of the year working on John Hall. They called him "Bad John Hall." When I looked at the transcript, I thought we were never going to get through. Everett Hall, his nephew, wrote over a hundred pages about his uncle. Luckily for us, Everett is a good writer. The only thing we had trouble with was correcting punctuation and grammar. Some paragraphs and sentences were out of order and we had to move them.

I had watched Tonja and Lisa closely as they edited the first forty pages of the manuscript and had listened to them as they made decisions about everything from placement of material to matters of punctuation and spelling, but when I asked them to describe those decisions, they didn't seem to recall much in any kind of detail. They were unable to describe the process that they had just completed.

One of the teachers in our writing program has told me that she learned grammar only when she began to teach it. There may be some truth in that. At least, it seemed to be true that students had not had much experience in looking at editing as we had defined it in a conscious or detailed manner. The first interviews that the student researchers conducted with the other students about the editing process often turned out to be just as general as Tonja's assessment had been.

We decided we needed to define in more detail the type of editing decisions that were being made. Being precise about what we were looking for and agreeing to a common vocabulary helped us all. Our definition of editing included decisions about content as well as about structure and wording. Finally, we reached a definition of editing in terms of (1) the material that would be included in the published interview, (2) the decisions students made about the structure and organization of that material, and (3) the mechanics of usage (including spelling and punctuation).

Tonja's Case Study: Editing the Spoken and Written Word

Tonja and her partner Lisa worked with a manuscript that Everett Hall, a retired storekeeper and one of our best contacts, had given to us the year before. He was an old friend whom we had interviewed several times and he had given us an important gift. The manuscript was an account of the life of his uncle, a man who had become infamous in the area for his gun battles during the early 1900s. One winter Everett wrote down everything that he knew about his uncle and presented the result to the class for publication. Tonja's and Lisa's work on Everett's manuscript formed an important contrast to the rest of the class, who were editing oral interviews. As Tonja began her editing, she noted, "Everett had already given our material an order. When you're working with a transcription, you have to create that order."

Although Tonja and Lisa didn't have to deal with the problem of giving form to a transcription, they did have to work with the author of the piece. He visited them frequently, sometimes bringing material that he thought needed to be inserted into the text or clarifications that he wanted made. In the beginning, they looked to me to provide them with solutions to some of their problems. As the work progressed they made more decisions on their own, partly from necessity and also because I was making a conscious effort to give them more responsibility. That became an important factor in how they felt about the work. As Tonja told Amy, one of the researchers:

> The hardest part of the class — I thought — was the transcribing, but now I know that was easy. I started editing and it's major rough (laughs) because there are two teachers and thirty students in the class. There's not enough time for both of them to help. You've got to figure things out on your own ... look it up yourself. I really think that is an advantage. I've learned English that I didn't know before and I've been in English class for four years, I had to look things up myself and remember them and use them over and over again.

Two of the greatest problems in Tonja and Lisa's editing work on Everett's piece were dealing with the author's wishes to add sections after the major portion of the work had been completed and experiencing the gradual influence that the style of the writer had upon the two girls' own writing. From the beginning, both students were aware of the author's investment in the piece. They didn't want to hurt his feelings through the suggestions that they made about his text. When he brought them a long section that he wanted inserted into the manuscript near the end of their work, however, they expressed their reservations. They felt the story had coherence as it was and they didn't want to break that continuity by inserting additional material.

Eventually, they managed to persuade him to agree to add the section as a postscript in the final installment of the story. Tonja decided that since the manuscript was so long, we needed to print it in two sections: one installment in the fall issue of *Mantrip* and one in the spring issue. The girls chose a particularly climactic moment in the manuscript as the ending of the first section so that "people would want to read to find out what happened later." It seemed to work. There were many days when I would look across the computer room to see Tonja and Lisa sitting with Everett and discussing sections that they had trouble understanding or that they thought the reader might find difficult, trying to clarify the meaning with him; and he continued to do research and to add small sections to the manuscript almost up until we sent it to the printers.

When Tonja and Lisa began to write the piece that the editor of a magazine had requested from us, both of them asked for some additional time, claiming that everything that they wrote tended to sound like the author whose work they had just finished editing. Everett's style was often dramatic, similar to that of the regional local color writers of the early nineteenth century and characterized by a great deal of action. In the one hundred pages that he had written, he moved his character through forty years of his life. Tonja and Lisa had to identify Everett's writing style in order to work within it. We talked about the difference between Everett's writing and the language in the interviews we had done with him. In spite of the fact that his writing took on the flavor of early romantic novels, it also contained a great deal of information — both direct and indirect quotes that had been handed down over the years. We watched him move back and forth between the written and oral tradition in his writing.

Through Tonja's work with Everett's manuscript, we became aware of some of the very real differences between written and spoken language and discovered, as Tonja kept telling us, that something different was happening with the students who worked with written language and those who worked on oral interviews. Grounded in the philosophy of Vygotsky, British writing theorist James Britton (1987) has asserted that there is an integral connection between learning and language. In "grafting" written language upon spoken, Britton argues, students demonstrate a distinctive thought process. When writers begin to put thoughts into written form, they are making connections, often doing a type of thinking that does not occur in spoken language.

Throughout the course of the year, we found that we were "grafting" the constancy of the written word upon spoken language in some important ways. When we looked at the transcripts, we talked about what happened when students recorded the words of the people they had interviewed and tried to impose a structure. Statements that are perfectly clear in the context of an interview need clarification or structuring when they are written down. People don't speak in neatly structured paragraphs, and, at least on the surface, don't follow the same kind of deliberate, complex organization that is possible when they write. Annie Dillard (1990) has said that when you write, you are a Seminole alligator wrestler trying "to hold and tie a sentence's head while its tail tries to knock you over" (74–75). In spoken language, the alligator is not on the floor. Through Tonja's work with Everett's writing, we were able to look at what happens when the oral tradition is combined with the written one. When Everett sat down to "write," he put away, to some degree, the language that we had heard in interviews. He wrote sentences that attempted to explain more complex thoughts: "Had they known John [his uncle] only had his rifle and two more rounds of ammunition, and had they not left, chances are there would have been three more dead men on the little battleground in Branham Hollow — two of the posse and John, because John was not going to be taken alive and he was going to take two more of them with him." And he assumed a style of words that was less natural. His writing is a curious blend of the romanticism of local colorists and the action that drives a narrative.

We also talked about the revision that spoken language undergoes. We have listened to storytellers who never told the same story in quite the same way. Although the basic story line remained the same, a second telling always seemed to involve more details or more dialogue. Our research questions allowed us to look at the way the people in our community used language as well as our own efforts at working with it. In studying the writing, we found examples of words that students ran across in plays by Shakespeare, "holped" for "helped" for example, and abundant examples of similes and metaphors in some of the tales told by the area's better storytellers. In his writing, Everett made extensive use of an extended metaphor in accounting for his uncle's turbulent life, attributing it to his mother's contact with a hornet's nest. Students, at first, were surprised by the use of the metaphors. Why did Everett need to use them? How was it possible for someone without a great deal of education to have this kind of access to rich language? Studying the language and how it was being used was something that we hadn't consciously done before. Language in itself, language in real, powerful ways, became the focus of discussion.

An analysis of the different drafts that Tonja and Lisa were working with revealed that although they were having to do less work with structuring and ordering the content of Everett's piece, they were making some of the same decisions as students who worked on oral interviews. Although the usage errors that they corrected belonged to Everett for the most part, the analysis revealed that these were areas that students were having problems with in their own writing. When students transcribed interviews, they formed a kind of road map of their own weaknesses in usage. If they had problems with spelling or punctuation, that could be seen clearly. While we expected to see a great number of basic editing decisions such as the correction of spelling and punctuation errors in both the interviews and Everett's manuscript, those were not the most frequent kinds of decisions that students were making. Even in the final drafts, most of their decisions centered around the content and organization of the material in the interview. Student researchers, finally, distinguished textual decisions (clarity of language, structure, and coherence of information) from surface errors (punctuation and spelling).

Tona's Case Study: When Spoken Language Interferes

Understanding the thought process of the person speaking in interviews was often not easy. Tona, one of the black students in our class, undertook as her first real assignment an interview that we had done with a retired policeman the year before. Tona had not been part of the group that had done the original interview. This became a distinct disadvantage. She hadn't been there to hear the actual inflection or observe facial expressions and had to rely on the words alone for her interpretation. One section in particular caused Tona serious problems. The original transcript was sixty-some pages long. In two paragraphs of the interview, the policeman talked about his efforts to keep the townspeople out of trouble by closing down some establishments and by imposing a temporary curfew before trouble occurred. On the first reading, Tona thought that the policeman was simply saying the same thing twice, but later, after looking at the paragraphs, she realized that he was implying a cause-and-effect relationship. In other words, because of his action and that of other police officers, people were prevented from getting into trouble.

When the student researchers looked at the drafts later, they realized that Tona and her partner were dealing with two sets of problems: (1) how to arrange the content — the information that belonged to the person being interviewed — and (2) how to correct punctuation and spelling errors that they (the transcribers) had created.

Tona learned how to rearrange information by color-coding repeated categories. On the first interview, she worked without an outline so she had to read and reread, testing the sense of each sentence or section in her own mind before she moved the material. By the time she began to work on her second interview, she was color-coding all the information and was even working with other students showing them how to order their information. Later Tona wrote:

> I've found the most efficient and the easiest way to locate the information is to color-code it with markers. For example, you have this interview that has these subjects: early life in Middle Town, college years at T.S.U., and the marriage that didn't work. Choose a color (red, for example). From this point on all information dealing with Middle Town will be marked by red and so on. Color-coding will enable you to easily pick out the information on that topic. More often than not, interviews usually begin with the person's birth and go in chronological order from there. But from my experience, I had to rearrange the article in order to bring out the focus of a particular magazine issue which was a little difficult.

Year after year, color-coding is a method that I have seen students originate on their own. Although some students do all of their work using the clipboard on computers, Tona chose color-coding because she said that she liked to be able to look at the interview as a whole as she worked with it.

Once she had identified all sections such as "growing up," "jobs," or "marriage," and had moved the information into those sections, Tona looked at the overall structure. The drafts show her deleting those sections that she thought had to be removed. In an interview with Pam, she identified the next step as that of refining: checking each paragraph to make sure that it was unified, rearranging in some cases so the thought within the paragraph moved more smoothly, and looking for sentences that could be transposed to act as transitional sentences into new blocks of information.

Tona also had to learn to spell and punctuate spoken language. One of the major problems that Tona identified with her editing was spelling. She had recognized this from the beginning and discussed it with Amy, one of the researchers. One of the pieces of writing she did for the project dealt almost exclusively with her feelings about her own inability as a writer:

> I have a problem conveying words from my mind to paper. I can't spell. This is a problem when writing because it interferes with your train of thought. Someone might say, "Well, use a dictionary." The problem isn't the dictionary. When you're writing, by the time you have looked up the word in a dictionary, your thought has gone. Sometimes, I just think of another word that means the same thing but one that I can spell and use it instead. Then there are the times when I'm writing and I think of this great sentence, but I can't spell one of the words then that's when I begin to guess at the spelling of the word. Most often, I'm wrong. It really does become a problem after a while because it makes me frustrated and angry. I get so angry with myself that I'm unable to write anything. This is the main reason I don't like writing letters—because of my spelling.
>
> About fifty percent of the time I know when I wrong, but it's that other fifty percent that worries me all the time. For example, when I was younger and I had written my god-parents a letter just before Christmas, and my cousin had read it. That summer when I was visiting them, he asked me how to spell "get." I said "g-e-t." He looked at me and said, "Do you know when you wrote Momma you spelled it 'g-i-t'?"
>
> I said, "No." Well, he dropped it, but I didn't. When I got home, I looked at some of my many letters that I never sent off and I noticed "get" was spelled "g-i-t" every time. I hadn't realized it, but when I thought "get," my hand wrote "g-i-t." Even though when someone asked me, I spelled it correctly, I wrote it wrong. That bothered me for a while, but I began to watch myself more. I would no longer just spell it. I began to spell it out loud. Then if I still wasn't sure, I would ask someone or look it up myself. The funny thing is that the more syllables a word has, the easier it is for me to spell it.

At one point in my career as a teacher, I would have simply marked spelling errors and thought little more about them, but Tona's problem became one that I did a great deal of thinking about, especially since we were looking at the whole process of editing. The word that Tona spelled incorrectly is "get." It is pronounced "git" in this region. Her statement about her brain thinking "get" and her hand writing "git" is a significant one. Most of the educated students in Appalachia work with two languages: the one that they hear every day (the dialect) and the one that they encounter in school, the written language. We talked about the fact that it was quite possible that Tona's mind was seeing a mental image of "get" while another part of her was writing down the piece of dialect — "git" — that she had heard. Longer words didn't create the same kind of problem because she had encountered them the first time in written, not spoken, form.

While most Appalachian students continue to speak with a dialect, the speech of black students in our school usually contains little or no trace of that dialect. Many black children in our region spend vacations and summertime in the cities of Kentucky and the Northeast, which may explain why blacks are not as easily identified by their speech as are white Appalachians. Tona told Pam, one of the student researchers, that she had never "experienced being called a hillbilly before and no one really knows where I am from until I tell them."

Ann Berthoff has said that as teachers, we sometimes forget how difficult some of the things are that we ask of students or how intricate the processes are that they go through. Many of the students that I teach work very hard to destroy whatever language differences may exist between themselves and the rest of the world in order to escape the stereotypes that they feel others have about them. One session in which the students involved in the research project talked at great length about dialect ended on a very emotional tone. Two of the girls had tears in their eyes at the end of the conversation. They talked about how tired they were of being laughed at because of their speech. It was an issue they were not willing to let go of. In fact, when I listened to the interviews Amy had conducted, I found that she had spent a great deal of time asking, not about editing, but about how the students felt others perceived Appalachians. It turned out to be a question that she was deeply interested in researching and was not willing to abandon. It was much more important to them and the project than I realized.

James Britton, in "A Quiet Form of Research" (1987), quotes from the conclusions made by teacher researcher John Richmond about his study of a group of Jamaican teenagers at the London Comprehensive school in 1982: "If children sense confusion and contradiction around their language, they are likely to use it less well than if they sense approval and security around it .... It is not a coincidence that poverty, nonstandard dialects, and alienation from school are often to be found in the same area" (17). Richmond's conclusions applied to my students.

I understood in a deep way what was happening to Tona primarily because of my own experiences. When I left the mountains of eastern Kentucky for the first time, at age eighteen, I learned that part of my language did not exist. I learned not to say "chur" for "chair," and I spent a great deal of time trying to make myself heard. Dialect had nothing to do with my ability to think, but making others hear what I wanted to say over that dialect was another matter. One of the issues that we spent a great deal of time on once we began the research project was dialect and how it created an internal editor in Tona's head that she turned to as she began to write. She had learned to mistrust her own use of words and to watch herself as she wrote, so it was not surprising that writing became unpleasant for her.

The first interview that Tona worked on underwent about five or six different drafts. In November, we neared the point where material had to be taken to the printer, and decisions therefore had to be made quickly to reduce the length of the article. Such decisions are usually based on two factors: the special knowledge base of the person being interviewed and how that ties into the focus of the entire issue. Student editors decide on an underlying thread that runs through each issue of the magazine. This time it had been the violence of the region and the people. The students initially have a difficult time understanding why they need to do several interviews with a subject or how it is conceivable that they could end up throwing away over three fourths of the material they have gathered and transcribed. They learn to study all the material they have, to find the heart of the interview, to come up with a way to fit sections together coherently, and to throw the rest away or save it for another purpose.

Up to the last revision, Tona was shifting the order of sentences and paragraphs, skills that any writer must make use of. In addition, she was constantly rereading and rethinking how those added to the total effect, as she told one of the student researchers. The students know that they cannot change the words of the person that has been interviewed but they can transpose, tighten up, and give a sharper focus to the material with which they are working. In some ways, it is like working a puzzle — fitting the pieces together — but with words, the emphasis was on doing it in a coherent way.

Growing Independence

One of the questions that both Tona and Missie (the third case subject) asked me frequently at the beginning of the year was "How does this sound?" It was as if they wanted me to tell them the words that they thought they needed to state a thought, and I could feel their exasperation at times when I would not do that. What I did do was ask them to talk to me, to put the thought in their own words, and then transfer that back to paper, returning in a way to step one, the spoken language with which they communicated, and then grafting the written one onto that. I didn't realize till later how much I was doing in this project to try to put a whole number of things in the control of students.

Tona told Amy that she usually relied on me to make the final decisions about editing during the first part of the year. It was a fact that I only became aware of as a result of the research project. By the time Tona began her second interview, events had changed in the way that we worked together. In my journal, I noted that I was spending less time working with her, but I'm not sure that I would have been conscious of the amount of influence I was having on her decisions if it hadn't been for the student research. During the second semester, however, she was making hard copies and taking them home with her at night and using students in the classroom to assist her with editing. Her attitude at the end of the year was more confident.

Tona became more assertive in her decision making. I suspect that part of the change was a result of the fact that through her experience, she felt more comfortable with the work, but I also believe that some of the change was related to the nature of the work and the amount of control she felt she had over it. When I questioned in a marginal note if a particular statement had been recorded inaccurately, she wrote back to me, "No, she said it as it is stated. Here she's talking about her mother's father." She knew the text well enough by this point that she was willing to debate the question of structure with me or anyone else. As she wrote at the end of the year,

> There have been times when I have disagreed with my instructor, not over grammar but about story content. The one case where we had a difference of opinion was with an interview I did with my aunt. She had decided that we should include information about how black families stick together and help one another. Of course, there was nothing wrong with this, but the problem was that it had little to do with the main focus of the interview. Then even more conflict came in. If I did it her way, that would exclude one of the subjects that I found to be very important [racial trouble — Tona wanted to include an emphasis on the trouble that had occurred when the high school at Wheelwright was integrated for the first time; pickets marched and the school was shut down for a week]. I also believed her choice was in direct contrast to the main focus of the interview. I presented my case and explained why I felt that it was important for the trouble about integration to appear in the story. She read the interview again and after reading it, she found I was right.

When I reread Missie's final essay, which was about the devastating effect Vietnam had had on her father and which she had entitled "I Am Beginning to Understand," I was reminded of a theory that Ken Macrorie has that even the simplest person in times of a tragedy speaks with great eloquence. Tona entitled *her* final piece of writing about the research project "I Know." Have my students been empowered as a result of this project? I received a letter from Missie not too long ago. She was enrolled in summer courses at a college in the central part of the state, far away from home. She told me that she didn't understand what was happening to her: "I really don't want to pick up a major in English. I want to be a surgical nurse, but I also want to write." Writing has become a way for her to deal with the meaning of her life.

Reflections

We expected our study of editing to reveal a heavy emphasis on student decisions about correct usage. Although student interviews gave us a good picture of the mechanics that they had not mastered in their own writing, the editing work for the most part dealt not with mechanics but with their efforts to interpret and construct meaning. In the manner of professional writers, students were having to distinguish between those sentences or passages that helped create a central focus and remove those that did not. "Which is the work," Henry James asks in *The Spoils of Poynton*, "in which he [the writer] hasn't surrendered, under dire difficulty, the best thing he meant to have kept?" (Quoted in Dillard 1990, 5) When students reduced material in an interview from a hundred or seventy-five pages to seven, some of them felt that they were surrendering some of the things that they should have kept, but in doing so, they were discriminating about the value of the information. Reading skills were being put to use again and again as students tried to condense material. They spent a great deal of time trying to make language clear by what they chose to include, how they ordered that material, and what explanations they added. Practice in physically manipulating text seemed to give students more control over their own writing and over their own emotions and thought processes. Language became a powerful tool that allowed them to make connections. Some students were able to structure their own writing better. I could see that improvement in the writing they did.

One of the most important things we learned was how much students need a sense of approval about their language and an understanding of it, a knowledge of how it works and what it can do. When students spend a great deal of time in school having their language corrected as they attempt to talk or write in a classroom, something damaging happens. They lose confidence in themselves as writers and the connection with themselves and the words they need to communicate. As in Tona's case, they are having to perform additional tasks as they try to write — having always to stop and translate, in a way. Thus, a pathway is closed or, at best, blocked. Students who were able to listen to people who used the dialect to convey meaning and emotion became better writers.

During the course of the project, I learned a great deal about my relationships with my students. I know now that I could have given my students even more responsibility in the process of conducting the research. Although I had been willing to involve them in the research I had pulled all the results together, combining what they had discovered with my own notes and observations. Part of that happened because we ran out of time, but I also wonder how comfortable I would have been with their assuming that responsibility. Like my students, I have been conditioned by the relationships and the power found in the traditional classroom.

Throughout the research project, however, things were happening — moments in which I watched students simply take my breath away with the maturity I saw, moments in which I listened to Tona and Tonja talk about themselves and their work, and I know that none of it would have happened if we had not entered the new relationships made possible by the research project. We shared what it is like to be writers. I learned from them. We talked about growth with an awareness that it was something we were doing together. I learned that when I stopped thinking I had to make the agenda and establish the objectives, I was in a different classroom where a different kind of learning was taking place. My job was not to plan activities or to move students along a continuum of growth to where I thought they should be, but to assist them in doing that for themselves. In education, we talk a good game. We toss around words like "higher thinking skills," but little that we allow students to do calls for them to reflect on the experiences they have had and then move to that next level that John Dewey has described. We do it for them. We decide what form that next step should take. Maybe it is impossible to convince anyone that "school" limits what children can do, but I know that my students are quite capable of looking not only at *what* they are learning but *how* they are learning it. The shame is that we do not let them do more and that in some cases we do not believe they can.

Recently, I was able to sit in a classroom at the college where Missie, our third case subject, is enrolled. She spoke to a group of education students about the work we had done together. Part of what she said that day was, "Your words don't have to be fancy. They just need to be true. There are wonderful people in your community if you will just take the time to find them and talk to them." Amy, one of the students who had helped conduct the research project, was also there. There were tears in her eyes as she tried to explain to the students why it was sometimes so hard being from the hills of eastern Kentucky and how language was tied into that. Both of them were confident, honest, and articulate. I have never been prouder of them. Later, one of the teachers at the college told me that Missie had come to them believing that anything was possible for her and that we had given that sense of confidence to her. I didn't argue the point, but I know that is not the case. That is the kind of gift that could only come from Missie herself. I believe that on that day both Amy and Missie felt empowered. They own their words, and I'm counting on the fact that this is a kind of power no one can take away from them.

Because of the classroom research project I conducted last year, I am less certain of many things that occur in my classroom, things that I would have accepted at one time without reservations or questions. I am always just a little off center. That realization can be a little frightening. Before I allow myself to become too frightened though, I remind myself that teaching is a human activity. It is not about what I can orchestrate or manipulate, but rather about what I am able to observe in a room in which people are engaged in meaningful, important work. What my research project turned out to be, more than anything, was an attempt to understand the students in my own classroom and myself as a teacher as I interacted with those students.

Works Cited

Britton, J. 1982. *Prospect and retrospect*. Ed. G. Pradl. Portsmouth, NH: Boynton/Cook.

———. 1987. A quiet form of research. In *Reclaiming the classroom*, ed. D. Goswami and P. Stillman. Portsmouth, NH: Boynton/Cook.

Calkins, L. 1983. *Lessons from a child*. Portsmouth, NH: Heinemann.

Dewey, J. 1910. *How we think*. New York: D. C. Heath.

———. 1938. *Experience and education*. New York: Macmillan.

Dillard, A. 1990. *The writing life*. New York: HarperCollins.

Macrorie, K. 1987. Research as odyssey. In *Reclaiming the classroom*, ed. D. Goswami and P. Stillman. Portsmouth, NH: Boynton/Cook.

Martin, N. 1987. On the move. In *Reclaiming the classroom*, ed. D. Goswami and P. Stillman. Portsmouth, NH: Boynton/Cook.

Response One

James Moffett

Carol has the wisdom to place decision making at the heart of this account of student writing. Composition consists mainly of choosing — from subject matter and organization to sentence structure and diction and on down to commas and spellings. I have long recommended transcribing as a functional, well-motivated way to learn the "basic skills" and start to make the writer's decisions without yet having to take responsibility for drawing the material and forging those sentences from within. Whether transcribing interviews for publication or improvisations for scripts, the purpose is clear and real and raises for students the many psychological and social issues enmeshed in language that Carol documents here and that make oral history more than just a good way to ease kids into writing (which alone would justify it). Transcribing and editing other voices leads wonderfully into writing down and revising one's own inner voices.

The beauty of learning through activities like oral history that are not mere exercises done only in school is that they naturally give us insights into real life, because that's where they come from and feed back into. Thus I believe that nearly all of the perceptions Carol's students gained about themselves, language, and human relations that she attributes to the research project are in fact natural effects of the primary activities themselves, the interviewing and transcribing and making of a magazine, especially as these entail in turn other good learning activities. The very valuable discussion, for example, that took place to refine the definition of editing needs to occur in preparing interviews for publication, whether or not the editors are also objects of research. Carol felt that her students were unable to make editing conscious and become able to talk about it until the research process forced them to. If that's true, then the magazine process was missing something it should have had — more editorial discussion to induce just such awareness so members would know better how to proceed. But actually they did look at transcripts together and talk about "what happened when students recorded the words of the people they interviewed and tried to give it a structure." Insights about composition and about differences between oral and written language go with the territory of oral history. The students realized from looking at interview drafts that they faced two sets of problems — a text comprising their own transcription faults and the content or information belonging to the interviewee. The very nature of the task practically programs this realization — if the editorial process includes group discussion, as practicality demands.

The same, it seems to me, for the other sorts of learning that Carol documents so well. The errors the students corrected in Everett's manuscript echoed their own. As Carol neatly states, "When students transcribed interviews, they formed a kind of road map of their own weaknesses in usage." But in saying that the "analysis" revealed this, she seems to be crediting the research with what the assignment itself can readily bring about. Transcribing and editing are slow activities that require, as she makes clear, decisions at every step. Besides activating the will, the great thing about making decisions is that it makes you think all the way. "Our research questions allowed us to look at the way people in our community used language as well as our own efforts at working with it." Doesn't doing oral history, by its nature, allow or even require this? Similarly, the valuable perception that Tona was translating into standard dialect as she wrote was triggered by her act of transcribing her own speech, which forced her to compare her pronunciation with her spelling. Awareness of this "internal editor" brought out in turn her mistrust of her own language and negative feelings about herself as a speaker of a disparaged dialect. Carol's fine job of working one-to-one allowed Tona to deal with her reactions to the policeman just as it enabled her and Missie to have their words given back to them so they could synthesize their oral and written expression into more effective communication. Coaching or consulting one-to-one is a basic teaching method independent of any research project and important to writing generally.

In other words, I think that the students would have, or could have, learned the good things they did without the case studies of the editors, which were really a research project initiated by the teacher for her own, understandable purposes. She already knew *Mantrip* was an effective learning task, but, as she says, she felt she did not know how the good things happened, how deep they went, and how she might defend or explain them to outsiders. There are two issues here: one concerns what we mean by joint research with students, and the other takes us back to students' decision making.

A teacher has a right to do her own research to clarify something or reassure herself. The students agreed to go along with Carol's project (five of the six were girls), but the impetus for it did not come from them. And in her honesty Carol acknowledges that she had been more directive than she knew. "I know now that I could have given my students even more responsibility in the process of conducting the research." It was she who pulled all the notes together at the end, but it was also she who originally wanted to know more about what was happening in her magazine classes. I would guess that students would have thought up a very different research project. We get a hint of a possible one in the way that Amy shifted her interviewing of the editors from editing to "how the students felt others perceived Appalachians." "Being laughed at because of their speech" was so deeply felt that two of the girls cried over it. "It turned out to be a question that [Amy] was deeply interested in researching and was not willing to abandon."

It is much to Carol's credit, in fact, that her charges felt free to bend things their way and that she allowed herself to learn from this. "Tona became more assertive in her decision making" and came to rely less on Carol for final editing, all of which Carol became aware of, she says, only through the research project. The magazine carried over material from one set of students to another, but this had seriously constrained the one obliged to edit it. Like the teacher's initiation of the case study project, this had limited the students' decision making.

From Carol's honest presentation we can see how important it is that joint research of students and teachers be jointly initiated and conceived. Who wants to know what? Students are less likely to want to know how the classroom activities are functioning than what's happening in that world outside school. My impression is that teacher research so far often tends toward introspection about language, verbalizing about verbalizing—a degree of self-consciousness more appropriate for teachers than for students just really starting to sort out the various possibilities of language beyond social communion. It is true that puberty forces adolescents to go inward and *start* to examine the inner life, but it seems to me that if the learning activities are sound, like oral history, and are carried out *interactively* among students and teachers, such activities will induce as much awareness of the personal and social verbal life as students of that age will take. If students play a larger role in deciding the subject and purpose of joint research, we don't risk doing what professors too often do with their doctoral candidates—enlist them into the service of their own ongoing research goals.

Carol's teaching instincts seem excellent to me. I think that her uncertainties about activities that appear unconventional and unproven in schools prompted her to launch a research project that in some measure went against her own belief in the empowerment of students. The life of a *good* teacher is nothing if not a series of self-entrapments! What other teacher doesn't identify with Carol when she says, "Like my students, I have been conditioned by the relationships and the power found in the traditional classroom"? I think that as teachers become more accustomed to authentic activities in school and to student decision making, we will incline less toward research consisting of self-notation and cross-talk about these new phenomena themselves. This focus is a measure of legitimate teacher anxiety that as we accumulate experience and confidence will yield, I believe, to those things that students really want to investigate.

Response Two

Vera Scarbrough

There's a saying I'm reminded of when I read Carol Stumbo's work. "What the eye sees better, the heart will feel more deeply." Carol's work with her students shows a teacher thinking and caring about how researchers—and learners—wrestle with tough issues of language and change. If real learning is to take place, then teachers need to permit students to share control over what they write, research, and publish. Carol transfers her teacher power to Tona and Tonja, as well as her student co-researchers, who discover that nothing is impossible, and they gain self-confidence along the way.

Nowadays many teacher-disciplinarians would raise their eyebrows and balk if told to allow students to take over and occasionally get off the beaten track. I know a lot of teachers in my district would because they still adhere to the old school of teaching that believes "teachers teach and students learn"; that's what they think is happening when actually the student and teacher plunge deeper into what both feel is academic success. The rigid curriculum guides (often made by "experts" who have never taught in the classroom) cause us to concentrate on the problem rather than fix the problem. I enjoyed seeing the quotation marks Carol used when she spoke of "experts" because I knew just what she meant. But Carol took the risk and her students gained more confidence, learned more grammar and writing skills than if they had been in the traditional classroom ... and most important of all ... they understood what was happening.

The writing program at Vermont's Bread Loaf School of English inspired me to explore various teaching and learning styles and thereby ensured success for my students because I relinquished my teacher power. I must be honest, however. For me to surrender my authority and lay down all those methods to which I had been accustomed didn't come overnight. After three summers of study with writing experts Shirley Brice Heath, Nancy Martin, and Dixie Goswami, I realized I had been scaring away my English students who were not book-oriented. I remember what Heath said to us that first summer at Bread Loaf: "Don't focus on what the students do not know but what they do know and the knowledge they bring to the classroom. Some will never learn what's in the textbook." At that time I remembered thinking, "What

147

in tarnation do these kids know anyhow!" I had some who were never successful with proper punctuation, writing essays, or simply understanding basic grammar. All my method classes in college had told me to drill, drill, and drill some more. So in my pursuit of being a good teacher and their quest for success I went back to the curriculum guides and started all over. Sometimes it worked, sometimes it didn't. Many times we both became more frustrated.

Every teacher in the country has stories to tell of students who would never be motivated to learn or get fired up, even if the teacher got on top of the desk and did a hula dance. But taking them from what they did know to what they didn't know would be the key to their success and the end to both our frustrations. It would take us more than three years, but we all would learn the eye would see better when it entered the heart.

In a program very much like Carol's cultural journalism project in Kentucky, I have been working with students to publish the unrecorded history of our town, Oakdale, Tennessee.

Our story began in 1987 when thirty-three students and I decided we would write our own English book, one that we could use and study in the classroom. This book wouldn't be a school yearbook or a school newspaper or magazine, but a hardback, professionally printed book chock-full of photographs and intriguing history about Oakdale. It would focus on long-ago days when Oakdale was once a vital and thriving community made famous in the area as a railroad town. In 1983, when I first enrolled at Bread Loaf, I had learned from promotional material that grants were available for "teachers and students who because of their cultural and geographic isolation have inadequate education resources to support them." I applied for funds and was awarded an initial $2,000, which I used over the next year or two to purchase tape recorders, tapes, books, classic films, and various other materials that would enhance the classroom. I then approached the Morgan County Board of Education about something that was unusual in Tenessee's secondary schools, a fifth year of English. Board members didn't oppose me, but they said I would have to get state approval first and I eventually did. English V was offered at Oakdale High the following fall.

We learned, though, that you just don't write a book overnight and we would have to decide what we would tell. We decided to stick strictly to the history of the town, the railroad, the churches, and the various communities. We would gather histories as we could, visiting the newspaper offices, interviewing old-timers, and searching through libraries. We needed a lot of time outside the classroom for research; because we knew we would not be very popular leaving school during regular school hours every day, we set aside Fridays for our dismissals.

The rest of the week we would do projects at school, spending more time on the book as we gathered more material.

During the first year the students and I planned the directions our newly created English class would take. The first thing we decided was that the class could be taken for credit but would not substitute for a required year of English. Any student in grades 9–12 could take the class, and since we had no book we also agreed we would undertake activities that had to do with English, like improving our writing, speaking, listening, and reading skills. We knew this would make the authorities and experts happy. I particularly encouraged students who didn't do well in English to take the class, and we wound up with a remarkable cross section of the student body.

In surrendering my power to the students and letting them decide which directions the class would take, I was surprised that the first thing they did was to make rules. Together we made the rules that would govern the class, starting with the criteria for receiving credit and ending with the procedure for various grade levels. Students didn't want to go below a C, and they felt the only way one would make below that would be if he or she didn't show up, did absolutely nothing worthwhile toward making the class successful, or worse, as one student said, "took us all hostage." Right away I felt the class would be a success because the students wanted no one to make below a C. The students made an evaluation sheet containing ten questions, each having a point value from 0–10, which they filled out weekly. The questions could be changed to fit what the student was doing at a particular time. One such question they made up was, "Did I spend my time wisely in class this week, accomplishing at least one goal daily toward the project?"

During the first semester a junior and a freshman worked on writing skills with first graders. The two led the children as they acted out skits and then helped them write about what they had just done. Their project was so successful that they went to all students in grades 1–3 the next semester. Two seniors helped sixth graders publish their own poetry book and were responsible for getting some to publish their work outside the classroom. A group of sophomores made collages and gathered local histories and exchanged them with a group of sophomores from New Jersey, where a fellow Bread Loafer taught. Two more students helped kindergarten children keep learning logs about plants they had grown in the classroom, while others helped a seventh-grade class research and eventually draw the average Oakdalian. They compared them to the Mulungeons, a race of people who were thought to be a part of Sir Walter Raleigh's Lost Colony, and at one time had lived in Oakdale. Their project would eventually wind up in a science fair and give them a first-place prize.

I was truly amazed at what my students were thinking up to do and at what they were actually doing. Here they were teaching other students, gathering information for a book, and making waves across the school district. They were not an ordinary class! "Focus on what they do know," Heath had said. "Have them write about their success and tell of it," Martin said. "And don't throw away any of their writing . . . keep it all," Goswami said. Their success was tremendous. We had a lot to say, we were proud of what we had done, and we were keeping it all. When the editor of the county paper did a story on our class and wrote that as publication of our book drew nearer more money would be needed, a local bank came to our aid and made a $1,000 donation to allow the project to continue.

Aimee wrote in her journal that she kept in another English class, "I don't always feel motivated in some of my other classes, but English V places the responsibility on me rather than the teacher to get the job done." Another student, Brad, who never used a comma correctly in his life, said to me, "Here I've listed a whole bunch of dates and places about the railroad. What's the rule for the commas? I know I need some." When a large newspaper out of Knoxville heard about our class and came to do a story, Jeff, a three-year repeater in English II, told the reporter: "This is the only English that was ever interesting and that I've passed first time around out of all my years in school." I could have hugged him right then and there. Another student admitted to the reporter that he could have given himself all A's, but he didn't, because "I don't feel like I deserve them." There were times that I felt some of the students were too hard on themselves and I occasionally raised grades. In rare instances, I had to lower some, but always with an explanation. No one failed English V.

Our book came out in May of 1989. We called it *Oakdale: 1880 to the Present*. A Knoxville TV station told our story across the Tennessee Valley Region and we printed five hundred more books. We connected all that we knew to the outside world. The initial students have now graduated but they had a wonderful legacy to take with them. Others are left to tell their classmates about what we do.

So we started dreaming and made another wish. We took the money left over after we paid for publication, freight, and taxes on our book and made Oakdale pictorial note cards and postcards. We sold them to generate revenue for our next book, *Oakdale's Second Generations Tell Their Stories*. Now I go to teachers' meetings and smile when "experts" speak of curriculum guides.

9

Cross-Age Tutoring in South Carolina
PART ONE
Before the Millennium
(Student Becomes Teacher)

Ike Coleman

Background: Cross-Age Tutoring

Children have taught other children as long as they have been living, playing, and learning together, but the idea of older children teaching younger children has caught on more recently in formal education. In the 1790s, Andrew Bell dismissed most of the teachers at a school for troubled boys he directed in India and devised a system for the older boys to become the teachers. Joseph Lancaster transported the idea to England, and a forerunner of what we now call cross-age tutoring gained a foothold for a while there in the early nineteenth century. And, as a number of writers have noted, in more recent history the idea that older students can be responsible for the learning of younger students permeated the life of one-room schoolhouses throughout the nineteenth and early twentieth centuries.

Cross-age tutoring blossomed in the 1960s with educators like Peggy and Ronald Lippet, who showed that allowing older troubled students to tutor younger children had the potential to transform the older students and nurture the learning of the younger students. In *Children Teach Children*, a compassionate and persuasive book, Gartner, Kohler, and Riessman (1971) write about the theory and practice of cross-age tutoring projects. Large and highly acclaimed programs such as Mobilization for Youth, Youth Tutoring Youth, and Each One Teach One inspired these three writers. They say, as do most of the proponents of cross-age tutoring, that the idea benefits both the tutors and the tutees, but especially the tutors, who are placed in a position of trust and responsibility, and who must learn in order to teach. Because of the benefit to the tutors, many cross-age programs have employed as tutors students who themselves need extra help. And because many of these students have been told, explicitly and implicitly, that they have nothing of value to give in school, tutoring can be a powerful way for them to see their worth — as well as to learn.

In the 1980s Shirley Brice Heath began a cross-age tutoring project where nonnative English speakers in California, at Fair Oaks Elementary, tutored younger nonnative English speakers, in English. In Heath's project (discussed in an upcoming book, *Children of Promise: Literate Behaviors in Classrooms of Linguistic and Cultural Diversity*), the older students not only tutored but analyzed the linguistic progress of the younger students, kept field notes, corresponded with an outside adult, and wrote a manual for the project. In 1986 Heath proposed and directed an interactive writing project in South Carolina, which became part of the South Carolina Cross-Age Tutoring project, now directed by Elspeth Stuckey, whose article, "Coming of Age: The Cross-Age Tutoring Project," is a companion to this essay.

In South Carolina

For the past three years at Tamassee-Salem High School, a school of about three hundred fifty students in the foothills of South Carolina, the project has linked older remedial reading students, generally high schoolers from grades nine through twelve, as tutors with younger remedial students, most of whom have been sixth graders.[1] The older students not only tutored the younger students, they also were responsible for planning the activities, keeping track of the tutoring in a journal, and corresponding with the tutees and with an interested outsider who wrote back to the students. (Last year I was the interested outsider, but I also visited the class regularly — usually once every week or two — and wrote observations of those visits. In addition, because I was based at nearby Clemson University, I helped to find outside resources when the students asked for them, including video equipment, books, materials, and a professor from Clemson willing to talk to the students about history.[2]) The younger students also kept journals and wrote letters, and to a greater or lesser extent, they helped the tutors in planning.

Ms. Alexander, one of the school's remedial reading teachers, took on a crucial role in the project. Though she was not free from the constraints of the regular remedial reading curriculum, she opened the class to the project one to two days a week. The project would quickly have died without her active support as a facilitator. Her support, for instance, involved setting aside time for journal writing or giving the tutors time to plan activities within the everyday life of the classroom. One of the reasons for the project's success was that Ms. Alexander was willing to take the risk to make cross-age tutoring central to the work of the students in her course.[3]

To understand how valuable the project has been, it's necessary to know a bit about remedial education in South Carolina. Here, students who score below a certain level on standardized tests must be "remediated" in some way. Frequently—and this is true of Tamassee-Salem—remediation takes the form of special classes for students who have done very poorly on the tests (below the 25th percentile, for instance, on the CTBS, the Comprehensive Test of Basic Skills,[4] though students in some grades are also placed in remediation on the basis of another test devised by the state). The work for these classes typically involves workbook exercises, computer-assisted drill, and multiple-choice questions in preparation for the tests. I am no longer surprised when I enter a remedial reading class with no real books whatsoever—only workbooks. In South Carolina public education, the job of many teachers is to teach, and that of students is to learn, the sequenced skills of the curriculum. Particularly in remedial programs, the idea that students might have something to contribute to their own learning and that of other students is rarely considered.

I learned a great deal from the project. I won't, however, try to measure the success of cross-age tutoring at Tamassee-Salem by the usual measures used to quantify educational success in South Carolina. I don't know how the students fared on standardized tests, and I don't want to. If I did know, I wouldn't quote the statistics here, even if they were positive, because using the data from such tests is a validation of those tests—tests that too often convince students they can't be learners. And fundamentally, I believe tests utterly miss the most important kinds of learning, and it is that learning, on the part of one student and me, that I want to address.

The students in Cross-Age Tutoring at Tamassee-Salem became language researchers, charting in their journals evidence of the language development of their tutees. But the close language research that the project can make possible was difficult. At Tamassee-Salem, many of the tutors and the tutees live in a local foster home, and so throughout the project students moved in and out of the school, making stable pairs impossible. In nearly every one of my visits students had left or entered the class, although there were no more than twelve students participating at most. This problem was more than logistical; in a project that involves the friendship that arises out of collaboration, such changes are traumatic. Nevertheless, as happened throughout the project, students adjusted and devised their own solutions, so that instead of pairs, they worked together in small groups of three or four. As a result, the kind of careful language research of each tutee's development that is done with stable pairs of students was not easy. Instead, students spent a great deal of their energy planning for activities, writing in their journals about the activities after they happened, and corresponding.

The project was fully under way in December — late, but not surprisingly so for a project that requires such flexibility in scheduling. Especially in such a small school, it was difficult to arrange the schedule so that two remedial classes of the same subject, with an appropriate age difference, could meet at the same time. And yet, even in little more than half a year, the project made a difference to the students.

During the first year, 1987−88, the project at Tamassee-Salem had no content focus — the students helped each other on any kind of reading they chose. Elspeth Stuckey, the statewide project director, mentioned the need for some sort of focus, but in 1988−89, the students solved the problem themselves — without prompting — by choosing a theme. After reading a very condensed version of *Anne Frank: The Diary of a Young Girl*, they chose to read the full version of the book, and from the beginning they considered acting out some piece of it — or the entire condensed version.

One Student

Though all the students in the project participated fully in the work and said they liked it — and most said they loved it — I chose to focus on one of the eleventh-grade tutors, Rick Byrd, because he liked it a great deal, worked hard, thought about it in and out of school (and still thinks about it), and because I believe, judging from his letters and his testimony, he has gained as much from it or more than most of the other students. Plus he writes great letters. Yet in some ways he's not an outstanding example of what the Cross-Age project can do. Rick is not unusual in the way he has developed as a writer through the program. His life as a student has not been turned around by the project. But reading and writing is not the center of what I want to discuss.

Here is part of one of Rick's early letters:

1−2−89

Dear Ike;

The tutoring session was a great day, tim [Rick's tutee] was reading
[ready] to work as soon as I walked in the roon   Tim as [has] really
got attached to those books   he really like those books. We missed
you today in the tutor class. Tim as [has] came up with some terrific
ideas for the tutor class. Mrs. alexander told us this morning that we
can do a play in the Action Magazine   it is a wonderful play   I was
thinking about video tape it. like I told you before. I am glad I am
helping the 6th graders out on their reading skill   I wish you would
came today. because the kids was asking about you this morning . . . .
thank you a lot for the brochure [Rick had earlier asked for a
brochure about Clemson University]. it was very interesting   I was
thinking about going on a field trip at Clemson University English
Department one day before school is out   the tutors going & the kids
in the tutoring class   it is a great idea to do this. did you re-
seve [receive] my letter . . . the session today went outstanding Mrs.
alexander has a class full of students now so when you come Wednesday
you will see the difference. (more kids). do you tutor anyone else
besides here at the school   this [thanks] for the letter and take care
of yourself it was a wonderful day   Well I have to go   see you
Wednesday morning   have a nice weekend; and take care of yourself.
see you later   Thanks for everything

Rick E Byrd

Clearly, at the time he wrote this letter, Rick would have had real
trouble on a standardized test. But just as clearly, the letter shows
much of the richness of a project that is not geared toward preparation
for standardized tests, as is the usual fare of workbook exercises,
computer-assisted instruction, and other work on isolated skills that
often happens in South Carolina's remedial reading classes.

First, Rick obviously loves what he's doing. He has been entrusted
with the learning of another student. And he focuses on Tim, observing
and noting his behavior ("tim was [ready] to work as soon as I walked in
the room.") Even more gratifying, he credits and praises Tim for his
"terrific ideas," though it's not completely clear what those ideas are —
perhaps the play in the *Action Magazine*. (I found throughout the
project that in such a warm and close collaboration it was difficult to
trace the origin of ideas to specific people.)

Further, in this letter and in all of his others, Rick is full of ideas
and suggestions for the future. That many of those ideas may have
come from other students shows that the project has become a community, where ideas and know-how are shared. In this project, students
believed their ideas could count so they shared them. One of my main

tasks became to try to keep up with their ideas and if possible do what was necessary to bring them to reality.

Rick's letters taught me something too. Had I not known Rick, and if my role toward him were different, the mechanics in his correspondence would have put me off — would have terrified me, in fact, had I felt solely responsible for his language learning. But the deep humanity of his writing broke through my English teacher's defenses. Rick helped me *feel* the truth of something I had come to believe — that the human connection of this kind of communication was infinitely more important than periods and capitals, or even content.

But I didn't have to settle for an either/or choice: From reading and from years of working with Bread Loaf teachers, I knew that the best way for students to learn language was to be actively engaged in using it for real communication — and Rick was certainly engaged, having written a one-and-a-half-page letter, closely following another one just as long. And perhaps because of the safety of the communication, Rick experimented with language. And, though he hasn't mastered the conventions, he has a great deal of linguistic sophistication. He uses subordinate clauses confidently and well; though he doesn't use paragraphs, he generally makes sensible and clear transitions; he can switch tenses correctly; he asks questions, makes suggestions, hints in order to be polite ("We missed you today in the tutor class"), knows the social conventions of letter writing well enough to end warmly. If I were to make two lists, of all Rick can do with language, in opposition to all he can't do, the first list would be *much* longer. In short, Rick knows a great deal, even about language, that a standardized test would miss.

But through the communication, he's experimenting even with the conventions. In the opening he uses a semicolon, probably because he has noticed them in my writing (I use too many of them). Though of course he doesn't use it correctly, he's trying it out, just as children learning to talk experiment with sounds.

I answered all the students' letters, as fully and as quickly as possible. The role of the outsider, the person — or people — who reads the students' letters and journal entries and sends prompt, full answers, is crucial to the project. That person does *not* have to be a researcher. One year I found a number of people in a nearby home for senior citizens who cherished the chance to write letters to students. But some kind of outsider, in addition to providing an audience for student writing, helps students find the perspective necessary to see the value of their enterprise.

Following is my answer to Rick's letter — no great insights, but it's a fairly typical reply:

1/23

Dear Rick,

I'm sorry I haven't written this in time to get it to you in the mail; I'll just have to give it to you in person.

Your letter is one of the very nicest I've ever gotten. I showed it to both my officemates, who were just as impressed as I was. Then — and I hope you don't mind — I sent it over the computer network I'm on. Thank you, thank you, thank you.

I can't tell you how much I appreciate your concern for Tim, and for the Cross-Age Tutoring program; the project depends entirely on the concern and motivation of people like you. Keep thinking about how to make it more enjoyable for Tim, and for everyone else in the project — your ideas will truly make a difference.

Take care. I'll see you in a couple of days — or just as you get this letter.

Sincerely,
Ike

Of course, in letters to students I did more than praise. I joked, gave advice when students asked for it, asked for more information — all the things human beings really do in letters.

From early in the project, the students planned to do a play based somehow on *Anne Frank*. Many of the plans for the play are to be found in Rick's letters — ideas that were not Rick's alone, but which arose from the community. But reading through Rick's letters in preparation for writing this article, I realized that they serve wonderfully as documentation for the project because they contain so many of the ideas that later happened.

As I began to see, the project became more and more the center of the life of the classroom. At the students' request, Ms. Alexander set aside more and more time for the tutors to work in preparation for the tutoring sessions. In addition to planning for the play, the students were reading *The Diary*, making up crossword puzzles with words from World War II, planning a trip to Clemson to talk to a history professor, and doing their own historical research in the school library. These activities were in stark contrast to what they would have done in other remedial reading classes: workbooks or computerized skill and drill tests.

Perhaps Rick's letter has already made the point obvious, but I want to add that not only was the work rich and varied but it was the students who initiated almost all these activities. Showing none of the passivity, or rebellion, so characteristic of students in remedial classes, these kids asked the librarian if she could show them a World War II map of Germany, or offered in letters to use their own money to buy videotapes for use in recording the play they were to write, or asked me to find a professor at Clemson who could tell them more about the history of the time.

Here are two more of Rick's later letters, alluding to some of their activities:

3–8–89

Dear Ike;

    hey I thought I would write you to tell you about today's lesson in the tutor class   Tim had some very good news that we could [use] for the tutoring class. Everyone missed you today Did you read my last letter   I hope so. us tutors is practicing the play now after we come back from spring back [break]   we are doing the play March 29, 1989   it will be a very excited day. So be here on this date   we had read about 6 pages in the diary of Anne Frank. and also we are planning the [crossword] puzzles of Anne Frank they are excited about all of this. We had a Map where Anne Frank was from and they were very excited. So this play will be fun for the tutoring class. this will be a very good project to do for the tutoring class   have a great weekend   take care

Sincerely,
Rick Byrd

3–28–89

Dear Ike;

    hey it feels like I have'nt seen you in a long time. but here is a few lines. Well our play is getting sumed up   we already got posters and our plays written already. We are doing our play April 5th 1989. [The play was delayed several times.] I hope you get to come. Did you here about ben is in the hospital [Ben, one of the tutors, was diagnosed with leukemia — and at this writing still has it.]   his family is worried about him   everone here hopes he gets better soon something about white blood cells and red blood cells. Did you have a wonderful Easter vacation? I sure did. We had a good time. any way we are working hard and preparing for this play   everone is working and getting ready for it   everone here is very excited about this. Well what have you been doing lately? everone here said hello from the tutoring class. Everone here is preparing and working very had to organize this play   we are thinking about putting the play on tape and that sounds like a wonderful idea   Mrs A is very excited to about doing the play too. have a wonderful week

here is Ben's address at the hopsital
William Benson Price Room 524

Greenville Memorial Hospital
701 Grove Road Greenville, S.C. 29606

Sincerely,
Rick Byrd

I don't need to point out Rick's joy in the activities. I think improvement in the conventions of language is also plain — there is more end punctuation, capitalization is somewhat better, and the spelling and syntax, though not always right, are at least clear enough to give little problem in understanding. But much more important, I think, is Rick's — and the entire project's — concern for Ben. The tutors began corresponding regularly with him while he was in the hospital, and they were particularly conscientious about keeping him posted on the progress of the tutoring project. I think it's significant that none of Ben's other classes last year kept up with him — though I don't think such lack of contact is surprising, especially in a school where students must become hardened to the loss of friends who come in and out of the local foster home.[5]

But I believe the project was the reason the students stayed in contact with Ben. Reading the diary of a girl with the compassionate humanity of Anne Frank had some effect, but I believe the friendship and collaboration of the project helped model the empathy and concern they showed for Ben. [After shorter and shorter periods of remission, he is back in the hospital, possibly for the final time.]

As Rick's letters show, the activities of the tutors and tutees, with the guidance of Ms. Alexander, were still focused on *Anne Frank* and its historical background. The tutors designed crossword puzzles with words from the book, found maps of the area, read history books from the library about Nazi Germany, and most of all planned for and wrote the play. But none of the letters from the tutors discussed the content of the play, because they wanted it to be a surprise, for me and the tutees — even for their teacher — who were to be the main audiences.

Before the play, the tutors — at Rick's urging — also invited in two members of the community, Ramona Edney, a librarian, and William Squires, who served in World War II, to talk about the war. By this time, the students were working so much on their own that I didn't even know about the visit from Ms. Edney and Mr. Squires until I got this letter from Rick:

4−17−89

Dear Ike,

We all missed you last Wednesday   everone here said hello. We had a wonderful morning in the tutoring class. We had Mr. Squires and Mrs. Edney come in and talk about *Anne Frank and adolf hitler* the class was very excited about what was going on they enjoyed having a film and talking about Anne Frank why was she in the attic. I thought it was very excited and everone in the class was anxious about seeing the film. They loved it Ever one was very anxious to see you I wished you could have been here. Are we still going to Clemson? I hope so we are just about to do our play. Do you [know] that my sister had her baby last week she had a little girl named Annie. I thought I would share that with you Tim Loved last week's lesson. everone had enjoy it but I wished you were here to see it I hope I get to see you this Wednesday. The tutors are very happy of doing a play for the 6th & 7th graders have you ever meet Mr. Squires he is a outstanding person well I have to go hope to see you Wednesday

> Sincerely,
> Rick E. Byrd

I see now that this letter was not only as warm and informative as the earlier letters, but there was a great deal of improvement mechanically and syntactically — a comma instead of a semicolon in the opening, a much improved sense of what a sentence is (though he still has a long way to go), and better capitalization. I also notice that he was experimenting with underlining as in a title, though again he hadn't figured the problem out yet. And in this letter, for the first time, Rick had taken time to edit, changing the letter in a number of places visible on the original.

But I must admit that last year when I received the letter, I enjoyed it so much I didn't notice the grammatical points — much as I listen more to *what* my four-year-old son says than *how* he says it, trusting that he can learn language without a lot of help from me except as an audience interested in what he has to say.

Here was my answer:

Rick,

What a wonderful letter! ... I'm really sorry also that I missed seeing Ms. Edney and Mr. Squires. Thank you so much for arranging such a fantastic experience for all the students. What did Ms. Edney and Mr. Squires know about Germany? Had they been there during World War II? Was the movie good?

So you're an uncle! Well, congratulations! I didn't become an uncle till I was well into my thirties. Young children are one of the richest things in life, I think. Make sure you spend lots of time with the little girl if you can. And don't forget one of the lessons of the project: You can be a tutor for her also. Children LOVE to be read to.

Yes, I still want to go on the trip to Clemson. I'll make sure to arrange for a van on April 28th, and I'll come to Tamassee-Salem and pick you up. We all need to be thinking immediately about what we want to do when we're here. I'll talk to one or two of the professors about meeting you and telling you about the university, but you and the other students should also think about what kinds of things you might want to do here. I will also try to arrange for a history professor to tell you and answer your questions about World War II and Nazi Germany. I'll get back to you soon with more specific plans. ...

Sincerely,
Ike

Soon after the visit from Ms. Edney and Mr. Squires, the students wrote to me that the play was ready and asked me to videotape it. The tutors, down to three by this time because Ben was in the hospital and another student had moved, each had written the draft of a short dramatic piece, and then they had combined their ideas for a whole play, accompanied by construction paper programs they had painstakingly cut out and written. During their historical research, the tutors had found information about German education at the time, and they wrote about a classroom scene in Nazi Germany, where a student refuses to salute Hitler the required ten times and is sent to a concentration camp.

The tutors, as Rick's letter shows, were ecstatic about the chance for performing for their tutees — a much different kind of activity from the tutoring sessions. Though the play was very short, and the students, without any coaching in drama, had not understood the need for characters to have motivations, they masterfully incorporated what they had learned into the plot. For example, they read that even math problems to be done by students referred maliciously to Jews. From this knowledge, the students composed the following problem: "A bus holds fifty people. There are ten superior officers, ten common Poles, and five Jewish pigs. How many seats are left?"

In May, a week or so after the play, as an end-of-the-year reward, we all, tutors, tutees, and I, took the trip to Clemson University, doing all the things the students asked — touring the campus, eating ice cream made by the agriculture department, climbing the stadium. For students in a place as isolated as Salem, South Carolina, the trip was a marvel. (One sixth-grade student asked me if the university had a principal. "No," I said, "but it does have a president." "Does he paddle kids?" asked the student.)

And we also visited one of the history professors, to talk once more about Nazi Germany. I learned here too — not about history. Instead, after a lecture filled with horror stories, backed up by pictures of the most horrifying scences from death camps, I began to see the possible problems of letting students guide their own discoveries — a new issue for me; all the effects I'd seen until now were positive. As I watched the face of one of the young tutees I saw a look of fear, a look that later settled into sullen anger at the brutalities. I wondered, and still wonder, if I would allow students to explore such atrocities again. I've come to think I would strongly suggest another topic, especially for young students.

One Year Later

A couple of weeks ago, I visited Tamassee-Salem once more to interview Rick. You can imagine what I hoped for. I wanted, and half expected, to learn about his turnaround in school. I've seen the project do that for students. I thought perhaps his teachers might tell me what progress he'd made since last year. I wanted to see samples of his writing that would show continuing progress, and I hoped he would be reading voraciously now, as many of the tutors and tutees reported after a year with the project. Finally, I wanted Rick to tell me about his transformation eloquently and articulately.

I was disappointed in all those expectations. Rick was doing fairly well in school, though not marvelously. One of his teachers was surprised I was doing a case study on him, and wondered if I could get any information from him in an interview. In fact, I didn't get nearly as much as I'd hoped. His answers were usually a few words. What did he do on a typical day in his regular reading class—not the project? I asked him. "Just sit and read," he said. Other questions got similar answers: "I don't know." "I guess so." "I don't remember." But his longest answer was about a typical day in the Cross-Age project:

> We go and get what we need for the class—get some interesting stuff about what they like to do. Then you ask them what type of stuff they want to do in the tutoring class. They say, "Well, just go and get us some fun books to read," and we do that, because we know they like it. We read to them, and the next Tuesday we ask them questions about it, and then after we make questions, we make some crossword puzzles.

I also wanted to see some samples of his writing this year, expecting to find progress. He didn't have any, he told me. Instead he pulled out an envelope, looking brand new, that I had used last year to send him a videotape of the play. In it, he had saved for a year a stack of documents from the project of the previous year—a leftover program from the play, xeroxes of some of the historical information, and all the letters I had sent, carefully folded. As he showed them to me, and I realized he didn't have any of his writing from this year, but had saved *everything* from the project, I came to understand what I've insisted on here—how valuable the project had been, a value aside from, and in addition to, linguistic or academic progress.

But the meeting gave me more than sadness or nostalgia. Even with very little funding this year, the project has continued, though more sporadically, and Rick was even more excited about the present activities than he was about last year's. He and the other tutors, at their own insistence, wrote another play, a Christmas play this time, a copy of which Rick promises to send me.

When the millennium comes, the system of education in this state and others will make concrete the realization that *all* students can learn and care when allowed some direction over their own learning, and the chance to contribute to the learning of others. Then there will be no need for such a project. But in the meantime, the Cross-Age Tutoring Project can provide a context where roles are fluid enough to make room for all to be teachers and learners — and to show their caring for each other.

Notes

1. Cross-Age Tutoring at Tamassee-Salem has been funded and supported by the Bingham Trust for Charity, the Bread Loaf School of English, and the Clemson University Department of English.

2. For the last four years I have been director of the South Carolina Rural Writing Network, affiliated with the South Carolina Cross-Age Tutoring Project.

3. Although in this article I've said some harsh things about South Carolina schools, I must add that the project would never have flourished in the state's present climate of fear and accountability if it were not for the fact that Tamassee-Salem is a truly exemplary school, with a warm atmosphere and a creative and dedicated staff, particularly Sam Bass, the principal when the project described took place, who has since moved to another school; Joan Tunstall, the librarian and nurturer, of students and of the project; and Michele Alexander, a dedicated teacher who was willing to risk trying something new. In addition, and most of all, I would like to mention Den Latham, a former English teacher at Tamassee-Salem and coordinator of the Cross-Age Tutoring project there in 1987–88. Den is one of the most innovative teachers I've ever met, and the success of the CAT project in 1988–89 is directly attributable to Den's work.

4. Though below the 25th percentile on the CTBS sounds abysmal, from my own experience with the test, and after talking to dozens and dozens of teachers, I firmly believe that in the low ranges, CTBS scores are meaningless. The test is not only difficult, but there is little, if any, progression of difficulty. The students are defeated from the first, and many make no effort after the beginning. Others try their best, but because there is little progression of difficulty, they simply can't do any of it.

5. In the following year, 1989–90, as Ben's cancer worsened, the senior class began to rally for him. They organized fund drives, sent letters to him, and cheered him wildly as he graduated from high school in June. However, in the year I write about, none of his subject area classes, nor his high school class as a whole showed the concern that the handful of tutors and tutees did for him.

Selected Bibliography

Allen, V. 1976. *Children as teachers: Theory and research on tutoring*. New York: Academic.

Gartner, A., M. Kohler, and F. Riessman. 1971. *Children teach children: Learning by teaching*. New York: HarperCollins.

Goswami, D. 1989. Teaching students and interactive writing projects. *Bread Loaf and the Schools*. Summer.

Goswami, D., and P. Stillman, eds. 1987. *Reclaiming the classroom*. Portsmouth, NH: Boynton/Cook.

Heath, S. B., and L. Mangiola. In press. *Children of promise: Literate behaviors in classrooms of linguistic and cultural diversity*. Washington, D. C.: National Education Association and American Educational Research Association.

Martin, N. 1989. *The word for teaching is learning*. Portsmouth, NH: Boynton/Cook.

Wagner, L. 1982. *Peer teaching: Historical perspectives*. London: Greenwood.

Walker, S. 1989. "I love helping these students out on their reading": The Cross-Age tutoring project. *Bread Loaf News*. Fall/Winter.

PART TWO
Coming of Age
J. Elspeth Stuckey

The letter came in two versions. The first was a computer printout whose sentences columned down the page. This version ended with a request:

> MS. STUCKEY, IF IT'S NOT TO MUCH TO ASK OR YOU I WOULD LIKE FOR YOU
> TO SEND ME SOME PENCILS, PAPER AND CRAYON, AND MARKERS. I NEED A
> LOT NOT A LITTLE BECAUSE THEY USE PAPER SO FAST UNTIL IT'S A SHAME.

The second version of the letter was in pencil. It was written on two pages of lined paper and filled up all the writing space. This letter also ended with a request:

> Mrs. Stuckey is there anyway that you could get me a computer of my
> own? I could write on like yours. that doesn't cost you a whole arm
> and an leg. if you can't that's okay. but i will be upset if you tell me
> (no!) because I would like to go home and sit down and write all your
> letters on my very own computer and that would help me learn and
> do ... Mrs. Stuckey if you get me one out of your money or whatever I
> will give you my allowance every month to pay you back for the big
> favor. Please, please do me that favor. Love always.

Both versions were signed *Johnessia*.

If ever there was an example of the angst of literacy, this letter was it. There were two versions of the letter because the writer was caught between two writing systems. For three days, beginning on 29 October 1987, the writer wrote out the penciled version. For the next two days, she proceeded to input the letter on a computer at her elementary school in Branchville, South Carolina. She had never experienced a keyboard before. She used one finger to locate each key. On the second day of inputting, the teacher called it quits. Otherwise, the student would have been at the computer until midnight, hacking away with one finger.

Technology has its limits, of course. This writer, however, does not.

This writer is a seventh-grade student at a rural school in South Carolina. She has failed two grades. She is black. She is poor. She is a participant in the South Carolina Cross-Age Tutoring Project, and her story is the argument for humane, student-centered linguistic education in the schools. Such education is the purpose of the South Carolina project.

In cross-age tutoring projects, groups of older, at-risk students tutor younger at-risk students in reading and writing several times a week. The older students record field notes concerning the tutoring sessions. Once a week, the older students write to the director of the project to report their activity. The director responds to the students with questions and suggestions. The agenda is linguistic improvement for the older students.

Theoretically, the project proceeds on the assumption that when students learn to analyze and to interpret and to explain the purpose of written language they also learn to control written language. A further assumption is that when students engage in linguistic investigation, they escape the skill-driven type of activity that limits linguistic development. Their linguistic analysis and interpretation occur via their field notes and letters.

In South Carolina, the project is just two years old. It includes five sites. Four of the sites involve rural elementary and middle schools. The fifth site involves an urban college and high school. ("Urban" is used a bit loosely here — the schools are urban for South Carolina!)

The South Carolina project is based on a model developed by Shirley Brice Heath and others in a program to encourage the acquisition of literate (American) behaviors by Spanish-speaking children in northern California. Yet the theory and practice of cross-age tutoring are clearly generalizable. What the project really harnesses is an explosive possibility for learning when students of varying backgrounds and knowledge and experience come together to reach a common goal.

The urban site in South Carolina furnishes an example. This site involves students in a chemistry laboratory. Ninth-grade students in a predominantly black high school travel to a historically black college once a week to work with undergraduate science majors who are conducting experiments as part of their normal course work.

The ninth-grade students write lab reports:

> Today in lab we did an observing experiment. This experiment involved looking at things, writing them down, asking, and trying to answer our own questions.
>
> Today in the lab we were dealing with soda and food. The name of the soda is 7-Up, the types of foods that were used are raisins, grapes, cranberrys, beans, and macaroni.

The director points out interesting features of these lab reports:

> Well, kids, this write-up is a monument to mediocrity. As far as I can tell, none of you really knew what was happening. Nobody gave me any details about what the experiment looked like, what you did, what you said, what you thought.

The students try again:

> Today I don't know what really happened step by step in the lab, but I know by reading the worksheet it was about the solvay process — preparation of sodium bicarbonate.

An undergraduate tutor writes about her tutees:

> The both of them have complained about having to do so much writing. I explained to them the importance of communication and expression. They seemed to agree with my "speech." Other than those few things, we are progressing and not regressing which I know is very important.

The site coordinator writes, "I have been thinking about one way to determine whether the tutees are learning and that is by asking them to write something I should have asked from the very beginning. What is an experiment?"

Within this matrix of scientific experimentation and networked communication, the possibilities for education are real. The students are learning to be wise and able scientists as they learn to read, write and interpret laboratory information. They are learning to analyze and explain the radical differences between scientific discourse and real-world language. They are noting the difference between lab talk and lab reporting. They enjoy jargon. Recently, they got a computer, and the first thing the women did was to write to the men that "you fellows can do much, much better in the lab" (which provided a nice introduction to gender politics in science). The situation can promote opportunities for budding scientists; it can also promote a student examination of science itself.

The other sites demonstrate rich possibilities, as well. One site matches tenth through twelfth graders with sixth graders. They are reading and writing and rewriting short stories. Another matches sixth and seventh graders with first graders to help the first graders learn their ABCs, read sentences aloud, compose stories, and so on. The sites are limited only by the usual restrictions of time (school bells and buzzers) and conformity.

Perhaps a note on that is in order here. Conformity is a serious, undermining problem. The rigid, imposed schedules and systems and testing and tracking undercut any effort to be flexible or creative in classrooms. They shut down the very thing they presume to allow: the opportunity for education to afford better lives. In South Carolina, where thousands of the state's students live in rural — and racial — poverty, that is of particular importance. The students whose linguistic cultures and habits diverge from the usual white standards are the students shunted into the most confined, highly disciplined classes in the school system. The effect on the teachers of these students differs little from the effect on the students. Both groups are demoralized, angry, and at odds with each other. But the effect on the Cross-Age Tutoring Project is profound, also. The project must always do battle. The reason to keep battling is that the project shows that education and linguistic improvement can be a source of hope.

The poverty of the students in the South Carolina project is an overarching fact. The average annual family income of 75 percent of the students at the college in the project is under $8,000. At four of the sites, almost all of the students are black. With almost no exception, all of the students are from rural backgrounds. Twenty percent of the students at one of the most isolated sites live in a school for unwanted and abused children.

The project asks a lot of these students. Learning to analyze, interpret, and control language is not easy to do. The only reason that many people can do it is that they belong to the class of people who make the rules (thus they rarely need to analyze language). The students in the project clearly do not belong to that class. Nevertheless, these students have the abilities to penetrate linguistic mysteries. That is something that education for better lives has to do, penetrate mysteries.

We have to be careful, however, when dealing with populations of students like this. There is something very persuasive and extraordinarily moving about individual moments in this project. A student stands up to read before a class for the first time. A student draws hearts all over a letter. A student drags you by the arms and begs you to take her home with you where she can write books. But these are not the moments that fuel the project, and they are not the moments that will effect institutional change in the schools.

The final letter in the fall of 1987 by the writer whose letters opened this essay testifies to larger goals. The letter came all packaged up in a self-contained wad of notebook-paper engineering. On the front was a flap and written on the flap was the word PULL. So, I pulled.

The letter began, "Yes, Mrs. Stuckey, I would like to have a celebration. A rock party is the best kind to have." Then, the writer listed five items to bring to the party (for the children she and her classmates had been tutoring). The writer also included another list of the materials the project needed. "We need notebooks," she said, and pens and money. She added a P.S.: "I hope you have a nice Xmas, okay. And I still want that computer."

The letter is remarkable for linguistic reasons. The writer, after less than three months of the project, is writing longer, more responsive, more articulate letters. Johnessia is telling me what I need to know.

The letter is remarkable, also, for its role in expanding the limits of linguistic possibility. Accompanying Johnessia's letter is a letter from another student — one of Johnessia's classmates. The columned, all-cap sentences look suspiciously familiar:

DEAR MRS. STUCKEY

HOW ARE LIFE TREATING THESE DAY. MRS. STUCKEY LET ME GET TO THE POINT ABOUTYESTERDAY. ISALLY TRY MY BEST TO HELP THOSE KIDS OUT BUT, SOMETIME IWISH THAT ICAN JUST STAY WITH THEM FEW LONG.

This is the first letter this writer has composed on the computer. She was taught by the first writer.

The message from "I Sally" is a tentative version of the message from Johnessia. Sally does not yet ask for a personal computer. She simply wants a few long more minutes to spend with the first grader she tutors — a reasonable request.

Education should foster such linguistic development, a development that will empower students. Right now, Johnessia and Sally request computers, crayons, and rock music. One day, they will come of age and their requests will change. As they do, they will develop as persons in a social context, and, by example, they will challenge that context and expand the meaning and forms of education.

On this basis the South Carolina Cross-Age Tutoring Project goes forward. On this basis, too, it will come of age.

Response

Shirley Brice Heath

It is rare that we see learning. We look for it not in its coming, but in its outcomes — testimonies, test results, pieces, and promises. As adults, we easily equate what we label "learning" with what we think we have taught.

In cross-age tutoring, youngsters often labeled by their schools as unable to learn become those who enable others, and they then in turn reflect on the process of learning as they have created it in a collegial unit. The older learners describe, explain, narrate, and argue their ways of presenting information, promoting motivation, and controlling nonchalance (or worse yet resistance) from younger learners. They accept their own varieties of expertise and see themselves as key influences, necessary translators, and reliable sources of information for the younger students. Enfranchised as capable of facilitating learning for younger students, they take up responsibilities for explaining their process to make learning observable and knowable for others — adults outside the immediate scene.

The accounts of cross-age tutoring from Ike and Elspeth document how the "reporting out" to adults from the youngsters involved in cross-age tutoring stands as a key frame of learning. The students' accounts of what they have done with the younger students and of what they hope to achieve show us learning. Their accounts should erase any illusion that merely pairing two learners and telling the older to tutor the younger will bring about the same kind of learning as that which comes when older students tell adults what they see in the learning of younger students. The letters between Ike and Rick as well as those between Elspeth and Johnessia contain abundant evidence of what researchers label as affective, cognitive, and social dimensions of learning; the tutors hold up for viewing the practice of these abstractions. These exchanges allow adults to see also the extent to which the tutors reflected on how learning was a personal challenge in both intrinsic and material terms. Watching themselves watch and record the younger learners enabled the older students to acknowledge the nonmaterial components of learning (play, practice, patience, etc.) along with the material supports (paper, crayons, computers, etc.). Perhaps most important, they admit the importance of their active

170

roles in their own learning as well as in facilitating that of their younger partner.

But Ike and Elspeth do more here than tell us of the achievements of the cross-age tutors in the processes of learning. They face up to two harsh facts about such enriched occasions in schools: 1) learning within such experiences does not necessarily move over into "regular" classroom life; and 2) affective involvement, and even task-tied cognitive growth, may not be captured by the usual methods of *seeing* (measuring) overall academic achievement.

Rick's cross-age tutoring experience, valuable as it may have been for his temporary social self-esteem in an academic task, did not enliven his interest in the routine life of school. Rick's authentic writing in the tutoring exchange did not create a breakthrough in his school writing, and a year later, he had not activated for his "regular" classwork the agentry, control, direction, and affect he had exerted in the tutoring project. There is nothing wrong with the "theoretical" assumption that Elspeth notes: ". . . when students learn to analyze and to interpret and to explain the purpose of written language they also learn to control written language." However, contexts with some element of similarity may be necessary to reactivate the analytical, interpretive, and explicative purposes that come so naturally in authentic tasks that call for full engagement of all kinds of abilities: dramatic, managerial, and facilitative.

As tutors, Rick and Johnessia had to call in all of their abilites to persuade, sustain interest, plan ahead, manipulate authoritative powers, and ask for what they needed. The activities of Rick's classrooms a year later did not appear to him to call for such a range of involvement, and his minimal answers to questions about what he did there make it appear as though he saw no possibility of translating life there into descriptions that might interest Ike. For Rick and Johnessia, learning and doing could not be untangled in their tutoring.

Johnessia tells Elspeth that she knows that writing will help her "learn and do." Researchers of writing talk a great deal about "writing and reading to learn" as the key focus of education rather than the usual "learning to write and read." In cross-age tutoring, writing and reading not only comprise the central *doing* of the social interaction, but writing and reading also contain the seeds of *future doing*. After receiving many letters such as Johnessia's, Elspeth coached the tutors in ways to ask for supplies: 1) specify what you need and what you think the costs will be, 2) indicate how you will store and keep track of the supplies, 3) describe what you expect to accomplish once you have the supplies. Elspeth developed a one-page form for students to use to request supplies; planning the *doing* with supplies, ranging from books and paper to computers and audiotapes, reflected ways that the tutors envisioned learning as interaction among materials, learners, and language. The theorists' notions of "mediated learning" became for these tutors articulated through supply requests, plans, and concerns about helping younger students make connections among books, their immediate experiences (such as becoming an uncle), and distant persons and places (such as Anne Frank and the nearby university).

Because wide-ranging *doing* from and with knowledge is rarely seen (measured or tested) in schools, the abilities of Rick and Johnessia would receive little notice in most classrooms. Mandated "minimal competency" tests, standardized tests, and other narrowly based tests of factual knowledge cannot tap the breadth of cognitive and affective growth that cross-age tutoring promotes. When we test only to *see what students have learned*, we close our eyes to *how students know about learning*. Seeing how they know about learning requires enabling them to *do* with and from their learning. Thus authentic tasks in which students not only act from what they have learned but also write about how they have learned and plan to use that learning allow us to see learning as a continuum rather than as a point of measurement.

Rick and Johnessia, no doubt, brought from their out-of-school experiences most of the learning skills and means they displayed in their tutoring roles. For example, they display in several ways their understanding of human relations (note Rick's characterizations of individuals in his school) and a sense of the need to justify exceeding the unexpected (note Johnessia's offer to conserve supplies and to try to pay for the computer she requests). For many adolescents such as Rick and Johnessia, parenthood often precedes a stable and satisfactory entry into the adult world of work. There — in factories, fast-food establishments, offices, and on construction sites, as well as in corporate offices and governmental positions — there are tests of social awareness, planning skills, and ability to follow through on tasks, and such "skills" appear repeatedly on lists of "desired employee characteristics" that employers provide for job training programs. Many job-entry and job-advancement tests offer vignettes to which applicants must respond in order to demonstrate their potential as socially aware and capable planners within a corporation, an office, or a service establishment. In short, the adult world of work acknowledges that we see learning best when individuals act and plan from and with their learning.

In an essay entitled "The Origin of Extermination in the Imagination" (1985), humanist William H. Gass writes:

> In our society, where the murder of the mind is as common and everyday as the comics, in which the lie sets the standard for truth, in which falsifying ameliorations are epidemic; one thing at least ought to be clear, as the pattern of our public acts betrays it: Among us, war is willed, while peace is only wished. (242)

Learning from Elspeth and Ike, as they in turn see Rick and Johnessia learn, makes us consider rewording Gass's final sentence as: Among us, children's failures are willed, while their successes are only wished. Cross-age tutoring and the holistic ways of seeing that it encompasses show us that we can do much more than wish for the life success of students such as Rick and Johnessia. We can set about to will changes of ways of seeing and of enfranchising these students if we want to make schools bridges and not barriers between adolescence and adulthood.

Work Cited

Gass, W. H. 1985. The origin of extermination in the imagination. In *Habitations of the word*. New York: Simon & Schuster.

Section Two:
Teachers Learning

This section focuses on teachers who have been changed by listening to their students. As in the first section, the roles of student and teacher are not easily defined. In Chapter 10 two teachers enrolled in graduate school — one black, one white — become students of each other, as they explore together what it means to have to adjust discourse to meet the different cultural expectations of the academy. In "Talking About School: A Two-Part Invention," a teacher and student (who teaches) examine a course for teaching assistants that went wrong. Chapter 11 describes how a group of university and classroom teachers learn together as they puzzle through their opposing reactions to an incident among their black students one summer day in Detroit.

Other chapters advocate shared inquiry for teacher preparation and professional development. In Chapters 13 and 14 student teachers and their teachers collaborate in writing about projects that changed their view of education and themselves. Chapter 15 extends our argument for shared inquiry to using it as a means of professional development in the Philadelphia public schools. Collaborative inquiry for the teacher in this section means questioning assumptions, negotiating power, studying the sometimes painfully difficult process of matching well-intentioned theory to practice, becoming more responsive to how students *and* teachers learn, and gaining control over professional lives.

When teachers learn in these chapters, contradictions and problems are examined, not ignored. This is not passive learning or passive writing. As David Wilson reminds us in his comments on Chapter 13, we teachers are shaped by the multiple contexts from which we have come and in which we find ourselves. But "when we use reflection and collaboration to uncover and examine our assumptions about the nature of learning, teaching, and language," he says, we can be transformed.

As teacher research becomes more collaborative, so must our way of reflecting it. Thus these chapters suggest the range of collaborative writing as well as collaborative research, from dialogue (Murphy and Kazmierczak; Diamondstone and Merriman) to multivoiced essays written by a single author (Schaafsma) to coauthored single-voiced pieces (Lytle and Fecho) to essays in which two or three writers' voices trade off (Taylor and McIntyre; Cochran-Smith, Garfield, and Greenberger).

As in Part I, chapters are followed by responses intended to extend the conversation to the readers of this book.

10

Walking That Walk, Talking That Talk (Learning to Collaborate)

PART ONE

Doing the Do at a Tête-à-Tête

(A Portrait of Struggles over Academic Texts)

Judith Diamondstone

the tigers of wrath are wiser than the horses of instruction
William Blake, *Marriage of Heaven and Hell*

i cant count the number of times i have viscerally wanted to
attack deform n maim the language that i waz taught to hate
myself in/the language that perpetuates the notions that cause
pain to every black child as he/she learns to speak of the world
& the "self." yes/being an afro-american writer is something to
be self-conscious abt/ & yes/ in order to think n communicate
the thoughts n feelings i want to think and communicate/ i
haveta fix my tool to my needs/ i have to take it apart to the
bone/ so that the malignancies/ fall away/ leaving us space to
literally create our own image.
Ntozake Shange, foreword to *Three Pieces*

The expectations and canons of core black culture are
attributes of Black intracommunal status and style. Walking
those walks, talking those talks, walking those talks, talking

those walks, doing the do, keeping that cool, showing the
turn, are some of the salient items in the qualities which go
towards making of a proper core black culture.

Nanzetta Merriman, course paper

When Zan argues, when he jokes, when he performs as classroom
teacher, his vocabulary of movement defies cataloging. His eyes, brow,
mouth, his whole head, his upper torso, his whole torso, his hands, his
fingers go to work, carving the air, mimicking, defining, signaling the
subject of his thoughts and positioning his statements in relation to
each other. He often seems larger than he is because of his dynamic
presence. A strong man keeps coming on —

> The strong men gittin' stronger
> Strong men —
> STRONGER — (Sterling Brown, in Chapman 1968, 419)

Zan has told me he sees himself growing stronger, rising on the dreams
of his family, on their shoulders, like the smoke king that W. E. B.
Dubois (Chapman 1968, 359) sang about. He is a Harlem-raised black
man, the son of a Granada-born father and an Afro-American mother.

I met Zan when he was teaching a lively and unusual seventh- and
eighth-grade classroom in Cambridge, Massachusetts, which I visited
weekly throughout the year as a novice researcher during my first year
of doctoral studies at the Harvard Graduate School of Education. The
city magnet program attracted students of American black, Jamaican
black, Puerto Rican, white, Asian, and mixed parentage backgrounds;
they moved freely about the room, sat at desk clusters talking to each
other, and talked back to Zan, who walked around the room chewing
gum, engaging, exhorting, teasing, insulting, goading students, sometimes in street language or a bit of patois or Spanish. Sometimes he
spoke teacher talk, calling students to attention at the beginning of a
task.

My field notes, taken in the fall of 1986 and later revised, give a
closer glimpse of the classroom:

> The room is hexagonal-shaped. A big trash can beside a littered desk
> is overflowing. The clock above the door reads 6:00. It always reads
> 6:00. It is 10:20 a.m. Students at desk moved together into clusters
> are taking a test on the 1954 Civil Rights case, Brown v. Board of
> Education.
>
>   One boy raises his hand; Zan walks quickly to his side, leans
> over close to him, talks quietly. Another student asks, "Do you want
> me to give some examples?" Zan answers, "Very good, very good.
> You're not as dumb as I look." He checks another student's test:

"What else? — something more, that has to do with this person here — "
The student pauses for a moment, then looks at Zan and says something.
Zan: "Yeah, now explain it."

Pretending to be exasperated at something another student says,
Zan throws a piece of chalk across the room. One student calls out,
"Oh nice, nice. Real nice." Zan notices another boy wandering across
the room. He calls out, "Sam! How you doin'? Saw moms and pops
last night — want me to tell you about it?" Sam: "No."

During the year I observed this classroom, teacher and students
organized a mock trial of the 1954 Supreme Court case, Brown v.
Board of Education for the Northeast Regional Social Studies Conference. The trial was commended in the *Boston Globe*.

The following year, Zan was accepted into the Harvard master's
program in education. He entered the institution with the uneasy
knowledge that its prestigious doors had opened to him despite his
academic record. The schools where Zan grew up "don't give nobody
no hope. ... You can only go so far. ... — High school was the end of
the road [to] a good job working for the transit authority as a sanitation
engineer or going to the military. ..." But at home Zan was told he
could do anything. He had a strong belief in himself, and he saw his
parents take great strides in their own lives. Zan left his neighborhood
and over time became a successful and committed educator. When he
submitted his application to Harvard he included a fat portfolio documenting numerous school and community projects he had been involved
in over the course of fourteen years.

Knowing where his strengths came from, Zan told me stories
about his childhood. In Harlem, he had moved up through the ranks of
status in the streets, and now he reminisced about those times with
animation, laughter, and pride. I asked him, "So you made it big in
that world. ... How come you didn't stay there?"

Zan: " — Islam. Knowing who my mother is. Being scared. ... I
saw someone stomped to death. ..."

And, Zan said, if you had dreams, you knew you had to "get out
or die."

But Zan was not prepared for writing course papers at Harvard.
Diagnosed dyslexic in high school, he spells poorly. Reading is a
chore. Nevertheless, he completed course work for a B.S. from Bridge-
water State, with a major in "Early and Elementary Childhood
Education."

Fall 1987

Zan meets "the big H" with a furious singleness of purpose, ready to
do battle. He plans to grab whatever he needs, including "A's" in
seven courses for a double certification and thus a chance at any

principalship he wants. Friends and faculty try to reason with him, to propose a more manageable program extended over the summer; Zan is bitter at their skepticism and lack of support. "At least they have stopped stopping me," he says. (Zan was able to get credit for one of his courses based on past experience, and thus actually finished "only" six courses.)

We are sitting in the upstairs back room of a restaurant at a table for two against the wall, negotiating our commitments. Zan needs help on his writing, and I want to look closely at the writing process, so we have agreed to arrange weekly tutorials, which I will audiotape. I add a skeptical warning to the ones he has already received that his work load is too heavy even for students who are better prepared for Harvard. Zan reminds me that his wife, Kay, is working two jobs; his two girls, Thandi and Naledi, need shoes, "and all I've got is ten months for them to eat cream of wheat." I remind him that if he flunks he throws away ten thousand dollars, which won't help his family. He answers flatly, that flunking is not a possibility. "If I can hang on the block, I can hang here."

Thandi, a wily seven-year-old, and Naledi, two years older, both "caramel-colored" — their father's word — blending their parents' skin colors, clamber up the back staircase of the restaurant, flourishing cookies from Mike the manager. "When can we eat?" they want to know. It's dinnertime. Zan attends to his children and I to my notes.

> One perspective: Living in a world of others unlike himself, Zan travels through a looking glass rippled with distortion. He is about to undergo a series of accommodations to the language of the academe. He will do so with self-acknowledged fear — and with ferocity; in defensive anger and frustration — and with furious determination. He will not let go of his right to rage that others around him will never work so hard and perilously to maneuver on his terms. In his own dialect and in the language of the senses, Zan is a powerful communicator. But in the Harvard classroom, his behavior is seen by many as extravagant, challenging conventions and stirring resentment, impatience, and wry commentary. Zan has embarked on a deeply frustrating and paradoxical project: to make academic discourse, which contradicts his own communication strategies, serve the interests of others like himself. In practical terms, he will be obliged to engage texts he considers irrelevant to past and future experiences, to be explicit about what he considers obvious, and to treat the moral and political commitments that infuse his life as decomposable objects.

Zan arrives at my Somerville apartment late Sunday morning in early October; sprawls onto a chair while I make coffee. After opening banter, Zan grows serious, but never unzips the nylon satchel filled with books and legal pads and scribbled notes that he has brought.

Instead, he gets up to talk, charting the ways of white man's talk: it's bull; it evades the real issues; it's deceitful; it's a game — if you play it, "You invalidate your own shit."

I object to his "either-or" terms. His brow furrows. The rhythm of his speech accelerates. He articulates the space around him with emphatic movements.

Zan: It isn't either-or business. What has it been on their terms? (*His rich, resonant voice rises in volume*) What has it been in their terms? (*And continues to rise*) The man write his shit down in history! (*He pounds the coffee table*) He write it down!, baby. And — what the FUCK has he been doing? (*Zan's face is a mask of rage*) He has — been setting up his goddamn courts, he has set up the books, he controls the present, he KNOWS what's going to happen in the future. There's no ... mistake about it. He KNOWS what the hell he's doing. Legislative law canNOT (*pounds*) and everybody agrees, canNOT (*hit*) change (*hit*) morality (*hit*). You cannot legislate morality. (*Loud and angry*) No, you can't. The only two options you have is to change the consciousness of that individual. If you cannot change the consciousness of that individual, you BURN. HIS. ASS. (*A mask of rage again*) Period. And you CONFRONT him on those terms. Because this is NOT a tate ah tate. This is NOT a tea party. THIS is a revolution. Whether it be through WORDS, through ACTION, through art, through drama, through music, through education. That is what it is. It IS to transform. ... And whatever methodology you USE in that transformation — HAS TO BE GROUNDED — in action, and reflective action of — straight up and up, what Jesus loves: the truth. And if they can't hang with the truth — (*His voice grows very quiet*) How you gonna talk to a liar? (*Pause*) How you gonna talk to a thief? ... So I'm gonna walk into the man's house, I'm gonna be like the man. I'm jiving, he's jiving. (*Zan is acting like two people now, his body turning and bending as they move in relation to each other*) He's got his separate agenda, I've got my separate agenda. What kinda — games?

Judith: Those games make a difference.

Zan: No they DON'T. Those games are grounded in ... lies, THAT'S what those games are grounded in. They're grounded in DECEIT. That's what they're grounded in, baby. That's what they're grounded in.

Judith: And when you figure out how the deceits work, you can make them work against the deceiver.

Zan: (*High-pitched, frustrated*) I'm not playing the — game. (*Shaking *his head vigorously*) That's the whole deal! I'm not goin' to play your game! I'm not PLAYING that game. That's the trick they PUT you in. BE LIKE ME. BE — Here. Here. You know, be like me (*he sits in my reading chair with hands clasped and legs crossed, his face upturned, mouth pursed, brow raised, a parody of primness*) and if you're not like me, I'm goin' to hurt you for it. I'm goin' to reeally hurt you bad. I'm goin' to really hurt you an' don't you say nothin'. 'Cause I'm goin' to hurt you — . . . Games of maneuvering — I've gotto play that shit? HELL no — IF I PLAY LIKE THAT I AM! THE MAN. An' how can I BE the man and try to transform the man! Uh UHH. UH UHHH. UH UHHHHHH. I'm SORRY!

My objections fall flat on the rug. I retire to a sitting position on the couch. Zan's rage dissipates in concern for me. He lowers his voice.

Zan: You think the games can be undone from the inside. If I believed in God, I would pray that she could help me see that reason. But I — have lost part of my mind — have almost ruined my family, by trying to play the games on the INSIDE. And yes, I agree I may be ignorant — I may not be able to see how to work from inside the structure. But I don't want to look like that man. I don't want to act like that man. Yes, I — would like to be a global person. I am a human being. What you say and what he says to the pillow are the same thing as what I say to the pillow. But — I've got to change his consciousness. (*Then in a hardly audible whisper*) No no no no — listen listen listen listen. I know what you're saying. OK? I've spent the last couple of hours exposing my spit. There are ways of doing what you're saying — so you can confront an individual on his own language. That does not take away from —

Judith: (*Finishing for him*) From the rage.

Zan: From the rage. My right side is saying what you just said to me. But what I have done for the last hour or so is give you my left side . . . (*Softly*) There's certain times when you open up. It's like, sometimes . . . you want something so bad (*with rising, lingering intonation on "so" — drops on "bad"*). And you want to be recognized so bad. And you want your thoughts to be heard and reflected upon and you want to be read, you know. And you want to progress up a certain ladder. You want to make your own way in this man's world. Because it is his world, and you're not going to change that.

* * *

On a crisp October morning, I turn onto Massachusetts Avenue from the Lexington exit off Route 2, where I am regaled with the deep, brilliant color of autumn. There was no sumptuous foliage in spacious lots set back from the road where Zan grew up. This suburb announces its station well above the median on a certain ladder. I drive slowly along gentle bends in the road until I reach the school converted into low- and middle-income housing where Zan lives. I park in the rear lot and walk through crisp air to his ground-level apartment. Inside, Stevie Wonder is playing on the stereo. Books and papers are stacked on the dining room table, on the work table along the wall which holds an IBM clone computer, and on the rug. Eric, who lives next door, is finishing a joke.

Zan laughs in raucous glee as Eric leaves. Still in laughing mode, he switches to a sidetrack to ask if I would like to go with him to the laundry room. I follow a laughing Zan up the carpeted stairwell. He calls to Thandi and Naledi to bathe while he attends to laundry. We exit through a door in the upstairs hallway and walk up a ramp on one side of a huge interior. I remember that we are walking through what was once a school. On either side, closed doors indicate apartments; below us, the former gymnasium has been converted into a senior center. I see an open door to the laundry room in front of us.

A young blonde mother leaves pushing a stroller and carrying a laundry basket. I help Zan fold the last of six loads into a fifty gallon plastic trash can on wheels. When we return to the apartment, Thandi and Naledi are wet and giggling with towels wrapped around their middles in the bathroom doorway. They couldn't find a washrag so they used Naledi's shirt. Zan jokes sarcastically with them. The girls come downstairs to join us for scrambled eggs, home fries, and toast, and retreat noisily upstairs when Zan and I begin to work.

Zan formulates his thoughts on racism and the Constitution for an article he wants to write, discussing his pedagogical aims. Education has to include a "moral or primitive" component. By primitive, Zan refers to "the gut feeling of communal life." In the classroom he tries to create an environment in which students engage each other cooperatively and competitively, where they learn to rely on each other as resources to solve real problems. "It's not good enough to know what the 14th Amendment says — but to know that down the road you can own (it) — You can use it, but you've got to TAKE it." Learning and communication in and out of school must involve you at the gut level, or else you play into the man's agenda, which is his alone. To change the agenda, you have to become an activist. But activism on the political level is not enough, since you cannot legislate morality. If the man's agenda is built into the Constitution, the Declaration of Independence asserts that "it is the right of the people to alter their form of government, or to ABOLISH and institute new government."

* * *

Zan visits my house to get help outlining the paper on Racism and the Constitution. We talk about academic writing, who the audience is (the Harvard professors), what their terms are (that students write for their professors), what they expect of Zan (who does not accept their terms—instead, he refuses to be like other students: he insists the professors should meet him halfway).

"But see, Judy, I understand," Zan says as he surveys items on my bookshelf arranged for display. One of them is a photograph of the cast for a play produced at a New England summer program for teachers of English. I was one of the students enrolled there that summer and had acted in the play. "You didn't even look at the camera. Everybody else lookin' at the camera." Zan slides off the subject of professors—but stays right on target: "Got a lot of black folks in that troupe."

"You noticed." I take his jibe. There are no blacks in the cast.

"I can see that multiethnic shit just runnin' through that performance," says Zan.

I laugh. There were very few people of color among the students at the school that summer, and none of them tried out for the play. I try to remember if there were people of color among the authors assigned to us.

"We read some, um, we read Richard Wright."

"No shit. Read him, huh? All RIGHT. Tha's good. Tha's good to know, Judy."

"Toni Cade Bambara. Nothing too radical."

"Hell no. You gotta ease in on that. You can't just, you know—"

"I'll tell you what I did read for the first time a couple of years ago was Frederick Douglass."

"Fred?" Zan giggles. "You know what you should do is read yourself some brother Malcolm."

"Yeah, right."

"So OK. Fine." Zan gets impatient. "We gonna get this outline?"

I am worried that Zan does no writing on his own. I tell him he is afraid of expository writing. "It's like philosophy, and you're very philosophical." The next time he arrives at my house with a course paper he considers done. Written in passionate, poetic rhetoric, it's hard for me to follow. I apply tests of accuracy and reliability to each sentence. Zan has written:

> Black art is necessary to replace the colonized Negro culture of which most our lives are an example. Black people are colonized Negroes. Controlled by others. Lacking self-determination, self-definitions. Controlled politically and economically by Europeans ... Black art is an expression of black life. But revolutionary art? Revolutionary art could be black art. Revolutionary art would make a statement against. That would mean a transformation of the Negro into revolutionary black art.

> Black art is collective. It must express a whole people. Come
> from a whole people and speak to a whole people. It is functional like
> a gun. Its specific use is a specific use in the struggle to liberate
> ourselves. Committed. Committing in that it commits us to the struggle.

Zan and I settle on the living room couch with a jam jar cap for an
ashtray and mugs of coffee. I read what he has written, sentence by
sentence, asking for explanation wherever his meaning isn't clear. He
is frustrated at the request for more information than his own language
provides. When I tell him his professors won't understand a particular
passage, he insists they can if they want to — the meaning is there! on
the page. I insist that they won't be able to figure it out; he must make
himself explicit.

Zan: Am I writing to idiots?

Judith: Yes.

"How does black art commit you to the struggle?" I ask Zan.

Zan: It's art.

Judith: So HOW does it commit you to the struggle?

Zan: Did you hear all that above here?

Judith: Tell me now again.

Zan: What do you mean, tell me now. It's right there.

Zan and I continue in this vein for several minutes before we work out
the sentence completion: "Black art commits us to the struggle *by
adding the definition of the struggle to the culture*."

Zan and I spend most of that session arguing over a passage that
begins, "The notion that the particular could not be a universal is
not accurate scientifically, but it is a cover-up for racism. ..." I
tell him there is a knot in the words, not in his thinking.

He says, "You see, you're trying to break something and explode
something out when there isn't — there isn't a translation. ... Zero
is like nothing."

"But *the particular cannot be a universal by definition*," I try to
explain, imposing a particular tradition of English analytical philosophy onto his words, as if it embodied the truth — as if that particular
were the universal. I draw two big circles (universals) and two little
circles (particulars). "You're saying that each particular is tied to its
own universe — is that what you're saying? Each particular is tied to its
own universe — "

"Right," Zan says.

" — and EACH universal is tied to the particulars within it. So to say
that a universal isn't tied to the particulars within it is a cover-up for
racism."

"Right," Zan says, looking for a cassette to play and complaining about my music selection.

*   *   *

Zan tells me that I'm helping him. He had never realized that "the man" might not understand what he was saying. When I show my confusion and say what it is that I do not understand, he can see the difference between what he means and what I've heard. Now he concedes that he has to learn the language of his audience.

Zan: I NEVER wanted to use the man's words but I did want to let the man hear. And I wanted to do in my writing what he did to us.

Judith: You have to do it with his words.

Zan: I will use his words. I will use his words. — BUT! I will use my words too.

Judith: That's it.

Zan: I will use language that black folks are used to ... IN the man's words. They will look different in print. They will mean the same thing. But (*he takes a drink of coffee*) I want the Harvard professor, I want the oppressor to read the words. And I want to cause him some discomfort. That discomfort [will take the place of] a different language, a different syntax. So when the brother or sister who is young, who is an undergraduate, in high school — or the brother or sister trying to find themselves, they will see something very familiar ... in the thought, but also in talking that talk, walking that walk.

Judith: Right.

Zan: One must constantly reevaluate oneself in keeping forward and speaking the truth, in keeping forward and speaking the truth. Speaking the truth and going forward, the man will understand. Going forward means, we'll advance you. Truth, he understands that. Talking that talk, walking that walk, talking that walk, walking that talk, I've said the same thing. So it's how to, not compromise, but how to have those co-mingle.

*   *   *

I drive to Zan's on a bitter cold Saturday evening in late October. Naledi greets me when I walk in the door. She and Thandi are wearing white Betty Boop sweatshirts. Scraps of material surround them on the rug. A tiny, calico kitten cocks its head at me. Grover Washington is playing on the stereo. Kay is at work. Zan looks relaxed tonight, in baggy jeans and Harvard sweatshirt. We eat steak and home-fried potatoes with Zan's next-door neighbor and the girls, shoving stacks of books and papers to the center of the table.

After dinner, Zan's neighbor leaves; Thandi and Naledi get down to the litter on the rug, while Zan shows me his notes. He has written down his thoughts in cohesive sequences on pages of green, lined paper, stapled together by theme. During this session, Zan sits beside me reading from his notes while I type at the computer; as we work we make up terms for some of the procedures in expository writing. As before, we work on "saying more," and "linking," but we add "circling back," and the concept of making something that hangs together from the inside. Zan works with me, searching for and finding precise, specific words on his own. I cue him to "say more" with syntactic hinges like "so that —"

Judith: OK, could you say that for me again, please? As a principal I will make sure that teachers and students understand the nature of the oppressive problems created by an oppressive culture, SO THAT THEY CAN get behind, or whatever it is that you're going to say —

Zan: Be involved more fully in the avocation of teaching and counseling our children. See, teaching can be a vocation. It's something you buy into, but the way I understand it, if it's your avocation, this is what you really want to do — so it's an avocation, not just a vocation.

Judith: OK, so you've just explained that — to be sure that I understand it? You could do the same thing in this presentation; give it a place, to make sure that it gets across — (*The clause becomes: "so that they will turn their vocation into an avocation and become more effective in teaching and counseling our children."*)

*   *   *

Zan and I have learned how to learn from each other. But while we are fighting and laughing together, in the classroom, he remains outside the conversation, which seldom focuses on inner city children, class, race, or ethnic differences. To turn the conversation to his concerns, Zan is expected to present a logically consistent argument from his seat. He is not supposed to walk around the room, dramatize his relationship to his audience, or use any resources but logic and recorded evidence to win the engagement of others. He is supposed to perform on the terms he challenges. Instead, professors note that Zan often has a "revolutionary way of talking — that can cut him off from changes he wants to make."

Zan confides to me that his "left side" is leaking out in certain classes.

Zan: My left side is only seeking what my right side is saying, but it's going to the bones. The reason [my participation] is merging over to my left side is because my right side is like (*shrugs, grimaces*) not doing an adequate job or something — you see what I mean?

The right side is trying to do something within a certain cultural constraint and it's not getting anyplace. It's my frusTRATION — so my left side is saying, Well, you know, you ain't doing too good that. Try THIS!

In one particular class, Zan objected to his professor's rephrasing of the term "rotten to the core," which Zan used in reference to the inner city schools: "How do you go into a system and change that system if the system is rotten to the core?" The professor qualified the phrase: "Because I would attribute socially redeeming factors ...." Thereafter, Zan, the professor, and a number of students argued about the kind of language and the kind of logic that is appropriate and useful in institutional interventions. During the discussion, Zan spoke in a confrontational, challenging tone, and imputed conscious design to social ills, a design embedded in the Constitutional legacy of colonial America. The professor engaged him by:

1. Positioning Zan's comments within the theoretical framework of the course — "I have difficulty connecting the origins of the Constitution to today's inner city school systems. Now I've read articles that make the connection, but my preference for how to go about getting at your concern is for you to illustrate a system that is rotten to the core today, because whether or not it came from the Constitution, I can do without knowing that."

2. Establishing counterpoints — "My attribution is that — there are many sincere efforts to respond to the needs of the nonaffluent. And they are insufficient; but — I attribute you missed the good-intentioned, sincere efforts — and that will cut you off from having influence in the system — "

3. Asking questions — "Could you illustrate a system that is rotten to the core?"

Other students responded to the exchange, commenting on differences in Zan's and the professor's ways of talking, making meaning, and getting points across to the other.

Zan brought a transcript of the discussion to my house one night. I remarked on how productive the discussion had been in getting some of Zan's issues addressed, but Zan complained that the discussion had to happen at all — it was just a game, and a deceitful one, because the professor knew all along what Zan had meant by calling the system rotten to the core — yet he had insisted that Zan express his opinion in a linguistically explicit manner, so that its logic could be examined.

"He knew what I meant from Jump Street, Judy. He was locked into his universe, and there was no particular outside that universe. It had to be in with his universe. If it wasn't with his universe, then it

didn't exist, and I know it's jive. I suppose if it is that expository
thang — if it is that multilingual speech, that multilingual universe without
my universe within that universe or part of — the whole, (*whisper*) then
what — good am I?"

*   *   *

In February 1988, Zan and I dramatized our struggles over academic
writing at the University of Pennsylvania "Ethnography in Education"
conference. There he met women of color who told him flatly that
using the tools of the dominant culture would not change him. He
could use those tools to change the culture. Their words marked one of
many turning points in our conversations. In June of 1988, Zan
graduated from the master's program at Harvard with A's or A-'s in all
courses but one, in which he received a B. The following year he
served as interim principal in a K−8 urban magnet school. Today he is
principal in a suburban elementary school, where he is committed to
empowering students, staff, and parents.

But school districts do not typically make equity the centerpiece of
school structure and curriculum. Zan continues struggling to transform
seer and seen. I continue in my program, shaking frames.

Work Cited

Chapman, A., ed. 1968. *Black voices: An anthology of Afro-American literature.*
New York: New American Library.

PART TWO
Vision of a Field Negro
Nanzetta Merriman

Introduction

It may be unclear to the reader whether my vision is a phoenix or in metamorphosis. If they think it is ethnocentric they will see a burning phoenix. There is a core black tradition that I follow. That tradition comes straight from my mother and my father and their mothers and fathers. This vision comes from them and will eventually evolve into something greater. I know that my vision is in metamorphosis. I can't tell what part of the continuum my vision is on in relation to my family structure or the educational needs of society.

It is rumored my father never progressed further than the fourth grade. My mother started her advanced education after she had raised my Uncle Carl (her younger brother) and her three children. I'm the first person in my family to have earned two university degrees. I now know where this leads my children and their children — to find out how good they can really be. I did not begin this journey. My father began this journey in Granada, in the early 1900s. Then he knew he wanted indoor plumbing, a floor not made of dirt, and a better life for a family. The contributions and achievements that my children, my caramel angels, will make to society will be focused through the vision that is bound by tradition. I got here on the blood, sweat, tears, and love of my ancestors, parents, sisters, my wife and children.

I got my vision from seeing my parents' development and seeing and listening to their disciples. My father was a disciple of Garvey; my mother was a disciple of Martin Luther King. I'm a disciple of Malcolm X and of my family.

As far as our society is concerned, I believe that there is a need for more positive models for all youth and I believe that the African-American experience is one that ought to be championed as a source for positive models. Those positive models also change — some of what Garvey, King, and Malcolm said is no longer relevant to the battle at hand, but that does not negate the truth they bring to the dialogue.

192

The vision has to become something different — because knowing your vision means keeping your eyes open, listening, caring, learning from what you see, hear, and feel, and giving back. When situations change, that is, when the oppressed have developed their own power, or when the oppressor awakes — when the relations between them have changed — then the vision changes. It is always in metamorphosis.

The Vision

There were two types of Negroes in the antebellum South. The house Negro slept in the Master's house, ate the Master's food, assisted the Master in his tasks. If the Master's house was burning, the house Negro would say, "We are on fire." The field Negro lived in a community of shacks, ate pig tails, pig feet, neck bones — whatever the Master threw away. He had to be beaten to do the Master's tasks. If the Master's house was burning he would pray for wind. If the Master was sick he would pray for his death. Being a slave meant giving away your will or hiding it in secret prayers or acting in secret.

Today there are two types of Negroes in the American landscape. One is the colonized house Negro, who remains a slave to a system of inequity and prejudice. The other is the field Negro, whose identity refutes the Euro-American definition of Negro as thing. The field Negro's voice today defines core black culture.

> The sense of nationhood among blacks is as old as our abhorrence of slavery. Black nationhood is not rooted in territoriality so much as it is in a profound belief in the fitness of core black culture and in the solidarity born of a transgenerational detestation of our subordination. ... Rare is the black family without its proverbial charter for principled survival in the infinity of tight places occasioned by racist oppression. (Gawaltney 1980, xxvii)

Blacks who enter the mainstream without losing their identity in core black tradition take the project of the field Negro one step further. Their vision is truly to release the will of black people in America. I share with my brothers and sisters a vision of education as an instrument of black consciousness. I speak especially to black educators and other school leaders. I believe a clear vision is necessary to replace the consciousness of colonized Negro culture of which most of our lives are examples. Colonized means controlled by others, lacking self-determination, self-definition.

Education is an important element in the struggle for all human rights. It can be the means to help our children rediscover their identity and thereby increase their self-respect. Education is the passport to the future, for tomorrow belongs only to the people who prepare for it. Whoever controls the present controls the future, but whoever controls the past controls the present.

A major tenet of a vision that takes control of our legacy is to popularize the way black Americans have reinterpreted the Constitution to black Americans over the centuries because they have reconstructed the framers' intent in order to guarantee the rights of all citizens.

> The antebellum blacks who pledged allegiance to the Founders' Constitution perceived the all-important point that words do not speak for themselves. They realized the importance of interpretation. They revelled in the plasticity of language. They refused to be intimidated by those who insisted that Constitutional provisions can have only one possible interpretation. They understood that the Constitution is as decent or indecent, as progressive or reactionary as "we the people" make it. (Kennedy 1987, 7)

> Let me give you a word of the philosophy of reform. The whole history of the progress of human liberty shows that all concessions yet made to her august claims have been born of earnest struggle. The conflict has been exciting, agitating, all-absorbing, and for the time being, putting all other tumults to silence. It must do this or it does nothing. If there is no struggle there is no progress. ... (Douglass 1857, 200)

An educational vision that extends and legitimizes the legacy of black Americans advocates that the black experience in America, growing out of Nubian warriors, slaves, colonized Negroes, voices of core black culture, leaders in business, politics, law, and education, teachers of our children, should initiate the process of cultural reconstruction and ought to provide a primary model for all aspects of the curriculum and for good citizenship. Furthermore, adherents of this vision would argue that the Constitution enjoins all citizens to continually engage it as a living document, and to reinterpret it as exemplary black Americans have done. Finally, I urge black educators to enact this vision in the framework of an urban community where we can work with community members to empower our young people to take control of the constitutional legacy.

As educational leaders, we should make sure that teachers and staff understand the nature of the problems created by an oppressive culture so that they will turn their vocation into an avocation and become more effective in the teaching and counseling of our young children.

Standard textbooks state little about the great contributions of Afro-Americans to the growth and development of this country. When we send our children to school in this country they learn little about us to change the image of ourselves as cotton pickers. As professional educators we can make sure that students learn that their grandparents were Nat Turner, Hannibal, Malcolm X, Toussaint L'Ouverture, Cleopatra, Shirley Chisolm, and Angela Davis. Their grandparents' hands helped to forge civilization and rock its cradle.

Schools do not adequately educate members of the community. Therefore, there is untapped power in the community, even where the school is ever-present. While social service agencies come and go depending upon political fads or funding opportunities, the school remains, often dormant but potentially a catalyst for change. This is why we must possess the schools to tap the power of the community and to affect/effect social change.

"Gemeinschaftsgefuhl" is a German word that is untranslatable into English. It has been rendered as "social feeling," or human solidarity, with a wider connotation of a "sense of fellowship in the human community." This is what schooling ought to promote. Education should be one vehicle by which oppressed people can overcome established structures and manifest a concept of wholeness, grounded in solidarity. The democratic mission of the school will be met only when both skills and moral consciousness are found among its graduates.

More typically, schools resemble banks much more than communities of learning — banks where certain knowledge is treated as valuable tokens to be dispensed by some people (the ones who hold the knowledge, who believe themselves predestined in their privileged roles) to others who are ignorant, who have no knowledge, whom they evaluate as illiterate. This vile necrophilia negates education as inquiry into the nature of culture and as making knowledge necessary for cultural reconstruction. Banking education creates a caste system where administrators, teachers, and students are polarized and so is the school, which holds the knowledge, from the community, which is perceived to have none.

If schools are to avoid the function of perpetuating existing race, class, gender, and caste division, they must be guided by theories of education as transformation rather than as remediation. To do this, these questions must be asked and answered:

- What is studied?
- How is it studied?
- By whom is it studied?
- Toward what end is it studied?

We must struggle against all ethnocentric pedagogy that is preconceived, idealized, and monoethnic, and resist all oppressing and oppressed values and behaviors that students are expected to practice in school. A pedagogy of liberation that promotes black consciousness recognizes all races, colors, and creeds, while advancing the black experience as a model for cultural reconstruction. A revolutionary pedagogy develops habits that are nonreactionary: habits of proaction — action based on reflection and deliberation.

My view of the role of the educational leader, based on the tenet that the culture must be reconstructed, is to guide all members of the school community, including parents, teachers, and staff, in the process of becoming agents of change. That means that they should act as models and encourage teachers, parents, staff, and students to collaborate, communicate, make decisions, organize, and support each other. Just as teaching as banking will not work in the classroom, administration as banking can never elicit genuine change. Teachers treated as technicians, stuck in a vocation that is not central to their lives, will sabotage change, whether consciously or unconsciously, and cannot develop a committed engagement with the community.

This vision is antiracist, antisexist, anti-imperialist, anticapitalist, anticontrol by those who now have power; it is an attempt to change those who have power by making the black experience a primary part of American culture and consciousness.

Extremism in the defense of liberty is no vice. Moderation in the pursuit of justice is no virtue. I am not a racist. I am against every form of racism and segregation. I believe in human beings, and that all human beings should be respected as such, regardless of their race, color, sexual preference, or creed.

Therefore

"I am an extremist" (Malcolm X, 1964). I believe in intellectually directed extremism, extremism in the defense of liberty, extremism in the quest for liberty, extremism in education. I firmly believe in my heart, soul, and deepest being that the moment we take an uncompromised step, we can put a halt to injustices. We must realize that we are within our moral rights, when our freedom and dignity and that of others is being jeopardized, to take any means necessary, whether violent or nonviolent, to overcome. If I am wrong, and the model of core black tradition does not liberate all people, then I am a racist. But if I am right, I am a radical, and you who do not want to hear me are the racists.

My father Nanzetta was called Sam. The people he worked for called him that. Sam is short for Sambo. My father Nanzetta married one fine, sainted woman, Marie Banks. Marie (we called her Mummy) would hold us, love us, scold us, making sure she told us everything she could. FEEL. And now I feel that spirit deep down in my soul, and it makes me think back to my ancestors who lived a long time ago. When I feel that spirit deep inside my soul it makes me think of ancestors who ruled the world and all of its gold. My father came to this country from Granada because he believed in the American Dream. He labored to support a wife and three children; he worked three jobs until his death. They called him SAM. My father married one fine sainted woman, Marie Banks. Marie, Mummy, would hold us, love us, scold us, making sure to tell us that they would never know what it is we need. When I hear that spirit deep down in my soul, it is a blessed message that is part of my vision. My father's dream was indoor plumbing and linoleum on the floor. My dream is the reconstruction of my father's American dream. People call me Nanzetta.

Works Cited

Douglass, F. [1857] 1972. If there is no struggle there is no progress. In *The voice of black America*, ed. P. Foner. New York: Simon and Schuster.

Gawaltney, J. L. 1980. Drylongso. New York: Vintage.

Kennedy, R. 1987. Working paper. Cambridge Harvard Law School.

Malcolm, X. Presentation to Oxford Union Society debate, December 3, 1964. Aired on the BBC.

Response (A Dialogue)

Judith Diamondstone
Nanzetta Merriman

Nanzetta: So what is a collaboration? I suppose collabortion could be more or less like love. We both have to be honest and give up certain facades, slide our egos to the side in order to work with one another. Collaboration means trust. And I suppose that in collegial behavior people do begin to take on hierarchical relations. When one person's knowledge or sense is more accurate, the other person has to nod to that person's ability in that realm. But everything is cyclical. In a collaboration you feed off of and challenge one another.

Judith: Collaboration is not an easy dance — you have to want the growth that comes out of it in order to feel committed.

Nanzetta: Do you remember when you asked me to critique your first draft? I asked, Whose portrait is this? And you said it was yours. I said, If I take the brush and make some brushstrokes, then it isn't yours anymore, is it? What was important about collaborating on my vision and on my writing in general? I was only using one voice to articulate what I felt needed to be heard by all people. Consequently, it would not be heard by the multitude; it would probably have been looked at as ethnocentric without a cause that would inspire people who are not of color. Therefore I needed a sounding board. I needed someone who at least had insight into the qualities of language behavior that the academic would respond to. Hence our working together: in collaboration with you I found words or phrases that would bring other people into the fold.

Judith: When I was collaborating with you, I felt immersed in your contest with academic discourse. So the portrait focused on our writing sessions. The way I thought of it, the portrait was not about you but about your struggle with the academic institution that I mediated for you as a writing tutor. I believed that we were telling a story of resistance to academic writing that all those who do not actually SPEAK academese could relate to. Since the image in the portrait is of my way of seeing you (grounded with glimpses of our actual interactions), it is incomplete as a story of our collab-

198

oration without your *Vision of Education*. The *Vision* is not only one of the texts that we were working on in the portrait of your struggles with academic writing, but it is also your image, your own vision. So even though it's not directly concerned with collaboration, it is central to OUR story. This is the framework we want to give the chapter. As for the portrait, it marks the beginning of a learning process across different experiences, different histories, and in spite of our own limitations.

Nanzetta: One aspect of this learning process is that I have discovered that there are inroads to maintaining one's voice and style. Voice is who you are. It's your vision, your purpose. It should always remain in a paramount position. Style is like the manner in which one chooses to express oneself.

Judith: You say to keep your voice but adjust your style; the academics would have it the other way around—shift your voice, try out different voices, but keep your style intact. They would be very happy if you used the literature available in the university in your own way, in your own style. I think they find it more difficult to accept your vision, your voice, because you speak from your experience.

Nanzetta: I find limited support for my voice in the university literature. Therefore I turn to tradition, to my background. My power comes from grounding my writing in African-American resources. I've learned ways that one can alter the style but not divorce oneself from the voice. One should hold onto one's voice. To have people hear it and listen to it and understand it requires changing the style in which it was presented. But the message still stands. There are times when your voice demands your style; when it can only be said in one way or one fashion, or when you choose to do that and you stand by it. Style is the map and the roads in the map are your voice. What I've learned is that you can set a familiar map for the reader and change the road so that it goes where you want it to go until you change the map itself and the reader is on your territory. This is reciprocity.

11

Eating on the Street
Cultural Conflict in Detroit

David Schaafsma

This is the story of one perplexing and illuminating incident in the experience of teachers and students working together on a research project at the Dewey Center Community Project in Detroit in June of 1989.

The Dewey Center is a new alternative K–8 whole language school in Detroit's troubled inner city. The first summer workshop of the Dewey Center Community Writing Project involved thirty fifth-through seventh-grade students who live in or near the Jeffries Homes (also known as the Projects), working with seven University of Michigan and Detroit Public School teachers. The writing project continued the following year and into the next summer. Plans are to expand the project over five years to four inner city school sites.

The research project was designed to help students explore and develop with their teachers better ways of helping students learn to read and write. We see it as a collaborative, interdisciplinary project where students and teachers plan, write, talk, evaluate, and learn together. The students we have worked with are primarily what some people have labeled "at-risk." The teachers are from diverse backgrounds, four with extensive commitments to the inner city: Toby and Debi, two white veteran teachers; Jeanetta, a black veteran teacher; and Dana, a black first-year teacher; and three from the University of Michigan: Susan, a black teacher and former urban administrator, and George and I, two white teachers with little experience in the inner city.

On the third day of the project, we split up into groups and attended Children's Day at the Cultural Center in Detroit. Jeanetta's and George's group included Dora, Tameka, Farrah, Aquileth, and LaShunda. At our teachers' meeting, Jeanetta explained how she was personally bothered by seeing the above-named kids "eating on the street." As a teacher, she would never allow that.

George said he hadn't realized it was such a big deal. "I probably eat on the street all the time," he said. I said I did, too.

"But you can do that," said Jeanetta. "You are white teachers, and these are black students. Here they were in their white T-shirts, representing the Dewey Center, and they have this food (she mimicked exaggeratedly and comically) dribbling down their chin.

"No," she said. "No! Maybe it's just me, but that really bothers me."

We all laughed.

"No," I said, "You should bring it up, that's what these sessions are for."

Jeanetta said we all had different standards than she did in the classroom. She reminded us she had a reputation for being a tough teacher, but said she had been trying to "hang back" during the summer project in order to learn. She said she had some problems with the way some of us failed to discipline students for certain things. Susan said that she was upset about that, too.

This report focuses on several stories, teacher and student versions of the incident that occurred during the third day of the Dewey Center Community Writing Project. Our conflict of interpretation, based in part on our cultural differences, indicates the complexities we face when we work in multicultural settings and try to come to understand and celebrate cultural differences.

Teachers Telling Stories

"All truths being multiple, it is not surprising that the true version of any story is also multiple" (O'Flaherty 1988, 64).

Susan: Tough Love

Born and raised in Tallahassee, Susan got her B.A. in secondary education from the almost entirely black Tuskegee Institute. Of this education she says, "It was kind of a traditional setting, in the sense that the teachers were like the kind of teachers my mother had had. Some of them were still there that had taught my mother. They were very strict." Susan received an M.A. in Education from Stanford and from there became a teacher and administrator of an urban school in Texas.

In a phone interview several months after the conclusion of the

program I asked Susan what her memory of our conflict had been, and
how she now interpreted it. She explained:

Susan: It's very difficult for white people, and other people who are
not part of the black experience, to understand some of the things
that set us apart. And, for us, growing up in the South, we have to
suffer so many stereotypes as blacks, such as being associated with
smelling bad, laziness, and things like that. Or, seen as walking
around not knowing how to eat without dribbling food. For many
of the blacks who grow up in those type of situations, parents and
teachers and everybody else work hard to make you aware of the
things that had been very detrimental to our race, to our people.
We did not, as educated blacks, want to be associated in any way
with the things that would make us be seen as somehow inadequate.
We were seeking to set ourselves as educated people apart from
what had been said about us as a race. And the issue of hair-
combing—that nappy-head black boy, or that nappy-head black
girl—I think that many blacks grew up fearing that stereotype,
too. And naturally you wanted to appear wherever you went as
clean and as neat as you could. You didn't want to be associated
with those old ideas about what black people were like. Do you
understand what I'm saying?

David: I sure do.

Susan: OK. So this is what we have been striving to work for, and
certainly this is a major issue with blacks down South, because you
were constantly faced with that by white people, with their saying
these things about us. And those blacks, and particularly at such
institutions as Tuskegee, this was an issue that we as blacks made
it a point to emphasize. We made a commitment, many of us, to
train our people, lift our people, and not let those kinds of things
be said. So when I came to Detroit, there were some things that
were very disturbing that were going on there. We noticed, for
example, that the children were bringing their snacks and such
from their projects, and they were walking down the street, with
greasy bags and such, allowed to eat this food directly on the
street, and this was unacceptable for some of us, because of our
upbringing, our background. You wouldn't do anything to demean
yourself in this way—eating and snapping food and just walking
along the street with potato chips and sandwiches. We want them
to know that where it takes 75 percent for our brother, for our
white brother to get in, it's going to take 150 percent even now, in
1989, for our black children to get in to certain settings. You're not
going to be the anchor person, you're not going to be in the bank,
dressed all sloppily, eating food in this sort of way, you're going to
have to really really be up to par.

Susan's position on conventional behavior carried over to her views on language, particularly black English:

Susan: I think I said I felt that black English does not exist in the sense that we have white southern English, New Orleans English, New England English. I just don't see why we have to bear another label. I resent that as a black. I've been labeled enough. I don't want any other labels on me. Again, I feel that this is an issue that takes a lot of love and care where we're concerned. If you want to say black English exists and that there are certain patterns of speech that unfortunately have been developed among black people, that's fine. We need to be aware of that, as we try to teach English, and as we try to get people to speak and write effectively. But don't keep that label there as a crutch for my people. To say "It's OK for you to say that, because we all know that you speak black English." Because black English is never going to go in the United States, and we all know that. Nobody wants salespersons and teachers and others who speak and write ineffectively, regardless of color. We need colorless English, as far as I'm concerned. Because that's what we have, that's the kind of people that they want. They want people who can speak standard English, period. So that's my position on that, and don't use that, don't even give such a crutch to kids. Don't let folks think that you can get away with anything like that, because it will not work.

A key to Susan's view of teaching was her faith:

Susan: You know, David, I believe in tough love. And I also credit my grandmother, who was a very influential person in my life, and she was a tough woman. She didn't put up with things that were not right, and if she felt that we were doing something wrong, she told you that you're doing this wrong, I don't like this. And to me, that was the most loving thing a person could do, to try and make sure you get on the right track. And if you stay on the right track, find out what it takes to be successful, and we know what it's going to take to be successful. You have to have some faith. You have to have self-confidence. And that's what a lot of black children don't have. They do not believe in themselves.

Susan brought to the program a perspective on life and learning that all of us benefited from. Her discipline is one informed by a strong religious faith, and a belief, inspired by, among others, Booker T. Washington, the founder of the Tuskegee Institute, that observing the social conventions of the middle class remains the best means to social success in today's society. Her view depends heavily on models for these high standards of correctness, taken from her own modeling of behavior as well as from stories of the past and present. It is a view that Janice Hale-Benson (1986) explains: "Black parents have always stressed to their children the importance of their exceeding white children's behavior and performance because falling short would reflect unfavorably upon the group" (48).

While my own perspective on black history had been informed largely by those who have pointed out injustices, more recently, after having worked with Susan, I have been influenced by writers who have helped me see the strength of black culture to not only survive but endure. My view of black language use had been and continues to be informed by my work with African-American students, but also by the work of writers such as William Labov and Geneva Smitherman, who help me see the importance of celebrating a multiplicity of black and other dialects. I have been persuaded by writers such as Henry Louis Gates (1989), who says: "Eager to 'domesticate' the African slave by denying him and her their language, their religion, their values and belief systems, and indeed their entire sense of order, the slave owners, first, forbade the usage of African languages on their plantations" (15). I am eager as a white middle-class teacher to participate in a celebration, and not a further renunciation, of African-American language and culture. But through Susan's stories, I see the complexity of simply celebrating difference in a society that doesn't yet do so.

Susan's voice reminds us that a perspective on language must be developed with traditional and progressive educators of all races. Her story, her perspective, reminds us that to be truly collaborative in reshaping notions about learning and teaching requires negotiating different perspectives. There is no one answer to any problem, and many views, even seemingly contradictory ones, need to be heard in an approach to solutions.

Jeanetta: Hard-Nosed

Jeanetta radiates strength in her voice, in her firm stance in the class-room, and in the strong opinions she freely shares. A nineteen-year veteran of the Couzens School, Jeanetta had also been its union rep-resentative for all of those years. Known as a tough union negotiator, she was also admittedly proud of her reputation as a tough teacher. She volunteered to teach in the program after the Whole Language Seminar for Couzens School teachers in the Winter 1989 term.

In an interview with Jeanetta in late August, six weeks after the summer program, I asked her to tell me about her background, and what she felt had shaped her views as a teacher.

Jeanetta: My parents were educators. My mother was a schoolteacher. Daddy was the principal of the school, and when they stopped having segregated schools, and integration came, they put her out of a job, so she took the test to be a social worker. She became the first black social worker in Montgomery County, and I think there hasn't been another one in that county since she got the job. So some feelings are hard to talk about. It's just hard. Then when integration started they burned the school down where my daddy was principal.

David: Where was that?

Jeanetta: In Mount Sterling, Kentucky. They burned the black school down. This was during the time of integration, in the sixties. But when you live through something like that, that affects you, believe me. In other districts they let other black principals be assistant principals of white schools, but not in Mount Sterling, Kentucky. And my father had his master's degree in administration. But they put him back in the classroom as a history teacher. For a year they let him do nothing, just kind of filling files, working with records. So you get a little uptight. But the black-white relations with our family in Mount Sterling were good, generally. We didn't have many problems. Both my father and mother were involved in everything, like the Chamber of Commerce, everything. My family was very involved in the community, you know, visible. I mean, I haven't had a lot of ugliness.

Jeanetta began teaching in Kentucky, married, moved to Detroit, and has taught for more than twenty years. She very much agreed with Susan on the issue of eating on the street:

Jeanetta: You know where that comes from? When we were little children growing up and going uptown, that was a thing that mother knew. We would buy candy and she would not let us eat the candy until we were on the way home. And if she ever saw us eating on the street she'd say, "I hate that. I detest that. You look like . . . whatever."

Jeanetta explains how this incident changed her perspective on collaborative teaching:

Jeanetta: We all learned from that discussion. That's the value of team teaching. You learn from each other, right? You talk about team teaching as negotiating, like power struggles, and I never thought of it that way. I never thought about it as negotiating. "Team teaching" is just my term, my name for it. To me it means the meeting of the minds, coming together with one specific goal that's workable. That's my idea of what it means. But I hadn't looked at it that way before. You see, when I think of negotiating, I think in terms of union negotiating or negotiating with the principal. You see, I look at it more like that. "Collaborative" to me is a team

teaching sort of thing, where you sit down and discuss your plans
and everyone comes to an agreement. But that day we were
definitely not in agreement, and there we had to learn from each
other's disagreements.

I asked her if it was difficult for her to think of teaching in terms of a
negotiation. In her experience, she had always made the plans herself,
and there was no negotiation necessary.

Jeanetta: At first I said no, but then I felt like I was a part of it.

David: You see, if you have to make decisions, then it's yours.

Jeanetta: And that made me feel more a part of the team. At first, I
had not been to any of the meetings, like Toby and Debi, because
I joined a little later. I had never been up to Ann Arbor like they
had. And I really didn't start feeling a part of it until I came to a
meeting in Ann Arbor, too. But then more and more I started
making suggestions and telling things from my way, my experience,
and you all seemed to like what I had to suggest, so I knew I had
something to offer.

David: And you're not normally shy.

Jeanetta: (*Smiles*) No, I'm not shy. You'll know what I think.

Jeanetta's stories reinforce what she calls a traditional perspective
on teaching and learning. That many black and white teachers see traditional methodologies as essential for assimilation into mainstream
culture further complicates the task of changing schools. Lisa Delpit
says, in "The Silenced Dialogue" (1988):

> Many liberal educators hold that the primary goal for education is for
> children to become autonomous, to develop fully who they are in the
> classroom setting without having arbitrary, outside standards forced
> upon them. This is a very reasonable goal for people whose children
> are already participants in the culture of power and who have already
> internalized its codes.
>
>   But parents who don't function within that culture often want
> something else. It's not that they disagree with the former aim, it's
> just that they want something more. They want to ensure that the
> school provides their children with discourse patterns, interactional
> styles, and spoken and written language codes that will allow them
> success in the larger society. (89)

As Delpit says, it is not an issue of "either/or": "They must be encouraged to understand the value of the code they already possess as well
as to understand the power realities in this country. Otherwise they
will be unable to work to change these realities." As she puts it,
"There is a political power game that is being played, and if they want
to be in on the game there are certain games that they too must play"

(97). Those of us who taught in the program generally agreed with Delpit's perspective, but we disagreed at times about what that meant for teaching our children that summer.

After many years of teaching, Jeanetta finds her kids increasingly difficult to deal with, and she doubts, even after what she agreed was a successful summer program, whether a whole language approach will necessarily be successful with poor black children. But she is determined to try to change her classroom, because she sees the need to change, and because she saw successes in the summer program she would like to see occur in her own classroom. She taught in the program's second summer, and continues to make use of more writing and more group work and individualized instruction than ever in her classroom.

Hers is a testimony to the usefulness of collaborative teaching, but it is also a tale of ambivalence, of contradiction, of doubt, of the difficulty of adapting to new concepts about teaching after a lifetime of teaching another way. It is no fairy tale of change through collaboration, but an indication of the need for support in teacher change, and for continued dialogue that does not silence contradiction, but welcomes it, as narrative conceptions of learning must surely do.

George: Making Friends

George, a lecturer with the University of Michigan English Composition Board, was the "spiritual hub" of our teaching team, loved as a trusted friend, and respected by all of us for his love of kids, and his advocacy of their individual styles of learning. He and I had worked in a similar program in rural northern Michigan, the Huron Shores Summer Writing Program, but we both welcomed the challenge of adapting such a program to an urban setting with our friends from Detroit. In November 1989 I talked with him about his perspective on the eating incident:

David: So in terms of your comment earlier about conventions, this doesn't disturb your personal notion of the conventions of eating.

George: Not at all. In fact I didn't even notice it until Jeanetta drew my attention to it. So Jeanetta and I talked about it as we progressed toward Wayne State. She, more and more tempted to say something to the kids, and me, just happy that I was walking along, getting to know them. As we got closer to Wayne State, perhaps due to Jeanetta's more and more constant banter about it to me, the eating became a bit more noticeable to me, and actually in a way irritating. The kids were carrying these purple plastic things, plastic containers of grape juice, and as they drank it and spilled it on themselves, you know, they did take on the appearance of being a bit sloppy and all. I began to think of them and the way they looked, more — like, hey, we're "going out," in a way, you don't want to get that stuff all over you. I would have told my own kids the same thing.

David: Toby might have stopped them from eating on the street because she hated the junk food they were eating.

George: But I would have taken a practical view: You're going to spill that stuff all over you, and we had a good snack coming up, so why don't you at least wait until we all get together to eat. The complaint of Jeanetta's finally was that it was a matter of the attention that it brings on a person, and that these are young, underprivileged kids, from the inner city, who will draw negative attention to themselves, because they're eating in the street. She tried to illustrate this to me, as we got closer to the Cultural Center, when she insisted that the kids put this food away, and she said, "You see, George? No one else is eating in the street here." And I looked around, and sure enough, no one else was eating in the street. But I said, "Jeanetta, white folks do that all the time." "You can do that," she said, "yeah, but, black folks can't. White folks can get away with that because no one really pays attention to them." She said, "This is a double standard, my being harder on these black kids than the white folks, but there is a double standard being held by this country and you have to be aware of it." So she spoke about it as a matter of culture, that it's not acceptable among black folks who want the best for their kids. Because black folks have more to face, the road is harder for them. So that to act out in the same way even a white person would do is less acceptable for a black person; they have more to prove. And all of this of course says a lot about Jeanetta. It's the way in which she's raised her own kids, and it's the way in which she herself had been brought up to be.

David: At the very least this made us more sensitive to cultural differ- ence. In some sense, I think I felt at the time, that we were being told that we as white teachers, all of us, couldn't really understand what it was like to work with black kids, in the same way that black teachers could, and our only option was to look at black teachers for how to work with black kids. But if you really disagree with the way the black teachers are dealing with black kids, then what do you do?

George: But we do need to look to black teachers, and they need to look to us. And we all learned some things from working together. We went in saying that we would accept them, and their ways of language, and wanted to work with their ways of learning. And we do, but now because we have talked, we know a little better, that it's more complicated. But you can get in trouble either way, being authoritarian or liberal in terms of encountering another culture. I just didn't want to get into any kind of authority thing, and neither did you.

George was enthusiastic about working with students and initially joined me in opposing, for instance, teachers' efforts to change students' language to make it consistent with "standard English" grammar. Ultimately, all of us, including George, came to a position of compromise with regard to this issue, and we all agreed to try to discourage students from eating on the street.

George's story of the conflict about "eating on the street," while it shared certain affinities with other teacher stories (he was sensitive to Jeanetta's perspective, as she was to his), was a different interpretation of the events. He learned through discussion with Jeanetta the difficulty she had with "public eating," and she learned to appreciate the various reasons why he seemed to have no problem with it, and why he was furthermore reluctant to discipline students for doing it. As an outsider, he was unaware of the cultural conventions attendant to poor black children eating on the street, conventions at least as perceived by these particular black teachers. He, like her, was caught in conflict, and by sharing in it, we all came to the kind of resolution we all must come to in such a situation, a decision that comes from the best of our collective understanding at that point. Both he and I, inexperienced in the inner city, needed to hear and learn from the stories from the strong black traditions of Jeanetta and Susan, and from the stories, too, of white teachers like Toby, who had taught many years in the inner city.

Toby: Mother Curry

Born and raised in Detroit and having taught for more than twenty years exclusively in the inner city of Detroit, Toby was a highly successful teacher at Burton International School for more than ten years before fulfilling a dream with her friend and colleague Debi in establishing an alternative whole language school in the inner city. Having heard her and Debi speak at the National Council of Teachers of English in Los Angeles in November 1987, on the use of family histories and community ethnographies in their classrooms, and talking to them about their work afterwards, I felt they basically shared George's and my perspective on language learning and students. When they heard us speak at the same conference about the Huron Shores program and were enthusiastic, I was even more confident of our shared beliefs. When George and I first discussed the possibility of developing a writing program in Detroit, they were the first people we talked with.

I know Toby as an exciting teacher, highly energetic, passionately committed to having her students learn in meaningful contexts. I talked

with her about the program in late November, focusing on the issue of
eating on the street:

Toby: Even though I read lots of black authors and historical fiction,
and other texts about blacks, and had taught in the city for years, I
still didn't know what the allusion was because I'm not black. It's
like the way you carry yourself out in public in a basically white
world, and how you're perceived. And you don't want to be
perceived as slovenly or sloppy. I think that was the general thrust
or worry, of how these black kids were perceived out on the street.
And then I think there was something about, someone said something about white teachers not being able to understand black
standards, or black kids, and I remember I got defensive about it.

While Toby here comments on her perceived differences between a
black and white perspective, she had been complimented by Susan for
being an example of a white teacher who upholds strict standards for
behavior of black children. Susan praised Toby specifically for "being
tough" with students with regard to trash disposal on the day following
Children's Day at the Cultural Center. Though she is supportive of
individual students' needs, and is personally "not bothered" with eating
on the street specifically, Toby makes it clear that her standards for
students' behavior in certain situations, with adults on class trips in
particular, are exacting. She consistently broadens the issue of cultural
conventions. This is an important point for those of us who teach
literacy in multicultural settings to consider in learning to deal with
cultural difference.

Toby: [Susan and Jeanetta] do have a point there, though it personally
doesn't make me scream to see kids eating on the street, as a rule.
But I go on field trips, and I've been doing this for years with my
kids, I expect them, I tell them it's like being out with Mother
Curry, you know, it's like being out with your parents in public,
and I have certain perceptions or expectations of how people are
going to behave. And we've been to plays and been the quietest
group in the audience, and with raucous white suburban schools
that are just active and obnoxious like calling out to the actors,
inappropriate things. I make it clear to my kids that if they don't
like the performance they can just sit quietly and we'll discuss it
later, they can criticize it in a paper or something. But I've taken
numerous groups to Orchestra Hall, and everywhere, and I don't
ask the kids to dress a certain way. I think that violates their civil
rights. But I expect them to maintain a certain level of behavior.

David: These standards you have, Mother Curry, they have nothing to
do with race or class, or do they?

Toby: No. It has to do with how you should behave when you're out in public, in an audience. You shouldn't be talking whether you're screening a movie or talking to a neighbor, you know. So I didn't do anything — at Burton, I didn't have a majority — well, gradually we got to be about 50 percent black there, but this is the way I've been doing things for years.

Toby's approach, in some respects similar to Susan and Jeanetta's, asserts the need for teachers to help students of all cultures to an understanding of the expectations of a "standard English world." She also makes it clear, however, that even her many years as an inner city teacher have not given her "all the answers" to the issues; many remain unresolved, and she demonstrates that she is eager to learn more from others.

Toby: I feel the need to help kids edit for publication. And I think that's a real consideration. I don't care if they're black or white or Hispanic, I want them to be able to succeed in the broader world, which is a white standard English world. And I don't want them not to be able to get a job, or apply to a college, because they can't speak standard English. And 99 percent of the time when I ask a kid to rephrase something in standard English, and I do it frequently in the classroom, they do it. So it's not an issue in terms of they can't — it's like it's OK to talk a certain way with your friends, when you're hanging out. And I encourage that a lot. I've had kids who have written in dialect for different plays. Like I had two girls that wrote a play about two old slave women who were sitting on their rockers. They were eighty years old and they were talking all in dialect. And that was real appropriate for the setting.

David: I wonder if there isn't a connection between the insistence on manners for black kids, like not eating on the street, and the insistence on —

Toby: Standard English? Maybe. But you know what it is with me is I've had so many different ethnic groups in the last ten years. I mean lots of kids have lousy manners. It has nothing to do with whether they're black, white, or Asian. I've had to chastise kids out in public, for acting like morons, because you're not supposed to act like that in public. If you're with your friend in the mall, that's one thing, but if you've got an adult with you then I expect a certain kind of behavior. In fact, I have had a lot of excellent black kids, and many of them were the strongest and best-behaved in the program, so it wasn't generally the black kids who were the problem. It was the Cass Corridor white population that was acting the flakiest on my field trips at Burton, and in our summer program,

too. You know, I see it just as a class issue, with Susan and
Jeanetta and Dena, not in socioeconomic terms, and not exclusively
in terms of race. I'm not sure, but that's what I think. But I would
imagine there's a real strong connection between their perception
of language and their perception of behavior, you know, the social
graces, and all. Well I just see kids from so many different backgrounds, they're kids, first of all.

I admire all of the teachers in the Dewey project for their deep
commitment to teaching in urban settings, but our stories about our
work differ. What I think is clear is that teachers committed to collaborative teaching can learn about teaching literacy in multicultural classrooms through the stories they tell each other. When we argued about
cultural conflict in our teaching, teachers told anecdotes to support
their positions. Each teacher's perspective is constructed with and
through their stories, constructed in terms of their experiences as
teachers. For instance, feeling challenged about her legitimacy and
commitment, Toby told a series of brief anecdotes about her teaching
at Burton International School, and when George felt it necessary to
lighten the tension, he told a story on himself as a sloppy eater.

The conflict itself began with a story, an interpretation of experience
told by Jeanetta, and supported by the stories of Susan. Many of us
shared our own stories in response to this particular interpretation of
"eating on the street"; but unless we had heard each story, told from
particular perspectives, we might not have begun to understand important issues of cultural difference. In collaborative teaching and
learning, we need to hear each other's stories in order to broaden our
own interpretations and understand a more complete context.

Student Versions: The Generation Gap
and Issues of Authority

But collaborative teaching and learning is impoverished if it stops
without including student perspectives in the process. Several months
after the summer program, I asked some of the students who had been
there to tell me what they recalled about their experiences of that day.
LaShunda, who was in George's group, and Allen, who was not, both
black students, responded in this way:

David: What do you remember about Children's Day, Allen?

Allen: It was boring, Dave. And hot. Too hot.

David: What else do you recall about the day? Anything you want to
say.

Allen: Nothing. It was terrible. The teachers all made us go and some
of us didn't want to, but we had to anyway, and we had to walk

about twenty miles and it took about three and a half hours. It was terrible, Dave.

David: LaShunda, what do you remember about Children's Day from last summer?

LaShunda: We walked to the cultural area, and it was hot, and we couldn't buy snacks. Mrs. Thomas [Jeanetta] wouldn't let us, but I had already had some along from home. We watched some dancing with drums. There was a parade with a man on stilts. We walked home and I don't remember what else happened.

Without my having prompted either of them, and not knowing about the teacher discussion about the cultural issues involved in discipline, both Allen and LaShunda recalled issues of disagreement with teachers about power issues on that day. LaShunda specifically recalled being denied by Jeanetta the opportunity to buy snacks. But I didn't ask either of these students to expand upon or explain their answers.

In talking about the issue with Dora, however, in February 1990, I asked about the specific issue of eating on the street, and told her that it was an issue that had been a source of conflict for teachers.

David: I wanted to ask you about this eating on the street. Some of the teachers didn't like it. Can you figure out why?

Dora: Yeah, they say little kids who eat stuff on the street, when they buy chips and stuff, they pass it around, and they share it with their friends, and you don't know what your friend had, and then teachers will tell you that you can go back and get your chips and you can just sit. If you sit then you miss out on school and if it's in the summertime you miss out on fun things to do. Also, they don't want you to get sick, because I guess you can get that by eating on the street.

David: So that would be the problem with eating on the street. So you think that's what they might have been upset about. Let me say this: they said they thought it was sloppy, that it made a bad impression if they see people eating on the street, especially little kids.

Dora: It's not sloppy to eat on the street, because little kids get hungry more often than what grown-ups did when they was little. Adults don't understand the way that kids be like.

David: So you think that's all right, that's what kids do. So you think that adults just tell kids that they don't like to see kids doing that?

Dora: Because they didn't do it when they was little.

David: It's just an example of adults not understanding the way kids are today, maybe?

Dora: Yeah.

For Dora, like many of these fifth- through seventh-grade students, the day involved several sticky issues of freedom and self-determination. Dora didn't seem to characterize the conflicts of the day in terms of issues of race or class, but as an issue of age (younger people should have the right to "be themselves" and are misunderstood by adults), as a matter of a difference of opinion about what constitutes "sloppiness," and as a function of the usual student/teacher power relations (teachers, like most adults, tell you what to do, how to live). Besides, she says, teachers do not realize how hungry students get, implying that not letting kids buy food on this day is being insensitive to their different physical needs. The student versions conflict with some of the teacher versions in some important ways and thus enrich our storied understanding of Children's Day at the Cultural Center. They remind us that in imagining new notions about literacy learning, we would be wrong to leave student stories, student voices, out of our evolving story. In any conception of collaborative research into literacy, it is crucial to let them speak with us, and help us shape the future.

The conflict about eating on the street happened on the third day of a fifteen-day program. Having the opportunity to discuss these delicate issues together led to other discussions, other sharing of conflicting stories, through which we got to know each other, and also learned from each other. We agreed as a group to confront behavior such as eating on the street if we thought it was inappropriate, but we also agreed that these rules were shifting, provisional, grounded in specific situations, and that continued negotiation would be necessary. In other words, we decided no absolute rules for any group or situation. In a multicultural setting, the rules have to change because the contexts are rapidly changing. One of the virtues of collaborative teaching is that it unsettles our assumptions about what students need. We need to work together to begin to question ourselves. In our program, we continued to discuss issues of difference, including ideas about black English and student authority, how much freedom we should give students to decide their own use of time, and how much "structure" to give conferences and writing groups. And we maintained our commitment to involve students in such talks.

Collaborative Myth Making, Teaching, and Learning

"The object of understanding human events is to sense the alternatives of human possibility" (Bruner 1986, 53). One of the reasons multiple versions of events are important is that they tell us more about the nature and importance of tellers and storytelling in the context of collaborative learning. Wendy Doniger O'Flaherty, in her book *Other People's Myths* (1988), says, "All truths being multiple, it is not surprising that the true version of any story is also multiple" (64). When you truly examine others' myths, you also to some extent must begin to examine your own, and begin to see the mythical or constructed nature of what you believe and experience as truth. People teaching and learning collaboratively in a multicultural setting such as we were in during our summer program, people intent on not silencing each others' voices, who are working together on common goals of learning and teaching, both transform and are transformed in the act of sharing stories. This is a view of myth making, and of history, as communion, not just communication (O'Flaherty 1988, 148), a kind of collaboration that does not eliminate conflict, but that makes use of differences for growth.

An important aspect of our collaborative myth making, with regard to the preservation and celebration of difference, was its orality. The teacher stories I have shared here were spoken, and that fact, which reinforces their very provisional and contextual nature, helps us to see the useful conflict that's at the heart of the collaborative process. As Kieran Egan (1987) points out, "Oral cultures engage the emotions of their members by making the culturally important messages event-laden, by presenting characters and their emotions in conflict in developing narratives — in short, by building the messages into stories" (455). Glassie (1982) sees this, too, in his work with Irish storytellers: "Stories embody argument over important ideas and push toward the frontiers of culture to provide the outsider as well as the insider with a means for constructing the culture in its own terms" (291). He goes on to say that the stories told in Irish "ceilis" don't merely confirm the ideological unity of the people present. They "use social unity to raise the truth that confines ideology and calls doctrine into question" (298). Stories, Glassie is saying, can be told to build unity and heal wounds, but they can also be important in exploration, in learning. These stories preserve conflicting voice where closure is obviously not achieved.

We were a strong-willed group of teachers, with strong, and we knew, sometimes divergent opinions. Though we shared a desire and an enthusiasm for teaching together in the program and developed a close friendship (which continues), we also did not avoid sensitive issues in our frequent talks together. We used the opportunity to talk about important matters pertaining to our passionate interest in urban literacy, and our love of teaching this particular group of children. We took the opportunity daily to share stories about our students, stories that stressed our shared interests, but also some of them painful and conflicting, which contributed in equally important ways to building our community.

Collaborative learning is messy, not neat and linear. It's complicated and enriched by stories of experience. The story of our teaching collaboration, unlike most carefully written stories, has no fixed beginning or ending. It's a slow, and apparently "inefficient" process of construction, with inevitable starts and stops, and sometimes outright failures to understand or agree. The talk is tentative, a form of thinking-in-process, ephemeral, constantly changing. In the summer program we were dealing with complex, cumulative, often contradictory processes, representing many interests, and these interests are often conflicting and always changing. Narrative learning, especially oral narrative learning, was largely the way we negotiated these complexities in our summer program.

The Dewey story about literacy, like many other stories about literacy in many different school settings, depends on the stories of cultural conflict about such issues as eating on the street. Multiple perspectives are needed to inform and construct this story, and negotiating these cultural conflicts together in *conversation*, where they could best be addressed, has been crucial to our learning about these issues. These stories that we share are not "relative" but committed — toward students, toward the preservation of the best of culture and community, and toward changing what needs to be changed. This larger story, comprised of our collective stories, is a kind of act of imagination that is committed to change, to teaching and learning, to social justice.

Works Cited

Bruner, Jerome. 1986. *Actual minds, possible worlds*. Cambridge: Harvard University.

Delpit, Lisa. 1988. The silenced dialogue: Power and pedagogy in educating other people's children. *Harvard Educational Review* 58(3): 280–98.

The Dewey Center Community Writing Project. 1989. *Corridors: Stories from inner city Detroit*. Ann Arbor: Center for Educational Improvement Through Collaboration.

Egan, K. 1987. Literacy and the oral foundations of education. *Harvard Educational Review* 57(4): 445–72.

Gates, H. L. 1989. Narration and cultural memory in the African-American tradition. In *Talk that talk: An anthology of African-American storytelling*. New York: Simon and Schuster.

Glassie, H. 1982. *Passing the time in Ballymenone: The culture and history of an Ulster community*. Philadelphia: University of Pennsylvania.

Hale-Benson, J. E. 1986. *Black children: Their roots, culture and learning styles*. Baltimore: Johns Hopkins University.

Labov, W. 1972. *Language in the inner city*. Philadelphia: University of Pennsylvania.

O'Flaherty, W. D. 1988. *Other people's myths*. New York: Macmillan.

Polakow, V. 1985. Whose stories should we tell? Critical phenomenology as a call to action. *Language Arts* 62(8): 1–16.

Robinson, J., and P. Stock. 1990. The politics of literacy. In *Conversations on the written word: Essays on language and literacy,* by Jay Robinson. Portsmouth, NH: Boynton/Cook.

Smitherman, G. 1977. *Talkin and testifyin: The language of black America.* Detroit: Wayne State University.

Response One

Hazel Lockett

David Shaafsma's account of eating on the street in Detroit and different teachers' responses to the incident reminded me of the old image of America as a melting pot. I wonder what the person who coined the cliché would make of the stew that's described in this story about the Dewey Center Community Writing Project.

The conflict among the teachers about eating in public reflects the complexity of attitudes towards behavior, highlighting the fact that there are no right or wrong positions and that we have strong feelings about what seem to be quite insignificant cultural practices. And everybody's got "reasons" for their views. Joyce could certainly justify her position; Susan could justify hers. It's not the differences of opinions about what's good behavior that matter in this account, though; it's the fact that the group talked, wrote, and argued about their differences. I want to suggest that having a climate that's open enough to encourage people to talk about these matters is essential: It's what we teachers and our students need to be able to do if we're to survive—even prevail—in classrooms that are culturally diverse.

Like all teachers, I've had to make difficult (on-the-spot) decisions and take unpopular actions in light of my judgment about what the public perceives to be good behavior. On one occasion several of my (mostly black) students, who were on a three-day field trip, were scheduled to eat dinner in a cafeteria. To make sure that they all knew how to handle themselves, we had pre-trip sessions to answer questions and to give students examples of every possible kind of situation in which they might find themselves. We wanted them to look good and feel good about their behavior on that trip! But the actual visit to the cafeteria presented a problem. When students finished eating, they moved from table to table, talking to their friends and enjoying the action. My co-chaperone and I told a few students that it wasn't acceptable to table-hop in this restaurant and asked them to spread the word. No complaints! Students seemed to be grateful that a possible problem had been solved before the situation became unpleasant.

Aside from consideration for other people in the cafeteria, our motivation was similar to Joyce's and Susan's. We did not want people in the restaurant to think that our students were just another group of black kids who hadn't been trained to eat out, that they didn't care how others perceived them—that they hadn't been brought up to be courteous in public. In the back of my mind, perhaps, was the concern that some people find black youth inadequate for most public occasions, no matter what choices they make, and also that some think poor behavior by *any* black represents poor behavior by *all* blacks. (I don't know if white teachers feel this way about white students.) The idea is always in my mind that the destructive fire of prejudice does not need additional fuel in the form of my students' unconventional behavior.

Accounts such as David Shaafsma's remind us that teachers from all cultures need to be aware that neither we nor our students are "finished." We should also admit that mainstream adults in the USA are neither likely to be tolerant of teenage blacks and other students of color who act in culturally different ways nor to have high expectations of them. From my own experience as a black teacher and student, I have observed the looks of surprise on some of my peers' faces when I've contributed to the classroom discourse.

I teach in a district that is overwhelmingly black, which is not an unusual circumstance in urban schools these days, but I find that I must be very sensitive to cultural practices to avoid friction and mis-understanding. A few years ago, I had an African-American student who was a Pentecostal Jew (this fact I did not know). One day he appeared in class wearing a yarmulke. I jumped to the conclusion that he was somehow mocking a Jewish practice, and I asked him to remove the yarmulke. I doubted him when he told me that he was celebrating a ritual that required him to wear the yarmulke, and it took repeated assurances from the student and two of his friends to convince me that he had a good—religious—reason for breaking my rule that males are not to wear headgear in my classroom. After reading David Shaafsma's narrative, I see that I missed an opportunity to examine with the entire class our cultural "rules" about wearing hats or covering our heads. In retrospect, I see missed chances for interviews, library research, and real dialogue and learning.

It's worth mentioning that in my class, in a school that I've described as "overwhelmingly black," we had—to my knowledge—Muslims, Christians, and an African-American Jew. Can you imagine what it was like when we tried to plan a party? So most of our classrooms are "melting pots," or perhaps they're more like cultural stews—or, as a friend says, mixed salads: each group brings to the bowl its own unique ingredient that has the potential to create a new taste without losing textures and flavors.

I don't imagine that many of us are going to have access to collaborative teams such as the one operating at the Dewey Center to help us change our teaching environment through critical reflection, but we can — in all our classrooms — use some of the group's techniques to enrich our understandings of each others' behaviors — eating, dressing, writing, and so on. I'm imagining classrooms where students — and teachers — talk and write informally to each other about their daily experiences and about learning and teaching. Classrooms where inner city teachers and students tell each other stories about their lives and discover common ground among the differences.

I read "Eating on the Street" not so much for information about how the collaborative event at the Dewey Center worked but for ideas about how my own classroom functions as a place where our learning about each other as individuals with cultural and social histories changes and improves the way we learn math, English, and other subjects. "Eating on the Street" also gives me a way to think about what happened in my own classroom in 1989—90 when, using the workshop approach described by Nancie Atwell, I asked my students to write on topics of their choice in genres of their choice. I did not demand "correctness," and I did not mark individual pieces of writing — new departures for me. Under these circumstances, my students wrote more and wrote better than any students I've worked with before: they produced four portfolios with as many as twenty-five pieces of writing in each folder. They talked about themselves and each other as writers — and they became writers. Of course I want my students — all of them — to be able to produce carefully edited writings that we are proud of, but I am reconsidering the proposition that they will learn to do so in "rule-governed" classrooms.

Response Two

Ken Macrorie

When asked to write this response, I was told that the editors weren't looking for a customary analysis or critique, but rather for comments that go beyond what the writer has said, or take off from it, in other words, to show the consequences of the writing in a reader's mind. I accept the invitation.

1

As I read this case history again and again, I found myself enjoying most what these teachers and students had to say in interviews. Their words were clear and moving. Often the statements made by scholars whom David Schaafsma quoted were unclear or verbose. And so were some of David's generalizations.

I sensed the irony in the fact that in the Dewey Project he seemed to want school to respect the mother tongue of black English while still helping students learn standard English, and yet at times he and the scholars he quoted were writing in an "academic discourse" difficult to understand partially because it has little relation to anyone's mother tongue.

2

Behind the surprise that white teachers in this case history felt about two black teachers' responses to black students eating on the street lies the fact that in a multiracial or multicultural society members of the most powerful group seldom know much about the culture of less powerful groups. This has always been true. Colonized people are forced to take jobs as servants or slaves. They live and/or work in the homes of the colonizers, doing their bidding, often helping to raise their children. The reverse is not true. The colonizers do not take jobs as servants or slaves to the colonized. They do not live or work in the homes of the colonized. So the colonized know much more about the culture of the colonizers than vice versa. George Bernard Shaw brought out this truth humorously in his play *Arms and the Man* (1894), which is written from the point of view of knowledgeable and thoughtful servants working for a "noble" family in an imaginary European country.

3

Often in contemporary America, educated whites, when pressed, resent suggestions that they read the literature or learn the language of small African-American or Native cultures within the larger white culture. They say they already have enough to do to keep up with the literature and language of their own culture.

Now in the United States many writings by Africans, African-Americans, and Native Americans are available, yet their numbers are not overwhelming. For example, reading just the following five books would furnish a considerable insight to white readers into black culture: *Narrative of the Life of Frederick Douglass* (1845), *What the Negro Wants* (1944), *The Autobiography of Malcolm X* (1964), *Talkin and Testifyin: The Language of Black America*, by Geneva Smitherman (1977), and *Invented Lives: Narratives of Black Women 1860–1960* (1987), edited by Mary Helen Washington. A reader of these books can see how well the African-American authors and editors know the white culture in America.

I don't mean here to sound as if I, a white American, have a wide or deep knowledge of nonmainstream cultures in the United States. I haven't here mentioned the Hispanic or Latino culture or its literature because I am very little versed in either.

4

Often I like to think of what's fair, or just, in human interaction rather than what's decreed or established as the right thing to do or say. Is it fair that so-(badly)called members of "minority" cultures are expected to master a dialect of the "majority" culture called standard English? And that members of the "majority" culture are not required to master the black English dialect of African-Americans? Oh well, I know that the power games in any society are played out in more or less standard language, but I'm talking about fair and just, not required, prescribed, patterns used as ways to put down people or keep them in their place. I'll even take *logical* as a criterion. Say "If a person is one-tenth black, then he is a black." And, "If a person is one-tenth white, then he is a white." You see the logic of that.

One difficulty of the language problem that comes lurching up in this case history about "Eating on the Street" is that most citizens have little knowledge of how much anyone's mother tongue is an unconscious power of every human being. The linguist Edward Sapir said, "Language is human behavior."

5

Another point about fairness. In David Schaafsma's next-to-last section of "Eating on the Street," students talk to say what's on their tongue rather than to figure out what a teacher would like to find there. Dora says:

> It's not sloppy to eat on the street, because little kids get hungry more often than what grown-ups did when they was little. Adults don't understand the way that kids be like.

I wonder what Dora is basing that first assertion on. I'm guessing that she has no factual basis for it. But I think it's fair and just that her words are being heard in the Dewey Center in Detroit and are reaching us readers wherever we are. She may be feeling a deep resentment against grown-ups. I would ask her to write freely how she feels that adults are treating her and her peers. It won't do to dismiss her feeling because she expressed it in exaggerated terms.

I'm grateful for the invitation to say these things.

12

Talking About School
A Two-Part Invention

Jill Kazmierczak
Richard J. Murphy, Jr.

This essay is a joint effort. It represents a conversation carried on over two and a half years. We are both teachers now, but when our talk began, we were teacher and student. Connected by institutional chance in an academic course and a teacher-training program, we were trying in our separate (and conflicting) ways to make school work for us. This account of our talk traces our experience inventing a relationship whereby we could work together. It is a personal story.

Recent discussions of power and authority in the classroom, of class or gender relations in school, and of the pedagogy of writing instruction have tended to disregard the personal. Instead, they present teachers and students as abstract values in a systematic relationship. Paulo Freire's *Pedagogy of the Oppressed* (1970), to take one example, is a sustained essay in abstraction. According to Freire, for instance, "teachers and students (leadership and people), co-intent on reality, are both Subjects, not only in the task of unveiling that reality, and thereby coming to know it critically, but in the task of re-creating that knowledge" (56). Such abstraction is due in part to the fact that the writer is articulating generalized analysis of education. In the interests of advocating broad political change or curricular reform, such universalizing language is desirable. The abstract style is also due in part to the difficulty of rendering persuasively the particular experience of individual teachers and students. We believe, however, that generalized analysis will only have value — can only be understood and can only inspire reformed practice — so long as it is grounded in the complex experience of particular persons.

224

In order to contribute to this grounding experience, we offer the following story about ourselves. We have written it to make apparent the complexity of the transaction between student and teacher. Its themes are not new. They inform every classroom and at one time or another are the experience of every teacher and student. Although curriculum design may be based on abstract models of cognition, moral development, the nature of knowledge, and the processes of learning, it is implemented by persons who fear and hate, respect and love one another. In focusing on such themes, we must admit our own self-absorption and the extent to which it disabled us in our work. We also risk distorting our experience. The perspective we take disregards most of our daily functioning amid the enormous number of ordinary tasks school sets for both teachers and students. We believe, however, that the usual business of school is always interwoven with feeling and that the dynamics of teaching and learning are always personal. For this reason, we want to challenge the tidiness of systemic analysis by insisting on the tangle of our own experience.

Murphy: The Writing Across the Curriculum Program at Radford University arranged an end-of-the-year workshop for a group of faculty to write about their teaching. I was one of the participants. We had been meeting with each other throughout the year, talking together about our plans for our courses, and collecting materials to use in writing retrospective accounts of how they worked. The workshop was scheduled for the week in May after graduation.

I had great misgivings. I had agreed to participate and write, but the course I was to write about — a graduate course in the teaching of writing — had failed. No one outside of it knew how badly. It had disintegrated.

When Dixie Goswami came to Radford University in late February to talk with our faculty group about teaching, she told us we could learn from our students. We could ask them to review their own notebooks, to look for specific passages where they saw themselves learning, and then to write to us about those moments. We could draft tentative descriptions of our courses or of some elements in them and then give those drafts to our students for their comment. We could ask them to write companion descriptions to ours, setting next to each other our different accounts of how learning and teaching occurred. "Ask your students," she said.

She gave no assurances. The answers we got might be thin or unintelligible. They might be discouraging. But the promise of her simple suggestion was obvious. If we asked our students about our teaching and their learning, we might gain insight into our classrooms that our own analysis and reflection alone would be unable to provide.

It is not clear to me now what sort of insight I supposed that might be. But if I was going to try to analyze my own teaching, then it immediately seemed right that I should ask my students what they thought. My unsuccessful course, the obligation to write about it, and Goswami's suggestion converged: I should ask students to join the inquiry.

Still, it was not until two months later, during the last week of classes in the spring, that I decided to ask Jill Kazmierczak, one of the students in the course, if she would work with me. She had come to my office for something else — supplies, the photocopier auditron, something — and I suddenly found myself doing it, cautiously, not knowing how to say what I wanted, not knowning what she would say in reply.

We have been writing back and forth to each other ever since — freewriting, letters, the essay for the Radford faculty, a conference paper, and drafts of this chapter. We have each returned time and again to reflecting on that moment.

Kazmierczak: I paused outside his door, as I usually did, and listened for voices. Often, if Rich were conferencing with students or talking on the phone, I'd come back later. Though his office door was usually open so we could get supplies or borrow books about teaching and writing, I rarely just walked in. This time, though, the whir of his computer and the tapping of keys let me know I would not be interrupting a conversation, so I went in. As I picked up the pen to sign out the auditron, he turned, his hands leaving the keyboard as he began to speak.

I don't remember his exact words when he asked me to work with him — "I am going to be writing an essay about our course last fall for a writing-across-the-curriculum project." I do remember that he spoke quietly, slowly, as if he were selecting each word and placing it before me. "I thought the course didn't go so well," he said to me, "and I was wondering if you would help me talk about what happened."

He looked serious. He was not nodding and telling me how this promised to be a valuable learning experience for me. He was not suggesting that my experience as a writer would be broadened. He wasn't trying to sell me on this. He was simply asking.

Murphy: Eleven new graduate teaching fellows were enrolled in English 551: Teaching Expository Writing. I had assigned seven books, a presentation, a long paper, and weekly journal entries reflecting on the reading, their course work, and their teaching. At the end of the fourth week of the semester, Jill closed her journal entry with this terse sentence, "I hate what's going on here."

Kazmierczak: It was not as simple as that sentence sounds.

I watched him teach at the beginning of the year. In one of our earliest classes, he made a presentation about student writing that astonished me with its energy and concentration. I remember walking out of the building with a classmate into the night air and saying, "*That's* how I want to be able to teach. *That's* what I want to be able to do."

But as much as I admired his mind and style, I was suspicious of some of his ideas. As we were preparing for the fall semester to begin, he recommended that I not grade my students' papers. We were standing in the hall outside the secretaries' office where other members of the department were lined up, running off their syllabi. "The grade will get in the way," he said.

"Why?" I asked. I had never had a teacher who left my writing ungraded.

"Well, if we want to encourage students to revise, we have to regard these as drafts," he said. "If we grade them, the students will be more concerned with pulling their papers up a letter grade than with rethinking."

He was very emphatic, but I was not convinced. It sounded vaguely dishonest to me. I thought that students would want — and deserved — to know how they had done, to know where they stood.

One afternoon, still early in September, as he was passing through our office, I asked him how many words long our journal entries should be. I had read the assignment description he handed out. It was ambiguous about length — 1500 words a week, more or less, as a ballpark figure, a target to shoot at, and so on. His answer was more ambiguous still. "I'm not going to count the words," he said. But then why bring up the number of words at all? I thought. What struck me more than his answer, though, was his tone. A sort of irritation, impatience, a condescending smile, as if I should know better than to ask about such a thing. As if I had done wrong to try to figure out what he meant.

In class the week before I wrote that journal entry, Rich put a transparency of a student paper up on the wall. Then he divided us into groups and asked us to examine the paper for looseness and redundancy. "Cut massively," he said, and away we went, slashing with abandon.

I was shocked. I couldn't believe he was doing that, criticizing the paper projected up on the wall in front of us, belittling it like that, years after it was written, totally out of the context in which it had been composed. It seemed to me that he was laughing at it, urging us to laugh at it, each time we found another word or phrase to cut. All I could think about (as I sat there appearing to do what he had asked) was that he could do that to me and to my writing, too. It made me think for the first time that he didn't really respect his students the way he said he did.

I cannot speak for the other graduate teaching fellows, but in spite of my regard for his reputation and authority and my initial respect for him as a person, I began very early to distrust him.

Murphy: Frustration and animosity in the course were widespread. Instead of becoming catalysts for productive inquiry and exchange, the reading and writing assignments had become hollow tasks. Class discussions had become strained and superficial, suffused with what felt to me like a vague but almost constant hostility. The students complained about the journal — said its purpose was unclear, its length too long, said they didn't know what I wanted them to write. I asked them to prepare a presentation designed for an audience of other writing teachers and to rehearse it with the members of the course. Then I encouraged them to propose their presentations the following spring for the program of the state association of teachers of English; no one did. I was unable either to create or foster within the course a conversation about the teaching of writing. The talk that developed among the students outside the course was a result more of their sharing an office and the common job of teaching than of their being members of a classroom community.

I could not understand what was fueling the class's negative energy. It seemed clear to me that, in their first semester of both graduate school and teaching, there were a host of different reasons for individual anxiety and uncertainty, but these did not add up to a coherent group complaint. I continued to ask everyone to bring me their questions or concerns, but few actually did, and the tone of the class grew even more sour. By the tenth week of the semester, sitting around a large table, a number of students voiced seething anger, nothing was resolved, and we adjourned. In a few weeks, the course ended similarly: the work was finally over; we disbanded. It was not how I thought the course would end. It was not what I hoped for when it began.

Kazmierczak: It is hard now to recall the trepidation I felt when I began the graduate program. Opening the envelope, holding my breath as I unfolded the letter to read "pleased to offer you admission . . . ," and then reading it again, "offer you admission," and again, just to be sure, "offer you admission. . . ." "I'm in! I'm in!" I yelled as I danced side steps from the mailbox to my house. An offer for a position as a teaching fellow and a tuition scholarship followed. I remember practicing my penmanship on the back of an envelope before I signed the teaching contract. I wanted so badly to do well.

During the summer before the program began, I made weekly visits to the university bookstore to buy the texts arriving for the teaching-of-writing course. I read Mina Shaughnessy's *Errors and Expectations* (1977) in the sun, marking pages with scraps of paper until there were so many white paper markers that my book looked like it had sprouted a head of white hair. I practiced telling my horse what she most needed to know to write her first essay in college. I worried about learning my freshman students' names, I worried about making friends with the other graduate teaching fellows, and mostly I worried about making good grades in graduate classes.

It was with all that fear and desire that I first shook hands with Rich, the program director. We sat in his office. He asked some innocent question — what brought me to Virginia? or something — and suddenly we were off, talking about my brother's mountain climbing in Nepal, about oriental rugs. I had thought he would ask why I had gotten a C in my undergraduate Romanticism class. I was waiting for him, trying to pick up any signal that I was on the wrong tangent, talking about the wrong things. But he was listening to me, asking me about the altitude of the base camp on Dhaulagiri, asking about the Sherpa guides, asking me about Kathmandu. I had no idea whether or not he thought I was capable of teaching a course in Freshman English, but this was unexpected. He was talking to me.

When the semester began, the reality of the task of graduate school and teaching was more than I had imagined on those sunny summer afternoons. By the third week, I was swimming in student papers, revisions, journals. I had already run out of lesson plans from the August orientation workshop for new teachers and was struggling to be inventive on my own. Assignments from my graduate classes were coming due. I was moving as fast as I could to get my work done, unsure how well I was doing, and I could not get from Rich a clear assessment of either my performance or my progress.

Rich would not give us evaluations until the end of the semester. Keep grades, he had said, in their limited and proper position — at the end; we wouldn't receive an evaluation of any kind until the last day. Ask Rich how you did, the question would boomerang back: "How do *you* think you did?" Persevere and ask again, he would square his shoulders and say through thin lips, "Fine."

Eventually I quit asking, but I never quit wondering if my performance as a student in his class and as a teacher in the classes he
observed was up to his standards.

Murphy: Every time I watched her teach I admired her work. She
moved easily, smoothly. Her voice was quiet and exact, yet full of
animation. "Is it beautiful out there today, or what?" she would
say with a smile as she swung her briefcase up onto the desk at the
front of the room. She had never taught before, but it looked like
something she had done in her dreams. The classes I visited were
organized and focused. She asked questions that got students talking
and then, listening closely, asked more about what they said. She
drew students in, noticed who was quiet, solicited their opinions
too. When she handed back papers, she had something personal to
say to everyone, connecting herself with them and their work in a
brief comment or exchange. Moving down the aisles, around the
room, changing the geography of the space. Everything quick,
nothing rushed. Everything clear and purposeful.

I cannot imagine not telling her that this is what I saw when I
watched her teach. When I look back now at the notes I gave her
at the time, they seem full of pieces of this picture. But I know
that it was months before I gave her something like my full impression of her teaching. As much as I wanted her to reflect on her
own work and evaluate it against her own sense of purpose, I was
not trying to keep my regard a secret. I thought she was very
skillful. I thought her teaching was very good. I thought her poise
and my appreciation of it were obvious.

She said she could hardly control the shaking in her hands,
and every day she expected to trip and fall there in the front of the
classroom.

Kazmierczak: I watched his reactions carefully. All the new graduate
teaching fellows watched him, and we all thought we saw the same
thing: Don't believe it when he praises you because he does that
too often, and besides he wouldn't tell you if you were doing
poorly. Give a great answer to a question, "Bravo!" Rich would
shine. Do a fancy maneuver to pick up a pencil that fell from a
student's desk in front of you, "Bravo!" would ricochet across the
room again.

One day a few of us were gathered in our office of blue
carrels. Someone arced a wadded-up page of writing into the
garbage can; someone else said, "Bravo!" Laughter. Suddenly we
realized we'd all been hearing the same thing; we'd all been wanting
to believe it. Another page of notebook paper wadded up and
slammed in. A chorused "Bravo!" Another and another. Glee,

satisfaction, scorn, mockery. More paper, more bravos. The joke
was cemented, the alienation complete. It was us against him.

Murphy: When the semester was finally over, the course ended, but I
was unable to stop thinking about it. I played it back for myself
again and again. Though it was just the thing I least wanted to do,
I began to think that I should talk with students from the course
about what had happened. Partly it was Dixie Goswami's advice;
partly it was vertigo. I decided to ask the one student who seemed
to me to have been most bitter and angry. Not the student who
was loudest or most frantic or saddest, but the one who seemed to
me in her stern silence the most deeply critical.

Around the table that day late in the fall semester, Jill had
looked at me and said to us all: "This work is impossible. It cannot
be done." Her face was colorless with fury. Her words felt to me
like spit.

Kazmierczak: I went to see a friend on the faculty, told him I couldn't
do this, told him Rich was driving me crazy. He wouldn't give us
grades. We didn't know what he thought. I was angry. I couldn't
even stop being angry long enough to sound sane. "Stop whispering,"
my friend said. "You don't have to whisper. The door's closed."

"I can't help it," I said. "If I don't whisper, I'll scream."

Murphy: When I asked Jill for her help in May, I was not so afraid she
would say no, although I thought it very possible she might. I was
more afraid she would say yes, but that behind her eyes would be a
secret distance, a secret judgment. I was afraid that even as we
worked together, we would be working apart, divided by our
memories. All the while we were handling the facts of the course,
we would be tasting that old bile. I imagined that beneath the
surface of our work, the past would be replayed again between us.

But in fact Jill did not hesitate. She spoke more directly than
she had ever been able to when we were both entangled in the
course. Yes, she said, it was a failure. Yes, it was like a forest fire.
Yes, exactly, our office became a camp, and you were the enemy.
Yes, we mocked you behind your back. Yes, we didn't trust you,
we couldn't get a straight answer out of you, we didn't know what
you wanted, we needed your help and you wouldn't give it to us.

I asked her if she would help me think about what had happened.
She said yes, and then we talked and talked about the past.
Without alienation, and at last without fear.

Kazmierczak: Some afternoons we talked at the computer, sitting in
front of Rich's screen. He typed questions, I the answers—silent
but for a nodding head and then a clatter of keys, or a long breath
and then another response tapped out slowly. Our hands shifted

back and forth over each other across the keyboard. We worked separately in our offices, too, writing what we each saw happening at individual moments during the semester. Sometimes we walked around the campus talking, arguing, putting so much energy into the talk that we would find ourselves paused, stopped in the middle of the sidewalk, laughing.

During one of those pauses, I found myself asking him why, when he saw the course failing, why he so quixotically refused to accept his role as authoritarian. "Why not get up there and BE the teacher?" I huffed at him.

"That's not the solution," he said tautly, through thin lips.

"I know, but what are the alternatives?"

"Don't talk alternatives," he said. "What's the dream?"

"You didn't get your dream," I reminded him. "You got worse. We all got worse."

Murphy: It wasn't easy talk. Every day our collaboration had to be remade, and any day either of us could put an end to it. We argued. The more we permitted ourselves to say, the more complex and difficult our subject grew.

Kazmierczak: When we try to reconstruct what it was that finally made our cooperation possible, we can recover at least one strand of its fabric. During the August workshop before the fall semester — and the course — began, Rich and I had worked together in a writing group, responding to each other's essays about our parents — his about his father, mine about my mother. The next spring, as the year came thankfully near its end, the two of us were in different groups.

By this time, Rich had distanced himself from all of us. He didn't come to our office, and I rarely saw or spoke to him outside our weekly meetings. But I had gone to his office to return the auditron I had used to make photocopies of the draft of my essay for my group. As I signed the tally sheet for copies, I remembered what it had been like to work in that August group with him. Our four desks were pulled close together in a knot so tight that our feet bumped if anyone changed position. One of the members had written about a teaching experience that affected her so deeply she found herself dreaming about it. "You had this dream?" Rich said to her. "Over and over like you said here? That's wonderful." All of us were together at that moment.

Murphy: As the graduate students worked on their essays in August, I worked on one of my own. The draft excited me with its promise. When I read it to the members of my group, it wasn't finished, but I could feel its pulse and momentum. The group could feel it too;

they encouraged me to keep going. When it was done, I took it around to them individually and read it and asked for their suggestions and reactions.

It was an essay about my relationship with my father, about my being, as he used to say, "his son, the writing teacher." It retold a story from his childhood that he had shared with me only in his old age. I tried to make both the story and his telling of it merge together for the reader with my sense — as his son — of what both meant. The writing absorbed and pleased me.

I remember sitting with Jill at her desk, ten days after the program began, going over it word by word, cutting bits she thought were clichéd. I remember asking her to help me with a detail: Did she know what that lever was called that was used to cock a BB rifle? The lever that wrapped around the trigger under the stock? It was a crucial detail in my father's story, but I couldn't remember what he had called it. Did she know what it was?

She didn't. No matter. We asked around the office. No one else knew either. "Call it a 'lever' for now," she said, and laughed.

Kazmierczak: Standing in his office in May, I thought about the changes that had come over us since then and said to Rich that it felt strange to be reading my draft to a new group. Copies in hand, I suddenly invited him to read it.

"Give me your essay," he smiled. "I'd love to."

I was glad to give it to him, glad to have him read it, thrilled he'd take the time to type a response, to respond at all. It reminded me of the verve with which we'd initially approached each other and our hopes for this program we'd be working together on.

Murphy: When we brought the first draft of our joint essay to the writing across the curriculum group of the Radford faculty, we received a criticism we didn't expect. It's too self-indulgent, they said. Too soft. So what? they said. The course was a bust, and now you're friends. What do you want readers to make of that?

We both knew they were right, and we have been working ever since to uncover both the grit of our experience and the wonder. We knew we would need to render more specifically the difficulties of the course.

Kazmierczak: It was a Monday morning. The end of September. I walked down the hall to the fountain for a drink of water, passed Rich at the copier, exchanged hellos. On my way back to my office, I noticed the black binder sitting on the paper feeder. I was three steps beyond the copier, through the doorway into my office when it registered — he's copying *my* journal.

I stood for a moment in disbelief. I had spent six pages telling stories about my students, sketching class discussions and what seemed to me to be important discoveries in their journal entries. Then at the end I wrote that the program, with all the bad feelings and complaining in the graduate office, was not doing justice to the small pleasures of teaching. I had missed a program meeting, and I had justified my absence by saying I was wonderfully busy with my students. I had ended the journal with "I hate what's going on here."

I stood there seething in anger and embarrassment, thinking that I should have known better than to have written something so critical of the program he directed, knowing I had walked by him twice without his even hinting at what he was doing. I wheeled around and went back to the copier where he stood.

Murphy: I copied her entry without asking her permission. She looked at me with such disgust that I woke in the middle of the night haunted by her face, hearing again her words: "I wouldn't sneak around copying *my* student's writing."

I tried to explain why I had photocopied her journal, tried to apologize, said I often made copies of pieces of student work, tried to tell her that I hadn't done so with hers because I thought she was "complaining" (her word for what she had written), but because the contrast between it and her expressed love for teaching in other parts of the same entry seemed so striking and puzzling to me. I gave her back the copy, promised to ask her permission in the future, tried to encourage her to continue to write freely.

No way, her face said: I'll just be sure to write from now on with awareness that what I write may be copied.

Sneak. That's what she said, and for all my talk, that's how I felt. I had misread her journal. I hadn't seen it as a complaint but as a lament. Then suddenly, she was out of reach, sitting at her desk, looking up at me as I stood at the door of her carrel, waiting for me to finish so she could get back to work. She had nothing more to say.

I wished she had not seen me copying her journal. I wished I had not copied it. I wished we could somehow bridge the guilt and anger and distrust, but talk was all I could think of, and there was nothing more to say.

Kazmierczak: We would pass each other in the halls and exchange polite greetings. He would observe the freshman classes I was teaching and take copious notes. I would attend his weekly class on the teaching of writing and keep looking down at my book.

Murphy: The night the class met to discuss Sondra Perl and Nancy Wilson's *Through Teachers' Eyes* (1986), the discussion felt especially dismal to me. One of the teachers described in the book, Ross Burkhardt, had had the worst year of his teaching life while he was being observed by researchers Perl and Wilson. I raised the question of his failure, asking the class to speculate about its causes, and to consider the place of his story in the book as a whole. The talk was lethargic.

What the teaching fellows apparently wanted to talk about instead was the journal assignment I had given them. Jill entered this discussion briefly, cryptically, suggesting that I eliminate the assignment. When I tried to examine aloud the implications of her comment, she seemed to withdraw, to look away, down at her notes, somewhere. She seemed to think that what I was saying bore no relation to her comment at all. After a few moments — annoyed that even *this* subject was going nowhere — I came back to her, asked again for her opinion. Her neck snapped a little when I said it, her eyes popping open, as if she had been publicly rebuked.

Kazmierczak: I had not read Perl and Wilson's book. I had *looked* at it and read the introduction, looked at the chapter about Audre Allison and at the kindergartners' handwriting. I sat for three hours wondering if it would be discovered that I had *not* done the assigned reading. It did not occur to me then that I had stopped learning, but now as I remember that evening I cannot recall the focus of the class, its issues or purpose. I was thinking of myself, feeling guilty and embarrassed. In reply to some comment I made, Rich said, "I don't know if this answers Jill's question; she's stopped looking at me."

I looked up, then down at my book, harder than ever.

Murphy: Some mornings, getting out of my car, I would see Jill's truck pull up and park on Fairfax St. I would watch her balancing her bag and briefcase and fast-food coffee, and I would try to calculate. Would our paths cross before we got to the steps of Washington, the building we shared? Should I delay and let her go first? If we met, we would have to walk together. What could we say to simulate cordiality? After "good morning" and the weather, our silence would be awful.

When she came to my office to talk about something specific — the presentation she was planning to make, for instance — it was easier. We had an agenda. She wanted help thinking about how to defend the modes of discourse or about how to talk about the uses of analogy in the teaching of writing. We could focus on the particular. But even as I seemed to be concentrating in these meetings on the business before us, I was unable to keep from calculating our paths, from trying to plan our courtesies.

Kazmierczak: I spent hours preparing my presentation, then raced through my examples and omitted a main point in my conclusion. My notes shook in my hand as I talked. I circled the room with my eyes, avoiding the corner where he sat. I was so disappointed in my performance, I stayed after class to talk to him about it.

Eventually the conversation broadened from my presentation to the context of the whole course. Rich asked me to talk to him about what I saw happening. I scoffed, "Oh, you mean, 'Let's share!'"

"That's my philosophy of teaching." He sounded disarmed.

Rich drew an analogy to a group of people climbing up a mountain with one person saying, "This can't be done. We can't make it." He was trying to prove that morale was the cause of the problems in the course. As he talked, I thought to myself, Look how smoothly he develops this group of climbers, how big he tells me the mountain is — difficult but manageable. It's a nice analogy. It fits. Look how he's trying to make me figure out for myself what he has in mind.

I thought he asked me to talk with him that night so he could refute me, defend himself, sway my opinion of him. I knew he would win if we got into a verbal battle. Yes, your argument is quite logical, I nodded. Yes, it is far clearer and more reasonable than my complaints.

Since then he has told me that our talk that night was very important to him — a "breakthrough," he called it. He thought it was a conversation we were having there. But the talk changed nothing for me. I remember driving back home then, my hands tight on the steering wheel, my knuckles white as the moon.

Murphy: In the course of our reflection on our experience, Jill was able to tell me what it had been like to be at the receiving end of my supervision. I scheduled visits to all the teaching fellows' classes three times during the semester. On each visit, I took detailed notes, recording as fast as I could the time sequence of the class, the instructions of the teacher, question-answer exchanges with students, occasional observations about student behavior or teacher manner, and as many specific names of participating students as I could catch on the wing. I also participated in the activities of the classes I visited, so sometimes my notes were more sketchy than others.

Whatever they were, I gave them to the teaching fellow after class, often without looking back at them myself and asked the teacher to make a copy for me for my files. These notes were the only written report of the class, and they were essentially descriptive rather than evaluative. The talk after the visit was informal and unstructured; it took as its subjects those features of the class that I or the teaching fellow found most striking. My goal was not to evaluate the class but to help the teacher reflect back on it and to speculate about its dynamics and effects.

Sometimes, the schedule of my visits precluded this immediate post-class talk. In such cases, I gave the teaching fellow my notes anyway, and we arranged a later time to talk.

Kazmierczak: Rich snapped off four pages of notes from the top of his legal pad as we headed out of my classroom. I knew most of what they would include — what was said in class; snippets of what the two guys in the back of the class were doing when I turned to write on the board. I thanked him and placed the pages in my folder. As we walked across the campus, we arranged a time to talk in more detail. Rich didn't have time now; he was scheduled to observe another teaching fellow's class.

We walked together to Young Hall, and as we started up the steps I asked him, "Could you tell me, just briefly, what you thought? I mean, how do you think it went?" He had stopped on the stair just below me; I stepped down. Instead of answering, he turned the question back at me: "Well, what did *you* think? How do *you* think it went?" I looked past his shoulder into the branches of the parking lot trees and thought: Oh, God, if I say it worked, he'll think it didn't and will think I'm just bragging or trying to influence his opinion. If I say it didn't work, he might have thought it went well and will revise his opinion. Besides, I'm not even sure if I know what works or not.

It seemed dishonest to me, his making me guess what he thought — as if he were evaluating not only my performance but also how close I could come to guessing *his* assessment of it.

"Can't you *just* tell me what you thought?" I said, trying to measure out my words without catching the aggravation I felt building.

"I thought it went fine," he said flatly.

Fine? I wanted to slug him right there on the steps.

"Okay," I said. "Thank you for coming."

Murphy: When Jill and I began at the end of the year to reconstruct our experience, we talked at every opportunity. We wrote to each other to focus our talk; we wrote afterwards about what we had said. We also read — other essays written by Radford faculty about their courses, published essays on the theory and practice of collaborative learning, articles on teacher research and the nature of academic work — and then we talked about what we had read.

One particularly helpful article was "A Discourse Not Intended for Her," jointly written by Magda Lewis and Roger Simon (1986). I was gripped by it. The two perspectives of the piece (Simon was Lewis's teacher in a graduate course) seemed arresting to me, daring. The two writers seemed willing to do something utterly fresh, to tell the story of the deep conflict between them. In generalizing their conflict as a gender issue, though, Lewis and Simon seemed to me to reduce rather than enlarge their story and to diminish rather than enhance its significance. Still their finding a way to collaborate seemed wonderful to me, and I thought we might try to follow their lead. As it has turned out, we have not only learned from their story and their analysis. We have borrowed, too, the antiphonal structure of their essay.

Kazmierczak: When I read the Lewis and Simon article, I saw better what it was we might do for the paper we were working on. It suggested a voice I thought we might assume in talking about what had happened. It presented a dilemma that sounded familiar. However much Rich tried to level his own authority with us, he could only do so from a position of authority. The forms of leveling he chose, therefore — asking us to call him by his first name, to sit in a circle, asking for our opinions on his writing, walking with us to the student union during class breaks — all came to seem to me contradictory.

At the same time, I did not want him to relinquish his authority. I wanted him to be the teacher and to take the responsibility to evaluate my work. Now when I look back over my whole experience of school, I see how heavily I relied on the judgment of my teachers, how my own judgments were significant to me to the extent to which they conformed to my teachers'. I realize I selected a field and chose classes that were of personal interest to me, but when I entered the classroom, I immediately, consciously or unconsciously, began searching for the teacher's standards. When clear evaluative standards were withheld — as Rich withheld grades — I found myself searching for evaluative feedback through informal remarks, marginal comments in my class journal, a nod of approval from the back of the classroom. Sometimes I asked point-blank, "How am I doing?" Being expected to ask myself that question seemed silly, knowing the final evaluation would not come from me.

During the semester in which I was his student, I was afraid of failing both as a student and as a novice teacher. Here was Rich, telling us not to worry about failing, not to think about grades and evaluations, because such thinking would limit us. Yet all I could think was that it was *my* grade, *my* fellowship, *my* scholarship at stake here: just tell me what you want me to do.

Working since with Rich has given me the perspective to say this is my education: here is what I think.

Murphy: During the semester in which I was her teacher, I was afraid of Jill because I thought she saw something wrong in me and in my work, but I didn't know what it was and she wouldn't (or couldn't) say. Across the distance between us, I felt her anger and disapproval, and they made me angry, in turn.

Our talk together later did not diminish her challenge. She made me see that my practice as a teacher has been riddled with contradiction. I have wanted students to read and write and think for themselves, to commit themselves to their work, and to evaluate themselves fairly and honestly. But I plan their schedule and structure their assignments as if they would not do it themselves. I treat them as novices, but I say that I consider them colleagues. In most circumstances, this contradiction makes my relationship with students ambiguous, and sometimes (as I think it did in the course we are describing) it can help ruin our work together.

In an early draft of our paper, I said that what Jill saw behind my eyes was an unwillingness to judge students and, in lieu of judgment, a latent scorn. She said she didn't think that was true. She cut it from the draft and said instead that what she saw — but did not understand at the time — was my fear of failing as a teacher. "It's ironic," she wrote, "your fear ignoring ours, missing mine."

When I asked her to help me think about what had gone wrong, I never imagined such a rapprochement as this. I had agreed to write a paper for my colleagues, but did not know what to say. I had taught badly but did not understand and could not explain either how or why. The failure of the course sapped both my energy and hope. I lost even the desire to teach. I did not suppose that if I asked Jill to talk with me about failure, she might say yes and in so doing transmute the experience into something whole and vital. I did not imagine that she would give me back faith in myself.

Kazmierczak: The retrospective talk between us at the end of that year was unlike anything I had ever experienced before. Fragile, sometimes bitter, more often gladdening — it felt reckless and free. As if all conventions were suspended, as if there were no rules. It felt to me as if we were inventing a language between us.

I did not know where we were going or how or if we would continue. Some days, some moments, I glimpsed the whole collaboration evaporating, us squaring off against each other. It shocked me — like suddenly seeing a gargoyle leering over the door of a church. And it frightened and saddened me because, for all its difficulty, this has been the single most valuable learning, thinking, talking I have ever done.

In constructing this version of our experience, we have tried to emphasize the concrete. We have selected only a few particular moments of interaction from the time during which we were, first, student and teacher, then collaborators in a conversation of thought, talk, and writing. We have underrepresented the context of our experience, said little about the bureaucratic structure within which we worked, given no space to the views of the other members of the course or the teaching fellow program. We assume that their experiences were different from ours; it is just the particular idiosyncracy of ours that we have found instructive. Our purpose was to recapture our working relationship in enough detail to permit us to examine in it some of the features and character of our own teaching and learning. But this means that our story is essentially personal. We have made it so deliberately.

Much of the recent literature about pedagogy and schooling is concerned with relations — power, gender, race, and class relations — among teachers and students and the social structures within which they function. Stanley Aronowitz and Henry Giroux (1988), for example, view pedagogy as "a deliberate and critical attempt to influence the ways in which knowledge and identities are produced within and among particular sets of social relations" (194). According to Roger Simon (1987), pedagogy is inherently political. "Talk about pedagogy," Simon says, "is simultaneously talk about the details of what students and others might do together *and* the cultural politics such practices support" (371). In such views of the relations between teachers and students, the emphasis is on what the personal *means* for politics or culture. The emphasis of our account is on what the personal *is*.

The tendency toward abstraction in the literature of pedagogy is criticized even among radical theorists of education. Elizabeth Ellsworth (1989), for example, takes Freire, Giroux, and Simon (among others) to task for the "high level of abstraction" of their generalized goals. According to Ellsworth, they all call for teachers to help students make deliberate moral choices, but they then provide "only the most abstract, decontextualized criteria for choosing one position over others" (300–301). And Harvey Weiner (1986), committed as he is to encouraging teachers to create collaborative learning opportunities for students, admits that it "is messier in practice than in theory; no one can *live* the theory as clearly as the model suggests" (60).

It is the mess of practice we want to represent. Our aim is to assert that because teaching and learning in school are so complex, the abstractions of the pedagogy literature are too limited. As we drafted our different versions of this account, we imagined a hostile reader throwing down our chapter and asking baldly — like our colleagues in the writing-across-the-curriculum workshop — "So what?" When we tried to generalize our experience, the answer eluded us. Our essay is about grading, we would tell ourselves. Yes, but not simply about grading. It is also about evaluations and authority, about the responsibility for learning, about risk and respect, desire and disillusionment. That is, it is about the personal dimension of the transaction of school — the dimension in which its structures are realized and its abstractions played out. We are one student and one teacher; we have come to know each other and ourselves better in our work. That is a world of knowledge. By tracing some of the vexing puzzle of its growth, we have tried here to represent only our personal answer: so everything.

Works Cited

Aronowitz, S., and H. Giroux. 1988. Schooling, culture, and literacy in the age of broken dreams. *Harvard Educational Review* 58: 194.

Ellsworth, E. 1989. Why doesn't this feel empowering? *Harvard Educational Review* 59: 300–301.

Freire, P. 1970. *Pedagogy of the oppressed.* New York: Seabury.

Lewis, M., and R. Simon. 1986. A discourse not intended for her. *Harvard Educational Review* 56: 457–72.

Perl, S., and N. Wilson. 1986. *Through teachers' eyes: Portraits of writing teachers at work.* Portsmouth, NH: Heinemann.

Shaughnessy, M. 1977. *Errors and expectations: A guide for the teacher of basic writing.* New York: Oxford University.

Simon, R. 1987. Empowerment as a pedagogy of possibility. *Language Arts* 4: 371.

Weiner, H. 1986. Collaborative learning in the classroom. *College English* 48: 60.

Response
Brenda S. Engel

This is the story, in two voices, of a misunderstanding—a painful, drawn-out misunderstanding. It provides the occasion for the authors (and readers) to reflect on some important issues: among others, the nature of the relationship between student and teacher, the ambiguous and often unrecognized effects of power and authority, sources of institutional change, and the relative usefulness of particularity versus generalization. Some of these issues are explicit, others suggested by the events recounted. Taking off, then, from my understanding of their misunderstanding, I will add another voice to the dialogue.

It's worth thinking about how such a missing of minds, resulting from differences in expectations between a teacher and his student, was possible for two people of obvious good will and intelligence. The phenomenon is common enough in education from kindergarten through graduate school. Most of the time, in such situations, there's little or no rapprochement: the students remain angry and contemptuous, the teacher self-righteous and unreformed. In this "Two-Part Invention" (wonderful subtitle!), however, the teacher was lucky enough to encounter Dixie Goswami and courageous enough to take up her suggestion, to "ask your students." The issues themselves are then "acted out" in the dialogue between teacher and student.

The explanation for how the misunderstanding was possible is contained in the dialogue itself which becomes something of a parable or cautionary tale. The dialogue is framed by two arguments, one at the beginning and one at the end, for the value of analysis "grounded in experience" as opposed to generalized or abstract analysis: "We believe . . . that generalized analysis will only have value—can only be understood and can only inspire reformed practice—so long as it is grounded in the complex experience of particular persons." The authors proceed to illustrate this belief by offering their own experience as a case study. Yet the events recounted tell the story of a teacher (one of the authors) who is himself a fool of ideology—of abstract pedagogical principles—which in fact causes his failure of rapport with the students in his course. If we think of ideology as abstraction, we have to understand that, in the essay, Richard Murphy is himself a case in point, an illustration of what nongrounded theorizing can lead to. It's not quite clear, however, that this is his intention.

I want to elaborate here an idea, a perennial favorite, which lurks behind the scenes in the essay. It has to do with the nature of institutional change: how paradigm shifts occur in the social sciences. In education, more than in the physical sciences, the rear guard seems to hold out and continues to dominate in the face of new knowledge coming out of experience and research. This results in an uneasy and incomplete relationship of practice to theory. To cite an example from elementary education, research and evidence from the last twenty years support a developmental theory of literacy learning: that new knowledge is built on old, that meaning is at the heart of learning, that children learn in different ways and at different rates, and that self-correction is central to intellectual growth. Most common practice influenced by the mythology of schooling, by institutional inertia in the face of change, and by standardized testing, still generally fails to take these ideas into account. Children are taught to read as though grade one were the beginning of learning, are given meaningless texts to decode and are required to practice meaningless exercises; their work is corrected by the teacher and they are expected to be at "grade level" on standardized texts. If a primary grade teacher is idealistic enough to forgo basal readers and workbooks in favor of literature, the children in her class are likely to come out poorly on the standardized tests.

My point is that a paradigm shift, to be effective, requires an entire reworking of the system. Partial, piecemeal change inevitably catches someone off base — usually the students. And evaluation is one of the system components that commonly lag. Practice may change — teachers become friends, students work, not for grades but to gain knowledge — but evaluation, like a dinosaur that has somehow survived from a bygone era, still looms and terrorizes.

Jill Kazmierczak was justifiably angry because the instructor imposed his own ideology, inconsistent with the still traditional practices of the institution — at least as far as evaluation is concerned — in which the course is embedded. It was also inconsistent with her experience and expectations and even, to some extent, with Murphy's own practice. He says, in effect, "I *want* you not to care about grades" — a bit like mandating autonomy.

What makes the account particularly sad is that Murphy, although an ideological fool, is also serious, high-minded, and (in my opinion) *right*. He aims to educate this group of students for change, so when they themselves teach, they will understand the difference between description and judgment and perhaps develop different, more mutually respectful relationships with their students. Education then can begin to change from a mindless, ritualized routine to a more rational, human activity.

There's a related subtext in the account, which is mentioned only briefly but makes it additionally painful: Richard Murphy's own insecurity. He seems almost to take refuge in ideology, withdrawing farther and farther from the students and, by his actions, denying their feelings, their natural and acculturated desire to know how *he* thinks they are doing. The repeated, somehow not quite authentic expression of approval, "bravo," reveals someone avoiding encounter, not coming out with a genuine, thoughtful response. And here it's hard to attribute his failure wholly to ideology. It looks more like personal uneasiness.

Hampered by ideology and perhaps by his own nervousness, Murphy failed to see the difference between giving a genuine response, informed by thought and considerable experience, and judgment from an institution-supported position of superior authority. "I was afraid of Jill because I thought she saw something wrong in me and in my work" and "what she saw—but did not understand at the time—was my fear of failing as a teacher." It was perhaps significant also that Murphy's own essay, which he showed individually to his students, concerned his relationship with his father, surely not a subject chosen haphazardly in that context. I was sorry that Jill Kazmierczak didn't comment on it in the essay and that we readers were not told its content.

Still, one can speculate that if the institution were not a qualifying agency, if Murphy were not constrained to give grades, if the student/teacher relationships were less loaded with institutional paraphernalia, a different relationship might have been possible. The students might have turned to Murphy for his experience and knowledge and he might then have been free to offer the kind of help Kazmierczak so poignantly misses: "We needed your help and you wouldn't give it to us."

I began by saying this is a painful story. One feels sympathy for both writers, caught in a situation that is mainly not of their making—where there's no really good solution because of the interfering demands of the institution. Somehow Murphy's claim near the end that their talks did "transmute the experience into something whole and vital" is not quite convincing; the language, coming from an otherwise straightforward, accomplished writer, seems too much a cliché. Kazmierczak's revelation, "It felt to me as if we were inventing a language between us," is more telling—and, finally, optimistic. A new language (although not neologisms) is needed—one that is grounded in, and emerges from, experience. This recognition allows the painful story told by these two writers to achieve at least a near-happy ending.

13

Negotiating the Curriculum
Children, Teaching Intern, and University Professor Together

Janet B. Taylor
Glynnis Glass McIntyre

Taylor's Introduction

Generally, we university professors are responsible for conducting and/ or directing research in order to contribute to the knowledge base of our discipline and are regarded as experts of that discipline. We are analytical and experimental in our research approaches as we attempt to contribute valid and reliable findings. In addition, we are entrusted with the responsibility of educating those who choose or are required to have some knowledge in our discipline. As a rule, we provide instruction through the traditional model of lecture, assigned readings, and laboratory assignments where applicable, and use graduate teaching assistants to grade our papers. We accept the notion that there will be a normal range of scores in each class and assign our grades accordingly. Rarely do we question the effectiveness of our teaching or wonder about those students who didn't make it. We consider the impact our teaching approach may have had on those results even less often.

On the other hand, elementary and secondary classroom teachers who prepare the students that frequent our classes have been the subject of much public scrutiny. Recent national studies (Carnegie 1986; Goodlad 1984; and others) have suggested the need to improve

Many thanks to Barbara Thompson for serving as the model teacher for the practicum, for sharing her wisdom, and for allowing us access to her wonderful kindergarten children.

the quality of the teaching at this level. Current educational reform is saying that these teachers can no longer accept the premise that "some will make it and others won't." Now, these teachers *must* wonder about students who are not "making it," examine the effectiveness of their own teaching, and find ways to modify their instruction in order to be more successful. To that end, some exemplary classroom teachers have used the "teacher as researcher" model of inquiry to learn more about the effect of their teaching. As they have shared their findings in published form (Branscombe 1987; and others), this model has developed a certain legitimacy as a means for examining and communicating knowledge about teaching.

Professors of teacher education have begun to take notice and support "teacher as researcher" as a way for classroom teachers to come to know and improve their practice, but few have moved beyond working as the expert university collaborator who advises classroom teachers as they conduct such research. Only a small number have been willing to consider doing such research on their own teaching.

I can make these statements because my ideas have changed about early childhood education. Before becoming a professor I taught for fourteen years in the public school setting. I left that setting only because I thought I could effect more change by teaching teachers and researching early learning at the university level. My doctoral program, like that of most of my colleagues, trained me to do experimental research. Furthermore, it helped shape my view of qualitative research as soft, subjective, and better left to the anthropologists. The teacher-as-researcher model was not mentioned. Thus, it is not surprising that when I began my first university teaching assignment ten years ago, I did experimental research, lectured, and functioned as a highly traditional professor in and out of the classroom.

This teaching style was not the style I used in my kindergarten classroom, nor was it consistent with the constructivist style (that is, to create a learning environment in which students can actively construct their own knowledge and to facilitate their interaction with the environment) I had expected my kindergartners to learn. My children and I were active co-learners, who valued one another's knowing. We talked, listened, shared, and collaborated on projects. We were problem solvers and decision makers. When we built houses, painted pictures, acted out plays, and baked gingerbread men, we worked cooperatively to resolve issues about obtaining and using materials. Not only were we active learners, but we also practiced self-examination and reflection, which were, in my view, two essential elements for thinking about learning. Because of this environment, we did not rely on outside experts to tell us what to do. We conducted our own inquiries, did our own readings, and then acted and evaluated.

Why had I reverted to a traditional approach of teaching at the university level? Why had I abandoned all that I had learned from the children when I walked into the university setting? My first five years of university teaching allowed me little time to consider such questions. My goals, and those of most other assistant professors, were to teach my classes, supervise student teachers, conduct research, write grants, publish, get promotions, make tenure, and survive at the university level. It was only as I began to realize that I would survive, that I began to question my teaching. I found myself longing for the active learning and collaboration that I had shared with the kindergarten children. I also found myself wondering how I could modify the teaching styles evinced in our graduates. As I questioned and reflected on my teaching, I began to make changes.

At first, my changes related to inviting students to discuss rather than listen to me lecture. Next, I began to include assignments that required them to be researchers of learning rather than practicers of teaching. At the same time I began to do some collaborative research with graduate students who were teachers in the field. Of course, I functioned in the role of the university expert, who guided and directed their research.

My first *real* collaborative research occurred when I was developing an idea about a shared writing experience for kindergarten and primary children. At first it was very difficult for me to acknowledge the contributions the classroom teacher made to the practice and to the research. As I eased into it, though, the experience became like my kindergarten experience — co-researchers examining and reflecting on practice.

I continued to do such research with other teachers over the next three years. In my opinion, this was genuine, collaborative teacher research. Because it examined the practice of others in their classrooms, however, I was distanced from some aspects of the teacher-as-researcher process. I was still safe. I had not inquired about my own teaching. I had not felt the terror or power of such research.

Five years later, I had the opportunity to take the last step in the process and engage in an inquiry about my own teaching. It happened rather serendipitously when Glynnis G. McIntyre, one of the most promising students I had encountered in our undergraduate program, asked me to direct her graduate level practicum, and I agreed. As my student in a ten-hour early childhood course that focused on constructivist language arts and social studies curriculums, Glynnis had "learned" the rationale and strategies for implementing shared journal writing, a process that I developed and researched with others. Additionally, she and her classmates implemented this process in a summer laboratory program for four- through eight-year-old children.

From my supervision of her during this experience, I anticipated that Glynnis would have a successful internship. I also thought that she would not only meet all of the classroom teacher's expectations, but also model constructivist teaching strategies, such as shared journal writing, in such an efficient and effective manner that it would influence the classroom teacher's practice. I was convinced that Glynnis was firmly rooted in constructivist theory about how children learn, and that she would base her instructional decisions on this knowledge.

I was shocked when I learned that my expectations were not confirmed. During her student teaching experience, Glynnis mistrusted the whole shared journal process, and believed that parts of it were questionable, and perhaps even harmful, with second-grade children. Her thinking about the practice was influenced by her own experiences with children and by the corroborating opinion of her classroom teacher-supervisor. I wondered how this could have happened, and what this suggested about my teaching methods.

When Glynnis began her graduate work, she discussed her concerns about the practice with me. By this time, she seemed to assume that the problem had been due to her failure to implement the strategies "correctly," or at least that is what I thought she assumed. Nevertheless, she wanted to do a graduate practicum that would improve her skill in the process, and answer some of the questions she had related to the practice. Needless to say, I was delighted to serve as "expert" once again and to supervise the practicum. I thought that this would give me the opportunity to reestablish Glynnis's convictions, and help her learn how to base her instructional decisions on those convictions rather than on vague emotional responses or some external forms of authority. In other words, I could "rescue" Glynnis.

Additionally, since I judged that I had been less than successful with her at the undergraduate level, I was interested in examining how I might be more effective in bringing about change. To that end, I set up her practicum by selecting four strategies that the literature suggested as effective change strategies for teachers. I placed Glynnis in a kindergarten classroom of twenty-two children with a highly competent model who had used the shared journal process for a number of years. Secondly, I asked Glynnis to keep a journal of daily entries that would allow her to reflect on her teaching and raise questions related to that teaching and the children's actions and responses. Next, I arranged for weekly conferences with me so that we could discuss her progress and address her questions or concerns. Lastly, I scheduled regular video-taping of her sessions with the children, so that Glynnis could observe her own teaching and the children's responses to that teaching.

The Inquiry

After our initial brainstorming session on September 28, Glynnis and I agreed that along with the practicum we would become co-researchers of learning; gather and analyze data and in that way explore if and how she changed her beliefs and practice, what contributed to that change, and if and how that change influenced the children. We planned to collect our data during the five-week practicum (seventy-five clock hours with the children) near the beginning of the school year in the public school of a small rural community in the southeastern part of the United States. We decided to analyze Glynnis's daily journal entries, transcriptions of the audiotaped conferences with me, transcriptions of the videos of her teaching, Glynnis's written reflections of the video viewing, and anecdotal records of her interactions with the classroom teacher, as well as my field note observations of her in the classroom. Glynnis and I used the data analysis as the final step of the study to fit practicum experience requirements.

Negotiation was to be the common theme for our research because just as Glynnis wanted to learn more about the role of negotiation and the value of having children exchange points of view within the shared journal process, I also wanted to examine the nature of the negotiation and interaction that took place among Glynnis, the classroom teacher, the children, and myself as we conducted our practicum. We decided that we would examine negotiation as it occurred when groups of individuals work together to reach some mutually agreed upon decision.

Negotiation requires individuals to explicate and share their reasoning either about what is true (in the intellectual realm) or what is right (in the moral realm). Cooperation and argument are essential to this collaborative process. From a constructivist perspective, cooperation and mutual agreement are possible only when all individuals in the group perceive their role in the decision-making process as equal. When equality is perceived, differences in reasoning can be argued in a forum that requires individuals to listen to and consider other points of view, and to resolve issues that are in disagreement. Through the process of conflict resolution, individuals advance their own thinking by moving to higher levels of coordination and by eliminating previously held notions that now are recognized as incomplete or erroneous. This kind of conflict resolution leads to mutually agreed upon decisions. When equality is not perceived, individuals who view their role as subordinate often will simply bow to a decision of the co-worker even though they don't really agree with it.

Within the shared journal process (Taylor 1984), negotiation occurs after two or three children have shared events they believe will be of interest to their classmates. Since shared journal is a collaboratively determined chronicle of events in their lives, the task during this negotiation is to decide which of the events shared should be recorded in the journal for that day. Theoretically, at the first of the year, teachers initiate this process by asking the children to suggest which events they want to remember through writing, and to explain to the class their reason for preferring that topic. The teachers then ask other children whether they agree or disagree with that suggestion and why. From their reasoning, the children must arrive at some kind of majority or collective decision about what is to be recorded in their journals that day. As the year progresses, the children assume more and more of the responsibility for the conduct of the discussion, and the teachers remove themselves from the discussion to observe the hypotheses the children use as they grow in their ability to establish and communicate a point of view, to support a point of view, to consider different points of view, and to select and present subject matter that will appeal to their audience.

As Glynnis's teacher, I was interested in examining the kinds of negotiation that would occur between us prior to, during, and after the practicum; if and how we collaboratively made decisions about the practice, the effectiveness of her implementation of the process, and the value of the change strategies I had selected; and if and how these decisions influenced the impact of the practice on the children. As a constructivist, I held that our negotiation would advance Glynnis's reasoning about the use and value of the shared journal process.

When we completed the practicum, both Glynnis and I were uncertain as to what we had accomplished. We both felt frustration, in that neither of us could boast about the effectiveness of our teaching. Thus we reluctantly began to analyze the data. The remainder of this chapter describes what we learned from our collaborative research. It recounts how issues related to competing agendas surfaced and changed over time. It also discusses how those agendas influenced the children's and the researchers' interactions in the negotiation of the curriculum. It points out ways those agendas were resolved and the outcome of those resolutions. Finally, it discusses the role of empowerment and autonomy in the process. Both voices are heard, so that the reader will understand how the competing agendas evolved.

McIntyre's Agenda

As a college student majoring in Early Childhood Education, I was on top of the world when I began my professional internship. I had learned so much during my undergraduate training that I thought I could turn my internship classroom (a second-grade classroom in a rural Alabama setting) into an exciting place for children. Most of my knowledge about education was based on the constructivist theory of Jean Piaget and his followers. However, it wasn't long before I realized that my supervising teacher's beliefs conflicted with mine. She was a traditional elementary teacher who was eclectic in her approach to education, and who anticipated that her intern would adopt her teaching style. I did not see my role as a student teacher who compliantly completed my assignments, filled in while the teacher took a break, and then graduated to my own classroom. Rather, I saw my role as an advocate, one who could demonstrate to this teacher, the principal, and myself that a constructivist approach to teaching was the best environment for young children's learning. Well, as one might expect, my "best-laid schemes" went astray.

The foreshadowing of my problem occurred when I decided to discuss using a whole language approach with my supervising teacher. I explained that I wanted to use the shared journal process (Taylor 1984) as my component for writing and the shared book experience (Holdaway 1979) as my component for reading. Her only comment was, "Well, you can try it, but I don't think it will work!" Of course, I was more determined than ever to prove her wrong, and to prove that whole language approaches such as these were the panacea for literacy problems in education. I realized later that this missionary zeal hindered putting my theory and approach into practice.

At first, the novelty of my inexperience worked well with the children. They loved the shared book experience and enjoyed the shared journal writing because it allowed them to use stories from their lives told in their own voices. However, this process caused me to question everything I had learned. My crisis came when a cute little teacher pleaser did not have her topic chosen during the shared journal negotiation. She cried for fifteen minutes, and my supervising teacher said, "I told you so!" I panicked. Although I had very strong ideas about education, I have a soft heart. I also maintain that the welfare and well-being of the children is my first concern. The child's crying bothered me so much that I changed the approach to daily individual journal writing. I reasoned, with the teacher's help, that if a classroom practice made children cry, it couldn't be in their best interests. I forgot all of my notions about natural consequences and about children learning from experience and from other children's perspectives. I ignored the fact that children often cry when they are learning and growing (for instance, when they fall while learning to ride a bike). I also forgot to use my strategies for helping this child learn to consider others' perspectives.

By the end of the three-month internship, I was confused and frustrated. The supervising teacher had won; I had lost. After the internship, I spent hours reflecting on the experience of seeing the child cry as well as my abandonment of my beliefs. I could sense that what I had done was wrong, but given the situation I felt that I had no other choice. I came to believe that it was the negotiation portion of the shared journal process that upset the children. Some of the children weren't able to cope with the criticism of the other children. Finally, I decided that if I were going to become a professional educator, I had to develop a better understanding of my actions and feelings and the actions of the children as they experienced negotiating points of view. So I went back to school to get a master's degree.

Because I had a personal need to know, a need to resolve the acknowledged conflict between what I had learned in school and what I had experienced with children, I asked Dr. Taylor to direct a practicum for me that focused on shared journal writing. I reasoned that since she had developed the practice, she was the expert who could help me better understand the process. But additionally, I thought that perhaps I was right and that she could learn more about it through me. At the time, neither of us considered how that dynamic would affect our collaboration.

After we held our initial planning session for the practicum, talked about the problems I had encountered during my internship, my agenda for the practicum, and the possibility of shaping the practicum into a collaborative research project, I eagerly and apprehensively started.

> *Sept. 9*: I was glad that Dr. Taylor agreed it would be helpful for me to observe Barbara for the first two days. Even though I've done journal writing with kids many times, I'm always a little apprehensive about the first time with a new group, so hopefully the observations will give me a little more confidence. I'm excited and a little nervous about beginning my practicum, but I can already predict that it will be a valuable learning experience for me as well as the children, and hopefully even Dr. Taylor will learn a thing or two.

Each day for three weeks, I drove the forty miles to the classroom and stayed for three hours. The first two days I observed the teacher, questioned her about her strategies, and worked with the children as they wrote in their journals. She was considered a master teacher who had used shared journal writing in her classroom for several years, and the children were accustomed to the process. Slowly, I developed the confidence to lead the children through the shared journal process and to allow my teaching to be videotaped. On Wednesday, October 5, I assumed full responsibility for shared journal writing in the class.

From the beginning of the project I had two competing agendas. They surface not only in the classroom but in my journal, during the conference sessions, and in my reflections and responses after viewing my videos of my teaching. At first, I felt pulled in two directions. Even though I wrote about them in my reflective journal and read them in the transcripts, I didn't comprehend their influence on our research until Dr. Taylor and I analyzed the data. The first agenda item was the one we had agreed upon at the outset — the development of my ability to lead the negotiation through questioning. The second, but unstated, agenda item was my need to assume a sense of self-reliance and to be able to control the children's behavior and thinking.

The first evidence we found of the conflicting items was the October 3 entry of my reflective journal. I focused more on classroom behavior than the students' negotiations and decisions:

> with regard to the negotiation — Barbara tried to get the children to talk to each other about their statements. When one child would tell why they liked a story, she would ask a few other children what they thought about the child's reasoning. This didn't accomplish the goal that it was supposed to, but if we keep on doing this maybe it will eventually.
>
> with regard to behavior and control — As usual, the story that I considered the most important did not win. The two things that really stood out to me today were: (1) The way Barbara had them vote, and (2) The class's short attention span. I guess there's not much you can do about the short attention span of the children. I just hope that I can handle it, and be observant enough to know when to stop and when to keep going.

This entry was typical of my entries for the next few days:

> *Oct. 4*: The discussion of the stories was short because the kids were starting to get restless. We did a Mouse-er-cize before journal writing today, and it really seemed to help them work off some energy before sitting down for journal writing. They were much more attentive for the first part but got a little restless toward the end. Overall, I thought journal writing went well except for the discussion of the stories.

Not only did my focus on behavior take up the majority of my reflective time, but it also took up time in my conferences with Dr. Taylor.

October 6 Conference

Taylor: ... talk about the comparison between what you thought was happening and then how it looked on the tape.

McIntyre: Well, I thought, when I did my first day, I thought it was worse than it really was when I looked on the tape.

Taylor: How did the video help you realize that it wasn't as bad as you had thought it was?

McIntyre: Well, I felt like they were a lot more rambunctious and not paying attention a lot more than they really were. They were paying more attention than I thought they were at the time.

Taylor: Can you think back to before you saw the video and try to
    recall what it was that made you think they weren't attending?

McIntyre: They were moving around a lot, I mean a lot, like from one
    side of the circle to the other. There was one group that I'm pretty
    sure were not paying attention because they were in their own
    little circle within the circle talking about different things. In the
    video it excluded the group that I thought was being the worst.
    Which was good and bad. Bad because I couldn't look back to see
    what they were doing, and good because it made it look better.

The first evidence we had of my need for approval from external
authorities and my sense of powerlessness to solve problems on my
own occurred when I wrote the following entries in my journal.

> *Sept. 28*: If I could only step back from situations and look at them
> objectively, then I could probably resolve a lot of questions myself
> instead of depending on Dr. Taylor to help me see it in a new light.
>
> *Oct. 5*: When we were discussing the stories, I felt that no one was
> listening to the reasons being given. It was frustrating, and I didn't
> know how to handle it.
>
> *Oct. 11*: Today was embarrassing! *Dr. Taylor* came in to observe, and
> even though I didn't feel nervous everything was wrong. I guess I
> wanted everything to be perfect, and when it wasn't I was discouraged.

Dr. Taylor was my mentor, and I needed her "stamp of approval"
so much that I didn't push my problem of classroom control nor my
lack of confidence in some of the things that she was suggesting. Such
role changes were too risky! These reflective journal entries show that
fear, that lack of power.

Although I discussed the agenda of behavior and control with Dr.
Taylor during these early sessions, I usually found a way to switch the
discussion to my questioning strategies and the children's poor negotiation ability, the intended agenda for our session and for the research,
instead of allowing us to resolve the control issue. On October 12,
Dr. Taylor even noted the agenda of my control in the classroom when
she said, "So now that you're feeling a bit more comfortable with the
control you can focus in on what kinds of questions you are asking."

When I asked for specific advice about my control problems we
both gave it cursory attention but never resolved it in a problem-
solving manner. Our interactions focused on my questioning strategies,
the research, and the children's use of shared journal. However, we
were still blind to the dynamics of the roles of teacher expert and
student learner. In many ways we were acting out our roles rather than
collaborating.

On October 12, I seem to have recognized that if I called on children who weren't listening, I inhibited the discussion. Furthermore, I realized that I was focusing on controlling their behavior, not on interacting and sharing ideas. This was the first evidence we found of my being able to use my own observations to problem-solve for myself.

> *Oct. 12*: I tend to call on kids who aren't listening; therefore they don't have anything to say. There's got to be a better way to get them to interact.

On October 13, I began to feel I had the right to comment on what worked and what didn't. Even though Dr. Taylor recommended using agree and disagree, I wrote in my journal:

> *Oct. 13*: After talking to Dr. Taylor yesterday, I really tried to remember some of the questions that I used during negotiation. ... I tried to get them to compare reasons by asking who didn't agree with the first reason. This didn't work well because I don't think they understood the concept of agree and disagree.

The following response to the video shows my first attempts at moving away from the subjective berating of my efforts to a more objective look.

> *Oct. 18*: As usual, the sharing wasn't as bad as I expected. It always seems worse than it really is. My questioning still isn't very good during the negotiation, but I think it gets a little better every day.

This seemed to be the second turning point in my practicum. It occurred in the third week of our research. I was beginning to feel that I had a right to my own teaching style and methods for behavior control. The October 19 conference with Dr. Taylor shows my attempt to shift control in our collaborative work and my attempts to control behavior issues for myself.

October 19 Conference

McIntyre: I realized that I was having a real problem asking questions.

Taylor: Good, how did you realize that?

McIntyre: Well, when I started to sit down and write the questions that I had asked, I was going — I don't think I asked any questions! And then I would try to think, What questions could I ask? But the situations are so different every day that you can't plan questions to ask.

Taylor: Then it would be real artificial because they have to come out of what the children are saying.

McIntyre: Right, and see, I'm having a real problem picking up on things. I have to get more in tune to the kids.

Taylor: You're probably sitting there thinking, "What can I ask next?" rather than listening to what the kids are saying.

McIntyre: That's exactly what I've been doing!

Taylor: And when you do that, you're blocking your mental processes from picking up on the kids.

McIntyre: And even when I do that—I sit there and I think I'm going to listen to this kid, and then I have to think of a question to ask. And then I start to write in my journal at night, and it's hard for me to remember what happened because I was really not listening. I was hearing, but I was not listening.

When I responded to the next videotape I continued to assume some of the responsibility for my feelings and their impact on the children.

> *Oct. 21*: This day seemed much worse than it looked. I was so frustrated and disappointed, but after seeing the video it didn't look as bad as it felt. I think that maybe I was the problem and not the kids. It seems so unfair that just because I wasn't in a great mood the kids suffered. How can a teacher monitor herself and allow for "mood swings"? How could I have compensated in different ways to be fair to the class?

Much like the small child who hesitates before leaving Mama's side, I hesitated before building the power to take control of my teaching. My journal describes this.

> *Oct. 25*: Today's journal writing was very exciting, especially after talking to Dr. Taylor. It helps so much to be able to talk about the things that have happened in journal writing. I guess it's just a form of moral support, but whether it's Dr. Taylor or Barbara (classroom teacher), or even my roommates at times, I always feel better after I've talked about it. I've found that writing in this journal does the same type of thing, but nothing can top *hearing* someone say that "things are going great" or "it's okay, I'm sure things will be better tomorrow." I think that one reason talking helps is that I still don't have an abundance of confidence in myself. I've found that the more I actually work in a classroom, the more confident I feel about getting my own classroom. I just hope that I have as much support then as I do now.

As I became more involved in the practice, I began to take more risks. When Dr. Taylor didn't reject my first attempts at assuming control over some of my decisions, I gained a little more confidence. As we watched the videos and talked, and as I wrote in my journal, I began to realize that my ability to conduct the shared journal experience wasn't as weak as I thought, and that although I wasn't perfect, I was making progress. I was able to disagree with Dr. Taylor and the classroom teacher to a certain extent, and to share the ways I was implementing shared journal.

October 19 Conference

Taylor: You could say, "Do you agree with Jake?"

McIntyre: Well, see, I've tried that. I've tried coming from that aspect "Do you agree with" — well, actually I think this is the way I did it. The first person gave their reason on why they thought a story would happen, and I said, "Is there anyone that disagrees? Does everyone agree with K, or is there someone that disagrees?" And they all looked at me and then they started raising their hands, so I picked on someone and they told me the same thing K had just told me, so I didn't think that they understood the difference between agree and disagree.

Taylor: They don't.

McIntyre: Well, then I couldn't think, on the spur of the moment — I couldn't think of another way to explain to them agree and disagree.

As any inexperienced teacher, my actions sometimes contradicted my own interpretation of negotiation. One example of this occurred when I tore a child's journal page from the book. On October 27, I told Dr. Taylor about this.

McIntyre: I did something today that I had never done before.

Taylor: What?

McIntyre: I tore a little girl's page out of her journal because it was such a mess. And I said, "Do you think this is good?" She looked at me and shook her head. "Does it look like scribble-scrabble to you?" She said, "Uh-huh." I said, "Good, me too. Let's tear it out and start over." So I did, and she went back, and she didn't do a very good job the second time, but ...

At the time this happened, I was attempting to interpret, implement, and coordinate several teaching strategies at once. For example, I was attempting to value the child's work, interpret the developmental stages of children's writings, resolve what I thought was correctness in writing, and motivate children to do their best. I was also considering the natural consequences a writer receives when a reader doesn't like what has been written. Finally, I was attempting to develop my own voice with classroom management. As a result, I tore the page out and said what I did. If I had to do this over, I am not sure what I would do. All I know is, this is what I did that day. It was a turning point for me.

As the practicum came to an end, I realized that I had resolved some of the issues that caused the study. For example, on October 27, Dr. Taylor asked me if I was seeing heartbroken kids when their topics weren't selected.

McIntyre: No! We've had one child that pouts a little bit sometimes when he doesn't win and it was J, and he didn't today. But sometimes he pouts and lies down and puts his head down. But he, I mean, then like that he's over it and writing about the other topic. I think part of the reason I had that problem in the second grade was that they weren't a community, and if you're a community it's OK if someone else in the group gets written about, but if *you're* not and *your* story doesn't get written about, then you feel like you're less important than someone else.

My last turning point occurred during the transcribing of the videos. When I merely viewed them, I responded to my teaching in a primarily evaluative sense. Through the transcription of the videotapes I realized that not only had I grown in my ability to lead a discussion, but the children had also assumed much more of the responsibility for interacting with each other as they negotiated the topic. A comparison of the tapes from October 5 and October 26 illustrates the changes in my strategies and in the children's participation.

October 5

McIntyre: OK, who can tell us why they think one of these stories was the most important today?

Student 1: Uh ... Keri's.

McIntyre: What story was that?

Student 1: About her Mama.

McIntyre: OK, why do you think that story was the most important?

Student 1: I like Florida.

McIntyre: OK, Brad?

Student 2: Jessie's.

McIntyre: What story was that?

Student 2: Mama had a wreck.

McIntyre: Why do you think Jessie's story was most important?

Student 2: 'Cause I like cars and everything.

October 26

McIntyre: OK. We're going to think about the story that's important to us today and will help us remember today the most.

Student 1: Jake has something to say.

McIntyre: What, Jake?

Student 2: I have something to tell the group.

McIntyre: OK, if you would like to tell them which story you think is most important and give me a good reason, I want you to tell the group.

Student 1: He didn't say nuttin'. I didn't get to see what he was trying to say.

McIntyre: OK, Brad.

Student 3: Rob's, 'cause I went to a state fair, 'cause I seen it on TV and I went to it yesterday.

Student 4: No, you didn't.

Student 1: It wasn't open yesterday. Not that state fair. It was another state fair.

Student 5: Uh-huh, I went to it last night.

Student 4: Well, you went to another kind.

Student 5: Uh-huh.

Student 3: Well, Jake, he works for my Daddy, and he went to the state fair when it was dark.

Student 5: I did too!

McIntyre: Does anyone have a different kind of answer?

Student 6: Cole's.

McIntyre: Why?

Student 6: 'Cause one time my grandma moved.

Student 7: Ohhhh.

Student 6: Not Papa.

This analysis suggested that I had helped move the children from interacting only with me as they responded to my questions with single words or phrases to interacting with one another in real discussions about the topics, the truthfulness of the stories, and the responses to one another's sharings, and the monitoring of turn taking to a certain degree. Additionally, they were negotiating with me about who should be called on for ideas.

Being a teacher researcher was frustrating and even demoralizing at times. I didn't like to think of myself as being less than perfect. However, through the research I learned about children's development. Additionally, I discovered that many of my ideas about children and how they handle negotiation were not necessarily true. If children have a teacher who allows them to make decisions and respects their points of view, then they will accept the class's decision, and sometimes even agree when the class votes against their story.

More importantly, the research helped me look at myself objectively and appreciate my progress rather than berate my lack of perfection. Analyzing the data helped me observe how what I was saying and doing influenced the children. Now I'm not as fearful of making mistakes and am more willing to openly discuss them with others. I've also realized that I can learn from these mistakes if I take an objective look at them. Although I know that I still rely on authority figures for support, I am more confident in my own ability to make instructional decisions and to support them with data from my own research.

Taylor's Agenda

As I analyzed the data I became aware that during the practicum I served as an external authority, judging the rightness or wrongness of practice. I planned the practicum study because I had experienced so much success with other students through this kind of work. Next, I selected the classroom setting that I thought would be most supportive of the change I wanted to bring about. Additionally, I used the first and subsequent conferences to "correct" Glynnis's thinking about the purpose and value of the negotiation aspect of shared journal. The transcription of the first conference clearly revealed that I did most of the talking, and that Glynnis compliantly acquiesced to my point of view with comments like, "OK, I get the point!" At no time during this conference did I attempt to assess the kind of knowledge Glynnis held about teaching in general, much less about the process she was beginning to study.

While I served as expert, and tried to reason with Glynnis about her implementation of the practice, I followed my own agenda — my investment in the shared journal process. That agenda took precedence over my need to understand what Glynnis really "knew" about the teaching-learning process. I had no idea how deeply embedded her beliefs were about the role of teacher, and how I, as expert, was modeling many of those same notions. For example, as expert I set up and guided the practicum to "correct" her thinking, rather than work collaboratively with her to determine what she knew, what she wanted to accomplish from the study, and how she thought she could accomplish it. When this became apparent to me, I wondered about the role I had served in past practicums, and during undergraduate internships.

Additionally, the analysis helped me realize that Glynnis had grown to mistrust much of what she had learned about teaching in her under-graduate program because when she attempted to apply aspects of her learning, the behaviors of the children did not fit her deeply embedded a priori notions about the role of the teacher and the role of the learner. The transcript of our conference on October 6 offered the first evidence of that.

McIntyre: They haven't been playing with the blocks, which was really strange to me. They play with the little cardboard blocks, but they don't play with the wooden blocks. Barbara says it's because they're too lazy to put them back up. But today, I thought, well I had this play class, I should try something I learned from it. I sat down with the blocks, just by myself, and started building with the blocks. And as soon as I started building, two kids came over. "What are you doin'?" "What are you doin'?" I said, "Well, I think I'm going to build a racetrack" and I was just building a road with bridges and different little curves and stuff, and then I got a car and started going around with it and they said, "Hey, great!" and they started playing with it. And I got up and they played almost the whole center time with the blocks. I was like "Great, it works! Something that I've learned worked."

This excerpt highlights Gynnis's expectation that application of a teaching strategy should bring immediate results, and her lack of confidence in strategies that don't have this effect. Glynnis "knew" that helping children learn to listen, argue, consider others' points of view, make decisions, support their own decisions with reasons, and mutually agree on decisions was developmental. However, in practice, she expected a change in her line of questioning to bring an immediate change in the children's behavior. When it didn't, she determined that the change wasn't "working."

Coupled with this expectation was Glynnis's unstated belief that there was a topic that should be selected through the negotiation. Her reflective journal showed that when children's topic choices and reasons for those choices didn't match her choice, she believed that her strategies "didn't work." On the other hand, when the children's decisions did match her expectations, she thought the children were becoming more "logical" in their negotiation.

Oct. 3:

topic selection: As usual, the story that I considered most important did not win.

negotiation: ... some children still said that they liked X's story because X told it. ... This didn't accomplish the goal that it was supposed to but if we keep on doing this, maybe it will eventually.

Oct. 4:

topic selection: Once again someone liked a story because they liked the person who was telling the story.

negotiation: Overall, I thought journal writing went well except for the discussion of the stories.

Oct. 11:
topic selection: The class voted to write about Leanne's playhouse being painted. I'm not sure why, but maybe it had more to do with the way the class feels about Leanne than the way they felt about her story.
negotiation: After forgetting to do the negotiation I was a little frazzled so I'm sure it didn't go as well as expected. I've been trying to get the kids to react to their classmates' reasoning but I'm not having much success.

Oct. 24:
topic selection: Finally, the kids and I agreed on a story!
negotiation: The negotiation was good today and I think that their reasoning for supporting a story is getting better and more logical.

Oct. 31:
topic selection: Brad didn't share much and this story was so great I was sure he would get written about. When the negotiation started I knew that he was going to lose. I couldn't believe that these kids didn't think that Brad's story was the "most important" and I did something that I never do: I told which story I thought was the most important and why! Well, of course this didn't work either and the class wrote about the two girls going to the carnival.
negotiation: I was distressed, discouraged, and disappointed at the time, but now I say *hurray*! This class just proved to me that they were thinking for themselves, being autonomous individuals, and forming a community. I still think that Brad's story was the most important but I'm very glad that the class didn't vote to write about it just because "the teacher" thought it was the best.

Rather than accept the children's decisions about the story they wanted to write, and rather than examine the hypotheses they were using to explain their decisions, Glynnis predetermined which story was the "right" or "best," and was frustrated when the children did not choose as she thought they should. Although she never overtly stated this, she seemed to believe that their inability to choose the "right" topic related directly to her inability to lead the negotiation. Consequently, in her mind what she was doing wasn't "working." Even on October 31 her entry reflects the continued conflict between her attempts to correct the children's thinking and her explicated goal of fostering their autonomous decision making.

As I reflected on the data, I noted that during the pre-practicum conference I "told" Glynnis that it didn't matter which story the children selected, because we were interested in the hypotheses the children used as they made their selections over time. Therefore I expected her to know that her goal was to help children advance in their thinking about the criteria they might use to determine interesting subject matter for sharing and writing. What was startling was the realization that I had tried to "teach" Glynnis in the same way that she had tried to "teach" the kids. I had predetermined the "right" goal, and had forgotten that like the kids Glynnis needed time and many opportunities to advance her thinking about the practice. She was just beginning to differentiate between her need to influence the topic selection and her goal for them to be autonomous decision makers by the end of the practicum. Her experiences with the children had caused sufficient disequilibration to make her think about *how* she was trying to "teach" them.

Instead of giving Glynnis the time to cope with her own disequilibration, I had been pushing her to respond as I had expected. I would go into our practicum sessions planning to teach her and answer her questions so that she would learn the "right" way to do shared journal. After each session, I would think, "This time she's got it. She knows what to do!" But, much to my dismay, she would return for the next session with the same script of one- or two-word comments or the same set of problems. Time after time we repeated this kind of session. Then when Glynnis left, just as she did with the children, I berated myself because I couldn't figure out what I was doing wrong! As I examined the data and reflected on the project, I realized how limiting a teacher's use of the right/wrong dichotomy can be. I also realized how static and artificial learning must be in order for such a dichotomy to exist. Yet, because of our prior experiences with teaching and learning, Glynnis and I used that dichotomy to evaluate our own teaching.

When we use the teaching dichotomy of rightness/wrongness and correctness/incorrectness, we are unable to observe children's and adults' developmental levels of learning. I always taught this developmental perspective to my graduate and undergraduate students; however, I did not realize that I was ignoring the developmental nature of their own learning while I was actually working with them. I became aware of the need for considering this as I attempted to deal with these competing agendas.

Although Glynnis compliantly agreed with my reasoning during her conferences, she also trusted what she had learned through her internship and had either consciously or subconsciously established her own agenda for the practicum. This agenda surfaced in her first journal entry following our initial conference when she wrote, "I'm very excited and a little nervous about beginning my practicum, but I can already predict that it will be a valuable learning experience for me as well as the children, and hopefully even Dr. Taylor will learn a thing or two."

Although they were never explicitly stated, Glynnis's journal was replete with attempts to disprove the things I was trying to help her observe. For example, I told her that our previous research suggested that children move through a variety of hypotheses about which story should be recorded, which in turn influences the kinds of stories they share. At first they base their decision on the popularity of the storyteller, and then on whether or not they have had a similar experience. However, as they move to a more sociocentered perspective, they begin to use what we have called "the bad hypothesis"; that is, if something bad happens to someone, that is what we should write about. On October 14 Glynnis wrote, "We had three kids share today. Jake shared a story about his brother getting hurt. Lanetta shared about a friend who was sick and couldn't come to school. Jerrie shared about his mother hurting her foot." She follows this with, "Once again, when the class voted, the bad hypothesis did not hold true. Jessie's story sounded a lot worse than Jake's, but Jake's story received the most votes. This was the closest the voting had been since I started doing journal sharing." Although the bad hypothesis was in every story shared, Glynnis denied its existence because the story she determined was the worst was not the one the class selected. However, on October 19, when a story about being sick and having to miss school was selected over a trip to an air show with accompanying poster, Glynnis did not acknowledge the bad hypothesis, but rather wrote, "I just hope that all the kids won't start bringing in toys and gadgets to share during journal time." Glynnis's determination to help me learn a thing or two (her agenda) caused her to view the children's early hypotheses as problems, and to ignore their movement to the use of the bad hypothesis. On the other hand, my determination to "correct" her thinking prevented me from recognizing her developmental need to be "a teacher." Thus, our conflicting agendas influenced our ability to be careful observers of learning.

I overlooked Glynnis's need to learn all that she could about teaching. Her questions related to a variety of concerns, such as procedures to use for voting and ways to manage the children's behavior in the classroom, to approach the physical aspects of writing, to use themes and daily routines, to please the classroom teacher and children, to make me proud of her, and to make sure the children did what was necessary to be successful in school. My responses related to strategies she might use in getting children to elaborate their questions, reason at a higher level, and expand their ways of knowing. Both of us were focusing on the methodological level of a classroom practice or activity; however, I was speaking as the theorist and she was questioning as the naive classroom teacher. Neither of us was coordinating points of view or coordinating knowledge. Instead, we were using our preconceptions of right and wrong, correct and incorrect, professor and novice teacher in our sessions. As a result, I was unconsciously trying to impose my notions on Glynnis's thinking so that we would share those notions.

She was trying to do the same with the children. We were creating a shared base of figurative knowledge about teaching but it was not mutually operational. As I analyzed the data I found that I was not relying on any kind of developmental notions about teaching. I knew what Glynnis was capable of being and wanted her to perform at that level immediately. I thought she was ready to refine a practice. What I had not considered in my teaching was requisite for a constructivist teacher. If we, as constructivist teacher educators, are to build on what our students "know" about teaching, we must first identify what that knowing is.

How could this have happened? How could I have been so blind to what Glynnis knew? As I read the data and reflected on the contents I realized that while I was serving as "expert" I believed that I was truly cooperating with this student. I thought that when I put forth an argument Glynnis would accept what she agreed with, and argue when she didn't agree. When she didn't argue, I assumed that we were in agreement. What I accepted as cooperation was merely Glynnis's acquiescence in the theories of someone whom she perceived as more expert. This acquiescence was most apparent in the data related to the issue of how Glynnis should initiate and focus the negotiation. Often teachers will ask, "Which of the stories is the most important?" I argue that the word important focuses on an evaluative rather than a substantive issue. I suggest that they ask, "Which story will you remember?" or "Which story do you want to write about?" or "Which story will we want to read about tomorrow?" This issue surfaced during our conference on October 6, and October 7 Glynnis wrote the following in her reflective journal:

> The sharing went much better today and the change in the way that I asked questions helped a lot. I think that when they get used to hearing the question asked in this way it will get even better. I've stopped asking them to think about the stories that they think are the most important, and I ask them to choose the story that will help them remember that day the best.

On October 26, however, Glynnis initiated the negotiation with the following statement: "We're going to think about the story that's important to us today and will help us remember today the most." And later: "Tell the group, not me. Convince the group to vote on the story that you think is the most important." Even on October 31 she wrote, "I couldn't believe that these kids didn't think Brad's story was the most important." These comments document Glynnis's unresolved conflict. At first, she yielded to my point of view and changed her questioning to conform to my expectations. Then she attempted to combine both perspectives into one question. But in the end, her statements reveal that she still believed one topic was more important than the others. From the data I realized that cooperation in the "true" sense of the term never existed in our collaboration. Glynnis and I never negotiated during the practicum. Actually, we were in conflict with each other because of our competing agendas. Neither of us would have been able to examine our frustration with the practicum had we not agreed to gather and analyze the data. However, because we honestly respected each other, because Glynnis was trusting enough to share the contents of her journal, and because we wanted to know, we were able to resolve our frustration and collaboratively learn about our teaching from each other. What I mistook for true collaboration was Glynnis's trust and belief that I would help her. From this study I have come to believe that as long as students view their instructor as expert, true collaboration is not possible.

Conclusions

As mentioned earlier, when we completed the practicum we both questioned what we had accomplished. Through the data analysis we learned about our competing agendas, our own teaching, and how that teaching influenced our learners. Because Glynnis was so preoccupied with issues related to control and to learning to teach, and because I was so preoccupied with "correcting" her thinking, we were unable to observe much of what was really occurring. However, our records of those events allowed us, as Ann Berthoff says, to "re-search" the accomplishments of the practicum from a more distanced perspective. This process allowed us to work cooperatively in the true sense of the term. Here, neither of us was the expert in practice. We used the data to comment on each others' teaching, and yet both of us were "expert" informants for each other.

As Glynnis transcribed the questions she had asked and the responses the children had made, she could concentrate on the substance of their replies, rather than on whether or not they were sitting appropriately in the circle. Through this process she began to observe the qualitative changes that occurred over time. She stopped making evaluative statements about the rightness or wrongness of her questions, and began to discuss them in relation to the children's responses. Additionally, she began to observe the kinds of hypotheses the children were using, rather than see them as problems.

Because the reflective journal allowed Glynnis to express her thoughts freely, and because Glynnis was willing to share her journal for the analysis, I came to know her as a teacher. But, I also came to know my own teaching. Unlike Glynnis, I felt no satisfaction. Rather, the analysis and my reflections on it have caused me to change my entire approach to undergraduate and graduate teaching supervision. The quarter immediately following our analysis, I began to implement different ways to supervise undergraduate student teachers, so that I was better able to identify and build on what they knew about teaching. Since then I have incorporated a variety of different constructivist strategies in the design of my courses, and am ever mindful of the "levels of wrongness" through which these beginning teachers must pass. The results of these applications far outweigh the discomfort I experienced as I studied my own teaching.

As for Glynnis, I recently talked with her by phone, and found that she is experiencing a rather successful first year of teaching kindergarten children. When I asked her what she felt most comfortable with, her response was an instantaneous, "Shared Journal, of course! I still don't have all of the kinks worked out of the negotiating aspect of the process, but even it makes more sense to me now and because of that is beginning to work for the kids."

When we had completed our conversation and I hung up the phone, I thought to myself, "Glynnis, you really did teach me a thing or two."

Works Cited

Berthoff, A. 1987. The teacher as REsearcher. In *Reclaiming the classroom*, ed. D. Goswami and P. Stillman. Portsmouth, NH: Boynton/Cook.

Branscombe, N. A. 1987. I gave my classroom away. In *Reclaiming the classroom*, ed. D. Goswami and P. Stillman. Portsmouth, NH Boynton/Cook.

Carnegie Forum on Education and the Economy. 1986. *A nation prepared: Teachers for the 21st century*. Report of the Task Force on Teaching as a Profession.

Goodlad, J. 1984. *A place called school: Prospects for the future*. New York: McGraw Hill.

Holdaway, D. 1979. *The foundations of literacy*. Portsmouth, NH: Heinemann.

Taylor, J. 1984. Shared writing experiences. Paper presented at the Alabama Department of Education Early Childhood Workshop, Montgomery. August.

Response
David Wilson

In their chapter, Taylor and McIntyre remind me that teachers and academics live their professional lives in very different places — schools and universities — and while universities are indeed a kind of school, the expectations in the two places are quite different. In graduate school and again early in my life as an assistant professor, I learned that my success was thenceforth going to be measured primarily by my contribution to scholarship and that that contribution was going to be determined in large part by the quantity and quality of the written texts I would produce.

The work of elementary and secondary teachers, on the other hand, is conducted largely in talk. As a high school English teacher, I was not expected to produce written texts. My work as a teacher practically forbade it. Instead, I was expected to talk and listen to students, and when I wanted to share what I knew with colleagues, I talked to them.

Perhaps, as Jim Marshall suggests, even the kinds of knowledge that these communities produce and use are different. Now, when I report the results of my research — even when it draws on observations and interviews in classrooms — I must do so primarily in written texts. I must transform my rich experience of those classrooms into the tables, figures, diagrams, and descriptions that comprise research results. In order to do this, I must strip away much of what I experienced in those classrooms.

While I now must move toward generalization in presenting what I know, as a high school teacher in Tipton, Iowa, I was drawn to the specific, the individual. Then I could not easily strip away features of my experiences in room 313. Everything was important. While I might occasionally see Circe or Darren as representatives of a kind of student in my attempts at understanding them, they and their classmates each asserted their uniqueness, requiring me to come to know and interact with them as individuals. While I now must context-strip in order to fashion generalizations that will stand above and across specifics, as a classroom teacher in room 313 I had to attend to the particulars of context in order to draw generalizations down to fit the specific circumstances of individual cases and faces.

For teachers, then, the written text is not an efficient or effective way to embody what they know. Instead, they represent their experiences primarily through stories—oral narratives rich with context and peopled with individuals. Those outside the teacher community too seldom respect or understand teachers' stories. These frustrate us, or we dismiss them as being "just stories." And teachers are often suspicious and distrustful of the written texts that academics use to represent their knowledge. Such discourse seems too abstract, too removed from the specific, the individual.

We inhabit, then, different discourse communities, and our memberships in those communities shape the ways in which we understand and share our understandings of the classrooms that become the subjects of our collaborative research efforts.

Taylor and McIntyre also remind me that we are faced with the traditional role of university academics as experts and evaluators, which makes academics and teachers unequal in the collaborative construction of knowledge. As Taylor explains, "Cooperation and mutual agreement are possible only when all individuals in the group perceive their role in the decision-making process as equal." My role as advisor or instructor in the graduate programs of the classroom teachers with whom I seek to collaborate can impede our efforts at collaboration. My context makes me different. I have, they believe, more opportunity for reading and reflection. I must know more. And my role makes me different. Ultimately, we both know, I must assign them grades in the courses they take with me, and I must write their comprehensive examination questions and evaluate their responses. To be truly collaborative, we must find ways to move outside or beyond our given roles and contexts.

These two writers also remind me that we teacher educators are not our students' only teachers; indeed, we are not the only—nor always the most persuasive—voices our teachers-to-be hear. At the university our students take courses in English and history and math. And our certification requirements have them working in schools for practica and student teaching. Recently, I received a telephone call from a young woman whom I had never met, but who is a student in the secondary English teacher education program that I direct. Elizabeth wanted to know what I thought about isolated, direct instruction of traditional school grammar. She was enrolled in two courses: one in the English Department on the teaching of writing, and another in the journalism program. "The books we're reading in my English class tell us to de-emphasize grammar and focus on the kids' strengths and their efforts at making meaning. But my journalism professor says kids have no business writing until they've mastered grammar. He says that teachers are copping out, that the lack of phonics and grammar instruction in the schools is responsible for the demise of our language and culture." Elizabeth's work in her English class had made her familiar with the principles and practices of language instruction advocated by Nancie Atwell, Frank Smith, and Donald Murray, and while she found them seductive, the voice of her journalism professor more closely resonated with her own vague assumptions about language and with her own experiences in language classrooms, and so she ultimately found him more persuasive.

Taylor and McIntyre also remind me that our students' teacher education programs begin long before they enter our university-level education courses. They come to us with years of experience in and around schools. Even before they enter kindergarten, they've heard their parents and older siblings talk about teachers and schools. And they've heard or read media accounts and seen television shows or movies where schools and teachers play roles. Willard Waller reminds us that adult conceptions of teachers are often extensions of childhood fantasies, experiences, and images. Over time the details of individual teachers fade; what remains is often a teacher caricature rather than a true teacher portrait. Our students are likely to enter our teacher education programs with such caricatures, caricatures which inform their expectations of what it means to be a teacher.

In my role as a teacher educator, I, like Taylor, have learned that I must acknowledge what my students bring to their education courses; indeed, I must often help them understand that they bring anything at all. They are often unaware of the unspoken assumptions about the nature of teaching, learning, and language, and the roles of teachers and students that they bring with them. As Taylor reminds us, when we ignore "what our students 'know' about teaching," we thwart our own teaching and our students' development.

In an ongoing study entitled "The Development of Knowledge of English and Teaching in Pre-service English Teachers" (1990), Joy Ritchie and I are hearing much from future teachers to suggest that many have a vision of literacy learning that is at best a patchwork of scraps pieced together from three broadly defined sources. From their English Department courses and from the wider culture, they've acquired a vision of "high literacy." From popular conceptions of literacy, from their own experiences as students, and from their perceptions of the prevailing status of English instruction in the schools, they've acquired utilitarian and pragmatic notions about language and learning. And from reflecting on their own experiences as readers and writers and from some of their course work, they've acquired constructivist versions of literacy.

Taylor and McIntyre write of their "competing agendas," reminding me of a case study of implementing writing across the curriculum conducted by Swanson-Owens (1986). Swanson-Owens spoke of teachers' "natural sources of resistance" to innovation:

> [We] need to look closely at the ways in which ... reform efforts interact with the practical knowledge or conventional wisdom that guides teachers' responses to such initiatives. ... We know that teachers are not passive transmitters of knowledge but rather active and adaptive agents who filter curricular innovations ... through complex meaning systems. In short, we know that the adoption of a new curriculum is conditioned by the degree of fit between the meaning systems of those initiating it and those implementing it. (71)

Natural sources of resistance come to light when there is a mismatch between meaning systems. Teachers' responses to innovation may seem "resistant" in that they violate the expectations of those promoting the innovation; these responses are "'natural' or appropriate if one assumes that they reflect teachers' commitments to effective practice as they know it" (74). The problem of "competing agendas" which Taylor and McIntyre describe can, perhaps, be attributed to the unarticulated mismatch between their meaning systems. Before we seek to introduce innovations, we must first move close to the teacher and her context, examining the fit between our meaning system and that held by the classroom teacher.

I have also learned that I must recognize that there are many sources of influence on my students' eventual practices and beliefs. In a study of secondary English teachers who had participated in the Iowa Writing Project, I saw how old assumptions about the nature of writing, teaching, and the teaching of writing may simply be joined—rather than replaced—by new and often contradictory assumptions.

Robin, a ninth-grade teacher who believed in the power of positive response to "affirm and encourage" and who wanted her students to maintain control of "their own processes and products," also believed that she had to give and justify a grade for writing. To let herself off the hook, she fell back on things like "standard written English" as criterion for evaluation. At the completion of a grading period, then, she found herself not affirming and encouraging, but "correcting ... mistakes" and telling students that they "shouldn't have put this sentence in" or they "should have used a different word." At the completion of a grading period or unit, roles and rules suddenly changed. Becoming an evaluator also changed her role as a responder in that her response, she felt, needed to justify the grade assigned (Wilson 1988, 1989, 1990).

McIntyre, like Robin, was caught within her own "competing

agendas." While she wanted to develop her own ability to facilitate the children's negotiation through questioning, she also wanted to assume a sense of self-reliance and be able to control the students' behavior and thinking. This project with Taylor provided her with a mechanism for reflection and articulation that enabled her, finally, to understand that she was engaged in such a conflict.

McIntyre's focus on behavior reminds me of another source of dissonance between a teacher's beliefs and practices, a source especially relevant for new teachers. Early in my career as a teacher educator I worked with one of the brightest and most articulate students I have ever encountered. Keith had read Dewey and Moffett and Britton, had reflected on his own experiences as a student and pre-service teacher, and moved into his first year of teaching with a coherent and strongly held set of beliefs about the nature of language and learning. But, he explained in a letter, "It quickly became a battle simply for me to survive emotionally. I was unable to realize my goals right away — to teach as I believed I should — because I had to learn how to preserve my self-esteem from students who really didn't care about what I was trying to do." A set of beliefs informed by Dewey, Moffett, and Britton gave way to one predominately informed by 120 thirteen-year-olds, a principal who liked order, and a faculty of well-established, older colleagues.

Dr. Taylor and Glynnis McIntyre, then, remind me of much that is important for me as a teacher and teacher educator. They remind me that teachers and academics live their professional lives in very different places and that our lives in those places shape the ways in which we understand and share our understandings of the classrooms that become the subjects of our collaborative research efforts. They also remind me that we are faced with the traditional role of university academics as experts and evaluators, which makes the collaborative construction of knowledge among academics and teachers difficult.

Taylor and McIntyre also remind me that we teacher educators are not our students' only teachers; indeed, our students' teacher education programs begin long before they enter our university classrooms. In order to do our jobs well, we must acknowledge and understand the many sources that influence their conceptions of learning, teaching, and language.

Most importantly, perhaps, Taylor and McIntyre have illustrated for me the personal and pedagogical power that are unleashed when we use reflection and collaboration to uncover and examine our assumptions about the nature of learning, teaching, and language. In their negotiations, Taylor and McIntyre have transformed both themselves and their classrooms.

Works Cited

Marshall, J. 1988. Two ways of knowing: Relations between research and practice in the teaching of writing. In *Ways of knowing: Research and practice in the teaching of writing*, ed. J. Davis and J. Marshall. Iowa City, IA: Iowa Council of Teachers of English.

Ritchie, J., and D. Wilson. 1990. Emerging definitions of literacy among pre-service English teachers. Paper presented at the MLA Responsibilities for Literacy Conference, Pittsburgh, PA.

Swanson-Owens, D. 1986. Identifying natural sources of resistance: A case study of implementing writing across the curriculum. *Research in the Teaching of English* 20(1): 69–97.

Waller, W. 1932. *The sociology of teaching*. New York: Wiley.

Wilson, D. 1988. Teacher change and the Iowa writing project. Unpublished doctoral dissertation, University of Iowa, Iowa City.

Wilson, D. 1989. In-service education and teacher change: A study of writing project graduates. Paper delivered to the American Educational Research Association, San Francisco.

Wilson, D. 1990. Independent curriculum development: Obstacles to implementation. Paper delivered to the American Educational Research Association, Boston.

14

Student Teachers and Their Teacher
Talking Our Way into New Understandings

Marilyn Cochran-Smith
Elizabeth Garfield
Rachel Greenberger

There is little disagreement that pre-service teacher preparation, especially student teaching, is a critical period in the development of teachers' theories, instructional practices, and dispositions for thinking about their work and their lives as teachers. However, most schools that prepare teachers are not involved in research on the processes of learning to teach (Goodman 1988), and much of what we know about student teachers' learning comes from research in which students are objects of study rather than participants in the generation of questions and interpretations. These perspectives are of course important, but they provide only a partial vision of the initial process of learning to teach, with little emphasis on the questions, forms of knowledge, and interpretive perspectives of the two groups most prominently involved — teacher educators and student teachers themselves. In this chapter we hope to enlarge that vision by sharing some insights from the research that three of us have been conducting together. Our collaboration is the work of one university teacher educator and researcher, Marilyn Cochran-Smith, and two student teachers-as-researchers, Elizabeth Garfield and Rachel Greenberger, seniors in the University of Pennsylvania's undergraduate elementary education program.

For the last two years, by meeting regularly to talk about teaching and by examining Elizabeth's and Rachel's student teaching journals, reflective essays, formal papers for education courses, and lesson plans with written commentaries about them, we have been exploring together how students learn to be teachers. This chapter is drawn primarily from our audio-recorded conversations, some among the three of us (student teachers and their teacher) and some between Rachel and Elizabeth (student teacher and student teacher). Our aim is to provide a sense of the ways that talk functioned for us as a vehicle for learning, or, as we suggest in our title, how we talked our way into new understandings about teaching, learning, and learning to teach. The insights that we share in this chapter were planned, talked through, and worked/reworked collaboratively by the three of us. But because we believe that each of us also has something to say that is distinct and that represents our own individual visions, we have identified our separate voices as well.

Following a brief description of the teacher education program that forms the context of our research, Marilyn provides a sense of who we are as teachers and researchers and describes how our collaboration came to be. Elizabeth and Rachel then discuss, from their own perspectives as student teachers, some of the *ways* they have learned as well as *what* they learned about good teaching by becoming researchers and learning to inquire collaboratively. We conclude with comments about the implications of our work and a postscript.

Teacher Education Program as Context for Collaboration

Elementary education programs at the University of Pennsylvania are intended to provide rich student teaching experiences carefully integrated with the curriculum of courses in education and to establish close links between the university and area schools. The goal of the programs is that student teachers will develop the skills and knowledge of effective teachers, the inquiry stance of reflective teacher researchers, and a critical perspective on teaching, learning, and schooling. The centerpiece of these programs is the notion of student teacher-as-researcher. Cochran-Smith and Lytle (Cochran-Smith & Lytle 1990; Lytle & Cochran-Smith 1990) have defined teacher research as "systematic intentional inquiry" in which teachers use writing and structured talk to reflect on, ask questions about, and make sense of, their teaching experiences through journals, essays, oral inquiries, and classroom studies.

In teacher-research-centered pre-service teacher education, students have many opportunities to be researchers by writing journals and essays, conducting "mini" classroom studies, and engaging in inquiry through planned and systematic talk with their cooperating teachers and fellow students. The aim of these activities is that students will learn to inquire about what is going on in classrooms from the perspectives of experienced teachers and that they will observe carefully and listen to the questions children and cooperating teachers ask. Further it is intended that students will learn to explore the assumptions underlying common teaching practices, to ask questions of description and interpretation before they ask questions of cause and effect, and to interrogate their own experiences as teachers as well as students. The programs are designed to provide the organizational and social structures within which student teachers may have the opportunities to learn to teach through inquiry and research (Cochran-Smith 1991b).

Marilyn: A Teacher Educator's View

As a teacher educator, I have for a number of years experimented with course assignments that would encourage my undergraduate elementary education students to begin to be confident about their own emerging voices as teachers and to construct their own meanings for what they were reading about and experiencing in their student teaching classrooms. Two years ago, Karen Misasi, a senior in the program, began her final essay for my course this way:

> I can't believe it's December already and my yearlong language arts course is nearly over. I can vividly remember my initial encounter with the theory of whole language last January. It took me a while to change some of [my] more traditional theoretical assumptions about teaching and language ... but in time I came to realize that the underlying assumptions of whole language made much more sense than those underlying more traditional [approaches to teaching reading and language arts]. Why should the acquisition of written communication [be treated so] differently from the acquisition of oral communication, as traditional approaches imply? Why should phonics skills be so far removed from authentic discourse that they become ends in and of themselves?
>
> My assumptions did not change all at once, but rather evolved gradually over time. For example, I was more readily able to accept new ideas about writing than reading and about more advanced reading than beginning reading. As I struggled with the issues of whole language and the beginning reader earlier this semester, I realized that my notion of how children acquire language proficiency was internally inconsistent. I knew that just as I couldn't treat the development of oral language differently [from] the development of written communication, I could not treat writing differently from

reading, or advanced readers differently from beginning readers.

Yet I was still confused about what, specifically, I should do with beginning readers. I actively attacked the readings, searching for "the" answer. The more I began to realize that I would not find the answer in the readings, the more I turned to you and to my peers for help. I thought I'd had enough theory. I thought I understood and accepted whole language. Now I wanted to know how to put the theory into practice. I was looking for a step-by-step guide. At first, your responses implied that you were not about to tell me what to do. Eventually, you even stated that there *was* no "right" way to put the theory into practice. Yet, I was convinced that you knew exactly what I should do, but you wanted me to figure it out for myself. I never once seriously entertained the possibility that you were being completely honest—that there was no magical formula to follow.

Last night at 2:00 a.m. I finished the readings [for this course]. The last two, Dyson's "Staying Free to Dance with the Children" and Graves's "The Enemy Is Orthodoxy" really hit home. Suddenly things started to come together. On the one hand, I was becoming increasingly aware of the dangers in the old orthodoxies [about the teaching of reading/writing] while, at the same time, I realized I was searching for new ones to replace them. It never dawned on me that certain dangers are inherent in any orthodoxy. Orthodoxies act as a substitute for thinking. They guard against new ideas and more current research. They take on a meaning parallel to that of phonics skills in that they too become goals in and of themselves regardless of their roles in the learning process. As Dyson notes, every classroom community differs with respect to its social, linguistic, and cognitive features, so how could there be one universally best way to put this [theory], or any sound theory, into practice?

I feel I've come a long way over the past year, and that my theor[ies] of the acquisition of language have evolved significantly. . . . In thinking about where I was a year ago today, where I am now, where I am going, and the means by which I am traveling, I am reminded of an analogy. . . . I am riding on a train through a long and dark tunnel. I see bright flashes of light that create the illusion that I am rapidly approaching the end of the tunnel. Then I discover that what I see [is not the tunnel's end, but] the headlights of another train coming to challenge my assumptions once again. . . .

As a teacher, I was excited by Karen's writing, which seemed to me to have unusual clarity and self-consciousness about learning. Karen had moved well beyond her insistence earlier in the year on the right answers, the list of tried-and-true methods, and the precise sequence of steps for teaching young children how to read and write. Instead she seemed to be in the process of constructing a theory of reading/language teaching (and maybe all teaching) that was based on understanding rather than procedure—on understanding the nature of language as a system, language learning as an active process, and children as individual language users within diverse linguistic and social settings. The view of teacher I saw emerging in her writing was that of decision maker and curriculum creator rather than direction follower and implementor of others' decisions. And I found it especially significant that she insisted that teaching was a skill one never mastered and that learning how to teach was a process one never finished, that instead she recognized there would always be new challenges to her assumptions and to the practices she would inevitably begin to take for granted.

The direction of Karen's learning seemed very much in keeping with our program's goals for student teachers and with the current research that suggests an image of teachers as "reflective professionals" (Clark & Peterson 1986). The research on teachers' knowledge indicates that teaching requires great breadth and depth of professional under-standing and judgment (Shulman 1986, 1987) in conditions that not only vary considerably across the diverse sociocultural contexts in which teachers work (Elbaz 1983; Feiman-Nemser & Floden 1986; Lampert 1985), but also — even within the relative stability of particular contexts — are inherently uncertain. Our elementary education programs at Penn are based on this view of teaching and are intended to provide students with opportunities to develop their own theories of practice, or ways to construct and use knowledge within the complex and particular contexts of their daily teaching lives.

But as I thought more about Karen's writing, I saw more questions than answers in it. What kinds of perspectives about teaching and learning had Karen had when she began her university preparation? Had she changed her ideas, or had she simply learned to be a "good student" in my class by raising the kinds of questions I privileged and reflecting on her own learning in the language I preferred? If she had genuinely changed her perspectives, what was the process through which she had come to hold new theories and reconstruct her knowledge? Would she, as a student, see the same changes that I saw in her perspectives? I realized that if I wanted to know more about these issues, I would have to take seriously the possibility that I could collaborate with student teachers as fellow researchers who would look with me at the processes involved in learning to teach.

These were the questions and interests that brought me the following semester to begin a collaborative project with Elizabeth and Rachel. I initially invited Elizabeth to work with me to explore the process of becoming a teacher because I saw her as a particularly articulate beginner in the program who wrote an engaging fieldwork journal filled with unusual attention to detail as well as interesting questions. I was also impressed by her willingness to stick with a difficult first fieldwork situation and, almost despite the odds, to function as a learner in that situation. Elizabeth soon suggested that we invite her classmate, Rachel, to join us. I had been intrigued by prior discussions with Rachel and by what I thought of as her "inquiry perspective on the world" as well as on teaching and would have agreed gladly under other circumstances. But especially because our research was designed to be collaborative and because I wanted Elizabeth to own it as much as I did, I felt it was her right to shape its direction. And so our research became a three-way endeavor.

It was much later that the three of us realized that although our research was from the beginning collaborative and mutual in certain senses, it was not in others. I wanted to know more about the interpretive perspectives and bodies of knowledge student teachers use to understand and analyze problems, issues, and questions. I was especially interested in the ways these would change and develop over time as students became teachers and began to practice in their own classrooms. Elizabeth and Rachel shared my questions to a certain extent. They were interested in exploring with me the ways that they as beginners were learning how to teach, and they were not simply agreeing to be helpful to me by cooperating as the "subjects" of my research. But they also had their own motives for the project. They approached the collaboration as an opportunity to become teacher researchers who inquire about their own teaching. They wanted the opportunity to think about teaching by meeting in a special context with their teacher, to unpack many of their assumptions about teaching and learning, and to dig through the layers of their interpretations and judgments about children and teachers.

Our research, within which intentional talk was the primary mode of inquiry, began for all three of us as a way to explore the process of learning to teach, and as we met we discovered that we were indeed talking our way into new understandings. But it was not until we began to analyze our months of talk that the research became collaborative in a deeper sense. As we worked together to hone questions and to plan what we thought of as a "rough analysis," we began to own the project in a different way. Our research shifted from collaboration in name, but really more mine than theirs, to much more genuinely "ours." We began to explore the process of learning to teach from their perspectives as student teachers as well as from my perspective as teacher educator. Our work became an effort to represent student teachers' perspectives from student teachers' perspectives rather than filtered through my perspectives and expressed in my words and analytic constructs, as a teacher educator. In the sections that follow, Elizabeth and Rachel share some of their perspectives on learning to teach.

Student Teachers' Perspectives

Elizabeth

As we have said, as part of a collaborative research project, we have been talking together about teaching over the last two years. Rachel and I bring to these discussions and to analysis of them the perspective of student teachers. This is a perspective that experienced educators can no longer have. Although we are inexperienced, we hope that seeing through our inquiring eyes will prompt more experienced teachers and researchers to form fresh insights or to make renewed connections about teaching. As we considered how planned talk helped us to learn about teaching and about ourselves as teachers, we found four inter-connected themes. The first two themes, which I discuss below, are *ways* we learned about teaching. The last two themes, which Rachel describes, are *things* we learned.

Edelsky (1989) has pointed out that genuine collaborative research is almost always embedded within a relationship that is larger than the collaboration itself. This was certainly true for us — our collaboration as student teachers began with our friendship. We were both college juniors when we decided we wanted to be teachers. That meant that instead of taking three years to complete the elementary education program, we had to do it in two. As all students know, there is usually more reading in an education course than any one student can handle, and we were taking four to five education courses per semester. This situation, coupled with our friendship, was the primary reason we began talking. Our first collaborative efforts occurred when we decided to split the assigned readings, read every other article, and then explain them to each another. Meeting every Sunday over coffee, we realized that our discussions extended beyond the assignments from class. Through our shared talk, we were not only learning the content of the readings, but we also found that we were gaining insights about ourselves as learners and thinking more critically about what we were reading. One example of how talk prompted me to read more critically was recorded in a reflective paper I wrote for our language arts course.

During one of our Sunday meetings, I began to explain to Rachel the concepts of an article that discussed the different kinds of questions students ask. I came to the realization that I had read the article, but had not thought about the underlying message. I had not thought deeply about what I was reading. In my paper I wrote:

> I began to go over my reading notes, and as I did this Rachel asked me several questions. What happened was that as I tried to answer her questions, I realized I had read through this entire article as if it were "gospel." ... Rachel's questions caused me to reevaluate what I

had read with a critical lens. ... It was through her questions that I
became aware of how much I really disagreed with [the ideas in the
article].

After we talked, I began to think more deeply about how I read
generally and about how this realization might apply to my teaching. I
realized that because I was not actively questioning as I read, I was not
actively constructing my own knowledge. I was merely trying to summarize the author's ideas. As a result of this discovery, I began more
actively and self-consciously to raise questions. Later in the same
paper I wrote:

> How are we as teachers going to create an environment in which our
> students can learn critical thinking if we do not think critically ourselves?
> I am one step closer to the goal of creating this environment for my
> future students by facing this issue now. I am challenged by the
> prospect of questioning all that I read and making my own evaluations
> of printed materials.

It is evident to me that through regular and planned talk with Rachel I
was coming to new understandings about how reading, thinking, and
questioning could contribute to my development as a learner and as a
teacher.

Rachel and I extended our discussions from the assigned course
readings to what was happening in each of our fieldwork classrooms.
Our discussions became more intense and frequent as they started to
include our student teaching experiences, and it became common for
us to talk four or five times a week for two or three hours. Sometimes
we recorded our discussions, at other times we jotted down notes. As
we became increasingly involved with each other's learning processes
and classroom experiences, Rachel became an essential contributor to
my learning. I realized that I wanted Rachel to join in my collaborative
efforts with Marilyn. If we were going to explore the processes of
learning to be teachers, Rachel and I both would need to be involved.

Rachel and I began to share our past and present written work,
which added a new dimension to our ever-changing perspectives as
student teachers. We found that sharing each other's dialogue journals
from previous semesters helped us raise new questions and prompted
new, perhaps deeper, reflections. An entry from Rachel's journal and
then a response to it in my own demonstrate the way in which our
talk and writing formed layer upon layer of reflection and inquiry.
Rachel had written in an early journal of her first experience with her
kindergartners:

> My cooperating teacher started to read a new version of "The Three
> Little Pigs" and a few pages into it, she asked if I would like to take

over and read. I said I'd love to, and it was an incredible experience. Reading to children is indescribable. I felt for the first time — or one of them — that I was ... (I want to say, "in control," but I wasn't because the children had as much control as I did). I guess it was doing something where I was on my own — [I was] *teaching*.

When I read this excerpt from Rachel's journal about her fieldwork experience the previous semester, it raised additional questions for me about the first experience I had had reading to the kindergartners in my current field placement class. After reading Rachel's journal, I wrote in my own:

> I felt [that] my first experience reading "A Very Busy Spider" last week could have been better. I felt I didn't "let go." My cooperating teacher sensed this as well. Yet when reading Rachel's journal, I realized she must have "let go" and really put herself into the story when she read. It's not that I was dead. It's just that I was not as animated as I would like to be. When I read Rachel's journal, I realized that she must be really great at reading with children. I am curious about how different the styles of all of us who are student teachers at Penn must be. It would be interesting to explore and compare our emerging styles. How much of our development is natural ability? How much is experience? How will we change in our presentation of materials to children? How will my story reading change over the course of the semester when I will really have my first [extended] experiences reading to groups of children?

It is evident to me that by sharing our written work, Rachel and I helped each other raise new questions, which prompted new connections in our teaching. One way we have been thinking about the function of our planned talk and writing is in relation to the dialectical notebooks we have learned to keep in our language arts course. By keeping notes on what we are reading, perhaps quotes, passages, or impressions on one page and then written responses to those notes on the facing pages, we realize that we are able to keep an ongoing dialogue with ourselves. We are able to keep track of our interpretations. As Berthoff (1987) suggests, this form of notation represents "a continuing effort to review the meanings we are making in order to see further what they mean." As we have worked together to analyze our months of talk about teaching, we realized that the two of us and sometimes the three of us have been engaging in a kind of oral dialectical notebook. By recording our conversations in writing and on audiotape, we have been able to return to many of our thoughts, questions, and issues. We have been able to monitor our interpretations and the meanings that we see emerging in our work. Through an oral search, we have been able to come to new understandings about what we see, think, and read as teachers.

Rachel

Elizabeth has touched on two of the ways we have learned to learn as student teachers—oral inquiry and written inquiry. In the pages that follow I have shared two understandings we reached by inquiring in these modes. First we came to understand that in addition to everything else it is, teaching is also an ongoing process of realizing who you are as a person. By this we mean that teaching is a self-conscious activity. We do not use this term in a negative sense. Rather by "self-conscious," we mean self-aware. We realize that as we inquire as teachers, we are becoming more introspective. As we look deeper into ourselves as people, we are looking deeper into ourselves as teachers.

I began to make the connection between the way I develop as a teacher and my own ongoing self-discovery after I served as a substitute in one of the science classes at the school where I am student teaching. The regular teacher had to go out of town unexpectedly, and I was left in charge of a science classroom for the first time in my teaching experience. The lesson plan the cooperating teacher had left for me required fifth-grade students to make collages of the four food groups by cutting out pictures from magazines and gluing them onto construction paper. It is an extreme understatement to say that the session was less than satisfactory. In fact I wrote in my journal:

> The students were out of control! They were running in and out of the classroom, pouring glue all over their hands and destroying experiments set up in the room. I felt I had no control despite my best efforts to bring some sort of order to the class.

Coincidentally I had a meeting already scheduled with Marilyn and Elizabeth directly following this experience. I retold the story to both of them, panicked because I would be substituting for the same class the next day. I certainly wanted to prevent the situation from recurring, and I wanted to do something authentic and meaningful with these fifth graders. But at the very least, I wanted to be able to leave the school with my sanity.

We talked at length about how I could restructure the lesson, organize the room, and manage several different activities. Through our talk I started to realize that managing a class had a lot to do with me as a person. This was part of our conversation:

Rachel: (*Determined*) I think what I have to do is somehow set up my limitations. I've *got* to get these kids to know my limitations.

Marilyn: (*Pushing*) What *are* your limitations?

Rachel: (*Very uncertain*) How do you verbalize your limitations?

Elizabeth: (*Helpful*) Well, you can say, "I won't put up with any—"

Marilyn: (*Pushing*) If you can't verbalize them, how are you going to tell the kids?

Rachel: (*Shaking her head, uncertain*) That's true.

Realizing the need for limitations in the classroom was only the beginning of a discovery for me. Our conversation helped me to see that I had to have limitations, but putting that concept into practice was another issue. I ended up actually writing down verbatim and rehearsing out loud the limitations Marilyn and Elizabeth pulled out of me.

Marilyn: (*Summarizing*) So, you're going to tell them your limits tomorrow.

Rachel: (*Resolved, emphatic*) I'm setting my limits.

Marilyn: Now, what *are* your limits?

Elizabeth: What *are* your limits?

Rachel: (*Laughing nervously, very tentative*) To have them not out of control?

Marilyn: (*Firm*) Yeah, but that's too vague.

Elizabeth: How are you going to define "out of control" for them?

Marilyn: What do you want to see? How will you know they are "not out of control"?

Rachel: (*Tentatively*) When I ask for their attention, they give it?

Marilyn: Okay, what else?

Rachel: (*Still tentative*) Um ... they stay in their seats and do what they're supposed to be doing?

Marilyn: Is that different from what they are normally expected to do?

Rachel: No.

These conversations make clear that at the very least I felt nervous and hesitant about establishing limitations in my classroom. I was being pushed to acknowledge the disastrous results that not having clear limits could have, but I was not really convinced that good teaching *should* mean limiting children — I didn't really like the idea. And even if I became convinced it was necessary, I was very uncertain about how to go about doing that. But it was not until two weeks later as I talked with Elizabeth about a personal issue that I realized that there was a direct connection between my unwillingness or inability to set limitations in my science class and my unwillingness to do so in my personal relationships. I finally came to see that I viewed setting limitations for myself as a weakness. I saw it as a way of cutting myself off, of no longer caring or giving to others. If I were to say to a friend, "I don't have time to listen right now," or tell a student in the classroom, "Just a minute, I'm busy," I felt it was a sign of my not caring for that person. It was not easy for me to define my limitations — it did not come naturally. But the reason I felt so insecure about setting limitations in my classroom was that I felt insecure about setting them in my own life.

Before I talked with Marilyn and Elizabeth, I had not believed that limitations were a necessity and a strength in the classroom and in personal relationships. I had understood the concept of limitation in theory, but not in practice — I had heard, read, and talked about limitations in many different situations, especially when I considered tactics of classroom management in some of my education courses. However, when it came time to apply my understandings of limitations in a classroom or in a personal relationship, I could not do it. I realize now that this insight has helped me to understand the personal nature of teaching. Teaching demands continual introspection. Each discovery I make about myself as a person is also a discovery I make about myself as a teacher. In this sense teaching is autobiographical: our teaching styles emerge from who we are as people.

The final theme from our collaborative exploration of how talk and writing helped us develop new understandings about teaching is what Elizabeth and I call "taking a second look." Over the past two years, Elizabeth and I have each been in three different teaching situations during our three semesters of fieldwork. We have discovered that in order to understand what is really happening in any classroom in any school, we, as teachers, will always have to look again. Through our talk and writing, we have learned how to ask certain kinds of questions that can help us do this. For example, instead of asking, "Are these children learning to read," we have come to ask first, "What does 'learning to read' mean?" and "What does 'learning to read' look like specifically in this classroom?"

One of my first experiences taking a second look by using this kind of questioning occurred during my first semester of fieldwork in a kindergarten classroom. After observing the children drawing and writing, I wrote in my journal:

> My cooperating teacher has the kindergartners use pencils with no erasers, which I thought at first was a good idea because children won't spend all their time erasing mistakes and trying to make [everything] perfect. But after watching a few children get so upset and frustrated because they made mistakes as they drew, it made me look at erasers in a different way. Maybe they're not such a bad idea. Without the erasers, children don't have a way to change what they think looks wrong. It puts pressure on them to [draw or write] perfectly the first time.

This seems to me to be a good example of using writing to take a second look. Although the issue of whether or not to give kindergartners erasers seems simple, I struggled with it in my journal for two pages. I did not reach any conclusions, but I used my writing as a way to wrestle with the issue. For me, what Lindfors (1987) has called "wrestle writing" became a vehicle for taking a second look and thinking more deeply about what I saw happening in a classroom.

Elizabeth and I also learned to take a second look through our talk together. An example of the way we wrestled orally with an issue occurred shortly after both of us began student teaching at a progressive independent school. In this school children were trusted and given a lot of freedom. There was time for social interaction because the philosophy of the school emphasized the development of the whole child. An excerpt from an early conversation we had about the school demonstrates the way we talked our way into taking a second look at what was going on there:

Rachel: I was just really shocked! I thought, "This is the most chaotic thing I have ever experienced!"

Elizabeth: Oh, I had this experience too! I can't believe it.

Rachel: I thought, "This is not really school. They don't do anything. There is nothing going on in these classrooms!"

Elizabeth: You didn't look behind the scenes, maybe.

Rachel: I know. I'm sure that's it. This is a first impression. I was just so shocked. I thought, "What's going on? Is there any learning going on here?" If I were an observer and had no experience or background in education and I walked into this classroom, I'd think, "This is ridiculous!" Now, being in this program, I am saying to myself, "Wait a second. Let's really look and see what's going on. Let's look at these kids, let's look at these teachers. Let's look at the dynamics of the classroom and really see."

Later on in the conversation, I told Elizabeth how I had thought initially that there was no learning going on in social studies class. I had observed as the students were studying ancient Egypt and preparing for a vocabulary test. But all they were doing was asking questions about the literal meanings of words on their study guides. As I observed, I was sure the students were studying only to pass the test and were not picking up any real content. It wasn't until I read a story written by one of the students later that day that my perceptions changed. The story was clever and interesting; it was full of detail about ancient Egypt, and it was drafted in language that indicated not only mastery of the vocabulary test words but also understanding of the concepts. I was forced to take a second look by thinking about what learning might look like at different times and in different situations.

Rachel: It was unbelievable. [In her story] she was talking about a palace and a pharaoh and how differently everybody was dressed.

Elizabeth: So how did that change how you looked at the class?

Rachel: It completely changed it. What I see in just walking in is a lot of chaos. But what I thought was chaos is not chaos. There is a lot of learning going on.

Elizabeth: So, what you're questioning now is maybe, "Is the right kind of learning [going on]?" Is that what you're saying, the right kind of information?

Rachel: No, no, not at all. I'm not questioning that at all.

Elizabeth: Oh, you've gone the other way now? You're saying, "I love this?"

Rachel: Well, no, it's not that drastic. Reading that girl's story completely shocked me. I was very impressed [by the content she had included about ancient Egypt]. I guess that there really is a lot of learning going on and that by not digging and trying to find [and understand] it, you won't see it. If I hadn't read that story and just gone on what I had seen that first day, I'd think this is the most unstructured school and that nothing goes on there.

Elizabeth pushed me in this conversation to pinpoint how my perceptions had changed. The point of our conversations was not whether or not vocabulary tests were the "right kind" of learning, but that we needed to look beyond the surface. Elizabeth noted this recurring theme of the importance of taking a second look when she wrote in her journal, about a week after our conversation, "A lot of behind-the-scenes thought and planning cannot be understood at first glance." For us, this has become a refrain that sums up our knowing that teachers need always to look again. Writing this article together offered us an opportunity to make sense out of our collaboration as student teachers, and in doing so provided us with the chance to take a second look generally at our process of learning to be teachers. We realize now that part of learning to be teachers is learning kinds of questions and forms of inquiry, such as taking a second look, that will last a lifetime.

Elizabeth and Rachel

Being involved in research has helped us develop our learning in several ways. First, it has helped us take control of our own learning. By becoming more involved in understanding how we learn, we have become more aware of ourselves as learners and this has in turn empowered us. We have also begun to feel confident about questioning what is presented to us in our college classes. Because we have become researchers who ask questions, we can no longer accept theories and practices simply because our teachers present them to us. To the dismay of some of our professors, we have even begun to question some of the ways our teachers teach us. We want to have control over what we learn. We have also learned something about the kind of teaching positions we hope to find as we leave the university and begin to look for work. Above all, we want teaching situations where we can continue to question and to reflect on our questions within a supportive environment. Although we are beginners, we have enough experience to know that this will not be an easy quest.

Implications

Our collaborative research suggests that student teachers may learn a great deal about teaching from opportunities to talk and write their ways into new understandings about teaching. Certainly the idea of teachers working together to reflect and inquire collaboratively about issues of teaching and learning is not a new one. Bank Street's teacher discussion groups, Bussis, Chittenden and Amarel's (1976) advisory services, Eleanor Duckworth's (1987) "moon watching" and other observation/inquiry activities with teachers, Patricia Carini's (1986) documentary processes with groups of teachers at The Prospect Center and School, Margaret Yonemura's (1982) notion of teacher conversations for professional growth, and the joint inquiry processes of teacher collaboratives such as the Philadelphia Teachers Learning Cooperative (1984) are examples of some of the many contexts in which this has happened before and happened quite successfully. Feiman-Nemser (1980) sums up some of the features of these successful collaborations by pointing out that "one develops the habit of reflection in teaching through varied opportunities to study and research practice in the company of reflective nonjudgmental colleagues. Similarly, one grows as a teacher in settings that value and support professional learning and offer accessible models" (138). It seems to us that in order to begin to learn to teach, student teachers need reflective and collaborative opportunities too—opportunities to add to their learning additional notions of self-conscious reflection about their own learning, or what Knoblauch and Brannon (1988) have called opportunities for "knowing their own knowing." Unfortunately, opportunities like these are not so easy to come by in the pre-service teacher education community, where "reflection" sometimes focuses on method apart from content or context, and supervisory discourse tends to emphasize procedures rather than inquiry (Cochran-Smith 1991a; Zeichner et al. 1988).

As we put away our notebooks at the end of the meeting we had convened to complete the final revisions for this chapter, we casually chatted about what we had learned about teaching by preparing a presentation and writing a piece for publication. Rachel and Elizabeth bolstered each other's satisfaction and enthusiasm:

> [Being researchers] gives us a kind of power. We know now that as teachers we *will* be able to find ways to write, to publish. ... There's no reason to think that we can't. The things that we write will have value, and our observations *will* matter. ... As teachers, we will have something to say to others. [Talking and writing collaboratively] give us confidence about our beliefs, our insights, and our realizations.

Few students enter the teaching profession as knowledge makers and question askers. We think this is an important way to begin.

Postscript

It has been a nearly a year since we put the final touches on this chapter and had our last discussion about learning to teach. Since that time Elizabeth has nearly finished her first year of teaching at La Jolla Country Day School in southern California, Rachel has almost concluded a year at Brookwood School in Manchester, Massachusetts, and Marilyn has continued her work as an educator and researcher at the University of Pennsylvania. The perspectives and voices of student teachers themselves are critical to, but almost always missing from, the literature on learning to teach. This argument is similar to one made elsewhere about the need for teachers themselves to have a way of getting their knowledge into the "official" canons of what is known about teaching and learning (Cochran-Smith & Lytle 1990):

> Efforts to construct and codify a knowledge base for teaching have relied primarily on university-based research and ignored the significant contributions that teacher knowledge can make to both the academic research community and the community of school-based teachers. As a consequence, those most directly responsible for the education of children have been disenfranchised. ... [Teacher research] makes accessible some of the expertise of teachers and provides both university and school communities with unique perspectives on teaching and learning. (2)

For a long time student teachers and their school and university mentors have been disenfranchised from the making of knowledge about learning to teach. Opportunities for prospective teachers to construct their own meanings, monitor their own interpretations, and research their own learning should become standard parts of pre-service programs. But just as importantly, part of the job of teacher educators is to provide opportunities for their students to read the work of other beginning and experienced teacher researchers as well as opportunities to disseminate their writings to others.

Since Elizabeth and Rachel graduated last spring, the manuscript for this chapter and a number of other pieces of teacher research written by student teachers and experienced teachers have become part of the reading required in our pre-service programs. New students read Elizabeth Garfield and Rachel Greenberger along with John Dewey, Carole Edelsky, Shirley Brice Heath, Ann Berthoff, and Paulo Freire. Students often choose to respond to Garfield and Greenberger in the reflective essays assigned for their courses. Some learn direct practical strategies about learning to be teachers by patterning study groups after Rachel's and Elizabeth's, dividing major responsibility for course readings and meeting to review, argue, and make connections among the various articles and their own experiences in student teaching classrooms. Some write about personal (and sometimes painful) insights that have become professional insights for them when they come to see, as Rachel did, that teachers teach what and who they are. Some compare first impressions with later reflections on children and classrooms, owning their erroneous and often unfair initial judgments, and describing their efforts to look again to try to see through other eyes. In short, when students read this piece and the research of other teachers and student teachers who have gone before them, they often see their own emerging ideas about learning to teach through the mirrors and windows of these experiences.

Reading the self-conscious reflections of other experienced teachers and student teachers who are learning to teach invites beginners into the intellectual community of teacher researchers. It tells prospective teachers that novices and experienced professionals alike are continually learning to teach, and it emphasizes that one of the best ways to link theory and practice is through a process of self-critical and systematic inquiry about teaching, learning, and schooling. When everybody in a community is a researcher, power is shared, knowledge about teaching is understood to be fluid and socially constructed, and the wisdom and language of school-based teachers are seen to be as essential to the knowledge base for beginning teaching as are the wisdom and language of university-based researchers.

Finally, the literature of teacher and student teacher research adds new perspectives to the information we have about learning to teach. It brings many new voices to an endeavor that has been dominated by the voices of university-based researchers who are removed physically as well as conceptually from the day-to-day work of teaching children. If we agree that understanding the process of learning to teach is "multivoiced," then it is clear that student teachers and teachers, who are the closest to the work and who have the greatest stake in the process, must have prominent voices.

Works Cited

Berthoff, A. E. 1987. The teacher as REsearcher. In *Reclaiming the classroom*, ed. D. Goswami and P. Stillman. Portsmouth, NH: Boynton/Cook.

Bussis, A., E. A. Chittenden, and M. Amarel. 1976. *Beyond surface curriculum*. Boulder, CO: Westview.

Carini, P. 1986. *Prospect's documentary processes*. Bennington, VT: The Prospect Center.

Clark, C., and P. L. Peterson. 1986. Teachers' thought processes. In *Handbook of research on teaching*, 3d ed., ed. M. C. Wittrock. New York: Macmillan.

Cochran-Smith, M. 1991a. Learning to teach against the grain. *Harvard Educational Review* 61(3): 279–310.

———. 1991b. Reinventing student teaching. *Journal of Teacher Education* 42(2): 104–18.

Cochran-Smith, M., and S. L. Lytle. 1990. Research on teaching and teacher research: The issues that divide. *Educational Researcher* 19(2): 2–11.

Duckworth, E. 1987. *The having of wonderful ideas*. New York: Teachers College.

Edelsky, C. 1989. The nature of collaborative research. Paper presented at the National Council of Teachers of English spring conference, Charleston, South Carolina.

Elbaz, F. 1983. *Teacher thinking: A study of practical knowledge*. New York: Nichols.

Feiman-Nemser, S. 1980. Growth and reflection as aims in teacher education: Directions for research. In *Exploring issues in teacher education: Questions for future research*, ed. G. Hall. Austin: Research and Development Center for Teacher Education, University of Texas.

Feiman-Nemser, S., and R. E. Floden. 1986. The cultures of teaching. In *Handbook of research on teaching*, 3d ed., ed. M. C. Wittrock. New York: Macmillan.

Goodman, J. 1988. University culture and the problem of reforming field experiences in teacher education. *Journal of Teacher Education* 29(5): 45–53.

Knoblauch, C. H., and L. Brannon. 1988. Knowing our knowledge: A phenomenological basis for teacher research. In *Audits of meaning: A festschrift in honor of Ann E. Berthoff*, ed. L. Z. Smith. Portsmouth, NH: Boynton/Cook.

Lampert, M. 1985. How do teachers manage to teach? Perspectives on problems in practice. *Harvard Educational Review* 55: 178–94.

Lindfors, J. 1987. *Children's language and learning.* Englewood Cliffs, NJ: Prentice-Hall.

Lytle, S. L., and M. Cochran-Smith. 1990. Learning from teacher research: A working typology. *Teachers College Record* 92(1): 83–103.

Philadelphia Teachers Learning Cooperative. 1984. On becoming teacher experts: Buying time. *Language Arts* 61: 731–36.

Shulman, L. 1986. Those who understand: Knowledge growth in teaching. *Education Researcher* 15(2): 4–14.

———. 1987. Knowledge and teaching: Foundations of the new reform. *Harvard Educational Review* 51: 1–22.

Yonemura, M. 1982. Teacher conversations: A potential source of their own professional growth. *Curriculum Inquiry* 12: 239–56.

Zeichner, K., D. Liston, M. Mahlios, and M. Gomez. 1988. The structure and goals of a student teaching program and the character and quality of supervisory discourse. *Teaching and Teacher Education* 4: 349–62.

Response

Betsy A. Bowen

When I first read this report of Marilyn, Elizabeth, and Rachel's collaborative research I found myself accounting for the project as a happy accident—the product of an unusual combination of dedicated students, a gifted teacher, and a rigorous but supportive environment. Together, these three participants had studied both the process of learning to teach and the talk they used as they studied that process. For two years they met regularly to talk, reflect, and write, trying to understand how student teachers learn to teach and how talk can function as a vehicle for learning.

But as I thought more about their project, I realized that my first explanation for the richness of their inquiry was inadequate, even dismissive, since it shortchanges both these researchers and ourselves as their colleagues. If we assume that the participants' situation by itself brings about research like this, we imagine a distance between ourselves and researchers and cut ourselves off from the process of discovering more about the enterprise we are all engaged in.

If, then, intelligence, good intentions, and a congenial context do not explain the fruitfulness of this research project, what does? What made it possible for these three researchers to carry out extended, self-conscious, and satisfying inquiry? Ann Berthoff's essay, "The Teacher as REsearcher" (*The Making of Meaning*, Portsmouth, NH: Boynton/ Cook, 1981) provides some clues. Early in that essay Berthoff comments:

> Educational research is nothing to our purpose unless we formulate
> the questions; if the procedures by which answers are sought are not
> dialectic and dialogic, that is to say, if the questions are not continually
> REformulated by those who are working in the classroom, educational
> research is pointless. (31)

Three features of Marilyn, Elizabeth, and Rachel's research strike me in light of Berthoff's assertion: first, that all three participants were involved in framing the questions for the inquiry; then, that the process of discovery was carried on largely through what they called "deliberate talk"; and, finally, that the questions they asked and the answers they came to were repeatedly reformulated as participants strove to "take a second look."

Marilyn, Elizabeth, and Rachel formulated research questions for themselves at numerous points in the project. Marilyn explains that the heart of the early education program at the University of Pennsylvania is the "notion of student teacher-as-researcher." The program says, in other words, that student teachers *must* formulate questions to investigate in the classroom. This is, as Marilyn points out, a decidedly untraditional approach to teacher education. It assumes that research — or thinking critically about the process in which you are engaged — is not something you do *after* you have learned how to teach. It is something you do *in order* to learn to teach. Perhaps Elizabeth explains this relationship between inquiry and effective teaching best in her journal entry: "How are we as teachers going to create an environment in which our students can learn critical thinking if we do not think critically ourselves?"

But Berthoff's exhortation to formulate our own questions applies in another, more specific way to the project. Marilyn notes that, while all three participants shared a commitment to inquiry, the questions that motivated them differed. Her interest was in the interpretive perspectives and knowledge about teaching that student teachers developed; Elizabeth and Rachel's was in the process of student teaching itself. As Jim Moffett points out in his response to Carol Stumbo's chapter earlier in this volume, such differences in teachers' and students' interests frequently occur in shared research projects. Teachers want to know more about language and learning; students want to know more about the world, in this case the world of being a new teacher. During the course of this project, the participants learned to accommodate these differences, most dramatically by enlarging the inquiry to include Rachel. I think that the ability to accommodate all three participants' questions and needs contributed substantially to the satisfaction that Marilyn, Elizabeth, and Rachel derived from their collaboration and to their ability to sustain the project for two years.

If Ann Berthoff is right that productive research must be both dialectic and dialogic, then it is not surprising that Marilyn, Elizabeth, and Rachel describe their research as a process of "talking [their] way into new understandings." Throughout the course of the project, Marilyn, Elizabeth and Rachel met regularly to discuss the process of learning to teach. These discussions, and the participants' subsequent reflections on them, served as the center of their inquiry. Similarly, the collaboration between Elizabeth and Rachel began as purposeful talk: they talked as a way to manage and make sense of their readings for class. Other reports in this volume testify to the power of talk to help us make sense of our observations in the classroom. Sara Allen, for instance, formed a discussion group of colleagues who reviewed videotapes of classroom discussion with her, jointly analyzing and interpreting what they saw.

But talk alone may not be enough. For these researchers, as for Sara Allen, it was important to reflect together on their talk. Marilyn, Elizabeth, and Rachel made that possible by tape-recording many of their discussion sessions. It was this reflection, Marilyn says, that made their work truly collaborative. This reflection also made their research dialectic because it enabled them to reexamine, and hence reinterpret, their understanding of experience. Marilyn, Elizabeth, and Rachel were each challenged, then, by their own earlier assessments of experience as well as by one another's questions and comments. In fact, Elizabeth even compares their talk and reflection to an "oral dialectical notebook" that enabled them to reinterpret their understanding of learning to teach. This cycle of reflection and opposition, leading to new understanding, is the core of what Ann Berthoff calls dialectic.

Finally, good research, Berthoff maintains, requires that we continually reformulate our questions, or, as Rachel explains it, that we habitually "take a second look." Berthoff and Rachel both urge us to scrutinize our interpretations of experience and the questions that guide our inquiry. Rachel illustrates this process in her discussion with Elizabeth of an apparently chaotic classroom. Nudged by Elizabeth's questions, Rachel eventually labels her initial judgment a "first impression" and forces herself to reconsider it, saying: "Let's really look and see what's going on. Let's look at these kids, let's look at these teachers. Let's look at the dynamics of the classroom and really see."

This deliberate effort to reconsider assumptions or first impressions occurs throughout the project. In fact, Marilyn reports that the entire inquiry began when she took a second look at Karen's journal entry and began to wonder if real change had occurred and, if so, in what way. By consistently questioning initial assumptions, Marilyn, Elizabeth, and Rachel complicate and enrich their inquiry.

15

Meeting Strangers in Familiar Places
Teacher Collaboration by Cross-Visitation

Susan L. Lytle
Robert Fecho

Much has been written about the isolation of classroom teachers, yet relatively little is known about what goes on in programs within schools that seek to remedy this situation. Diminishing teacher isolation and creating more collegial environments for learning is not a simple proposition. A secondary teacher in a large urban comprehensive high school describes her experience with isolation in the following way:

> I used to wonder if there were other teachers in the building. 'Cause I used to walk in — of course it was quiet — so you come in to your room. And the way my schedule goes, you know, I never really saw anybody. And there's no lunch time. And then when I'd open the door at 2:04 everybody was gone. So I used to laugh to myself and say it was — you know — I was the only person in this building *really*. There were no other teachers. It was a figment of my imagination. They just *told* me there were other teachers in this building. In terms of isolation it was great, absolutely great. . . . And no support. Nobody did anything really very much to make me feel comfortable or included. . . . It wasn't deliberate; it wasn't antagonistic. I think it's part of that whole syndrome. You get in your little room and you close your door and that isolation makes you very comfortable.

On the one hand, alienation from other adults is disturbing. Yet, as this teacher suggests, isolation also provides an opportunity for privacy.

The security of one's own classroom allows for teaching unobserved. Working in solitude means that, as teachers sometimes put it, "nothing gets put on the line."

In this chapter we describe a program designed by urban teachers to alleviate their own isolation and to provide a new context for collegial learning. Called "cross-visitation" by the teachers who suggested the concept, the program enables pairs of experienced K–12 teachers to enhance their own practices and intellectual lives through access to each other's classrooms. Through periodic visits, they have the opportunity to build long-term reciprocal relationships integrated with their day-to-day responsibilities. Cross-visitation is designed to promote collaborative inquiry into teaching and more specifically, into language, literacy, and learning in urban classrooms.

Research on cross-visitation is central to the model at two levels; teachers are not only documenting their experiences in the classroom but also helping to collect, analyze, and interpret data about the program as a whole. We have taken responsibility for designing the study documented here, for coordinating data collection and preliminary analysis, and for writing this summation. To these activities we bring the perspectives of a classroom teacher who has been involved in cross-visitation for four years and a university-based researcher and teacher educator who directs the writing project. Drawing on interviews and teachers' writings, we describe from the perspective of teachers their experiences in struggling to "fold back the classroom walls" (Fecho 1987).

Peer Coaching, Reflective Practice, and Collegial Learning

On the surface, cross-visitation would seem to have some similarities with peer coaching, a practice that has recently gained considerable acceptance in many school districts. As described by Joyce and Showers (1982), peer coaching is necessary to transfer skills learned in staff development sessions effectively to the classroom. The peer coaching model that begins with theory, demonstration, practice, and feedback requires "social support" so that teachers can implement the new strategies in their classrooms over time. Based on an athletic metaphor in which complex behaviors are broken down into component skills and then, with overlearning, integrated into the classroom environment, peer coaching aims for teachers to gain executive control so that these new behaviors become automatic.

The notion of peer coaching, we argue, is based on a set of assumptions about the nature of professional development for teachers that is less innovative than it appears. While collegial or collaborative work is clearly emphasized, the dominant image of teachers as learners is still outside in: staff development as a process by which teachers are trained (sometimes by other teachers) and then take what they learn — presumably acquired out of a classroom setting — back to their class-rooms. "Training" is what teachers are presumed to need, and although they may participate in the design of staff development, the thought processes acquired are regarded as the effects of this training, and not the sources or causes. Although Showers, Joyce, and Bennett do not exclude teachers' concepts about teaching from the content of training, the examples and models given imply that in staff development teachers absorb theory and research generated elsewhere, most often in academia.

In a recent critique of coaching, Hargreaves and Dawe (1989) argue that one form, which they call "technical" coaching, focuses on the learning and transfer of new skills and strategies and not on what teachers *bring* to the training: their meanings, experiences, and real-world problems. Hargreaves and Dawe argue that because technical coaching is not self-critical, it often perpetuates the status quo. For teachers to participate in generating the knowledge base for teaching (Cochran-Smith & Lytle 1990), they need to be involved proactively in their own professional development (Lambert 1989).

In contrast to peer coaching, cross-visitation is more closely aligned with views of staff or professional development that emphasize teachers' experiences and support reflection on practice rather than the view of teaching as the orchestration of technical skills applicable across settings. The design of cross-visitation is compatible with recent discussions of reflective teaching and practical theory (Schon 1983, 1987; Clark & Peterson 1986; Elbaz 1983; Feiman-Nemser 1980), which suggest that teaching involves making decisions based on teachers' own theoretical frameworks and not simply skilled practice. When viewed as a primarily intellectual (rather than technical) activity, teaching involves knowledge and judgment, uncertain conditions, and often unpredictable outcomes. Reflective teachers see issues in their complexity, question the routines of teaching, and search for new understandings of the classrooms from the perspectives of learners. The recent literature on teacher research builds on this view of teaching and argues for a more prominent role for classroom teachers in the generation of the knowledge base for teaching (Goswami & Stillman 1986; Lytle & Cochran-Smith 1988; Cochran-Smith & Lytle 1990). In reflective practice, teaching is regarded as a "highly complex, context-specific, [and] interactive activity in which differences across classrooms, schools, and communities are critically important" (Cochran-Smith & Lytle 1988).

The literature on teachers' professional relations and the culture of schools as a workplace has its own critique of what goes under the name of collaboration and collegiality. Little (1989) distinguishes among a range of teacher-to-teacher interactions, which differ according to degrees of interdependence. Some relations between and among teachers may be characterized as simply "storytelling," others as mutual aid or helping, and still others as sharing or joint work. "Joint work" is Little's term for teachers involved in collective action in which a collective view of autonomy is substituted for a private version. While we are beginning to have a theoretical understanding of these distinctions, there has been relatively little study of how teachers actually influence each other's thinking and thus few in-depth descriptions of collaborative work and decision making (see, for example, Rorschach & Whitney 1986).

Other research on teachers as colleagues argues that true collaboration may be relatively rare. Hargreaves (1989) distinguishes between what he calls the "collaborative culture" (similar to Little's 'joint work') and "contrived collegiality," which "can be little more than a quick, slick administrative surrogate for more genuinely collaborative teacher cultures" (19). Because collaborative cultures take time to develop, rely on trust and mutual understanding, and arise from both the day-to-day and the long-term relationships of the participants, too often school districts try to abridge the process by merely creating common planning periods or convening more teacher-led meetings. Hargreaves points out that the resulting collaborations take on a facile air in which the participants feel compelled to work together as opposed to seeking out each other for support. Such collaborations rarely, if ever, get beyond what Little describes as storytelling—short, ad hoc searches for information, commiseration, or affirmation.

Cross-Visitation as a Form of Collegial Learning

Cross-visitation provides the opportunity for teachers to make sense of and improve their everyday practice, not by imitating routines and strategies but rather by questioning, observing, documenting, and discussing their own work in relation to the work of others. It more closely resembles "collegial coaching," which Garmston (1987, cited in Hargreaves & Dawe 1989) describes as being "directed more to the context of teaching and to the processes of self-reflection and professional dialogue among teachers." Working from the original conception, teachers who visit each other seek to create a collaborative culture, one in which the participants voluntarily work with each other over time. These meetings are not the result of administrative fiat, but are based upon reciprocal needs, mutual respect, and the appreciation of complementary talents.

Cross-visitation assumes that by discussing alternative ways of professional thinking, teachers become both "more aware of their own thinking" and more attuned to the notion that "alternative ways of thinking are possible" (Floden & Feiman 1980; as cited in Zumwalt 1984, 228). In connection with these activities, participants may engage in various forms of teacher research, defined here as "systematic, intentional inquiry" and including journals, essays, oral inquiry processes, and classroom studies (Lytle & Cochran-Smith, in press). Teachers' perspectives on teaching and learning are conspicuously missing from traditional — and current — research in the field. The *Handbook of Research on Teaching* (Wittrock 1986), for example, contains no articles written by teachers nor citations to published examples of their research (Cochran-Smith & Lytle 1990).

Called "Teacher-Consultants" or TCs, program participants interviewed in this study are K−12 teachers and fellows in the Philadelphia Writing Project (PhilWP), an urban site of the National Writing Project located at the University of Pennsylvania. The one hundred seventy teacher-consultants currently in Philadelphia's cross-visitation program thus have in common (a) participation in one or more intensive summer institutes focusing on themselves as writers and on theoretical frameworks and practices related to writing, learning, and teacher research; and (b) ongoing participation in a teacher-governed urban writing and reading project, which holds monthly meeting and supports teacher presentations, publications, conferences, and workshops. The Philadelphia Writing Project builds on the notions that theory and practice are reciprocally related and that change in classrooms results primarily from teachers' systematic, critical inquiry into practice over time.

The cross-visitation program is one component of a Teacher-Consultant Program developed collaboratively by the university, the school district of Philadelphia (which funds the program), and a closely linked curriculum development organization set up with corporate and foundation funds (the Philadelphia Alliance for Teaching Humanities in the Schools — PATHS). Each of the seven subdistricts within the larger school district has been provided with a writing support teacher, a long-term substitute hired for this program by the central administration. By a system of referrals designed to be voluntary and to work through the teachers themselves (as well as through principals and supervisors), teacher-consultants link up with other teachers in their own buildings, in other schools in their subdistrict, or across the district as a whole. Arrangements are negotiated by the teachers for visiting each others' classrooms; the writing support teacher provides continuity by taking over the class of either the TC or his/her partner. Ideally, these support teachers get to know the TCs' students and curriculum, and function as team teachers rather than as conventional substitutes. Visits with partner teachers may take place once or twice each month, depending on the number of teacher-consultants in the particular district and on other factors to be described below.

Studying Cross-Visitation

To investigate cross-visitation, data are being collected by teacher-consultants and university-based researchers working collaboratively. These data include: (1) *teacher logs* — monthly records of patterns of participation in the cross-visitation program, e.g., partners, own school, or others, grade levels, subjects, strategies for initiating contact; (2) *teacher journals* — more detailed accounts of the content of particular cross-visitations including types of interactions in each other's classrooms, questions and concerns, changes in teaching that resulted; (3) *interviews* — more in-depth, retrospective accounts of different perspectives including teacher-consultants, partner teachers, writing support teachers, administrators, and students; (4) *surveys* — broad-based paper-pencil questionnaires completed periodically by teacher-consultants; and (5) *teacher writing* — essays, applications, reports of classroom studies, papers prepared for presentation at conferences and meetings. Standard methods of qualitative data analysis are being used: review of the entire corpus, identification of typical and discrepant instances by method of analytic induction, and content analysis of logs, journals, interview transcripts, surveys, and other teacher writing.

In this exploratory article, we describe broad themes suggesting what teachers themselves indicate they are learning — about teaching as a public and private activity, about reciprocity in collegial relationships, and about empowerment in large, urban school systems. To do this we draw primarily on fifteen extensive interviews with teacher-consultants who have been participating in the program for one to four years and on writings about cross-visitation, including essays in project publications and applications to the summer institutes. Through the eyes of teachers we show how cross-visitation has been understood and constructed by other members of the school community — in relation to the conception of the program as teachers had originally envisioned it.

We regard the study of cross-visitation as a form of collaborative action research (Oja & Smulyan 1989; Carr & Kemmis 1986). Many teachers have participated in the data collection, analysis, and interpretation reported in this exploratory study. Teachers interviewed each other, collated excerpts from teacher writings, and participated in oral inquiry sessions in which preliminary categories of data were discussed and refined. As Zumwalt (1984) points out, collaborative research of this type may be regarded as a form of continuing education for in-service teachers:

> Support is needed for the continued education of experienced teachers
> that goes beyond the usual credential collecting and workshop smorgas-
> bord. Collaborative efforts that involve practitioners, researchers,
> and teacher educators in the process of conducting research or exper-
> imenting with substantive findings in their own settings need to be
> encouraged. Projects involving collaboration and deliberation ...
> need close attention. All are based on the belief that research and the
> research process can inform practice. And all recognize and respect
> the problem-solving and decision-making capacities of practitioners.
> (247)

In the next section we explore some of the recurrent patterns that
these practitioner-researchers identified.

What Teachers Say: Recurrent Themes

The interviews speak both to the uniqueness and to the commonality
of teachers' experiences. While the particulars of classroom, grade
level, school, and subdistrict varied considerably, three themes were
interwoven throughout. The first relates to the teachers' image of the
act of teaching—as a fundamentally private process involving a set of
complex relationships with students inside the classroom, essentially a
world unto itself—or alternately, as a process integrally related to the
work of others, more public, and open to sharing. The second focuses
on the nature of collaboration; although teachers seek and expect
some kind of reciprocity when cross-visiting, unanticipated obstacles
often occur in negotiating new relationships. The third involves the
teacher functioning in the system, where various actors carry different
and often conflicting conceptions of what it means to collaborate about
the improvement of teaching. Tracing these overlapping themes in the
transcripts of interviews and texts of teacher writing reveals what
teachers are learning through this unusual process of connecting with
other teachers.

Public and Private

The teacher-consultants interviewed for this study include one beginning
teacher (three years), ten who have taught for fourteen to fifteen
years, and three with more than twenty years' experience. Although a
few have some limited experience team teaching, particularly at the
elementary level, opportunities to observe and collaborate with teachers
in their own buildings or in other schools in the district have been rare.
If these have occurred, they have typically been one-shot and non-
reciprocal. Many teachers in the writing project report never having
seen the teacher next door teach, despite fifteen or more years of
proximity.

The most obvious, yet we think nontrivial, effect of engaging in cross-visitation has been a broadening of participating teachers' knowledge base about what occurs in their own schools as well as in the district as a whole. Teachers report learning about other grade levels and other content areas, about students with special needs and about different school cultures. As one teacher puts it, "it matters to me that we continue to have some time to mix across grade levels and disciplines. The generic similarities of teaching are much more powerful than the content and contextual constraints that separate elementary and secondary teachers. Within the school system there has traditionally been a separation; I learn from the mix." Another tells why teachers are willing to risk revealing their practice:

> My collaborations with teachers within my own school have been particularly interesting. I don't have to establish my credibility because my colleagues know I teach five classes a day including advisory, and I teach everyone, from remedial ninth graders to college-bound twelfth graders. I invite teachers to observe my classes or to allow me to observe their classes — there's an intimacy that already exists because we share a large piece of our lives in the same place. They don't have to be afraid that I'll see students who are distracted, bored, or disruptive, because they know if Ronald Smith is like that in their rooms, undoubtedly he has exhibited similar behavior in my room.

After fourteen years in what she calls "a pretty secluded environment," another teacher-consultant says she thought she knew "what teachers are like." Leaving her small school meant a way to "broaden [her] horizons" and as a consequence to see possibilities in people and relationships she had written off as static and limited.

While teachers' interdependency was tacitly acknowledged before cross-visiting, one by-product of *going public* was that teachers saw how their own work with students depended directly on the work of others. The network of classrooms — the teachers the students had last year, the others they encounter each day, and even the ones whom they will meet subsequently — all are in a sense participants in one's own classroom. Continuity with students may be an unanticipated benefit:

> In my own school, I like the fact that I've had the opportunity to do demonstration lessons with children who are now in seventh grade that I taught last year. They were children I was very close to . . . and I like the idea of going in and doing an activity with them again. I knew that they enjoyed writing. I went in and I knew that I was going to get an enthuasiastic response. . . . I think they responded positively to the activity that I did and a couple of them mentioned it again in the hallway in the days that followed. So I knew that I had reestablished a link there. And sort of the reverse of that, I also did a demonstration lesson with a group of fifth graders I will probably have next year. I

like the idea of going in and establishing the fact that I'm a person who will be involved in their education next year, and I'm giving them a little preview of upcoming things that they're going to do in sixth grade.

Cross-visitation appears to make teachers more conscious of their membership in a school community; although much of professional practice is conducted in private, its effects are shared. Student expectations about writing in one classroom or subject area are in a sense informed by expectations — or the lack thereof — in all others.

Another consequence of "going public" is that teacher-consultants begin to see their own classrooms as more intellectually interesting and challenging. This comes from several dimensions of the experience of cross-visiting. By both being observed and observing, they find that what has been routine becomes less so:

I was able to see myself in ways that I had never seen myself before. It's very hard to see yourself through somebody else's eyes when you are the only one in the classroom and there are no other eyes there. When suddenly there are other eyes watching you teach, when suddenly ... you're inside someone else's little world, you can see yourself in [new] ways.

Teachers also report changing their routine behaviors and learning from their students:

We teacher-consultants have come out from the isolation of our own classrooms and into one another's, looking at and talking about those things that we do. I'm not the same teacher that I was. My exploration of and excitement about my own learning and writing processes have made me more sensitive to those of my students. I'm not there just to learn, but to learn about myself as a teacher. The students are not there just to learn, but to help teach me how to make them more effective learners. I write in class now. I write with, to, for, and about my students.

Stepping out is clearly a route to improving *what's in*. Experiencing diverse viewpoints about what is familiar, or even repetitive, seems to contribute to teachers' energy and investment into their daily practice. Part of what is learned is that classrooms are not simply "familiar places"; teaching is a context-specific activity in which there is not just one perspective on what occurs, nor is there necessarily one best way to function in the classroom. Cross-visitation can lead, as we have shown, to appreciation for the richness and diversity of practice.

Making teaching more public is not without its problems, however. Teachers frequently report conflict about the loss of privacy and security entailed in the program. For some, self-sufficiency as a teacher has been a long-standing value. Furthermore, the norm that good teachers are expected to "handle it" in their own classrooms is a feature of the school culture working explicitly against collaboration. Teachers feel vulnerable and thus not entirely sanguine about the possibility that others see their less than perfect practice. As one teacher put it, "I've spoken with other teacher-consultants and our approaches still seem to threaten well-established teachers who feel that is it 'shameful' to need networking." For others, a teacher coming in may be regarded, at least initially, as an intrusion. One partner teacher, who later became a teacher-consultant, expresses it this way:

> The more isolated you become, the more protective you become of your area and then you look at, as an intrusion, somebody coming into your room ... you become more prone to feel like you're being judged.

Many teacher-consultants report having qualms about leaving their classroom to work with other teachers. Even when their classes are covered by an experienced writing support teacher, teachers feel that they are losing time with their own students and losing control over their classroom. These comments remind us that part of the ethos of teaching is that good teachers are in their classrooms, have good attendance, and do not seek opportunities to be away from their students.

What seems clear from the data so far is that teachers often feel conflicted, as the following quote aptly illustrates:

> I have been for many years an in-my-classroom teacher, doing most of my best work in seclusion—not sharing it with anybody because I was afraid I would be laughed at, I was afraid I would be told you work too hard ... so you don't share anything because you're afraid of that slap.

Cross-visitation clearly involves a set of risks associated with the loss of privacy. Yet from the data we see that teachers who participate in cross-visitation are likely to view themselves more as members of a professional community. Instead of "knowing" their school through the lore of the teachers' lounge or making the assumption that one's own experience is universal, teachers through firsthand observations and interactions with their colleagues have acquired new insights that stimulate useful questions about practice. Negotiating relationships with colleagues unaccustomed to reciprocity has proven, however, to be a particularly challenging aspect of the program, as we show in the next section.

Giving and Getting

Analyzing teachers' descriptions of their collaborations suggests that among the teacher-consultants and their partner teachers there are a number of conflicting conceptions that function as constraints or obstacles to teacher-to-teacher collaboration. The first relates to the expectation that the teacher-consultant will function in the role of expert on the teaching of writing. The following quotations from the transcripts of several of the teachers interviewed suggest the pervasiveness of and some of the problems associated with this view:

> The school district model, of necessity, has been one person disseminating "knowledge" to other people ... you know, that is the model people look for.

> One of the disadvantages is that ... you are viewed ... as an expert. This is an expert that's come to talk about writing and they are going to provide you with all the magical answers to all the problems that you have ... I found I have to clarify that when I go into a school right away—that I'm not an expert and I didn't come here to talk to you, I came to talk *with* you.

> I was very sensitive to the fact that I wanted to go in, not as any kind of an expert, but just as someone who heard some things and interacted with some things that I found very interesting and perhaps they would too. ... I know I'm very sensitive to people coming in and, without any background on what I'm doing, giving me advice on how this ought to be done or that ought to be done.

> I've confirmed the fact that collaboration is difficult when collaboration is in a situation that might be perceived as collaboration among unequals. I see myself as another second-grade teacher coming to talk to a second-grade teacher (or whatever grade) but they see me as someone who is coming with some expertise attributed to me. And I think that needs to be downplayed in order for something to succeed, for it really to be a collaboration as opposed to an instruction.

> And this teacher was very content. She didn't talk too much to me. Even when we were conferencing there would be moments of silence because she didn't have any questions. She was waiting for me to tell her things, or waiting for me to suggest things.

While we see here the teacher-consultants being cast in the traditional role of "knower" by their partner teachers, we also see teacher-consultants unsure about how to interrupt these expectations and establish these relationships on a different basis. Their ambivalence or uncertainty stems in part, it seems, from their awareness that participation in professional development experiences such as summer institutes and their roles in staff development at the district level do make them more knowledgeable about some aspects of teaching than their peers. They "know" more about writing and about teaching "as a quiet form of research." Their partners, however, are not novices but rather experts about their own classrooms and students. This knowledge—

and the awareness that their own task as collaborators should be a shared inquiry or co-investigation into teaching—does not necessarily alter their partners' expectations. In addition, the name "teacher-consultant" carries a kind of valence of status, no matter what disclaimers they may provide. These unspoken expectations make it difficult to establish a reciprocal relationship in which both partners feel powerful and their perspectives mutually valued.

Parallel to these expectations about expertise held by teachers for each other, teacher-consultants and their partner teachers may hold different assumptions about teaching and learning, and in particular about the teaching of writing. TCs, for example, share the belief that teaching is not simply "telling" or transmitting information and that in learner-centered classrooms teachers also learn and students teach. If a partner teacher regards writing as the acquisition of discrete skills, then the role of the teacher is more likely to be the expert assignment giver and paper corrector. While the TC in the role of expert providing direct instruction fits comfortably with a more traditional pedagogy, the TC as co-investigator is congruent with a student-centered approach to learning, which may not, initially, be shared.

Other differences in pedagogy and philosophy may be both more subtle and more powerful. An experienced first-grade teacher-consultant whose science curriculum is unusually rich with hands-on experiences and writing, for example, recounts how visitors typically want her to codify her curriculum so that others can immediately begin to use it. This request comes without regard for the uniqueness of her entire classroom ecology and the distinctive ways in which she works with children. Another teacher reveals that her own classroom is hard to explain to someone else. Some people love it when they walk into it and want to know more. And other people walk in and say "Well, I can't do this at my school." That this teacher's classroom is a place where only some teachers feel they can learn limits collaboration. When a teacher who is visiting looks simply for activities that can be "transferred," the possibilities for co-investigation are severely con-strained. The intent here is not the transfer of ideas intact from one classroom to another, but rather discussion and analysis leading to the selection and adaptation of practices to another setting. Both examples point to the difficulties in collaboration that stem from differences, often unexamined, in fundamental beliefs about how teachers and how students learn.

A variety of other attitudes or expectations also function as obstacles to teacher-to-teacher collaboration. The teacher-consultants interviewed report variations on the theme of "the quick fix," i.e., teachers and administrators who seek instant solutions to complex problems. As one teacher puts it:

> The teachers who express an interest in working with me constantly expect to be recharged with high voltage strategies or their interest quickly wanes. These teachers with a "handout" orientation are often too guarded or too defensive to develop a true collaborative relationship with a colleague.

Other times teachers report that their colleagues open the conversation with a rather narrow question and then follow up with acquiescence rather than a reflective and critical stance on what they do and what they are learning:

> One of the questions people asked me after I talked at one school is, "Should we be having our kindergartners and first graders draw ...?" And I said, "Yes" and they said, "OK. Well, we're going to do that." And I realized that while I was delighted that they would do some drawing with their students ... the next person who came along could say, "Don't have them draw. It's a waste of time." And they would say, "OK. I'll stop." And there wasn't any way in this format to talk more about why.

Given the diversity of teachers, schools, and administrators involved in the program, it is not surprising that people have different expectations about this form of collegial learning. As a result, teacher-consultants find they need to develop a variety of strategies for initiating and sustaining relationships with other teachers who may be working from very different assumptions about the nature of teaching and learning.

Unlike "technical coaching," long-term cross-visitation often begins in very informal unstructured ways. As one teacher describes her visit to another school (accompanied by another TC):

> We spent the day in the teachers' lounge. And we had teachers come in during the recess periods, prep periods, lunch periods, and it was very informal. We brought a lot of kids' writing with us, we brought a lot of the books we were using, and we just talked about things ... And we listened to some of the teachers' concerns, and we planned to do a little staff development on using literature in writing.

This notion of working with teachers' articulated concerns, of inquiring into what teachers themselves make problematic about their own practice, recurs throughout the data. Teachers found they needed to listen for each others' agendas and then frame their interactions inside the classroom so that the teachers feel comfortable taking public risks:

> If teachers and I plan together and if I listen to what they express as *their* need rather than what I interpreted as being their need, perhaps the faculty will become more involved in using writing strategies. Phenomenally enough, this *did* happen.

> We're using your room as a kind of laboratory and we're doing a little bit of experimenting and we want to talk about the things that are

happening. If you see me doing something or saying something to the kids that you question or don't understand, tell me. I would like to feel free to do the same with you.

Not only is there a kind of planned tentativeness in these arrangements, but there is also an openness to these plans allowing for spontaneity:

We started working together and the interesting thing about it was I would never know what her class was going to be like. We would plan things beforehand and she was the kind of teacher where if things were not going according to plan, she could go with whatever was, and make the most of that. And the enjoyable thing about working with her was that she would suggest things to me — "Well why don't we try this" and "What do you think of this." I really liked the way that worked. She would constantly give me feedback about what was going on in her class. And I could do the same thing with her. ... It's successful for me, if I don't feel like I'm doing all the work.

It's nice to go and work in somebody else's kitchen ... when Sandy and Mary came to my room, they were in there with the kids within ten minutes, asking the kids questions, helping them a little bit, finding out what they were doing. And I did the same thing in all of their classes. That I think is a part of it — not just sitting there watching.

In these examples, teachers engage actively in the events of each other's classrooms: they work directly with children, they raise questions, and they find they can improvise without upsetting the classroom routine. When this works, the pair conducts a collaborative inquiry in which two perspectives are merged but neither is subsumed. When TCs and their partner teachers co-plan the same lesson, what occurs can "make the familiar strange":

It was fun watching Mrs. S's classroom and seeing how she used the same piece of literature I used. Although we had planned our lesson together, hers seemed completely different from mine. She was more dramatic, more "on stage." Also, she ended up doing a completely different writing response than the one we planned.

This opportunity to observe another teacher's students learn, to see how another teacher adapts a plan on her feet in order to respond to what transpires, and then to have the luxury of talking all of this through with a colleague — all are taken-for-granted forms of collegial sharing in other professions such as medicine and law but extremely rare in education.

In an excerpt from a teacher's essay, Fecho (1987) describes the evolution of one collaboration over time, showing how he and another teacher gradually worked through their differing perceptions and negotiated some common ground:

> The dynamics of our initial meetings were based on a giver-receiver relationship; I was offering instructional suggestions that she would implement. The relationship was further complicated by my years of experience as opposed to her lack of the same. When I first visited her classroom, it was difficult to shed the observer/observed feeling. A note in my journal alludes to her nervousness with my being there. This thread was carried later into the year in seemingly harmless, yet telling remarks:
>
> "I don't have any writing to show you yet," she said one day as we passed in the hall.
>
> "What do you want to see me do?" was her question when I offered to sit in on a class.
>
> "Is this what you want?" she said, handing me writing samples.

In this passage, Fecho shows how difficult it is for teachers to alter the expectation that someone is doing something "to" rather than "with" someone else. As the relationship between Fecho and the science teacher evolved, they found a way to shift those expectations so that both teachers became equal and active partners in the exchange:

> The science teacher tried some writing. She openly discussed successes and failures. One day, she showed up at my door with a pile of papers. "I was desperate," she said, "so I told my students to write me a letter explaining what they've learned about chemistry this year." She and I had never discussed this use of writing. She had a problem; she addressed it through composition. Her sharing with me was on her own initiative rather than at my request. I ended up reading a pile of interesting, honest letters and picking up a new strategy to use and share.
>
> In addition, our relationship had shifted. She was now giving back. Our stance was less giver to taker and more colleague to colleague. This change is important to the collaboration because without it, we would have had little reason to continue. What we have now established is open groundwork for future collaboration, one in which I might bring scientific theory into the English classroom. (4)

In an interview I had with this teacher, who later decided to attend an institute and become a teacher-consultant, she emphasized the importance of working from her own issues:

> I think it was a very slow, unfolding kind of process ... It fit into my needs. It went where I was going with it. If it was too directed, it wouldn't have done me any good because it wouldn't have had any real value ... [The TC] might have been looking for something other than I was. It wasn't going to connect until it connected in a way that *I* saw results.

Negotiating collaborative relationships, when successful, appears to have two interrelated consequences. First of all, teacher-consultants and their partner teachers receive some validation for their own skillfulness and thus become increasingly motivated to reflect on and improve their own practice. The second consequence relates to the internalization by teachers of negative views of their profession conveyed by those outside it. Directly or indirectly, teachers are frequently criticized and blamed for the poor performance of urban schoolchildren. At the simplest level, cross-visitation gives teachers access to their colleagues' classrooms where children are clearly learning and teachers are excited about teaching. In the words of one teacher:

> Teachers have no idea how good they are, how much they know, and how many ways they can use that. ... A lot of people's talents are somewhat restricted by their own self-image, and their image of what teaching — particularly elementary teaching — is all about.

When teachers have an opportunity through a program like cross-visitation to know more about their colleagues' work and to take some collective responsibility for the quality of that work, the vertical school organization, which usually functions to monitor teachers' performance, can be supplemented by a lateral system, which effectively gives teachers more control of their profession. Lortie (1986) relates this phenomenon to the need for more decision-making authority in individual schools and to the importance of learning from peers. High on our policy agenda, he argues, should be "fostering the sharing of practical knowledge among classroom teachers" (574).

We have seen from this analysis of teachers' efforts to open their classrooms and experiences to each other that sharing knowledge takes more than merely putting structures in place. As we will show in our discussion of how cross-visitation functions within the constraints and possibilities of a large urban school system, creating a professional culture in schools is both complex and promising.

The Teachers and "The System"

The complexity of the relationships surrounding this program of teacher-to-teacher in-service education through cross-visitation is partially explained by its evolution in the district. Although cross-visitation began as a teacher-to-teacher initiative, it quickly became evident that these activities would have to be integrated into the responsibilities of line and staff district administration. What may appear to be trivial matters of protocol assume considerable importance in such a large system. Unlike forms of staff development such as workshops and meetings, which typically occur outside of the regular school hours, cross-visitation alters the daily work life of teachers and students.

As a consequence, teachers needed to enter into new relationships with district administrators, and to function in *the system* in new ways.

For example, while principals were comfortable allowing teacher-consultants to work within their schools, they were less supportive about having teachers travel to other buildings. Teachers whose experience leaving the building during the day had been limited to occasional field trips now had to seek permission from their principal to work with faculty in someone else's building. Beyond the logistical considerations, the data show that everyone involved in the system — principals, supervisors, and teachers themselves — had some difficulty defining cross-visitation and distinguishing it from other forms of staff development. Two issues are prominent in the transcripts of the teachers interviewed:

The first relates to the process of initiating a cross-visitation and the designation of participants. The written guidelines for the program (composed by teachers working with administrators and university faculty) emphasize that this activity of cross-visitation is voluntary and that, optimally, contacts would be made teacher-to-teacher. In practice, in an effort to support the program, supervisors began to encourage particular principals to invite TCs to visit their building. This follows an informal but established norm of the subdistrict offices to respond to the needs of school-based personnel. According to the TCs interviewed, this practice sometimes resulted in requests to work with seven or eight teachers in a single day or to work with teachers who the principal felt were so-called problem teachers or marginally competent. This too conformed with an established procedure. The teachers' contract requires principals to demonstrate they are doing everything possible to help "weak" teachers. In the TC's view, they were being asked to work with too many teachers and often in what they perceived to be nonvoluntary relationships.

Many TCs reported, however, that even when these contacts were not optimal, it was usually possible to turn the situation around. As one teacher put it, "I didn't deal with them [teachers identified for remediation] as though I perceived them as having a problem with their teaching. I dealt with them as being co-teachers, as being teachers that deal with the same student population that I was getting, teachers from whom I could learn as much as they could learn from me." The difference in intent between administrators and teachers was echoed frequently in the interview transcripts. As one teacher explained, "A lot of administrators view the role of the TC as a spreader of the gospel of writing and not as teachers who are learning at the same time as consulting."

A second concern relates to what TCs expect and are expected to do once they begin working with other teachers. Many school district administrators, and teachers, equate in-class staff development with doing demonstration lessons. The theory here is that showing a teacher how to do something new in her classroom is the most effective way to produce change. Modeling is a form of direct instruction, assumed by many to be central to students' and to teachers' learning (Lambert 1989). Furthermore, the culture of teaching resists observations, associating them with evaluation rather than support. When a partner teacher requests a demonstration from a teacher-consultant, at least two agendas may be operating: avoiding the risks of an observation or testing the teacher-consultant's ability to cope with that teacher's classroom. The following quotations from the transcripts reveal some of the difficulties of "doing demos":

> I never thought that I would be in a position where a principal or a [supervisor] would be telling me to go do a demonstration lesson for Miss Jones, whom I've never met, whose classroom I didn't know. Just as if I were a supervisor and that I was going to do that and then call that collaboration.

> But the first period I was there, the science teacher right away wanted a demo lesson. I did it. I thought I would never do it, but I did say I would. I mean I wanted to reach this person, and I wanted to show her how wonderful it could be if you did certain things with kids. And so it was important to do that demo lesson. I don't think it will change what she'll ever do, but it got me credibility in the school.

> A lot of times I feel used, by being asked to do a demonstration lesson. I like doing demonstration lessons, and I don't mind doing them, if I know that I'm going to be working with the teacher for a while. Like in my school I do this a lot. But many times I feel that teachers ask for demonstration lessons to give themselves breaks. And when you're invited into that school and you don't have that time to sit down with the teacher afterwards and talk with that teacher about what happened—or when you sit down and you talk with that teacher and the teacher has nothing to say, then you feel like you've been exploited.

Given past practice, it is not surprising that teachers may simply equate staff development with doing demonstrations.

> I think there are many people who do a wonderful job with staff development, but that's really not my goal—to do demonstration lessons. Occasionally I would like a demonstration lesson to be the beginning of something—begin a kind of collaboration from that perhaps. With the demonstration lesson being an end in itself, I'm not interested.

Teacher-consultants seem to resent the limited conception of their role as "doing demos." While they can in theory refuse when asked, as these quotations suggest TCs are anxious to find common ground. Thus they seek ways to respond to what the teacher wants while still moving the relationship from what Hargreaves (1989) calls "contrived collegiality" toward a more "collaborative culture."

Teacher-consultants are particularly attracted to cross-visitation when it allows them personal and professional flexibility, input, and a certain measure of control. Gaining this ownership does not entail a loss of authority on the part of administrators but rather some newly shared responsibilities.

Conclusion

As unique and rewarding as it is for teachers to open their classrooms, we have seen that it is not done without complications — diminishing isolation also diminishes privacy, sharing ideas may expose uncertainties, and taking on new roles in the system invites new responsibilities. Because the dominant culture of teaching is one of "fragmented individualism" (Hargreaves 1989), going into the classroom of another teacher brings not only new rewards but often new problems.

This duality plays out in many ways. When a program of collegial learning is marked by open-endedness and flexibility, it both encourages teachers to invent new roles and places new demands on them. As Goodwin (1987) points out, "teaching is an uncertain activity and ... teachers are vulnerable as a result of the uncertainties. ... Effective staff development efforts may not reduce the uncertainties that teachers face, but they can give teachers vocational choices that enhance the way teachers view themselves" (35). In effect, the cross-visitation program has been designed to capitalize on uncertainty, so that teachers who participate can negotiate different relationships in different situations. A precise definition of what teachers must do would limit the program's possibilities, many of which are clearly being invented by teachers as it evolves. In practice, however, this ambiguity also allows all who come into contact with the program to fashion a personal conception of it, one that may differ markedly from the original idea and may sometimes limit what participants can do with the new structures provided. It is no surprise that school systems look for predictability and sometimes "packaging." In large urban districts with thousands of teachers and students, it is a constant challenge to respond to the needs of particular children, schools, and neighborhoods while maintaining some systemwide continuity. Programs encouraging teacher-to-teacher collaboration may require increased tolerance for variation and diverse outcomes. As Hargreaves (1989) indicates, however, "unpredictability can be a threatening prospect" (24).

Collegial learning is further complicated by an often imprecise link between collaboration and inquiry. Too frequently, what is intended to be collaborative inquiry never gets beyond the day-to-day business of classroom life and, as Hargreaves (1989) suggests, is neither "searching nor wide-ranging" enough to counter the deep-seated culture of individualism predominant among teachers. Apparently the connection between collaboration and teacher research does not occur often enough in practice, partly because of constraints related to time and differing expectations but also because the notion of teachers as researchers has yet to gain widespread understanding or acceptance in schools. New support structures and more participatory research on cross-visitation may be needed to make the program less a setting for the passing of information and more a context in which vigorous inquiry can take place.

A third complication relates to participant commitment to such a program of collegial learning over time. Reciprocity is central to teachers' continued involvement. When TCs spend most of their time focused on the needs and questions of their partner teachers, the collaboration may be, in Hargreaves's terminology, "bounded:"

> Bounded collaboration is collaboration which is restricted in its *depth*, in its *scope*, in its frequency or *persistence*, or in a combination of these things. It is collaboration which does not reach deep down to the grounds, the principles or the ethics of practice, but which sticks with routine advice giving, trick trading and materials sharing of a more immediate, specific, and technical nature. It is collaboration which does not extend beyond particular units of work or subjects of study to the whole purpose and value of curricular and pedagogical judgment. It is collaboration which focuses on the immediate and the practical to the exclusion of longer-term planning concerns.

While many exchanges that appear to be simply about materials or logistics or the routines of teaching, we would argue, are actually more substantive than they appear, if the conversations lack depth and reciprocity, over time, this becomes problematic. When TCs collaborate more as knowledge givers and less as inquirers, once the novelty of seeing others "in action" passes, they may feel they have little to learn from maintaining these relationships over time. To enhance the learning by teacher-consultants involved, group sessions focused on both the process and the content of these collaborative relationships can provide a context for struggling with some of the more complex issues in teaching and learning that emerge from the program. When teachers write about their experiences in cross-visitation, their texts become catalysts for further investigation.

We see evidence of this possibility in the data collected so far. When asked about what they have learned from the experience of cross-visiting, teachers interviewed most often responded with what they had learned about working with adults, about understanding or coping with the system at large, and/or about their own self-image as a teacher. What they said less often were comments about the specific effects of cross-visitation on their own classroom practice. While the interviews conducted to date may not have fully explored these effects, they do suggest that there may be problems associated with motivating long-term commitment to any activity that increases risk and workload without sufficiently enhancing competence and self-knowledge. Further research is needed to explore the impact of cross-visitation on curriculum and instruction.

Finally, evidence from the interviews and teacher writing about this form of collegial learning suggests that problem-solving about collaboration itself is a critical part of the process. Working one-to-one requires a collective or community as a support structure, one that provides a safe forum for working out concerns and critiquing approaches. A writing project — operating somewhat outside of the school system — can function as such a support system, as can in-district meetings if convened for this purpose. What seems to be required is a degree of trust and openness, a reflectivity and a willingness to risk exploring professional relationships that involve struggle without being judged by one's colleagues in the process. Giroux (1984) has suggested that "the democratization of schooling involves the need for teachers to build alliances with other teachers," which "develop around new forms of social relations" (39). The study of cross-visitation shows that building such alliances creates both new problems and new possibilities.

Works Cited

Carr, W., and S. Kemmis. 1986. *Becoming critical: Education, knowledge and action research*. Philadelphia: Falmer.

Clark, C., and P. L. Peterson. 1986. Teachers' thought processes. In *Handbook of research on teaching*, 3d ed. See Wittrock 1986.

Cochran-Smith, M., and S. L. Lytle. 1990. Research on teaching and teacher research: The issues that divide. *Educational Researcher* 19(2): 2–11.

Elbaz, F. 1983. *Teacher thinking: A study of practical knowledge*. New York: Nichols.

Fecho, R. 1987. Folding back the classroom walls: Teacher collaboration via cross-visitation. In *Work in Progress*, Philadelphia Writing Project. Philadelphia: University of Pennsylvania.

Feiman-Nemser, S. 1980. Growth and reflection as aims in teacher education: Directions for research. In *Exploring issues in teacher education: Questions for future research*, ed. G. Hall. Austin: Research and Development Center for Teacher Education, University of Texas.

Floden, R., and S. Feiman-Nemser. 1980. Should teachers be taught to be rational? Paper presented at the annual meeting of the American Educational Research Association, Boston.

Garmston, R. 1987. How administrators support peer coaching. *Educational Leadership* 44: 18–26.

Giroux, H. 1984. Rethinking the language of schooling. *Language Arts* 61: 33–40.

Goodwin, A. 1987. Vocational choice and the realities of teaching. In *Teacher renewal: Professional issues, personal choices*, ed. F. Bolin and M. Falk. New York: Teachers College.

Goswami, D., and P. Stillman, eds. 1987. *Reclaiming the classroom*. Portsmouth, NH: Boynton/Cook.

Hargreaves, A. 1989. Contrived collegiality and the culture of teaching. Paper presented to the Canadian Society for Studies in Education Conference, Quebec.

Hargreaves, A., and R. Dawe. 1989. Coaching as unreflective practice: Contrived collegiality or collaborative culture? Paper presented at the annual meeting of the American Educational Research Association, San Francisco.

Joyce, B., and J. Showers. 1982. The coaching of teaching. *Educational Leadership* 40(1): 4–10.

Lambert, L. 1989. The end of an era of staff development. *Educational Leadership* 47(1): 78–81.

Little, J. 1989. The persistence of privacy: Autonomy and initiative in teachers' professional relations. Paper presented at the annual meeting of the American Educational Research Association, San Francisco.

Lortie, D. 1986. Teacher status in Dade County: A case of structural strain? *Phi Delta Kappan* 68: 568–75.

Lytle, S., and M. Cochran-Smith. 1989. Teacher research: Toward clarifying the concept. *Quarterly of the National Writing Project and the Center for the Study of Writing* 11(2): 1–3,22–27.

Oja, S., and L. Smulyan. 1989. *Collaborative action research: A developmental approach*. Philadelphia: Falmer.

Rorschach, E., and R. Whitney. 1986. Relearning to teach: Peer observation as a means of professional development for teachers. *English Education* 18(3): 159–72.

Schon, D. 1983. *The reflective practitioner*. San Francisco: Jossey-Bass.

———. 1987. *Educating the reflective practitioner*. San Francisco: Jossey-Bass.

Showers, J., B. Joyce, and B. Bennett. 1987. Synthesis of research on staff development: A framework for future study and a state-of-the-art analysis. *Educational Leadership* 45(November): 77–87.

Wittrock, M., ed. *Handbook of research on teaching*. 3d ed. New York: Macmillan.

Zumwalt, K. 1982. Research on teaching: Policy implications for teacher education. In *Policy making in education*, ed. A. Lieberman and M. McLaughlin. 81st Yearbook of the National Society for the Study of Education. Chicago: University of Chicago.

Response

Gordon M. Pradl

In their report on the new program of teacher cross-visitations initiated by the Philadelphia Writing Project, Susan and Robert risk pointing education in a radical new direction. Indeed, I would boldly proclaim, the novel institutional structures they introduce and champion, if widely adopted, could hold more promise for extended educational transformation than all the innovative curriculum movements and individual teacher education projects that so actively vie for our attention.

I say this because to genuinely open up one's classroom to a peer would mean the end to the hegemony of privatized teaching. In short, it would mean at last delivering on the promise of a new kind of education, the kind of classrooms and teacher/student relationships implied by all the rhetoric of educational reform that emphasizes *collaboration*. While we have slowly come to realize that most significant learning involves a co-dependency among learners — the social mediation of motives and actions, the negotiation of intentions and procedures among students and the teacher in concert with other teachers — unfortunately, the ways schools are generally organized serve to segregate individual teachers from one another, and this pattern in turn encourages teachers to separate students from each other.

The barriers that arise from this isolation, both physical and social, have their cumulative effect, for naturally enough the longer we go without testing a situation — in this instance the nature of the learning in our classrooms — the more hesitant we are to stick our necks out and risk reprobation. As one teacher in the study put it, "The more isolated you become, the more protective you become ... and then you look at, as an intrusion, somebody coming into your room ... you become more prone to feel like you're being judged." Indeed no one wants to be judged, just as no one wants advice, for evaluation makes us vulnerable, and so it remains easier to keep one's own counsel. As another teacher in the study admits: "I have been for many years an in-my-classroom teacher, doing most of my best work in seclusion — not sharing it with anybody because I was afraid I would be laughed at, I was afraid I would be told you work too hard ... so you don't share anything because you're afraid of that slap."

Patterns and routines of survival, of coming to terms with the daily grind, gradually erode the best of intentions. Even a new teacher who may enter a school system bubbling over with both the desire and the need to talk about her teaching and what she is learning every day in her classroom soon enough learns the ways of quiet cynicism. Teacher educators may want to encourage collaborative behaviors in school, but they remain as outsiders to these institutional imperatives, which keep frustrating attempts to get teachers to act differently. Thus even though from Paulo Freire to whole language, the cry may be for working together, not apart, for anchoring the curriculum in the dialectics of existential social being, not in the privileged but mostly invisible ideologies of the dominant institutional structures, we as teachers are still able to close our doors to the world. Unless we initiate contact with our colleagues, almost nothing prevents us from carrying out our classroom affairs free of the intervention of shared professional dialogue.

In reporting teacher reactions to cross-visitation, Susan and Robert clearly demonstrate how resistant the existing system will be to openness. What the teachers' responses finally forced me to acknowledge was that reform simply founders at the major point where we actually deliver the goods of our educational system: the isolated individual classroom. For in this private space, with all its warm protection and security, we as teachers are sovereign as we play out the traditional adult roles that enforce hierarchical schemes of organization. We have been strongly socialized to respect authority and to see knowledge as flowing directly from us to them (you listen to me, not me to you), so it is difficult to imagine teaching situations where equal and reciprocal relations might obtain. Indeed some of the teachers interviewed in this study reinforce how teachers themselves can establish a pecking order of expertise, how teachers assert unequal relationships among each other, all of which reinforces the movement of information and attention in one direction only.

But still as teachers we often try to improve what we're doing and so we may become intrigued by alternate ways of engaging students in our classroom. Possibly we are trying to encourage approaches to writing that focus on process, that involve learners in generating their own assignments. Perhaps we are continually organizing our students into small groups for work and discussion. Maybe we are enjoining students to respond freely to poems, doing away with the correct interpretation as the one that comes from the critic via the teacher. Yet, in each instance, unless we live out the new interpersonal reality entailed by the change we are attempting in specific procedural practices, our relations with students — especially in terms of listening to them — will all too easily remain business as usual. In short, reform can come right up to our classroom door, can even knock and be invited to enter, but without the sustaining light of critical conversation, it will wither or in some manner revert to the safety of established routines. Without an ongoing collaborative dialogue of inquiry impinging directly on what is actually occurring in our classroom (as opposed to the obvious fakery that so often occurs when we receive a supervisory visit), what incentive is there for us as teachers to experiment with new adult roles we might possibly play out in the classroom?

But what new adult roles are possible? Quite simply, the challenge of educational reform that emphasizes collaboration comes down to one crucial role transformation for the teacher. The reversal in question involves the teacher becoming a *learner* once again. Only where this has happened have the learning conditions in actual classrooms changed dramatically. The old role of teacher as dispenser of knowledge, and judge of what has been vacuumed up, is reimagined when teachers actively become students or learners alongside those students or learners they are responsible for in their classes. And generally the first thing teachers learn is what's on their students' minds — what do they already know, think, feel? Placing the student on a more equal footing will naturally challenge conventional authority relationships for the teacher, but only by construing the world from the student's point of view can teachers begin to adjust the curriculum in the direction of inquiry and meaning making.

And this is the great promise of cross-visitation: it invites us in to participate in a new conversation, one that dissolves the "normal" hierarchies so characteristic of school and classroom interactions. By engaging teachers in collaborative planning and learning situations with their peers, cross-visitations encourage them to immediately prac- tice new social roles (listening, sharing, tolerating, hypothesis testing, imagining, reflecting, analyzing, celebrating), roles that are to be played out and extended in the classroom after the door is closed — though in an important sense the door will never be closed again. With their rooms wide open to their colleagues, and through trusting discussions of what seems to be going on, teachers might be obliged to move beyond power and coercion in defending their practices; they might become more responsible for evolving rational decisions, for attending to how one might mediate between the subject matter and the child.

Susan and Robert openly admit that the logistics of educational systems already in place can easily overwhelm any school trying to implement some plan of cross-visitations. But the new confidence and professionalism that are possible make any struggle here worthwhile, as long as we see to it that each teacher's vulnerabilities are acknowledged within a protected space that allows for trust to slowly develop. If it's true that mostly we end up teaching as we've been taught, then the initial opportunity for fostering any significant cross-visitation movement lies in pre-service education. All occasions for learning, including "practice" teaching, need to be *open* and *collaborative* at the pre-service level if beginning teachers are to start off with a social mind-set that expects them to be *reflective learners* in their own classrooms. Further, imagine new teachers coming to their first teaching jobs with the anticipation that they will be working with other adults and comfortable with the fact that their own practices will be open to scrutiny — clearly such teachers could be a vital force for change. And think what would happen if these new teachers started interviewing those in charge of the school systems, rather than the other way around, and in doing so, asked whether some plan for cross-visitation was in place. Well, if the superintendent's answer isn't right and the program Susan and Robert describe continues to grow and flourish, then new teachers might suddenly be able to use, in a different context, W. C. Field's rejoinder, "I'd rather be in Philadelphia."

Afterword

Jeff and Amanda and I began planning this book very soon after *Reclaiming the Classroom* was published. We hoped for a book that would be written by students and teachers for students and teachers, a book that would be read and used in classrooms and in communities where people were figuring out how to begin action research projects. We talked to Bob Boynton and Peter Stillman, who encouraged us to find a form for this kind of co-authoring, but we couldn't do it. (Although we weren't able to imagine a collection that would serve such a wide range of writers and readers then, we're still struggling with the idea — and the need to go beyond conventional genres and formats to include and reach different readers.)

In the summers of 1988 and 1989 we had conversations with many Bread Loaf teachers and faculty. Jim Moffett, Ken Macrorie, Courtney Cazden, Betty Bailey, and other Bread Loaf colleagues spent many hours helping us move from our original vision to an alternate plan. Both Ken and Courtney suggested that we embrace the notion that teachers would be our most important readers: the book should be for them — and it is. Jim encouraged us to organize the book, insofar as we could, as a conversation. The brief responses to longer essays and stories are intended to suggest a way to read the book: as a conversation intended to raise questions, as a process rather than a collection of results and findings. We're pleased that many voices are represented here — and none that claim to have the last word.

And neither do I wish to claim the last word. Instead I'd like to think on paper about my own present understandings of *Students Teaching, Teachers Learning*. The students and teachers writing here seem to be entirely comfortable with the tentative rather than the scientifically validated nature of their shared inquiries. They are self-directed: nobody found questions for them to work on; their work hasn't been co-opted or trivialized. They assume that their special knowledge needs to be examined critically, revised, extended. Their nonhierarchical collaborations reflect the essence of teachers as researchers: They're engaged in authentic (and sometimes difficult) student/teacher relationships, which are reflected in the way they talk to, with, and about each other. They are process-oriented. Their emphasis is less on producing generalizable theory than on analyzing how ideology shapes our classrooms and our consciousnesses.

As I think about the meanings of the stories and accounts collected
here, I worry that they are so moving and memorable that it may be
especially difficult to go beyond the narratives to value and use the
knowledge they represent about the educational process. To paraphrase
Elspeth Stuckey, in her account of cross-age tutoring in South Carolina,
moving moments don't often lead to critical analysis of the de-skilling
of teachers and students or to radical institutional change. Aside from
rhetoric, what programs, funded privately or publicly, take collective
action research seriously as a key tool for school reform by providing
support over long periods of time to develop centers for shared local
inquiries? What programs, in the nineties, are pledged to use teachers'
and students' knowledge for a democratic reorganization of the ways
schools work? Can teachers bring about change?

I find myself returning often to the story of Amanda Branscombe
and Charlene Thomas's ten years as co-researchers, including what the
children did and how Shirley Heath and others were in it with them.
They show how laboring together changed their lives. Their story
changed forever my own conception of shared inquiry.

"Charlene is beginning to believe that she must be more political
so that she can be heard."

And so must we all.

DIXIE GOSWAMI

Notes on Contributors

Sara Allen has taught sixth through twelfth grades for seventeen years at Springside School in Philadelphia. In 1988 she received an NCTE Teacher-Researcher Grant to study student-sustained discussion. She continues to reflect on her classroom research at The Prospect Center in Vermont, in her own articles, and as cofounder of the Adolescent Study Group in Philadelphia.

Nancie Atwell was a junior high English teacher for twelve years. In 1988 she became the first classroom teacher to receive the Mina P. Shaughnessy Prize for outstanding research in the teaching of English for her book, *In the Middle: Writing, Reading, and Learning with Adolescents*. Currently she directs The Center for Teaching and Learning, a model elementary school in Edgecomb, Maine.

Betsy A. Bowen is Assistant Professor of English at Fairfield University. Her dissertation and subsequent research have examined talk between students and peer tutors. She is coauthor of *Word Processing in a Community of Writers*.

N. Amanda Branscombe is currently Assistant Professor in Early Childhood Education at West Georgia College in Carrollton, Georgia. She has authored and coauthored several articles about the teacher as researcher and students as co-researchers and has conducted numerous workshops on literacy and the young child's construction of knowledge.

James Britton was Head of the English Department at the Institute of Education, University of London. He has taught at the Bread Loaf School of English for several summers and has presented lectures throughout Europe, the United States, and Canada. His publications include *Language and Learning*, *The Development of Writing Abilities 11–18: Prospect and Retrospect*, and *English Teaching: An International Exchange*.

Courtney B. Cazden is Professor of Education at Harvard University. In 1985 she was President of the American Association of Applied Linguistics, and in 1987 spent six months in New Zealand on a Fulbright Scholarship. Her most recent book is *Classroom Discourse: The Language of Learning and Teaching*.

Marilyn Cochran-Smith is Assistant Professor of Education and Director of Project START (Student Teachers as Researching Teachers) at the Graduate School of Education, University of Pennsylvania. Her work is in language and learning, emergent literacy, and teacher education.

After graduation from the University of Virginia, **Ike Coleman** taught English for five years in rural Virginia, while attending the Bread Loaf School of English in the summers. He is formerly the Director of the South Carolina Rural Writing Network, a project involving several rural schools, sponsored by Bread Loaf and the Clemson University Department of English. The SCRWN, with small grants to selected schools, has sought to break down barriers between students and teachers, to create partnerships that nurture learning.

Judith Diamondstone is a doctoral candidate in the Graduate School of Education at Harvard. She is a former editor of the Harvard Educational Review and has conducted research on Soviet–U.S. use of computers in schools and on literacy projects in rural Alaska and in Cambridge, Massachusetts.

Brenda S. Engel is Associate Professor in the Division of Advanced Graduate Study and Research, Lesley College Graduate School, in Cambridge, Massachusetts. Her field is qualitative evaluation with a special interest in literacy learning in the primary grades. She is also a watercolorist and has taught art in elementary school.

Robert Fecho teaches English at Simon Gratz High School in Philadelphia. A Fellow of the Philadelphia Writing Project and a recipient of an NCTE Teacher-Researcher Grant, Fecho is currently working with eight other teachers from across the disciplines in creating Crossroads, a project-oriented, writing intensive school within a school. For his doctoral research at the University of Pennsylvania, he is doing collaborative research with his students on language use in the school and local community.

Elizabeth Garfield and **Rachel Greenberger** are both recent graduates of the Elementary Education Program at the University of Pennsylvania who are actively involved in professional development, recruiting prospective teachers, and teacher research. Elizabeth teaches fifth- and sixth-grade math and science at the La Jolla Country Day School in La Jolla, California. Rachel teaches seventh- and eighth-grade science at Brookwood School in Brookwood, Massachusetts.

Dixie Goswami is Professor of English at Clemson University in South Carolina. She also coordinates the Program in Writing and the Writing Grants Program at the Bread Loaf School of English. She is coeditor of *Reclaiming the Classroom* (with Peter Stillman) and *Writing in Non-Academic Settings* (with Lee Odell).

Mary K. Healy is Research and Training Director for the Puente Project in the Office of the President, University of California. Puente is a writing, counseling, mentoring program for at-risk Mexican-American/Latino students now operating at twenty-five sites across California. In addition, she is coeditor of *English Education* and coeditor of *What's Going On? Language/Learning Episodes in British and American Classrooms*. Along with her work with teacher researchers in the United States, she regularly teaches a course on classroom-based research methods for Swedish educators.

Shirley Brice Heath is Professor of English and Linguistics at Stanford University. She is the author of numerous books, including *Ways with Words: Language, Life and Work in Communities and Classrooms*, and has been honored with a Guggenheim Fellowship and a MacArthur Award.

Patricia Johnston is a reading teacher and supervisor in the Centennial School District in Warminster, Pennsylvania. She also teaches at the University of Pennsylvania.

Jill Kazmierczak received her Master of Arts from Radford University in Virginia. She is pursuing her doctoral degree at Duquesne University in Pittsburgh, Pennsylvania.

Deborah E. Keyes, a graduate of the Bread Loaf School of English, teaches at Portland High School in Maine. She is Project Director for "Grants for Students," the Maine Liaison Officer to NCTE, and Past President of the Maine Council for English Language Arts. In 1990 she coordinated the Teachers in Secondary Schools Program at her school, and she has taught a course at St. Joseph's College.

For twenty-three years **Hazel Lockett** has taught seventh and eighth grades at the Vernon L. Davey Junior High School in East Orange, New Jersey. Through the Andover–Bread Loaf Project she became more involved in teaching writing and now conducts writing workshops for teachers in her school district as well as for elementary school students who attend a neighborhood community writing workshop after school. She is beginning a cross-age tutoring project between her students and others at a local college.

Susan L. Lytle teaches in the Reading/Writing/Literacy Program of the Graduate School of Education, University of Pennsylvania, where she also directs the Philadelphia Writing Project. Lytle is writing a book on teacher research with Marilyn Cochran-Smith and is coauthor of *Inviting Inquiry: A Framework for Learning with Language*. Her research interests include participatory literacy assessment and the professional development of teachers.

Ken Macrorie is Professor Emeritus of English at Western Michigan University and has taught writing at the Bread Loaf School of English campuses in Vermont and New Mexico. He is the author of *Telling Writing*, *Writing to be Read*, *Uptaught*, *A Vulnerable Teacher*, and *Twenty Teachers* and has served as editor of *College Composition and Communication*.

Anne Martin teaches kindergarten at the Lawrence School in Brookline, Massachusetts. She is the author of *The Words in My Pencil: Considering Children's Writing* and has had articles in *The Harvard Educational Review* and other publications. Her major professional concerns are classroom teaching, writing about children in the classroom, and working collaboratively with other teachers to deepen understanding of children's learning and to improve teaching practice.

Nancy Martin is former Reader in Education and Head of the English Department at the University of London Institute of Education. She has been a Visiting Professor at Rutgers University, the Universities of Western Australia and Alberta, New York University, University of Maine, and Bread Loaf. Her publications include *Writing and Learning Across the Curriculum*, *The Development of Writing Abilities 11–18*, *Understanding Children Talking*, *Mostly About Writing*, *What Goes On in English Lessons*, and *The Word for Teaching is Learning*.

Glynnis Glass McIntyre received her Bachelor of Science degree and her master's degree in Early Childhood Education at Auburn University. She is currently teaching kindergarten at J. F. Kennedy Elementary School in Indio, California. She has been involved in planning and implementing a two-week orientation program for incoming kindergarten students and their parents and in putting together a new handbook that will help parents better understand the whole language approach to teaching.

Nanzetta Merriman is the principal of the John Ward Elementary School in Newton, Massachusetts. He has taught in elementary, middle, Head Start, and alternative school programs, and is the cofacilitator of the New Principals' Group at the Harvard Principals' Center.

James Moffett is an author and consultant in education who does workshops with teachers and occasionally teaches at the Bread Loaf School of English. His books include *Student-Centered Language Arts and Reading*, *Teaching the Universe of Discourse*, and *Coming on Center*. *Storm in the Mountains: A Case Study of Censorship, Conflict, and Consciousness* represents his own reportage and research (about a textbook controversy in Appalachia), and *Active Voices I–IV* is a series of anthologies of student writing that include oral history and other kinds of original research.

Richard J. Murphy, Jr. is Associate Professor of English at Radford University. He is at work on a book of autobiographical essays on teaching entitled *The Calculus of Intimacy*.

A teacher researcher for all but the first two years of her teaching, **Cindy Myers** currently teaches eighth-grade English in Seneca Falls, New York. She has spoken at state and national conferences, directed a three-year writing project for teachers sponsored by Bread Loaf, and has written about her research in *Reclaiming the Classroom*.

Gordon M. Pradl is Professor of English Education at New York University, where he also serves as Director of Staff Development for the Expository Writing Program. He edited *Prospect and Retrospect: The Collected Essays of James Britton*, coauthored *Learning to Write/Writing to Learn*, and currently serves as coeditor of the NCTE journal, *English Education*.

Vera Scarbrough teaches eleventh- and twelfth-grade English at Oakdale High and English composition at nearby Roane State Community College in Harriman, Tennessee. She attended Bread Loaf School of English, where she received her master's degree in 1987. In 1989, she and her students published *Oakdale: 1880–Present*, a local history book that covered over one hundred years of the town's past. Currently she is working on another book that will focus on human interest stories told by Oakdale's second generation.

David Schaafsma is Assistant Professor of English Education at the University of Wisconsin. Before directing the Dewey Center Community Writing Project in Detroit, he taught high school and codirected the Huron Shores Summer Writing Project in rural Rogers City, Michigan. He is interested especially in the uses of narrative in learning and in literacy in multicultural classrooms.

Ellen Schwartz has been a primary teacher for seven years at Putney Central School in Putney, Vermont. Her work with emergent curriculum stems from her participation in seminars and institutes at The Prospect Center in North Bennington, Vermont. She is a member of an ongoing child study group and is a consultant with day care centers, schools, and teacher preparation programs interested in descriptive review processes about children and their work.

After teaching at Sewickley Academy outside Pittsburgh, **Jeffrey Schwartz** is currently Head of the English Department at Greenwich Academy in Connecticut. In 1986 he received a Teacher-Researcher Grant from NCTE. He is a coauthor of *Word Processing in a Community of Writers* and has published poems widely and in a collection from Alice James Books.

Wendy Strachan, of North Vancouver, British Columbia, is a full-time educational consultant to schools and colleges. She began her professional career as a classroom teacher and taught for fifteen years in grades kindergarten through college in Canada, Malawi, and Malaysia. As Director of the East Asia and Athens Writing Projects, she has led hundreds of writing workshops over the past ten years for teachers in Canada, U.S., Europe, the Middle East, and Asia. She has written articles on teaching writing, literacy development, and teacher research, as well as a series of literature guides for reading young adult Canadian novels.

J. Elspeth Stuckey is Director of South Carolina's Cross-Age Tutoring Project. As a Fulbright Fellow she taught in Liberia. She has lectured on literacy issues throughout the United States and has recently published *The Violence of Literacy*.

Carol Stumbo has taught for fourteen years at Wheelwright High School and for eight years before that at Alice Lloyd College in Kentucky. She has coordinated a writing program in her school district for four years and has written about her work in *Harvard Educational Review* and elsewhere. Carol's students have won a certificate of commendation from the American Association for State and Local History for their work in collecting oral history.

Janet B. Taylor is Associate Professor of Early Childhood Education at Auburn University in Alabama. She has written numerous articles about teacher education programs and about young children and their notions about literacy. She has served in various state and national leadership positions in organizations for young children and has presented numerous workshops about ways children construct knowledge.

Charlene Thomas is currently an unemployed mother of five children. She has worked with Shirley Brice Heath and N. Amanda Branscombe as a co-researcher about her children's language development. She is continuing to observe and write about her family's literacy acquisition.

Ethel White is currently Director of the Auburn Day Care Centers in Auburn, Alabama. She serves on numerous state and local boards, such as the United Way, Alabama Alliance for Children, and the Child Care Coordinating Council.

She graduated from Tennessee A & I University in Nashville and was Director of the Head Start Programs in Pensacola, Florida, for fifteen years.

After teaching English and journalism in public and private secondary schools in Missouri, Afghanistan, Pennsylvania, and Iowa, **David Wilson** is now Assistant Professor of English Education at the University of Nebraska—Lincoln. His teaching and scholarship generally focus on writing instruction and the sources and development of teachers' understandings.

Born in Alexandria, Egypt, of Greek parents, **Evi Zoukis** speaks Greek, English, French, and Arabic. For twelve years she has been teaching Greek and French at a middle school in Athens that includes about fifty-two different nationalities. Evi is a resource person for the National Writing Project in Greece and has written two textbooks for teaching Greek.